Studies of Business Law – Recent Developments and Perspectives

Cătălin-Silviu Săraru (ed.)

Studies of Business Law – Recent Developments and Perspectives

Contributions to the International Conference
Perspectives of Business Law in the Third Millennium,
November 2, 2012, Bucharest

PL ACADEMIC RESEARCH

Bibliographic Information published by the Deutsche Nationalbibliothek
The Deutsche Nationalbibliothek lists this publication
in the Deutsche Nationalbibliografie; detailed bibliographic
data is available in the internet at http://dnb.d-nb.de.

We gratefully acknowledge financial support by
Societatea de Stiinte Juridice si Administrative
(Society of Juridical and Administrative Sciences),
Bucharest

Library of Congress Cataloging-in-Publication Data

Perspectives of Business Law in the Third Millennium (Conference) (2nd : 2012 : Bucharest, Romania)
Studies of business law : recent developments and perspectives / Catalin-Silviu Sararu.
pages cm
"Contributions to the international conference Perspectives of Business Law in the Third Millennium, November 2, 2012, Bucharest."
Includes bibliographical references.
ISBN 978-3-631-64128-6
1. Commercial law—Europe—Congresses. I. Sararu, Catalin-Silviu. II. Title.
KJC2044.8.P47 2012
346.24'065--dc23

2013020989

ISBN 978-3-631-64128-6 (Print)
E-ISBN 978-3-653-03073-0 (E-Book)
DOI 10.3726/978-3-653-03073-0

Internationaler Verlag der Wissenschaften
Frankfurt am Main 2013

PKL Academic Research is an Imprint of Peter Lang GmbH.

Peter Lang – Frankfurt am Main · Bern · Bruxelles · New York ·
Oxford · Warszawa · Wien

www.peterlang.com

Preface

Editor
PhD Cătălin-Silviu SĂRARU
Law Department, Bucharest University of Economic Studies

This volume contains the scientific papers presented at the Second International Conference "Perspectives of Business Law in the Third Millennium" that was held on 2 November 2012 at Bucharest University of Economic Studies, Romania. The conference is organized each year by the Department of Law at Bucharest University of Economic Studies together with the Society of Juridical and Administrative Sciences. More information about the conference can be found on the official website: www.businesslawconference.ro.

The scientific studies included in this volume are grouped into three chapters:

- *Recent developments and perspectives in the regulation of business law at European Union level.* The papers in this section refer to specific procedures for the adoption of regulations by the EU institutions, utility of the European company (Societas Europaea - SE); principles governing public procurement procedures, state aids that are incompatible with the internal market of the European Union, and combating discrimination at the workplace.
- *Transposition of European Union directives into national law.* The papers in this chapter provide a comparative view of various aspects of business law: the criminal liability of legal persons, protection against discrimination in a business environment, fiscal measures implemented during the crisis, sanctioning unfair contract terms, the role of European Works Councils; electronic money, combating late payments in commercial transactions, and transposing regulatory requirements into national law.
- *Recent developments and perspectives in the regulation of international business law.* This chapter includes papers on: the need to develop a common law on international bankruptcy, opinions about the importance of international commercial arbitration, transnational adhesion contracts, and contemporary challenges facing dignity at work.

This volume is aimed at practitioners, researchers, students and PhD candidates in juridical sciences, who are interested in recent developments and prospects for development in the field of business law at European and international level.

We thank all contributors and partners, and are confident that this volume will meet the needs for growing documentation and information of readers in the context of globalisation and the rise of dynamic elements in contemporary business law.

Table of Contents

RECENT DEVELOPMENTS AND PERSPECTIVES IN THE REGULATION OF BUSINESS LAW AT EUROPEAN UNION LEVEL

Ioana - Nely MILITARU

Special Procedures for the Adoption of EU Legal Acts. 13

Felicia BEJAN

The European Company (Societas Europaea - SE), a Legal Instrument of Mobility for Companies in the European Union 25

Cătălin-Silviu SĂRARU

State Aids that are Incompatible with the Internal Market in European Court of Justice Case Law 39

Ioan LAZĂR, Laura LAZĂR

The Efficiency of Public Procurement Procedures. The Principle of Integrity 49

Cătălina-Adriana IVĂNUŞ

Aspects of Prohibition of Discrimination against Women in the Workplace in European Court of Justice Case Law 61

TRANSPOSITION OF EUROPEAN UNION DIRECTIVES INTO NATIONAL LAW

Florina Mariana HOMEGHIU,

Mihaela CONSTANTINESCU

Implications of Discrimination on Economic Agents' Activity 79

George GRUIA, George Cristian GRUIA

Criminal Liability of the Legal Person and its Implications: a Case Study in Romania and the Czech Republic 99

Camelia Florentina STOICA

Restrictions of Law Provided by the Jurisprudence of the Constitutional Court and the European Court of Human Rights 111
Mihaela TOFAN
Protection against Gender Discrimination and Equal Treatment in the Legal Framework of Romania 131
Vincenzo CARBONE
Brief Analysis of Fiscal Measures in a Time of Crisis 149
Mihaela AIRINEI
Legal Regime Applicable to Non-Refundable Financing Contracts within the Sectoral Operational Programme "Human Resources Development 2007-2013 (Sop Hrd)" 155
Liviu Titus PAVELIU
Analysis of the Sanctions Applicable to Unfair Contract Terms under Romanian Law 169
Iulia BĂDOI
European Works Council 181
Alexandru BULEARCĂ
Electronic Money, Means of Payment in Domestic and International Economic Exchanges. Statutory Changes at EU and EEA Level 195
Ivan TOT
Combating Late Payments in Commercial Transactions: Transposition of the EU Directives into Croatian and Slovenian Law 211

RECENT DEVELOPMENTS AND PERSPECTIVES IN THE REGULATION OF INTERNATIONAL BUSINESS LAW

Luiza Cristina GAVRILESCU
Considerations on the Need to Develop a Common Law on International Bankruptcy 239
Cristina SÂMBOAN

Dignity at Work - Contemporary Challenges 249
Carmen Tamara UNGUREANU
The Romanian Adherent, Party to the Transnational Adhesion Contract 261
Harsh PATHAK
Rising Importance and Significance of International Commercial Arbitration 285
Cristina FLORESCU
On Dissenting Opinions in International Arbitration 295

RECENT DEVELOPMENTS AND PERSPECTIVES IN THE REGULATION OF BUSINESS LAW AT EUROPEAN UNION LEVEL

Special Procedures for the Adoption of EU Legal Acts

Lecturer Ioana-Nely MILITARU[1]

Abstract

The article is divided into three parts and Conclusions. The first part summarises institutions in EU legislative decision-making positions in the establishment of the European Communities, while part two addresses the procedures for adopting legal acts in their evolution. The third part presents the ordinary, special procedures and legal procedures for adopting non-legislative acts. Findings highlight how the Lisbon Treaty introduced new elements to the procedure.

Keywords: institution, ordinary procedure (co-decision), special procedures, decision making, legislative, advisory, cooperation, conciliation, consultation.

1. Institutions in EU decision-making positions

In the European Union, the process of adopting legal acts, and legislative or non-legislative decision-making – the so-called decision[2] process – mainly involves the European Parliament and the Council, Commission, European Council, while the Economic and Social Committee and the Committee of the Regions play an advisory role.

Since the establishment of the Community, the legislative powers of Parliament have evolved from their initial advisory role.

Since the introduction of the "budgetary treaties" in 1970 and 1975, involvement in the budgetary procedure has progressed, and budgeting competence in the European Company is now shared with the Council as specified in Art. 203 of the Treaty of the European Economic Community (TEC). By introducing the cooperation procedure in Article 6, the Single European Act (SEA) recognised the competence to adopt laws. The introduction of the co-decision procedure in the Maastricht Treaty (TMs) gave the European Parliament the same legislative powers as the Council. The Amsterdam Treaty then simplified the co-decision procedure; the Treaty of Nice promulgated the qualified majority for all Council actions, thus strengthening its position in the procedure for adopting Community legislation.

---

1 Ioana - Nely Militaru, Bucharest University of Economic Studies, Department of Law, Romania, ioananelimilitaru@yahoo.com.

2 See Dan Vataman, EU Law, Legal Universe Publishing, Bucharest, 2010, p 162.

The Lisbon Treaty made the co-decision procedure ordinary procedure in the European Union (Art. 289 Paragraph 1 of the Treaty on the Functioning of the European Union - TFEU), thus strengthening the status of the European Parliament - with the Council - as legislator. The Commission is the institution that initiates legislative acts in the European Union. Thus, Union legislative acts may only be adopted by Commission proposal, except where the Treaties provide otherwise. Other acts are adopted on proposal where the Treaties so provide (Art. 17 Para. 2 of the Treaty on the European Union - TEU). Also, the ordinary legislative procedure comprises joint adoption by the European Parliament (EP) and Council of a regulation, directive or decision on a proposal from the Commission (Article 289 TFEU).

In principle, draft laws are the result of Commission initiatives. As an exception, Parliament may request the Commission to submit an appropriate proposal for adoption of a new act or amendment of an existing act (Article 225 TFEU[3]), or the initiative can come from other institutions or from Member States, in special proceedings (Article 289 TFEU). The European Council does not exercise legislative functions but has decision-making powers, adopting non-legislative Common Foreign and Security Policy legal acts under the TEU (Art. 24, Art. 31). The Economic and Social Committee (ESC) and the Committee of the Regions (CoR) fulfil advisory functions. In this regard, consultation of the ESC and CoR by the European Parliament, the Council or the Commission is compulsory where provided for in the Treaties, and in all cases where deemed appropriate by these institutions (Articles 304 and 307 TFEU).

2. Procedures used in adopting legal acts in the evolution of the European Union

Since the establishment of the Community, procedures have seen the following forms[4]: conciliation, cooperation, notification, consultation[5].

a) Conciliation procedure. Increasing the budgetary powers of Parliament meant that it needed to be associated more closely with development legislation that was likely to have an impact on the budgetary powers. For this reason, a "conciliation procedure" was introduced on 4 March 1975 by Joint Declaration

3 See Art. 42 Para. 1 of the Rules of Procedure.

4 In addition to budgetary powers. See Pierre Mathijsen, Compedium of European Law, ed. Seventh, Club Europe Publishing House, Bucharest, 2002, p 69 et seq.

5 "Consultation" is discussed in the section on the European Parliament, the advisory function of this institution, see in this respect, Ioana Nely Militaru, EU Law, ed. II, Legal Universe Publishing House, Bucharest, p 199 and seq.

of the Council and the European Commission[6] in order to empower the views of Parliament. The conciliation procedure was applied to proposals with notable financial implications and whose adoption was not required by existing provisions. If opposition to these acts arose between Parliament and the Commission's position or the opinion of the Council, a conciliation procedure could be established in a joint committee. The Conciliation Committee was composed of members of the Joint Council (or their representatives) and a delegation led by the President of the Parliament, while Commission participants oversaw agreement between the two institutions. If three months of conciliation failed to produce a new opinion or Parliament and the Council failed to reach a final decision, the Council had the last word[7]. Far from being enlarged[8] conciliation was restrained and finally replaced by cooperation and co-decision procedures.

b) The procedures for cooperation in making the right decisions. The procedure of "institutional cooperation"[9] was introduced by the Single European Act in order to facilitate the adoption of Single Market legislation (Art. 6 SEA) according to a strict schedule that ended in 1992. The Maastricht Treaty (TMs) was extended to new areas that were subsequently "deprived of all the profit of co-decision procedure[10]". Under the Lisbon Treaty, cooperation procedure was reconsidered in compliance with Art. 295 TFEU, according to which the European Parliament, the Council and the Commission shall consult each other and make arrangements to cooperate by common agreement. To this end, they may, in compliance with the Treaties, conclude inter-institutional agreements which may be binding.

c) The assent procedure was introduced by the Single European Act on association agreements[11] and applications for accession of new countries to the European Union [Art. 218 Para. 6 lit. a), i) TFEU, ex 300 TEC].

---

6 OJEC, n C 89 of 22 March 1975.

7 Conciliation did not produce the expected results, "because it was not completed (either Council was to agree with the view of Parliament or a late decision), and was open despite the request of Parliament". The conciliation procedure only applied to a small part of the legislative domain, see D. Strasser, Travaux de concertation legislative, in *Les finances de L'Europe,* Éditions LABOR, Bruxelles, 1984, p. 572; Guy Isaac, Marc Blanquet, Droit communautaire general, 8 ed., Dalloz, Paris, 2001, p 77.

8 According to the second conciliation statement on 16 December 1981, Bull. EC 3/82.

9 See Cornelia Popescu, Fundamentals of Community institutional law, Economic Publishing House, Bucharest, 2003, pp. 132-133; Fabian Gyula, Institutional Law Community, Legal Sphere Publishing House, Bucharest, 2004, p 183 and 184 and Guy Isaac, Marc Blanquet, cited work, p 77.

10 See Guy Isaac and Marc Blanquet, cited work, p 77.

11 The Treaty of Nice has maintained this procedure.

By using the phrase "with the approval of the European Parliament", both the Treaty of Maastricht and now the Treaty of Lisbon assent procedure have been extended to other areas, such as:

- European citizenship (Art. 19 TEU ex 13 TEC);
- agreements establishing a specific institutional framework by organising co-operation procedures, agreements with important budgetary implications for the Union, agreements in areas where ordinary legislative procedure applies, or the special legislative procedure, agreement on EU accession to the European Convention on Human Rights and Fundamental Freedoms (Art. 218 Para. 6 lit. a), ii, iii, iv, v, TFEU, ex 300 TEC)[12];
- rules for the election of members of Parliament if the Council determines necessary provisions on uniform voting for the election of the European Parliament by direct universal suffrage (Art. 223 TFEU, ex 190 TEC);
- or on detection of a serious risk of fundamental rights breaches in a member country (Art. 7 Para. 1 TEU was 7 TMs). The assent procedure obligates the Council, not only to ask the opinion of the European Parliament before making a decision, but also to take into account the Parliament's position, otherwise the act is not adopted[13].

Nowadays, conciliation, cooperation, advising and consulting, are more associated with some EU institutions exercising functions which contribute to the adoption of legal acts. Since the new treaties came into force, these principles have been subjected to numerous adaptations and replacements, ultimately producing the following:

- conciliation has been replaced by the cooperation and co-decision procedure;
- cooperation is expressly provided in a single provision of the TFEU, encouraging, in this sense, the adoption of institutional arrangements that can be binding under Art. 295;
- consultation is expressly provided through the functions of the European Parliament, according to Art. 14 TEU, although, in principle, the advisory functions associated with the adoption of legal acts belong to the Economic and Social Committee and the Committee of the Regions (Article 300 TFEU). Although the European Parliament (EP) is consulted, the institution is not bound by its opinion,
- endorsement of the advisory function of the EP; this time, however, the institution requesting the opinion is obliged to take account of "EP opinion".

---

12 According to Art. 90 of the Rules of Procedure.

13 See Dan Vataman, Union Law ..., cited work, p 169.

3. The adoption of legal acts in the EU according to the Lisbon Treaty

Currently, EU legal acts are legislative and non-legislative.

The adoption of legislative acts of the European Union corresponds to the legislative function which is exercised, in principle, equally by the European Parliament and the Council. Pursuant to Art. 289 TFEU, these two institutions adopt the following two procedures:

- ordinary legislative procedure, so-called co-decision procedure, which consists of joint adoption by the European Parliament and the Council of a legislative act (regulation, directive or decision) as proposed by the Commission. This procedure is defined in Art. 294 TFEU;
- special legislative procedure, which consists of the adoption of a legislative act (regulation, directive or decision) by the European Parliament with the participation of the Council, or by the Council with the participation of the Parliament, at the initiative of a group of Member States (Art. 7 Paras. 1 and 3 TEU and Art. 11 Para. 3 TEU[14]) or the European Parliament (Article 225 TFEU), on the recommendation of the ECB (Article 129 paragraph. 4 TFEU) or at the request of the CJEU (Article 252 TFEU) or EIB (Article 308 TFEU).

A standard procedure for adopting non-legislative acts is not provided, nor for the adoption of legislation under special procedures. For the ordinary procedure, as we have seen, there are rules laid down in the TFEU, such as the budgetary procedure.

3.1. Ordinary legislative procedure, regulated by Art. 294 TFEU, was introduced by the Maastricht Treaty by modifying the Treaty establishing the European Community (TEC).

The procedure was extended by the Treaty of Amsterdam[15], while the Treaty of Nice extended the co-decision procedure, substituting some cooperation and

14 Treaty refers to the corresponding third initiative “a significant number of Member States”.

15 The number of cases falling under the co-decision procedure increased from 15 to 37, of which 11 were previously subject to the cooperation procedure (e.g. Art. 12, 15 Para. 4, 175 Para. 1, 179 TEU), two to consultation procedure (Article 46 and 47 (2) TEU), 8 fell under new provisions introduced by the TA (e.g. Art. 135, 141 Para. 3, 255 Para. 2, 286 Para. 2 TEU). See Guy Isaac, Mark Blanquet, cited work, p. 77, and C. Reich, Le traité

consultation procedures. These substitutions "accounted for more than half of EU legislative activity". The co-decision procedure strengthens European Parliament legislative power – the procedures of acting by qualified majority and employing inter-institutional negotiations – introduced by the procedure of co-operation between Parliament, Council and Commission.

The Amsterdam Treaty accelerated the co-decision procedure to make it possible for a Community legislative act to be adopted at first reading, if everyone involved in the process agreed, thus strengthening Parliament's involvement in the pre-legislative phase of decision making[16]. In this respect, the three institutions – the European Parliament, Council and Commission – adopted a Joint Declaration on practical new approaches to co-decision procedure (1999)[17] that replaced the Interinstitutional Agreement of 21 October 1993, which was considered to be quite cumbersome and complex. Although this procedure extended to seven provisions of the EC Treaty, namely Art. 13, 62, 63, 65, 157, 159 and 191, the Treaty of Nice did not establish and shift to qualified majority voting when adopting co-decision. Also, common agricultural policy legislative measures adopted by a qualified majority did not fall under the co-decision procedure.

Through the Lisbon Treaty, "co-decision" has become the ordinary legislative procedure for the adoption of EU legislation.

Ordinary legislative procedure is an original combination that includes:

- technocratic proposals from the Commission, which obtains technical advice from experts from all Member States;
- Parliament representing EU citizens of participating Member States;
- Council, which represents governments of the Member States, and acts by qualified majority (according to Art. 294 TFEU, ex 251 TEC).

3.2. Special legislative procedure

The Treaties provided for a special legislative procedure in some cases for the adoption of legislation by the European Parliament with the participation of the Council, or by the latter with the participation of the European Parliament, or by a group of Member States, or by the European Parliament on recommendation of the European Central Bank, Court of Justice or European Investment Bank

d'Amsterdam et le champ d'application de la procédure de codécision, RMC, 1997, p. 665; L. Descot, L'affermissement du Parlement européen par la traité d'Amsterdam, l'exemple de la codécision, TPD, 1998, p. 38; O. Manolache, Treaty of Community law, ed. V, C. H. Beck Publishing House, Bucharest, 2006, p 201.

16 See O. Manolache, cited work, p 103.

17 OJEC, N. L. 148/1 from 28 May 1999.

(Article 289 TFEU). Special legislative procedure differs from ordinary legislative procedure in that:

- Parliament and Council work together, but each individually (e.g. Articles 19, 21, 25, 33, 64 Para. 3, 65 Para. 4, 81 Para. 3, Para. 82. 2, 83 Para. 1, 86 Para. 1, 87 Para. 3, 89, 108, Para. 2, 113, 115, 126 Para. 14, 127 Para. 6, 140 Para. 3, 311, 312 and other TFEU);
- the initiative driving a legislative act does not come from the Commission, but from another institution or a group of Member States (e.g. Articles 65 Para. 4, 108 Para. 2, 129, 252, 308, all TFEU).

If the provisions of the TFEU provide for legislative acts to be adopted by the Council in accordance with a special legislative procedure, the European Council may adopt a decision authorising the adoption of such acts in accordance with the ordinary legislative procedure (Art. 48 Para. 7 Para. 2 TEU).

Special legislative procedures are not covered by standard rules in the treaties, but are governed by different rules for each of the cases provided for in the Treaties. And in the special legislative procedure, the Council and the Parliament are still involved in passing legislation that is subject to different rules from those governing ordinary legislative procedure:

- in most cases, special legislative procedure requires unanimity in the Council and consultation of the Parliament (for example, Articles 21, 33, 64, 81 TFEU);
- in some cases, this implies unanimity in the Council and approval by the EP (e.g. Articles 19, 25, 82 Para. 2, 86 Para. 1 TFEU);
- there are also several cases where the Council votes by qualified majority and the European Parliament is only consulted (e.g. Articles 223 Para. 2, 226, 228, all TFEU);
- there is also a special legislative procedure for the adoption of the annual budget of the EU, which is based on the usual procedure but has been specially adapted to the particular characteristics of the budget process (qualified majority in the Council under Art. 314 TFEU).

3.3. Procedures for the adoption of non-legislative acts

Any action taken by the European Union through a – special or ordinary – legislative procedure is a "legislative act" (Art. 289 Para. 3 TFEU). Conversely, any measure that is not adopted by this procedure is a non-legislative act. In addition to the theoretical implications, the distinction between legislative and non-legislative acts also has practical implications, for example the European

Parliament and the Council shall meet in public when debating and voting on draft legislative acts, not being forced to do this when they discuss non-legislative acts (Art. 15 Para. 1 TFEU).

Non-legislative acts have their legal basis both in the Treaties (primary legislation) and in secondary legislation (derived).

Examples of non-legislative acts that are based on Treaties, (the TEU and TFEU) include:

- Article 74 TFEU on administrative[18] cooperation in which the Council adopts measures on proposal from the Commission and after consulting the European Parliament. Given that the Treaty does not provide for measures to be adopted by legislative procedure, they are therefore non-legislative acts;
- Article 81.3 Para. 2 TFEU, according to which the Council may adopt a decision determining those aspects of family law with cross-border implications which may be the subject of acts adopted by ordinary legislative procedure. The Council is therefore not obliged to adopt by legislative procedure in this area.
- A series of non-legislative acts have been adopted by the European Council, for example:
  - Art. 86 Para. 4 TFEU, according to which the institution may adopt a decision to extend the powers of the European Public Prosecutor.
  - Art. 24 Para. 1(2) and Art. 31 Para. 1, both TEU, on Common Foreign and Security Policy, stipulating that the "adoption of legislative acts shall be excluded" in the area of CFSP and therefore decisions in this area by the Council and the European Council are non-legislative acts.

The Council acted by qualified majority on a proposal from the High Representative of the Union for Foreign Affairs and Security Policy and the Commission, in accordance with Art. 215 TFEU. In this regard, the Council adopted "restrictive measures" required on penalties related to CFSP against natural or legal persons, groups or state entities.

The examples mentioned above show that there are no rules for the procedure to adopt non-legislative acts because:

- the Commission – an institution with legislative initiative in principle under Art. 86 Para. 4 TFEU – only has an advisory role;
- in some cases the Commission is informed, but not consulted (Article 215 TFEU), in other cases it is consulted (Art. 74 TFEU);

---

18 Appropriate "Area of Freedom, Security and Justice" (formerly Pillar II of the EU JHA, later, by the Treaty of Amsterdam, CPJP).

- since TEU provisions exclude the use of CFSP legislation, all measures in this area are non-legislative,
- the European Council adopted a decision amending all or part of the provisions of Part III of the TFEU (Article 48 Para. 3 TEU). The Council shall act unanimously after consulting the EP and the Commission and the ECB, in the case of institutional changes in the monetary area. The Council shall act according to the rules above, and within the simplified treaty revision procedure (Article 48 Para. 6 TEU);
- when negotiating and approving agreements between the European Union and third countries or international organisations (Article 218 TFEU), the Council shall adopt the decision concluding the agreement, in some cases after approval by the EP and in others after consulting the EP.

Non-legislative acts adopted under secondary legislation or secondary legislation are: implementing acts and delegated acts. Their legal basis is as follows:

- 291 TFEU, according to which, if uniform conditions are necessary for implementing legally binding acts of the EU, those acts (the base) confer jurisdiction on the Commission, or – in specific cases duly justified and in cases provided for by Art. 24 and 26 TEU – the Council[19]. It is up to the legislature, while fully respecting the criteria laid down in the TFEU, to decide in each case whether to give powers to the Commission in accordance with Art. 291 Para. 2 of that Treaty. To date, the exercise of implementing powers by the Commission is governed by Council Decision 1999/468/EC.
- 290 TFEU, which introduces delegated acts pursuant to the Lisbon Treaty. According to this article, EU legislation may delegate to the Commission the power to adopt generally applicable non-legislative acts to supplement or amend certain non-essential elements of the act.

Does not are general rules governing the procedure for adopting delegated acts, unless a Commission Communication of 9 December 2009 establishing a model for legislation that could be adapted on a case by case basis[20]. In this case, the Commission Communication considers that

> "delegation may be considered a means of better regulation, which seeks to ensure that legislation can remain simple and be completed and updated without the need to

---

19 See Regulation (EU) 182/2011 of the EP and the Council of 16 February 2011 laying down the rules and general principles concerning mechanisms Member States to control the exercise of implementing powers by the Commission (J Of L. 055, 28.02.2011, p 013-018).

20 COM (2010), C 81 E / 6, from 15.03.2011.

> resort to repeated legislative procedures, legislature may also retain critical skills and responsibility" (Preamble, lit. H).

There is no general rule for the adoption of delegated acts in that Communication (the letter I), thus

> "Article 290 TFEU does not contain a legal basis for the adoption of a horizontal instrument laying down the rules and general principles applicable to the delegation because those conditions must therefore be determined in each basic act (act of legislative nature, a.n.)".

4. Conclusions

Through the Lisbon Treaty, co-decision procedure has become ordinary procedure in the European Union (Art. 289 Para. 1 TFEU), with the legislative function being shared between the European Parliament and the Council.

Further, the legislative powers of the European Parliament are indicated by the special regulation adopting legal acts of the Union, namely the specific cases provided for in the Treaties in respect of the adoption of a regulation, directive or decision by the European Parliament with the participation of the Council, or by the Council with the participation of the European Parliament (Article 289 Para. 2 TFEU). Note that the TEU, when enumerating the functions of the Parliament, begins by specifying that "The European Parliament shall, jointly with the Council, exercise legislative and budgetary functions" (Article 14 TEU).

Since the establishment of the European Community, the Council has retained its status as the main legislative body of the European Union. In this regard, the Council performs legislative functions, either individually, by special procedure acting unanimously in most cases (Art. 19, Art. 21, Art. 65, Art. 108, Art. 113 TFEU), or with a participating role only by the European Parliament, or jointly with the European Parliament, through the ordinary procedure (of co-decision).

Bibliography

Descot, L.: L'affermissement du Parlement européen par la traité d'Amsterdam, l'exemple de la codécision, TPD, 1998.

Gyula, Fabian: Institutional Law Community, Legal Sphere Publishing House, Bucharest, 2004.

Isaac, Guy, Blanquet, Marc: Droit communautaire general, 8 ed., Dalloz, Paris, 2001.

Manolache, O.: Treaty of Community law, V ed., C. H. Beck Publishing House, Bucharest, 2006.

Mathijsen, Pierre: Compendium of European Law, seventh edition, Club Europe Publishing House, Bucharest, 2002.

Militaru, Ioana Nely: European Union law, chronology. Springs. Principles. Institutions, Second Edition, Legal Universe Publishing House, Bucharest, 2011.
Popescu, Cornelia: Institutional Foundations of Community law, Economic Publishing House, Bucharest, 2003.
Reich, C.: Le traité d'Amsterdam et le champ d'application de la procédure de codécision, RMC, 1997.
Strasser, D.: Travaux de concertation legislative, in Les finances de L'Europe, Éditions LABOR, Bruxelles, 1984.
Vataman, Dan: EU Law, Legal Universe Publishing, Bucharest, 2010.

The European Company (Societas Europaea - SE), a Legal Instrument of Mobility for Companies in the European Union

Assistant professor Felicia BEJAN[1], PhD student

Abstract

According to the Treaties that established the European Union, the completion of the internal market represents an absolute priority in the construction of Europe. Guaranteeing companies' freedom of establishment is essential for accomplishing this major objective. Nevertheless, regulating a legal instrument for promoting European companies' movement in the European space encountered real resistance from the Member States. The European Company represents the first legal instrument provided by the communitarian legislator to companies willing to give their activities a cross-border character. Having an original legal status, this new type of structure marked the beginning of companies' movement on the single market. Beyond its contribution to the modernisation of communitarian companies' law, the European Company remains in itself an important legal instrument, albeit perfectible, for exercising the freedom of establishment for companies in the European Union.

Keywords: European Company, mobility, cross-border merger, seat transfer.

1. Introduction

The regulation initiative for a European type of company belonged to France. In 1966, Professor Sanders[2], together with experts from five other Member States, designed a project shaping the status of the incorporated European Company, a project adopted thereafter by the European Commission through the 1970 Regulation proposal[3].

The proposed status was inspired from the German law model of joint stock companies, known to be one of the most rigorous. Among the provisions borrowed from German law, there were also those concerning co-determination –

1 Felicia Bejan, University of Bucharest, Faculty of Political Sciences, Romania, E-mail: bejanf@digi.ro.

2 The European Commission was the institution charging Professor Sanders, the dean of the Law Faculty in Rotterdam, together with other experts in the field, to come up with a project proposal. The document Etudes sur un projet de société anonyme européenne, Série Concurrence, 1967, was sent to the Council by the Commission in 1967.

3 The regulation proposal from 30 June 1970 regarding the status of the incorporated European Company, JOCE no. C. 124 on 10 October 1970.

the *Mitbestimmung*[4] model – a system under which employees are represented at the administrative level and contribute to the company's management. The objective for borrowing this model was to prevent unfair competition regarding social aspects. Due to the lack of standardisation in this matter, it was felt that the decision by the European Company on which Member State to choose for its registered office might be influenced by attempts to circumvent law systems that were familiar with the co-determination mechanism, at the expense of the employees' and the concerned states' interests.

Despite the strictness of the regulation and its innovative character, the 1970 proposal to introduce, together with the national categories of companies, a company model characterised by a fully transnational status, governed by a directly applicable regulation, and moreover inspired by the German law system, while excluding the application of domestic legislations, was not successful.

Actually it is well known that Member States are reluctant to adopt any initiative that implicitly involves relinquishing national sovereignty in favour of communitarian legal order.

Many other proposals have been submitted to the states, but none of them materialised in time.

It took Member States more than 30 years to give up their mistrust in the European Company. In 2000, at the Nice summit of the European Council, the Member States of the European Community agreed upon this new communitarian instrument following final identification of a solution concerning the employees.

On 8 October 2001, European Council Regulation no. 2157/2001 concerning the status of the European Company (SE)[5], and the 2001/86/EC Directive completing the former with regard to employee engagement[6], were unanimously adopted. Compared with the 1970 version, which contained about 300 articles, the 2001 text has only 70 articles, which made it easier to understand and apply.

The regulation was enforced on 8 October 2004[7], a date that represented the deadline by which Member States were obligated to transpose the 2001/86/EC Directive into national law.

Within the context of globalisation, adopting a normative act concerning European companies was considered highly important for ensuring cross-border

4 Mitbestimmung is the exact translation from German of co-determination.

5 Published in the Official Journal L 294/1 on 10 November 2001.

6 Published in the Official Journal L 294/1 on 10 November 2001.

7 According to Romanian law, the Emergency Ordinance of the Government no. 52/2008 published in the Official Journal no. 333/30 April 2008, the Romanian legislator adopted national norms to enforce the Regulation regarding European Companies by introducing a new title of the Law 31/1990, namely Title VII1 – the European Company.

movement and increasing companies' competitiveness within the European Union. In an optimistic perspective, Frits Bolkenstein[8], member of the European Commission at the time, declared that

> "the European Company will allow the development and the cross-border reorganisation of many companies, while avoiding endless bureaucracy and the costs engaged by the creation of a network of subsidiaries. This represents therefore a step forward in the effort of business integration on the national market, in the daily reality, and an incentive for a growing number of them to take advantage of this opportunity beyond national borders and thereby consolidate Europe's competitiveness according to the Lisbon objectives".

2. The legal status of the European Company (SE)

The European Company is an autonomous type of company created on European Union territory that takes the form of an incorporated European company without being a joint stock company in the strictest sense, and which is established under the conditions and by the means provided by Regulation no. 2157/2001. The legal regime of the European Company is a mixed one. The aspects which are not governed by the Regulation at issue are covered by the national provisions of the Member State where the European Company has its registered office, adopted in accordance with communitarian measures regarding SEs, in particular, or applicable to a joint stock company created according to the legal system of the Member State where the SE has its registered office[2].

The European Company's legal status is an original one, adapted to the interest provided by the regulation it is governed by. It is obvious that – from setting up to the moment of registration – this genuine legal entity demonstrates a series of particularities, some of which constitute totally new legal structures for characterising companies.

The regulation text contains rules concerning the creation and operation of the European Company, norms organising legal aspects such as means of constitution, legal form and company name, company capital, registered office, management and administration, publication formalities and the company's registration.

Ways of formation. Irrespective of the means of constitution, the creation of a European corporation is always based on the prior existence of some stock companies, subsidiaries or branches in at least two different states. As emphasised in an official report, "a European corporation cannot be created *ex nihilo*"[9].

---

8 Frits Bolkenstein was Commissioner for the Internal Market in 2004.

9 Noëlle Lenoir, La Societas Europaea ou SE: pour une Citoyenneté Européenne de l'Entreprise (2007), Rapports officiels.

At the same time, whichever the means of creation, the European corporation requires at least one foreign element.

Regulation no. 2157/2001 establishes four possible routes to creating a European corporation:

a) a European Company established by joining two or more cross-border joint stock companies, created under a Member State's legal system, with their head office and central management in the European Union if at least two of them are governed by the law of different Member States.

b) a holding European Company established by joint stock companies or by limited liability companies, with the head office and the central management on European territory, and which are situated in at least two different Member States or maintain a subsidiary governed by the law of another Member State or a branch on the territory of another Member State for at least two years.

c) establishment of a subsidiary European Company. According to the Regulation, all types of corporations with their head office and central management on European territory and situated in at least two different Member States or maintaining a subsidiary governed by the law of another Member State or a branch established on the territory of another Member State for at least two years can form a European corporation-type subsidiary.

d) transformation of an incorporated company into a European Company, if it was established under the law of a Member State, has its head office and central administration within the territory of the Community, and has been operating a branch in another Member State for at least two years.

Legal form. According to Article 3 of the Regulation, the legal form embraced by the European Company is that of an incorporated company, created in accordance with the law of the Member State in which the registered office is located. The European Company can create one or more subsidiaries under the form of single shareholder European companies, a situation in which national dispositions regarding single shareholder companies don't apply.

Company Denomination. To emphasise the identity of this new type of corporation, the Regulation provides that the name of the European Company has to be preceded or followed by the abbreviation SE – *Societas Europaea.*

Minimum subscribed capital. The European Company's share capital is expressed in euro, and cannot be less than 120,000 euro, as a rule. There are certain activities which represent an exception, in these cases the legislation where the European Company has established its head office with a share capital which exceeds this amount, and national laws thereby apply accordingly. As the exception is strictly interpreted and applied, it obviously won't apply when national norms expressly provide for a lesser amount of share capital than imposed by the Regulation when establishing certain types of companies.

As far as the use of the euro as benchmark currency is concerned in those Member States which haven't yet adopted the single currency, the share capital is expressed in the national currency, while maintaining the possibility for the European corporation to express its capital in euro.

Registered office. The office of the European corporation can be established in any of the Member States, provided that its central administration is located in that country, and can be transferred to another Member State. In fact, the possibility to transfer the office from the Member State where it was registered to another Member State is one of the main advantages of this kind of corporation.

However, establishing the registered office in one of the Member States does not imply automatic assumption of the nationality of that country, the European Company being essentially a legal entity that is superior to the Member States' national law systems.

Central management. Regardless of whether Member States apply the monist system or the dualist system, according to the Regulation, the central management of the European Company has to function in the same country where the company has established its head office. Moreover, Member States are allowed to establish their head office and central administration in the same place. As far as relocation of the central administration is concerned, the Regulation stipulates the Commission's obligation to submit to both the European Parliament and the Council a report analysing the opportunity to establish the European Company's central administration and head office in different Member States.

Double publication of the establishment of a European corporation. The establishment of a European Company is subject to two-fold publication: at both the national and European levels.

At the national level, publication is submitted to the legislation of the Member State where the European Company establishes its head office and results in the enforceability of the corporation establishment against third parties.

At the European level, the disclosure consists of a public notification for informative purposes, published in the Official Journal of the European Union and concerning the registration of the European Company.

The notification is communicated by the national register of the Member State where the head office is established, and contains information regarding the European Company's denomination, number, registration date and place, publishing date, place and title, head office and field of activity.

Legal entity. The European Company acquires status as a legal entity as soon as it is registered. The European Company is entered in the national register of the Member State where the company has established its head office; such registration can take place only after conclusion of an agreement governing employee co-determination and decision making according to Article 3, Para. 6 of the 2001/86/EC Directive, or if the negotiation period established by the Directive has expired without reaching an agreement.

3. Essential contributions of the European Company (SE) to company mobility in the internal market

3.1. Shaping a legal regime for cross-border mergers

The 2157/2001 Regulation regarding European Company status represents the first communitarian text providing companies in the European Member States with a set of material rules which have facilitated the establishment of the cross-border merger procedure.

Its merit increases as it marks an end to the long period of time when European companies were faced with numerous legal obstacles when trying to cross the borders of the states where their office or central administration was located.

In legal literature, the cross-border merger is considered the main legal instrument for establishing European Companies. Some authors even assert that the European Company was conceived as a facilitator for cross-border mergers in the European Union. Although such an assertion is hard to prove scientifically, it is certain that in practice more than half of the existing European Companies were established by merger.

Beyond all these opinions, we consider that the major asset of the Regulation regarding the status of the European Company lies in its contribution to the movement of companies, by shaping a legal regime for cross-border mergers.

Therefore, for the first time in the history of communitarian law, a normative act offers a definition of the cross-border merger and regulates its field of activity.

According to the Regulation, every stock company has to cumulatively meet two conditions in order to participate in a merger to establish a European Company: it must have been established according to the legislation of a Member State and it must have its head office in one of the Member States of the European Union.

To benefit from the legal regime established by the Regulation, companies merging to form a European Company cannot have their central management and head office in the same Member State.

What's more, according to Para. 23 of the Regulation, this kind of procedure is also accessible to companies established on behalf of the legislation of a Member State where their registered office is located, but whose decision-making headquarters are outside the European Union, provided that the company at issue has substantial and continuous ties with the economy of a European country[10].

As far as the establishment of the merger is concerned, Article 17 asserts that the merger procedure must take place according to Article 3 and Article 4 of the Directive 78/855/CEE regarding internal mergers. As a consequence, the merger can take place:

- by absorption procedure, when the absorbing company takes the shape of a European Company and
- by establishing a new company, in which case the newly established company becomes a European Company.

Article 20 of the Regulation is considered to be truly innovative and crucial for crossing the traditional limits of cross-border mergers as it provides that the elements of the merger have to be mutually agreed by the companies involved in the merger project, and establishes the mandatory aspects of this one[11]. Introducing a substantive rule of law to unitarily regulate the content of the main document for the cross-border merger eliminates the inconveniences caused by the cumulative application of national legislations to the clauses of the merger contract.

---

10 Such a connection exists, namely when a company has a functional unit in the country at issue.

11 According to Article 20, the merger project includes the following elements:
a) the name and registered office of each of the merging companies together with those proposed for the SE
b) the share-exchange ratio and the amount of any compensation
c) the terms for the allotment of shares in the SE
d) the date from which the holding of shares in the SE will entitle the holders to share in profits and any special conditions affecting that entitlement
e) the date from which the transactions of the merging companies will be treated for accounting purposes as being those of the SE
f) the rights conferred by the SE on the holders of shares to which special rights are attached and on the holders of securities other than shares, or the measures proposed concerning them
g) any special advantage granted to the experts who examine the draft terms of the merger or to members of the administrative, management, supervisory or controlling organs of the merging companies
h) the statutes of the SE
i) information on the procedure by which arrangements for employee involvement are determined pursuant to Directive 2001/86/EC.

In addition, a possible conflict of law is avoided with respect to the necessary threshold for approval of the merger by the shareholders of the companies involved. According to the Regulation, the shareholders' meetings of all companies involved in the merger must approve it. Decisions to approve cross-border mergers require the quorum and majority conditions stipulated in the national regulations regarding internal mergers which usually apply to the modification of constitutive acts. Since unanimous shareholder agreement is not required, the different national regulations governing merger approval majorities basically cannot block the transaction any more.

Another important innovation in the merger procedure is considered to be the stipulation that independent expert institutions examine the merger project for each company and issue a report to inform the shareholders. The objective of such a rule was to eliminate the application of those national procedures in some Member States which allowed subsequent examination and modification of the mergers' financial conditions, and which threatened to affect the legal security of the procedure.

For the same purpose of ensuring legal certainty of the procedure, the rules require a mandatory judicial review of the merger procedure for each of the merging companies. The competent authorities have to issue a certificate which clearly confirms conclusion, prior to the merger, of the necessary acts and formalities. The importance of the control of legality is even greater as, according to the regulations, mergers can no longer be pronounced null and void following registration of the European corporation. The only possible penalty in the absence of merger examination control is the dissolution of the European Company.

An analysis of the body of regulations that govern the establishment by merger of the European Company shows that the legal regime for cross-border mergers combines substantive communitarian norms with references to national legislation. The procedure is subject to substantive norms regarding the merger process; norms which apply directly and have a direct effect, eliminating, in principle, any possible juridical conflict with respect to the legal aspects they refer to. If substantive norms don't have a regulatory effect, they refer to the national procedures applicable to internal mergers in every Member State.

As national regulations regarding internal mergers of stock companies are aligned following transposition of Directive 78/855/EC, such a reference shouldn't generate a conflict of law that might jeopardise the cross-border merger. This doesn't mean there aren't differences between the European states' merger regulations, and that a conflict of law is fully excluded. Because the Directive is mandatory for Member States only insofar as the final result is concerned, leaving the European countries free to decide how this result can be attained, differences between national legal regimes might emerge as a result of the individual application of the Directive concerning internal mergers of stock companies at national level.

According to literature in the field, the applicability of national procedures that could still give rise to a conflict of law represents one of the major sensitive points of the 2157/2001 Regulation concerning the establishment of the European Company by merger.

Practice has shown that, although cross-border cooperation between companies with their head office in different European Member States was a feasible means of reshaping their activity and consolidating the single market, intra-communitarian mergers still faced numerous legislative and administrative hurdles in the European Union. National laws governing all companies that sought to establish a cross-border merger continued to represent an obstacle to completing such procedures.

To eliminate this disadvantage, the best solution was to subject the merger to a single substantive law. The adoption of an appropriate communitarian instrument, which allows the establishment of a cross-border merger in the best conditions, became an evident necessity.

A communitarian legislative project to harmonise the national legal framework in Member States regarding cross-border mergers and facilitate the reorganisation of European companies was initiated. On 26 October 2005, the European Parliament and the Council adopted Directive 2005/56 on cross-border mergers of limited liability companies[12].

It can thus be said, without being wrong, that besides the creation of a legal regime for cross-border mergers, the European corporation contributed to the establishment of a new communitarian act fostering the mobility of companies in Europe, known as the cross-border merger Directive.

3.2. Regulating the transfer of a European Company's registered office from the Member State where it was registered to another Member State

By regulating the transfer of the European Company's registered office, the Council's Regulation no. 2157/2001 establishes another novelty regarding the freedom of establishment for European companies[13].

According to Article 8 of the Regulation, the head office of a European Company can be transferred to another European state. European Companies

12 Published in the Official Journal L. 319 dated 26 October 1978.

13 The transfer of the head office is regulated in the 16 paragraphs of Article 8 of Regulation no. 2157/2001. According to Romanian law, provisions concerning the transfer of the head office can be found in Title VIII Law 31/1990.

that are in the process of dissolution, liquidation, insolvency, cessation of payments or other similar situations are excepted and cannot benefit from these provisions.

The transfer of registered office does not imply the European Company's dissolution and doesn't require the establishment of a new legal entity, as would be the case if a national company wanted to migrate its activities within the communitarian borders. Relocation of the registered office does, however, mean that the legal entity becomes subject to different national laws, and must therefore adapt to a new legal regime.

Transferring a registered office is governed by a procedure that requires the preparation of a transfer project respecting the regulation provisions; this transfer project must adhere to all the steps needed for a legal decision to be made by the shareholders' meeting and must respect all the stages and formalities needed to protect shareholders, employees and third parties[14].

Without doubt, Council Regulation no. 2157/2001 gives the European Company a legal framework that enables it to cross the borders of the territory on which it was established. Nevertheless, it is our belief that regulating the transfer of registered office only in the context of European Companies is discriminatory of other European legal entities. The freedom of establishment on communitarian territory implies, together with other rights, the stock companies' right to freely relocate their head office to another Member State. Thus, we see a need for special communitarian regulation governing head office relocation that has a broader field of application.

Although the need for harmonisation in the field of registered office relocation has been clearly recognised since the Daily Mail[15] Decision of the European Court of Justice, issued in 1988, delays in translating this imperative into a normative act have occurred.

Given the intensification of national and European initiatives regarding the transfer of the place of incorporation, new regulation might not be far away. On 2 February 2012, the European Parliament adopted a Resolution with recommendations for the Commission regarding the 14th Directive on stock companies' rights to transfer their head office across borders[15]. The recommendations at issue were mostly inspired by the Council's Regulation no. 2157/2001.

Accordingly, as with cross-border mergers, the European Company not only regulates the transfer of the registered office from the European state in which it

14 The transfer of the registered office is regulated in the 16 paragraphs of Article 8 of Regulation 2157/2001. In Romanian law, the provisions on transferring registered offices are contained in Title VIII of Law 31/1990.

15 Decision of the European Court of Justice from 27 September 1988, case C-81/1987, HM Treasury and Commissioners of Inland Revenue/Daily Mail and General Trust PLC.

was registered to another Member State, but it also influences the development of communitarian law in the field.

When regulation governing transfers of registered offices is enacted, it will complete, together with the regulation concerning the European Company and the cross-border merger Directive, the set of legal instruments designed to guarantee the mobility of companies throughout the European Union.

4. *De lege ferenda* proposals concerning the regulation of European Companies (SE)

Although the regulation concerning the status of the European Company undeniably contributed towards removing hurdles blocking stock companies' freedom of movement, usage of this instrument by its potential beneficiaries has proven to be scant in practice.

The rules governing the creation of the European Company by merger were often criticised. The general use of the European Company to enable cross-border mobility is impossible given that the only types of companies who qualify for establishment of a SE by merger are joint stock companies[16].

In the context of a narrow application field, regulated strictly, the only solution for other kinds of companies to benefit from the advantages of this type of European legal instrument is to become joint stock corporations, with all the consequences such a change entails.

The fact that not all companies comply with the eligibility criteria provided by the regulation, but only those whose registered office and central management can both be found in one of the Member States only amplifies the problem concerning the limitations on company mobility.

De lege ferenda, we strongly believe that it is necessary, first of all, to extend the scope of application regarding the establishment of a European Company by merger to include all limited liability companies. At the same time, one of the problems that has been invoked and which requires a future legal solution concerns the inclusion of European Company in the category of companies who are entitled to merge with joint stock companies from other Member States in order to set up a new European Company.

Another criticism brought against the regulation governing the establishment by merger of the European Company concerns the ways in which cross-border mergers take place in practice.

16 Noëlle Lenoir, La Societas Europaea ou SE: pour une Citoyenneté Européenne de l'Entreprise (2007), Rapports officiels.

As noted, the merger procedure can take place by absorption or by the establishment of a new company. In practice, the two types of merger – the merger by absorption and the merger by the creation of a new company – were considered insufficient to allow European corporations to adequately concentrate their resources in order to compete successfully at international level. *De lege ferenda*, regulating cross-border mergers through absorption of a subsidiary by the parent company as a means of establishing a European Company could represent a solution for eliminating all the bottlenecks invoked by practitioners in the field. The procedure distinguishes itself by the absorbing company having the quality of associate for the absorbed entity, which leads to certain particularities concerning the conditions, the procedure and the effects of such a merger.

The 120,000 euro minimum share capital for the European corporation constitutes one of the limitations of the current Regulation. According to European norms incorporated in Member States' legislation, the minimum capital requirement for a stock company is 25,000 euro. A larger amount of share capital is required for specific fields of activity. For example, equity and financial activities are exceptions where the subscribed capital usually has to meet stricter requirements.

In our opinion, the discrepancy between the effective capitalisation of stock companies seeking to create a European corporation by merger and the financial efforts they have to make in order to cover the capital requirements of such a corporation is more than obvious.

This unjustified lack of correlation between domestic capital requirements and European requirements discriminates in practice between large companies and small and medium enterprises, and makes cross-border mergers an impossible target for the latter to reach.

De lege ferenda, European legislation must consider lowering the share capital from 120,000 euro. Such a change is all the more necessary, given that current regulation contradicts premise 13 of the Regulation which provides that

> "In order to ensure that [European Companies] are of reasonable size, a minimum amount of capital should be set so that they have sufficient assets without making it difficult for small and medium-sized undertakings to form SEs".

Or, *de lege lata*, small and medium enterprises, despite being the most numerous within the European states, are, in the majority of cases, not benefiting from the Regulation's provisions.

A sensitive point of the Council's Regulation no. 2157/2001 concerns the request that the registered office and the central administration of a European Company be established on the territory of the same Member State. Paradoxically, a mobility instrument establishes limits concerning its own freedom of circulation. Moreover, it leaves the Member States free to decide whether they want to implement by imperative norms the European Company's obligation to establish the registered office and central management in the same place. The regulation is quite obviously contradictory because, while offering Member States excessive power to limit the movement of European Companies, it also provides the necessity of an opportunity analysis concerning the elimination of the rule that stipulates the establishment of both the office and the management in the same country. In our view, this incoherence of the European legislator must be rectified *de lege ferenda*. It is our belief that the optimum solution can only be administrative mobility, allowing the location to be different from that of the registered office, and elimination of the Member States' possibility to restrict the freedom of establishment.

Conceived as a cross-border mobility vehicle, and subsequently transformed into a benchmark for other legal instruments governing the freedom of movement, the European Company remains a single legal construction that plays a crucial role for the evolution of business law within the communitarian space. Notwithstanding this, as noted above, the European Company, as with any other kind of legal construction, is perfectible. We believe its legal regime must be modernised to keep pace with the reorganisation and mobility needs of the companies in the internal market.

Bibliography

Angheni, S., Stoica, C., Volonciu M.: Drept comercial, C.H. Beck Publishing House, Bucharest, 2008.

Lefter, Cornelia: Fundamente ale dreptului comunitar instituţional, Economic Publishing House, Bucharest, 2003.

Lenoir, Noëlle: La Societas Europaea ou SE: pour une Citoyenneté Européenne de l'Entreprise, Rapports officiels, 2007.

The Treaty establishing the European Coal and Steel Community.

The Treaty establishing the Atomic Energy Community.

The Treaty of Lisbon.

The EC Regulation no. 2157/2001 of the Council dated 8 October 2001 concerning the European corporation's (SE) status.

The European Parliament and the Council Directive no. 2005/53/EC regarding cross-border mergers of stock companies.

Law no. 31/1990 regarding commercial enterprises.

Regulation proposal dated 30 June 1970 regarding the status of European incorporated companies.

State Aids that are Incompatible with the Internal Market in European Court of Justice Case Law

Lecturer Cătălin-Silviu SĂRARU[1]

Abstract

This article examines State aid that is incompatible with the internal market. Based on constitutive treaties (now Article 107 of the Treaty on the Functioning of the European Union - TFEU) the Court of Justice of the European Union has established in its case law the conditions to be met for a measure to qualify as State aid: existence of State intervention or through State resources, the intervention must be liable to affect trade between Member States, the intervention must confer an advantage on the recipient, the intervention must distort or threaten to distort competition.

Keywords: State aid, internal market, the Court of Justice of the European Union, subsidies, competition.

1. Preliminary Considerations

According to Article 107 Para. (1) of the Treaty on the Functioning of the European Union (TFEU) (ex Article 87 TEC)

> "any aid granted by a Member State or through State resources in any form whatsoever which distorts or threatens to distort competition by favouring certain undertakings or the production of certain goods shall, in so far as it affects trade between Member States"[2]

---

1 Cătălin-Silviu Săraru, Bucharest University of Economic Studies, Department of Law, Romania, catalinsararu@yahoo.com.

2 Paragraph (2) of Art. 107 TFEU provides a number of exceptions considered compatible with the internal market:
(a) aid with a social character, granted to individual consumers, provided that such aid is granted without discrimination related to the origin of the products concerned;
(b) aid to make good the damage caused by natural disasters or exceptional occurrences;
(c) aid granted to the economy of certain areas of the Federal Republic of Germany affected by the division of Germany, insofar as such aid is required in order to compensate for the economic disadvantages caused by that division. Five years after the entry into force of the Treaty of Lisbon, the Council, acting on a proposal from the Commission, may adopt a decision repealing this point.
Paragraph (3) of Art. 107 TFEU lists types of aid that can be considered compatible with the internal market under the conditions specified herein:

be considered to be incompatible with the internal market.

State aid, as defined in the Treaty, is a legal concept and must be interpreted on the basis of objective factors. For that reason, the European Court of Justice must in principle comprehensively review whether a measure falls within the scope of Article 107 Para. (1) of the Treaty on the Functioning of the European Union (TFEU) (ex Article 87 TEC)[3], bearing in mind both the specific features of the case before it, and the technical or complex nature of the Commission's assessments.

2. The conditions to be satisfied for a measure to qualify as State aid

Article 92(1) of the Treaty (now, Article 107 Para. (1) TFEU) lays down the following conditions for a measure to be classified as State aid[4]. First, there must be an intervention by the State or through State resources. Second, the intervention must be liable to affect trade between Member States. Third, it must confer

---

(a) aid to promote the economic development of areas where the standard of living is abnormally low or where there is serious underemployment, and of the regions referred to in Article 349, in view of their structural, economic and social situation;

(b) aid to promote the execution of an important project of common European interest or to remedy a serious disturbance in the economy of a Member State;

(c) aid to facilitate the development of certain economic activities or of certain economic areas, where such aid does not adversely affect trading conditions to an extent contrary to the common interest;

(d) aid to promote culture and heritage conservation where such aid does not affect trading conditions and competition in the Union to an extent that is contrary to the common interest;

(e) such other categories of aid as may be specified by decision of the Council on a proposal from the Commission.

3 Case C-487/06, British Aggregates/Commission, www.curia.eu, See also Ileana Pascal, Ştefan Deaconu, Codru Vrabie, Niculae Fabian, Politica în domeniul concurenţei, Publishing "Legal Resource Center", Bucharest, 2002, p. 26; Ioan Alexandru, Cătălin-Silviu Săraru and others, Drept administrativ european, Lumina Lex Publishing House, Bucharest, 2005, p. 204, 205.

4 Case C-172/03, Heiser, www.curia.eu. See also Radu Cristian Muşetescu, The Economics of State Aid Control in the European Union during the Financial Crisis: the Challenge for a Post-Crisis Rhetoric, Theoretical and Applied Economics, Volume XIX (2012), No. 6(571), p. 179, 178; Marina Kesner-Škreb, Mia Mikiæ, State aid in the European Union and Croatia, Institute of Public Finance, volume 1, number 1, October 2003, p. 118.

an advantage on the recipient. Fourth, it must distort or threaten to distort competition.

2.1. Existence of State intervention or through State resources.

Only advantages granted directly or indirectly through State resources are to be considered aid within the meaning of Article 107 Para. (1) TFEU. The distinction made in that provision between aid granted by a Member State and aid granted through State resources does not signify that all advantages granted by a State, whether financed through State resources or not, constitute aid but is intended merely to bring within that definition both advantages which are granted directly by the State and those granted by a public or private body designated or established by that State.

Therefore, statutory provisions of a Member State which, first, require private electricity suppliers to purchase electricity produced in their area of supply from renewable energy sources at minimum prices higher than the real economic value of that type of electricity, and, second, distribute the financial burden resulting from that obligation between those electricity suppliers and upstream private electricity grid operators do not constitute State aid within the meaning of Article 92(1) of the EC Treaty[5].

The expression State resources in Article 87(1) EC Treaty (now, Article 107 Para. (1) TFEU) covers all the financial means by which the public authorities may actually support undertakings, irrespective of whether or not those means are permanent assets of the public sector. Therefore, even if the sums corresponding to a State aid measure are financial resources of public undertakings and are not permanently held by the Treasury, the fact that they constantly remain under public control, and therefore available to the competent national authorities, is sufficient for them to be categorised as State resources. That is the case where the State is perfectly capable, by exercising its dominant influence over public undertakings, of directing the use of their resources in order, as occasion arises, to finance specific advantages in favour of other undertakings[6].

Article 92(1) of the EC Treaty (now, Article 107 Para. (1) TFEU) is directed at all aid financed from public resources. It follows that aid granted by regional or local bodies of Member States, whatever their status and description, comes under said provision[7]. Also, in order to determine whether aid may be regarded as State aid for the purposes of Article 92(1) of the Treaty (now, Article 107 Pa-

5 Case C-379/98, PreussenElektra, www.curia.eu.
6 Case C-482/99, France/Commission, www.curia.eu.
7 Case C-248/84, Germany/Commission, www.curia.eu.

ra. (1) TFEU), no distinction should be drawn between cases where aid is granted directly by the State and cases where it is granted by public or private bodies established or appointed by the State to administer the aid[8].

All subsidies from the public sector that threaten competition are addressed by Article 92 of the Treaty (now, Article 107 Para. (1) TFEU), whether or not they are granted by the government or a central administrative authority of a Member State. A body forms part of the public sector when it has been established by the legislation of a Member State as a special body under the supervision and guarantee of the legislature, its tasks governed by statutory and regulatory rules, and its director general and other directors appointed by the head of State and the government of that Member State respectively; its public nature cannot be called into question by arrangements that are part of the internal organisation of the public sector, such as the existence of rules to ensure that that body remains independent of other public authorities. The legislative power to which that body is subject is one of the constitutional powers of a State, and Community law cannot permit the rules on State aid to be circumvented merely through the creation of autonomous institutions charged with allocating aid[9].

According to the case law of the Court of Justice, the condition that, for a measure to qualify for classification as State aid within the meaning of Article 87(1) EC (now, Article 107 Para. (1) TFEU), it must be imputable to the State, and cannot be interpreted in such a way that such imputability is inferred from the mere fact that that measure was taken by a public undertaking controlled by the State. Even if the State is in a position to control a public undertaking and to exercise a dominant influence over its operations, actual exercise of that control in a particular case cannot be automatically presumed. It is thus necessary to examine whether the public authorities must be regarded as having been involved, in one way or another, in the adoption of that measure. In that respect, the imputability to the State of an aid measure taken by a public undertaking may be inferred from a set of indicators such as, in particular, its integration into the structures of the public administration, the nature of its activities and the exercise of the latter on the market in normal conditions of competition with private operators, the legal status of the undertaking (in the sense of its being subject to public law or ordinary company law), the intensity of the supervision exercised by the public authorities over the management of the undertaking, or any other indicator showing, in the particular case, an involvement by the public authorities in the adoption of a measure or the unlikelihood of their not being involved,

8 Case C-303/88, Italy/Commission, www.curia.eu.

9 Case T-358/94, Air France/Commission, www.curia.eu.

having regard also to the compass of the measure, its content or the conditions which it contains[10].

The financial resources of a private company primarily owned by a public authority and acting under the control of the latter can be regarded as State resources within the meaning of Article 87, Para. 1, EC (now, Article 107 Para. (1) TFEU), since

> "they remain constantly under public scrutiny and therefore available to public authorities"[11].

Founding the existence of intervention by means of State resources in favour of an undertaking does not require that the undertaking must be the direct recipient. The fact that a Member State renounces tax revenue may, indeed, involve an indirect transfer of State resources, capable of being treated as aid to economic operators other than those to which the tax advantage is accorded directly[12].

2.2. The intervention must be liable to affect trade between Member States

As regards the second condition, there is no threshold or percentage below which it may be considered that trade between Member States is not affected. The relatively small amount of aid or the relatively small size of the undertaking which receives it does not, as such, exclude the possibility that trade between Member States might be affected. Fulfilment of the second condition does not therefore depend on the local or regional character of the services supplied or on the scale of the field of activity concerned[13].

The aim of Article 92 of the EEC Treaty is to prevent trade between Member States from being affected by benefits granted by the public authorities which, in various forms, distort or threaten to distort competition by favouring certain undertakings or the production of certain goods. Article 92 does not therefore distinguish between the measures of State intervention concerned by reference to their causes or their aims but defines them in relation to their effects, so that the alleged fiscal nature or social aim of a measure taken by a Member State cannot suffice to exclude it from the ambit of Article 92[14]. Thus, according to the Court of Justice, a measure by which the public authorities grant to a public undertaking a tax concession which, although not involving a transfer of State resources, places the recipient in a more favourable financial

10 Case C-482/99, France/Commission, www.curia.eu.

11 Case C-328/99, Italy and SIM 2 Multimedia/Commission, www.curia.eu.

12 Case T-93/02, Confédération nationale du Crédit mutuel/Commission, www.curia.eu.

13 Case C-172/03, Heiser, www.curia.eu.

14 Case 173/73, Italian Republic/Commission of the European Communities, www.curia.eu.

situation than that of other taxpayers, constitutes State aid within the meaning of Article 92(1) of the Treaty[15].

2.3. The intervention must confer an advantage on the recipient

As regards the third condition, it is settled case law that the concept of aid embraces not only positive benefits, but also measures which, in various forms, mitigate the charges which are normally included in the budget of an undertaking and which, without therefore being subsidies in the strict meaning of the word, are similar in character and have the same effect. In that regard, Article 92(1) of the Treaty requires determination as to whether, under a particular statutory scheme, a State measure is such that it favours 'certain undertakings or the production of certain goods' in comparison with others which, in the light of the objective pursued by the system in question, are in a comparable legal and factual situation. If it is, the measure concerned fulfils the condition of selectivity which is a defining characteristic of the concept of State aid. The fact that the number of undertakings able to claim entitlement under the measure at issue is very large, or that they belong to different sectors of activity, is not sufficient to call into question its selective nature and, therefore, to rule out its classification as State aid. Similarly, aid may concern a whole economic sector and still be covered by Article 92(1) of the Treaty. That would not be the case if a measure, although conferring an advantage on its recipient, were justified by the nature or general scheme of the system of which it is part[16].

A measure cannot be described as State aid within the meaning of Article 92(1) of the Treaty if it has not provided any advantage to the alleged recipient. The Commission was thus right, after carrying out complex economic appraisals, to decide that the arrangements made by the public authorities, whereby the body responsible for managing betting on horse races in one Member State, having deducted a levy on bets which it takes on behalf of the equivalent body in another Member State on races held in the second Member State, transfers a proportion of the levy to the latter body, do not constitute State aid, even though those arrangements are different from those applied in relation to bets on races run on national territory if, after an examination of all the arrangements governing the flow of funds between the two bodies managing, each on its own territory, betting on races, it reached the conclusion, without committing any manifest error of assessment, that the transfer of levy does not involve sums higher than

15 Case T-106/95, FFSA e.a./Commission, www.curia.eu.
16 Case C-172/03, Heiser, www.curia.eu.

the recipient body would have collected if it had itself taken abroad the bets relating to the races falling under its sphere of responsibility[17].

2.4. The intervention must distort or threaten to distort competition

As regards the fourth condition, aid which is intended to release an undertaking from costs which it would normally have had to bear in its day-to-day management or normal activities, distorts the conditions of competition[18].

Establishing whether the aid has a real effect on trade between Member States and that competition is actually being distorted is not necessary, only examining whether that aid is liable to affect such trade and distort competition. In particular, where aid granted by a Member State strengthens the position of an undertaking compared with other undertakings competing in intra-Community trade, the latter must be regarded as affected by that aid. Moreover, it is not necessary that the recipient undertaking itself be involved in the said trade. Finally, the relatively small amount of the aid or the relatively small size of the undertaking which receives it does not as such exclude the possibility that trade between Member States might be affected[19].

The fact that a Member State seeks to approximate, by unilateral measures, the conditions of competition in a particular sector of the economy to those prevailing in other Member States cannot deprive the measures in question of their character as State aid. Like all the rules of Community competition law, the Treaty rules on aid are intended to ensure, not perfect competition, but effective or efficient competition. Under those circumstances, compensation for structural disadvantages makes it possible to avoid categorisation as aid only in certain specific situations. Thus, an advantage conferred on an undertaking with a view to correcting an unfavourable competitive situation is not State aid within the meaning of Article 87(1) EC if it is justified by economic criteria and if it does not discriminate between economic operators established in different Member States. In that sort of situation, the Community judicature in reality applies the criterion of a private operator in a market economy. Similarly, an advantage granted to an undertaking which mitigates the costs which are normally included in its budget does not constitute State aid within the meaning of Article 87(1) EC where the advantage is intended to remedy the fact that the beneficiary undertaking incurs additional costs resulting from special rules which are not in-

17 Case T-471/93, Tiercé Ladbroke/Commission, www.curia.eu.

18 Case C-172/03, Heiser, www.curia.eu.

19 Cases C-393/04 and C-41/05, Air Liquide Industries Belgium, www.curia.eu.

curred by competing undertakings subject to the ordinary law under normal market conditions[20].

For advantages to be capable of being categorised as State aid within the meaning of Article 87(1) EC, they must be granted directly or indirectly through State resources and be imputable to the State. However, Article 87(1) does not distinguish between State interventions by reference to their causes or their objectives but defines them by reference to their effects. It follows that the concept of aid is an objective one, the sole test being whether a State measure confers an advantage on one or more particular undertakings. State resources do not cease to be so simply because the use of those resources is similar to that by a private investor. The question whether the State has conducted itself like an entrepreneur is a question relating to the existence of State aid and not to the examination of whether the resources in question are public in nature[21].

Through a Decision about the interpretation of ECSC (European Coal and Steel Community) legislation, the Court described as incompatible with the common market in coal and steel, subsidies or aids granted by states. In the same case, the subsidy is defined as a payment in cash or in kind made in support of an undertaking other than the payment by the purchaser or consumer for the goods or services which it produces. According to the Court, the concept of aid is nevertheless wider than that of a subsidy because it embraces not only positive benefits, such as subsidies themselves, but also interventions which, in various forms, mitigate the charges which are normally included in the budget of an undertaking and which – without, therefore, being subsidies in the strict meaning of the word – are similar in character and have the same effect[22].

The Court of Justice has established that the partial reduction of public charges devolving upon undertakings in a particular sector of industry constitutes aid within the meaning of Article 92 of the EEC Treaty if such a measure is intended partially to exempt those undertakings from the financial charges arising from the normal application of the general system of compulsory contributions imposed by law[23].

The Court also stated that the charging by a Member State, or an entity on which it exerts influence, of a tariff fixed at a level lower than that which would normally be chosen may be regarded as aid for the purposes of Article 92(1) of

---

20 Cases T-254/00, T-270/00 and T-277/00, Hotel Cipriani/Commission, www.curia.eu.

21 Cases T-228/99 and T-233/99, Westdeutsche Landesbank Girozentrale/Commission, www.curia.eu.

22 Case C 30/59, De gezamenlijke Steenkolenmijnen in Limburg/Haute Autorité, www.curia.eu. See also Ioan Alexandru, Cătălin-Silviu Săraru and other, cited work, p. 205.

23 Case C 173/73, Italian Republic/Commission of the European Communities, www.curia.eu.

the Treaty. In such circumstances, the State, or the entity on which it exerts influence, does not apply the preferential tariff as an ordinary economic agent but uses it to confer a financial advantage on certain undertakings by foregoing the profit which it would normally realise. On the other hand, a preferential tariff does not constitute aid if, in the context of the market in question, it is objectively justified by economic reasons such as the need to withstand competition on the same market. A preferential tariff system for supplies of natural gas, made available by a Member State to very large industrial users in a given production sector, does not constitute State aid insofar as, first, that tariff is justified by the need to withstand competition from imports from non-member countries in order to retain important existing customers and, secondly, the frontier price made available to a natural gas distributor established in another Member State enables that distributor to grant a comparable tariff to very large industrial users belonging to the same production sector in the latter Member State[24].

State aid, within the meaning of Article 92(1) of the Treaty (now, after amendment, Article 87(1) EC), covers measures which, in various forms, mitigate the charges which are normally included in the budget of an undertaking and which – without therefore being subsidies in the strict sense – are similar in character and have the same effect. A system under which certain undertakings are accorded the advantage of increased reductions in social security contributions relieves them of some of their costs and confers on them financial advantages which improve their competitive position. The social character of such State measures is not sufficient to exclude them outright from classification as aid for the purposes of Article 92 of the Treaty. Article 92(1) of the Treaty does not distinguish between measures of State intervention by reference to their causes or their aims but defines them in relation to their effects[25].

3. Conclusions

The competition policy of the European Union is to prevent intervention by member governments that can distort the free market by discriminating in favour of State companies or granting other aid to certain companies in the public sector/private sector (State aids)[26]. For this reason, the Treaty on the Functioning of the European Union prohibits, in principle, any form of aid that may distort

---

24 Case C-56/93, Belgium/Commission, www.curia.eu.
25 Case C-75/97, Belgium/Commission, www.curia.eu.
26 Marina Kesner-Škreb, Mia Mikiæ, work cited, p. 132.

competition in Member States on grounds of incompatibility with the internal market.

The Court of Justice of the European Union plays an important role in the application of the Treaty to concrete situations occurring among Member States, and has set benchmarks over time to strengthen the internal market.

Bibliography

Alexandru, Ioan, Săraru Cătălin-Silviu a. o.: Drept administrativ european, Lumina Lex Publishing House, Bucharest, 2005.

Kesner-Škreb, Marina, Mikiæ, Mia: State aid in the European Union and Croatia, Institute of Public Finance, volume 1, number 1, October 2003.

Muşetescu, Radu Cristian: The Economics of State Aid Control in the European Union during the Financial Crisis: the Challenge for a Post-Crisis Rhetoric, Theoretical and Applied Economics, Volume XIX, No. 6(571), 2012.

Pascal, Ileana, Deaconu, Ştefan, Vrabie, Codru, Fabian, Niculae: Politica în domeniul concurenţei, publishing "Legal Resource Center", Bucharest, 2002.

European Court of Justice case-law: www.curia.eu.

The Efficiency of Public Procurement Procedures. The Principle of Integrity

Lecturer Ioan LAZĂR[1]

Teaching Assistant Laura LAZĂR[2]*, PhD Student*

Abstract

The procedures related to public procurement rank among those government activities that are most exposed to corruption. The lack of transparency can seriously affect the integrity of these activities. Compliance with the principle of integrity is therefore essential for ensuring the efficient management of public funds. International efforts to establish the principle of integrity in public procurement procedures have been ongoing since 2004 and culminated in the adoption of the OECD Report on Integrity in Public Procurement in 2007. According to this document, the efforts of the international community should be guided towards enhancing transparency during public procurement procedures and establishing efficient control and liability mechanisms with regard to the spending of public funds. This paper focuses on the definition of the integrity principle in public procurement, mentions the major risks which can occur during the key stages of the procedures, the optimal level of transparency in these procedural stages and the major instruments which can ensure the integrity of public procurement procedures, such as accurate records, internal and external control, and the prevention of corruption and conflict of interest.

Keywords: transparency; principle of integrity; public procurement; public procurement control mechanisms.

1. Introduction

The institution of public procurement has a rich history stretching back to antiquity, with the first records of purchases in the public interest dating back to 2400-2800 BC.

Public procurement plays a very important role in society because it represents one of the main economic governmental activities. Thus, according to literature on public finances[3], governments are involved, in principle, in four types

---

1 Ioan Lazăr, "1 Decembrie 1918" University of Alba Iulia, Faculty of Law and Social Sciences, Department of Public Law, Romania, E-mail: avocat_lazar@yahoo.com.

2 Laura Lazăr, "Babeş -Bolyai" University of Cluj-Napoca, Faculty of Law, Department of Public Law, Romania, E-mail: laura_lazar@ymail.com.

3 see Robert L. Heilbroner, Lester C. Thurow, Economics Explained, Simon & Schuster, New York, 1987, p. 39; 100; 132; T. R. Jain and other, International Trade and Public

of economic activities: a) providing a suitable legal framework for the conduct of economic activity; b) redistribution of income in society through the collection of taxes and public expenditures[4]; c) provision of free public goods and services for citizens, such as national defence, public health system, education and infrastructure; d) acquisition of goods and services.

Public procurement is one of government's key economic activities[5] that is most vulnerable to corruption. Procurement represents a major interface between governmental and private sector activities and it provides multiple opportunities for both private and public players to divert public funds to their private gain. Therefore, the lack of transparency and proper allocation of responsibilities for any irregularities that occur are major threats to securing the integrity of procurement activities. The solution is to apply the principles of good governance[6] in public procurement procedures as well.

2. Ensuring the principle of good governance in public procurement

The principle of good governance in public procurement involves ensuring the integrity of the public procurement procedures, and the efficient administration

Finance, FK Publications, New Delhi, 2009, pp. 3-15; Harvey S. Rosen, Public Finance, McGraw Hill Inc., New York, 2005, p. 16.

4 Public expenditure and taxation, together with other methods of increasing public revenues, channel the public resources in the directions indicated by public policy. Therefore, public spending is able to determine the change in the nature and volume of production, resource allocation, income distribution, stabilisation of prices and employment levels, job increases and employment through economic growth. For details, please see Alan S. Blinder, The Economics of Public Finance, Atlantic Publishers & Distributors, New Delhi, 1989, p. 205.

5 Public procurement in the EU accounts for approx. 15% of EU 27 GDP. For details, please see OECD, Integrity in Public Procurement. Good Practice from A to Z, OECD Publishing, Paris, 2007, p.10, and also Council of Europe, Corruption in Public Procurement. Reports on the 2nd European Conference of Specialised Services in the Fight Against Corruption, Tallinn, 27-29 October 1997, Council of Europe Publishing, Strasbourg, 1998, p. 963; OECD, Fighting Corruption and Promoting Integrity in Public Procurement, OECD Publishing, Paris, 2005, passim; Sue Arrowsmith, John Linarelli, Don Wallace, Regulating Public Procurement: National and International Perspectives, Kluwer Law International, Haga, 2000, p. 83.

6 For a detailed presentation of the principle of good governance please see Emilia Lucia Catană, Principiul bunei guvernări. Evoluţii europene şi studii comparative, Universul Juridic, Bucharest, 2009, p. 136.

of public funds, along with ensuring fair competition among private actors in this field[7].

Speciality literature focuses mainly on the most important procedural stage in public procurement, i.e. the award of the public procurement contract through public auction. However, the transposition of the principle of good governance requires transparency – an essential condition of integrity, which must be fulfilled at every procedural stage of public procurement, from the very beginning of the public needs assessment to the last procedural step of contract performance. The above-mentioned principles must not be neglected even if the tender does not involve competition between bidders, or if contracts are signed in emergencies, or the value of the contracts is low, a situation that usually does not imply the use of public auction as a method for contract award anyway.

According to the OECD report on integrity, enforcing this principle and preventing and combating corruption is only possible by providing: a) transparency; b) professionalism; c) professional responsibility of the civil servants who handle public funds.

2.1. Transparency in public acquisitions

Ensuring transparency[8] in public procurement procedures is particularly important in terms of securing the integrity of these procedures. Transparency allows better control of how procedures are conducted, since it cannot be achieved without guaranteeing the right of access to documents of a public interest.

The main goal of transparency is to provide equal opportunities for competitors, through equal and free access to information regarding the public procurement opportunity, the method of allocation, selection criteria and the method for contract award, in order to ensure fair and competitive procedures[9].

---

7 See Satyendra Singh, Handbook of Business Practices and Growth in Emerging Markets, World Scientific Publishing Co. Ltd., Singapore, 2010, p. 276; Ognian Shenlov a.o., Anti-Corruption in Public Procurement, Center for the Study of Democracy, Sofia, 2011, p. 8.

8 In order to analyse the findings of a study on identifying the level of knowledge applied by the local community to the urban environment of Mures county with regard to the concept of public procurement and public perception of the implementation of procurement management in relation to transparency/integrity versus corruption, please see Catană, Marius Cristian, Achiziţii publice, Universul Juridic, Bucharest, 2011, pp. 246-249.

9 Please see also Elodie Beth, OECD Principles for Integrity in Public Procurement, OECD Publishing, Paris, 2009, p. 22.

Certainly, transparency involves costs for both public and private actors, but the benefits outweigh the costs. However, ensuring public access to documents cannot be possible without clearly protecting trade and business secrets, in order to achieve fair competition between suppliers – and also without protecting state secrets.

Exceptions to competitive procedures must be established in advance, based on clear criteria which serve to delimit emergency situations. However, it some specific thresholds must be set for contracts which are considered low value. Circumstances that may cause the use of simplified award procedures could be based on: i) the nature of the contract (e.g. in markets characterised naturally by low competition), ii) reduced value of the contract iii) exceptional circumstances (e.g. emergency situations) or iv) the protection of state interests (e.g. national defence). In these situations, transparency can only be ensured by strictly defining situations that can lead to simplified procedures, carrying out more detailed reports, etc.

Ensuring transparency has been facilitated by the widespread use of information technology in public procurement procedures. This new means of interaction between government and bidders allowed easy access to real information and a better oversight of these procedures.

A practical example of this could be the electronic auction system in Romania (the Extended Electronic System for Public Procurement - SEEAP), conducted by http://www.e-licitatie.ro portal. The project cost 4 million euro to implement and has been able to support online purchase transactions with a total value of more than one billion euros.

The project began as a pilot with 159 participating public authorities and seven product categories, whereas the portal currently has 12 845 public authorities as users and more than 37 259 registered bidders for more than 333 product categories. The project was a success and was referenced by the OECD in its report on integrity in public procurement, especially because the project was executed with strong political commitment, and at reduced fees for participation, and was backed by massive publicity campaigns and training courses that were organised for civil servants and other categories of users of the electronic system.

2.2. Ensuring professionalism in public procurement procedures

Performing public procurement proceedings in accordance with the principle of transparency does not in itself ensure the integrity of these procedures. Thus, public funds can optimally only be properly managed by qualified personnel[10] with the necessary logistical and materials resources to perform their tasks.

The process of professionalisation of the civil service includes: streamlining the number of civil servants, separating the responsibilities of the various categories of officials, facilitating control activities, ensuring adequate training and qualifications of officials, and preventing conflicts of interest.

Thus, the professionalism of civil servants[11] could be provided if the following conditions are met: a) consistent use of public funds; b) helping civil servants adapt to the changing environment; c) minimising the possibility of corruption.

In order to ensure proper administration of public funds, we believe that public officials must have the necessary qualifications, which can be obtained either through individual studies or professional training in project management and risk management. Drawing up an annual budget of proposed procurement procedures could ensure the transparency and predictability of the procedures and also fair resource allocation, with the possibility of achieving adequate funding.

Helping public servants adapt to the changing environment can be ensured through continuous professional training. Attracting specialists from the private sector should be facilitated by offering competitive salaries and motivational bonuses. Officials must be aware of the legal framework and be trained to deal with the risks that may occur during the proceedings.

The threat of corruption can be minimised by eliminating conflicts of interest, and by clearly defining responsibilities. Codes of conduct can also be developed. Incompatibilities may include family or business relationships, or previous work activities, incompatibility with other functions, etc. An adequate legal framework is essential to guarantee the confidentiality of information by regulating professional secrets.

As far as the development of ethical codes of conduct is concerned, a proposal has been drafted in our country. The Procurement Code of Ethics (CEAP) has been proposed in order to supplement the Code of civil servants and the

---

10 For more details regarding the importance of the professionalism of public servants, please see Ioan Lazăr, Administrația publică, managementul public şi sursele europene de finanțare în contextul noilor provocări impuse de conjunctura actuală a economiei mondiale, "Pandectele Române" no. 5/2009, pp. 73-84.

11 Please see also Jorge Martinez-Vasquez et al., Fighting Corruption in the Public Sector, Elsevier, Amsterdam, 2007, p. 153; Staffan Furusten, Andreas Werr, Dealing with Confidence: the Construction of Need and Trust in Management Advisory Services, Copenhagen Business School Press, Herndon, 2005, p. 170; OECD (2007), cited work, p. 70; Elodie Beth, op.cit., p. 119; OECD (2005), cited work, p. 114.

general Code of Conduct for Romanian officials with the aim of ensuring a supreme set of rules for officials involved in public procurement procedures.

The objectives pursued by the Code of Conduct adopted by the public authorities and private actors participating in procurement procedures include, for example, preventing personal gain by civil servants and the staff of companies involved in public acquisitions, optimising the resources used to maintain a standard of integrity, compliance with laws and contractual obligations.

The proponents of the ethics code also seek to establish essential principles in the performance of public functions, such as equality, non-discrimination, fairness, proportionality, impartiality, transparency, fighting corruption, rule of law, professionalism, accountability and the sovereignty. The principles mentioned above imply the observance of basic rules, including the ban on accepting gifts (other than acts of courtesy), avoiding conflicts of interest, respect for confidential information, reporting attempts at corruption, and participation in professional training programmes[12].

2.3. Professional responsibility of public servants

Public procurement is one means by which public money can provide value. The pillar of any effective public procurement system is therefore the availability of control mechanisms and their degree of efficiency[13]. We refer here not only to internal and external administrative controls and audit control, but also to the procedural mechanisms that enable administrative complaints to be filed against public procurement decisions by public authorities, and direct social control mechanisms[14].

---

12 Ibidem.

13 For more details regarding the importance of control in public procurement, please see Sue Arrowsmith, John Linarelli, Don Wallace, op.cit., p. 38 and next; OECD (2009), op.cit., p. 35; OECD (2007), op.cit., p. 16; Council of Europe, op.cit., p. 964; János Bertók, Public Sector Integrity: a Framework for Assessment, OECD Publications, Paris, 2005, p. 198.

14 One example is the direct social control carried out by the representative of an NGO that acts as an outside observer of public procurement procedures. The representative must be a public figure, respected, apolitical, with legal knowledge and without a criminal record, and must not suffer any conflict of interest. He or she will have access to all documents and information at the critical stages of the procurement process in order to ensure transparency and prevent corruption. For more details on access to public information, please see Ioan Lazăr, Laura Lazăr, "Garantarea liberului acces la informaţii de interes public în reglementări ale unor state membre ale Uniunii Europene", Pandectele Române no. 3/2010, pp. 70-90.

Public procurement is an element of government accountability to the public; insofar as the administration of public funds is concerned, citizens must be the ultimate beneficiaries of these procedures. Ensuring the objective of integrity in public procurement procedures would be impossible in the absence of concrete and accurate boundaries between different categories of civil responsibilities and procedures to ensure the existence of administrative, contentious or quasi-contentious complaints mechanisms to deal with possible abuses committed in the management of public funds. However, in order to increase the accountability of civil servants, social control mechanisms could be established - where civil society, consumers, the media and the general public are the main factors that ensure accountability of the perpetrators.

As far as the delimitation of professional duties is concerned, the majority of OECD countries have established special ministries or government agencies to manage public procurement procedures[15]. From this point of view, we can distinguish between states with a centralised system of public procurement authorities and those with a semi-centralised system of such authorities. Centralised procurement systems are controlled via ministerial agencies specially created for this purpose. Examples include countries such as Bulgaria, Hungary, Lithuania, Malta, Poland, Portugal, Slovenia and Romania. Semi-centralised systems are characterised by the presence of several institutions conducting procurement control in the field. In these countries special sections of the Chancellor's or Prime Minister's Office and a special government agency are usually set up for that purpose. Examples include countries such as Germany, Ireland, Italy, Sweden and United Kingdom.

Another very important aspect in this respect is the accuracy of the written or electronic public records, which is practically a prerequisite for assigning responsibility. Given free access to public information, public records are the main control lever allowing the general public to supervise public authorities. Citizens, the media and NGOs have the opportunity to check the extent to which decisions of administrative authorities are well documented, justified and compliant with relevant legal regulations.

---

15 These authorities are responsible for drafting legislation in the special field, advisory powers, international representation and control functions in compliance with the legal procedures and government policy. See in this regard the OECD (2005), op.cit., p. 140; For the aforementioned duties is responsible the Romanian National Authority for Regulating and Monitoring Public Procurement (see http://www.anrmap.ro) and the Directorate for Investment, Public Affairs and Services from the National Revenue Agency (see http://www.anaf.ro/public/wps/portal/!ut/p/c0/04SB8K8xLLM9MSSzPy8x Bz9CP0 os3gvY1PLEGczFzMP32ADAyMfPx93Z0sDQ39TA_2CbEdFABHXzN0!/).

As we mentioned above, effective control is not possible without ensuring access to administrative or judicial appeal, as appropriate – to enable decisions by public authorities to be submitted to judicial review. Procedures for controlling administrative decisions must also meet the requirements of independence and impartiality, as well as the criteria of celerity and efficiency.

In order to ensure the efficiency of appeal procedures, most states established a procedural delay between the decision to award a public procurement contract and its execution, although some states provided the possibility to contest contracts during execution (for example, Netherlands, Norway or the United Kingdom) or even after the execution of the contract (e.g. Sweden); in the latter case the appeal can be pursued only to claim for damages.

Also, some states[16] have opted for a special means of filing complaints by civil servants working in the field (the so-called "whistleblowers")[17]. They can report irregularities under the cloak of anonymity. This possibility of reporting cases helps to uncover those irregularities which are hardest to detect.

Most countries in recent times are therefore opting less for administrative or hierarchical control, in favour of administrative jurisdiction[18] or judicial review. There are, of course, examples of alternative conflict resolution methods, such as Belgium, where mediation is also a possible means of controlling administrative decisions by the public procurement authorities.

The success of appeals against decisions by public authorities depends very much on the range of remedies available, such as interim measures (suspension of the contract, for example), contract annulment, compensation, or even administrative penalties (lump sum or instalment fines).

3. Consideration of risks that can cause the principle of integrity to fail

The integrity of procurement procedures can be ensured only in the presence of the necessary means to prevent irregularities that could lead to corruption, lack of transparency or difficulties in assigning responsibilities for the irregular

16 Examples include countries such as Canada, Korea, United Kingdom and United States.

17 For details, please see OECD (2007), op.cit., p. 105; János Bertók, op.cit., p. 8; OECD (2005), op.cit., p. 158.

18 For more details regarding administrative jurisdiction mechanisms please see Ioan Lazăr, Jurisdicții administrative în materie financiară, Universul Juridic, Bucharest, 2011, pp. 224-305.

spending of public funds. Such risks[19] may occur at any stage of the procurement procedures.

Thus, the procedural stages which precede public auction are exposed to risks such as the wrong evaluation of public needs, which can result in incorrect scheduling of the procedural stages and the allocation of insufficient financial resources. Other risks could be the wrong definition of technical specifications, or choosing the wrong procedure for public award, which could mean the contract is awarded to a bidder who cannot satisfy the public needs. As far as public servants working in the field are concerned, it is particularly important to clarify and remove any conflicts of interests, which may lead to information disclosure and thus eliminate the competitive fairness of the procedures.

International experience has shown which irregularities occur most frequently at this stage of the proceedings. Examples include insufficient time to allow bidders to prepare their quotations; formulating technical specifications that fit only one particular bidder; inappropriate intervention by politicians or political parties in the proceedings; improper and abusive choice of what constitutes emergency procedures by the authorities; unnecessary or economically unjustified purchases, failure to consider environmental issues; overstatement of the value of goods and services provided by a particular supplier, etc.

The procedural stage of the tender attracts the most attention from authorities and specialists. However, this procedural step is not free from risks and irregularities as the lessons learned by the international community show us.

Most of the irregularities that can occur at this stage are related to procedural transparency in the process. They start with the despatch of the invitation for public auction and ends with the contract award decision.

In some situations risks to ensuring the principle of transparency may arise, such as failure to communicate the public announcement on the beginning of auctions, previous and discriminative disclosures of information about the organisation of public auction to a favoured bidder, which eliminates the correctness and fairness of the procedures and increases the possibility of collusion among companies participating in the auction, for example in order to maintain an artificially high price for the goods or services concerned. Other risks include the failure to establish prior criteria for awarding the public procurement contract (economic, social or environmental criteria), which can favour a named bidder.

---

19 For more details regarding the risks to integrity which can occur during public procurement procedures, please see Colin Nicholls a.o., Corruption and Misuse of Public Office, Oxford University Press, Oxford, 2011, p. 411; OECD (2007), op.cit., p. 21; OECD (2005), op.cit., p. 24.

Another aspect worth mentioning is related to the lack of public access to information on the contract award decision, which can hinder the possibility to submit the decision to control by the appropriate judicial authorities or administrative courts.

The procedural stage where the public procurement contract is enforced may also present risks for contract management and can result in the improper allocation of responsibilities if the contract is not properly enforced. Problems with subcontractor accountability may arise, for example, or with the way public officials are performing their obligations, which can lead to payments being offset, costs being billed twice or fictive migrations of costs between contracts.

4. Conclusions

The importance of public procurement as a main instrument of governmental policy has increased dramatically in recent years, and the value of public procurement contracts now accounts for a significant portion of a country's gross domestic product. Thus, public purchases have become a key element for ensuring effective management, and elimination of corruption of the public resources.

Consequently, the international community turned its attention to finding and providing the necessary conditions of integrity, concluding that the integrity of public procurement could not be ensured without transparency, the professionalism of officials, and effective mechanisms for assigning accountability for irregularities found in procedures.

As we have seen, special attention must be paid to issues such as guaranteeing public access to information, training civil servants and ensuring administrative, quasi-jurisdictional or judicial control mechanisms in order to fulfil each of the conditions mentioned above.

Also, the integrity of these procedures cannot be secured without preventing or eliminating the specific obstacles which may arise en route to ensuring the integrity of procedures. It is very important that public servants are empowered to prevent risks of irregularities and provided with the necessary monitoring or control levers to prevent or mitigate these risks.

Bibliography

Arrowsmith, Sue, John Linarelli, Don, Wallace: Regulating Public Procurement: National and International Perspectives, Kluwer Law International, Haga, 2000.

Bertók, János: Public Sector Integrity: a Framework for Assessment, OECD Publications, Paris, 2005.

Beth, Elodie: OECD Principles for Integrity in Public Procurement, OECD Publishing, Paris, 2009.
Blinder, Alan S.: The Economics of Public Finance, Atlantic Publishers & Distributors, New Delhi, 1989.
Catană, Emilia Lucia: Principiul bunei guvernări. Evoluţii europene şi studii comparative, Universul Juridic, Bucharest, 2009.
Cătană, Marius Cristian: Achiziţii publice, Universul Juridic, Bucharest, 2011.
Furusten, Staffan, Andreas Werr: Dealing with Confidence: the Construction of Need and Trust in Management Advisory Services, Copenhagen Business School Press, Herndon, 2005.
Heilbroner, Robert L., Lester, C. Thurow: Economics Explained, Simon & Schuster, New York, 1987.
Jain, T. R., et al.: International Trade and Public Finance, FK Publications, New Delhi, 2009.
Lazăr, Ioan, Laura Lazăr: Garantarea liberului acces la informaţii de interes public în reglementări ale unor state membre ale Uniunii Europene, "Pandectele Române" no. 3/2010.
Lazăr, Ioan: Administraţia publică, managementul public şi sursele europene de finanţare în contextul noilor provocări impuse de conjunctura actuală a economiei mondiale, "Pandectele Române" no. 5/2009.
Lazăr, Ioan: Jurisdicţii administrative în materie financiară, Universul Juridic, Bucharest, 2011.
Martinez-Vasquez, Jorge et al.: Fighting Corruption in the Public Sector, Elsevier, Amsterdam, 2007.
Nicholls, Colin, et al.: Corruption and Misuse of Public Office, Oxford University Press, Oxford, 2011.
Rosen, Harvey S.: Public Finance, McGraw Hill Inc., New York, 2005.
Shenlov, Ognian, et al.: Anti-Corruption in Public Procurement, Center for the Study of Democracy, Sofia, 2011.
Singh, Satyendra: Handbook of Business Practices and Growth in Emerging Markets, World Scientific Publishing Co. Ltd., Singapore, 2010.

Aspects of Prohibition of Discrimination against Women in the Workplace in European Court of Justice Case Law

PhD student Cătălina-Adriana IVĂNUŞ[1]

Abstract

The Court has consistently ruled that equal treatment between women and men is a fundamental human right, part of the general principles of EU law. European Court of Justice case law and European law have treated different aspects of discrimination on grounds of sex. The principle of equal treatment between women and men in the workplace encompasses remuneration, access to employment, vocational training and promotion, and working conditions. The European Court of Justice has ruled on controversial aspects such as discrimination on grounds of gender reassignment or sexual orientation. Particular attention has been given to maternity protection in the workplace.

Keywords: non-discrimination, equal opportunities, European law, labour law.

1. The principle of non-discrimination

In its constant jurisprudence, the Court has established that equal treatment between women and men is a fundamental human right, part of the general principles of EU law[2]. Respect for human rights is one of the general principles of EU law, the observance of which the Court has a duty to ensure[3].

Further, as has been held, equal treatment between women and men must be applied in relations between the EU institutions and their employees[4].

The principle of equal treatment is generally applicable and encompasses employment in public service[5].

---

1 Cătălina-Adriana Ivănuş, Bucharest University of Economic Studies, Romania, catalinaivanus@gmail.com.

2 Judgement of 15 June 1978, Defrenne/Sabena (149/77, ECR 1978 p. 1365).

3 For example, Judgement of 15 June 1978, Defrenne/Sabena (149/77, ECR 1978 p. 1365), Judgement of 20 March 1984, Razzouk and others/Commission (75 and 117/82, ECR 1984 p. 1509), Judgement of 26 February 1986, Marshall/Southampton and South-West Hampshire Area Health Authority (152/84, ECR 1986 p. 723).

4 Judgement of 20 March 1984, Razzouk and others/Commission (75 and 117/82, ECR 1984 p. 1509).

5 Judgement of 26 October 1999, Sirdar (C-273/97, ECR 1999 p. I-7403), Judgement of 11 January 2000, Kreil (C-285/98, ECR 2000 p. I-69), Judgement of 19 March 2002, Lommers (C-476/99, ECR 2002 p. I-2891).

2. Access to employment

On 9 February 1976, the Council adopted Directive 76/207 on the implementation of the principle of equal treatment for men and women as regards access to employment, vocational training and promotion, and working conditions. This directive broadens the scope of the equal pay for women and men principle to all aspects of labour relations as regards access to employment, including promotion, and to vocational training, and as regards working conditions. Directive 76/207 requires that the Member States shall introduce into their national legal systems all the necessary measures to ensure the principle of equal treatment for men and women as regards access to employment.

The Meyers case is an example of how the court interprets the Directive provisions. In its judgement, the Court held that equal access to employment covers not only the conditions prevailing before the employment relationship comes into being, but also all those influencing factors that need to be considered before the individual makes a decision of whether or not to accept a job offer[6].

So the payment of particular State benefits depending upon a level of income qualified for treatment within the area of access to employment because the candidate would be influenced by whether they would be entitled to this benefit when considering their decision to take up a post. Consequently, such a consideration had an impact on access to employment[7].

On the other hand, in the von Colson case the Court held that Directive 76/207 does not require discrimination on grounds of sex regarding access to employment to be made the subject of a sanction by way of an obligation imposed upon the employer who is the author of the discrimination to conclude a contract of employment with the candidate discriminated against[8]. In the case in question, Werl prison had two vacancies for social workers. Sabine von Colson and Elisabeth Kamann, plaintiffs in the main proceedings, applied for these posts but the positions were occupied by two male candidates. The plaintiffs requested that the defendant be ordered to conclude a contract of employment or to pay them damages amounting to six months' salary. The national courts de-

---

6 Judgement of 13 July 1995, Meyers/Adjudication Officer (C-116/94, ECR 1995 p. I-2131).

7 Handbook on European non-discrimination law, European Union Agency for Fundamental Rights, 2010, p.72.

8 Judgement of 10 April 1984, Von Colson and Kamann/Land Nordrhein-Westfalen (14/83, ECR 1984 p. 1891), Judgement of 10 April 1984, Harz/Deutsche Tradax (79/83, ECR 1984 p. 1921).

clared the claim inadmissible under national law and asked the Court of Justice to determine the applicable law.

European legislation establishes maternity protection, but leaves the national authorities free to choose the special and concrete form and methods for protecting women, particularly as regards pregnancy and maternity[9].

Another way to protect a female worker is to prohibit discrimination on grounds of pregnancy or maternity. The Court, in many cases[10], held that a refusal of employment on grounds of pregnancy constitutes direct sex discrimination. In these circumstances, the refusal to employ a pregnant woman is a limitation of access to employment.

Moreover, discrimination on grounds of pregnancy or maternity cannot be justified by citing the financial loss which an employer who appointed a pregnant woman would suffer during her maternity leave. For example, refusal of employment on account of the financial consequences of absence due to pregnancy must be regarded as based, essentially, on the fact of pregnancy[11]. Therefore, an employer violates the principle of equal treatment set out in Articles 2(1) and 3(1) of Directive 76/207 if he refuses to enter into a contract of employment with a female candidate whom he considers to be suitable for the job where such refusal is based on the possible adverse consequences for him of employing a pregnant woman[12].

In the Mahlburg case (C-207/98) the Court of Justice held that refusing to hire a pregnant woman for a permanent post because of a legal prohibition on employing a pregnant woman in certain posts is contrary to the meaning of Art. 2(1) and (3). In this case the post was a permanent one so it was disproportionate because her inability to work would be temporary[13].

In order to ensure that the pregnant woman's rights should not be illusory, the Court rules that the exercise of those rights cannot be the subject of unfa-

---

9 Art.2 (3) of Directive 76/207 states that the Directive shall be without prejudice to provisions concerning the protection of women, particularly as regards pregnancy and maternity.

10 For example Judgement of 8 November 1990, Dekker/Stichting Vormingscentrum voor Jong Volwassenen (177/88, ECR 1990 p. I-3941), Judgement of 3 February 2000, Mahlburg (C-207/98, ECR 2000 p. I-549).

11 Judgement of 8 November 1990, Dekker/Stichting Vormingscentrum voor Jong Volwassenen (177/88, ECR 1990 p. I-3941).

12 Judgement of 8 November 1990, Dekker/Stichting Vormingscentrum voor Jong Volwassenen (177/88, ECR 1990 p. I-3941).

13 Handbook on European non-discrimination law, European Union Agency for Fundamental Rights, 2010, p 53.

vourable treatment regarding their access to employment. Therefore, the result pursued by the Directive is substantive, not formal, equality[14].

In its 30 June 1988 judgement, the Court considered that the lack of transparency in the recruitment process is contrary to the principle of equal access to employment, because this lack of transparency makes it impossible to exercise any form of supervision by persons adversely affected by discriminatory measures or by national courts[15].

However, the equal treatment Directive can be read both ways. Hence men could suffer discrimination in comparison with women, as regards access to employment. Thus, in the Dory case[16], the plaintiff argued that women have the right of access to military posts but are exempted from the obligation to perform military service, while that obligation is imposed on men, which contradicted the principle of equality and constituted unlawful discrimination against men. The national courts referred to the Court for a preliminary ruling as to whether EU law precluded compulsory military service for men because the delay in access to employment and vocational training could constitute discrimination on grounds of sex.

The Court established[17] that the Directive 76/207 must be applied in regard to access to employment in the armed forces and can verify if the measures taken by the national authorities are appropriate and necessary to achieve the aim of public security.

However, the delay in the careers of people called up for military service is an inevitable consequence of the choice made by the Member State regarding its military organisation, and the EU cannot regulate even if sex discrimination regarding access to employment and delays in men's career progress does exist. The existence of adverse consequences for access to employment cannot have the effect of compelling the Member State in question either to extend the obligation of military service to women, or to abolish compulsory military service. Hence, EU law does not preclude compulsory military service being reserved to men[18].

---

14 Judgement of 30 April 1998, Caisse nationale d'assurance vieillesse des travailleurs salariés/Thibault (C-136/95, ECR 1998 p. I-2011).

15 Judgement of 30 June 1988, Commission / France (318/86, ECR 1988 p. 3559).

16 Judgement of 11 March 2003, Dory (C-186/01, ECR 2003 p. I-2479).

17 Judgement of 26 October 1999, Sirdar (C-273/97, ECR 1999 p. I-7403), Judgement of 11 January 2000, Kreil (C-285/98, ECR 2000 p. I-69), Judgement of 11 March 2003, Dory (C-186/01, ECR 2003 p. I-2479).

18 Judgement of 11 March 2003, Dory (C-186/01, ECR 2003 p. I-2479).

3. Recruitment practices

In the Belgian Centre for Equal Opportunities and Opposition to Racism vs. NV Firma Feryn case (C-54/07), the Court examined the direct discrimination concept. The Court had to consider whether direct discrimination exists when an employer declares publicly, within the context of a recruitment procedure, that it will not recruit employees of a certain ethnic or racial origin. The court answered that question affirmatively. Although it relates to discrimination on grounds of ethnic origin, the Court judgement may still be applied by analogy to direct discrimination on grounds of sex.

The Court of Justice found the fact that an employer publicly declares that it will not recruit employees of a certain ethnic or racial origin to be direct discrimination in respect of recruitment because it was clearly likely to strongly dissuade certain candidates from submitting their candidature and, accordingly, to hinder their access to the labour market. These statements constitute facts of such a nature as to give rise to a presumption of discriminatory recruitment[19].

According to EU law and EUCJ case law, the plaintiff must prove the facts that are presumed discriminatory. If a person establishes, before a court or other competent authority, facts from which it may be presumed that there has been direct or indirect discrimination, it shall be up to the respondent to prove that there has been no breach of the principle of equal treatment[20].

The precondition for the obligation to adduce evidence in rebuttal which thus arises for the alleged perpetrator of the discrimination is a simple finding that a presumption of discrimination has arisen based on established facts. It may constitute facts of such a nature as to give rise to a presumption of discriminatory recruitment policy statements by which an employer publicly lets it be known that, under its recruitment policy, it will not recruit any employees of a certain ethnic or racial origin. The employer could adduce evidence that it has not breached the principle of equal treatment, which it can do, inter alia, by showing that the actual recruitment practices of the undertaking do not correspond to those statements[21].

A question that arises[22] is whether direct discrimination exists even in the absence of an identifiable complainant contending that he has been the victim of that discrimination. The existence of such direct discrimination does not imply the identification of a complainant who claims to have been the victim. In his opinion, the Advocate General consider that – in such cases – it may be very

19 Judgement of 10 July 2008, Feryn (C-54/07, ECR 2008 p. I-5187).
20 Art. 4 (1) of Directive 97/80.
21 Judgement of 10 July 2008, Feryn (C-54/07, ECR 2008 p. I-5187).
22 Idem.

difficult to identify individual victims, since the people affected may not even apply for a position with that employer in the first place. The notion of victim should cover people who would be interested in applying and are qualified for the job. By publicly stating his intention not to hire people of a certain racial or ethnic origin, the employer is, in fact, excluding those people from the application process and from his work floor. He is not merely talking about discriminating; he is discriminating. Thus, the announcement that people of a certain racial or ethnic origin are unwelcome as applicants for a job is thus itself a form of discrimination[23].

As I stated earlier, the recruitment process should be transparent in order to comply with the principle of equal access to employment, but this does not imply that workers should have access to information about the person recruited by the employer. Directive 2000/78 and Directive 2006/54 must be interpreted as not entitling a worker – who claims plausibly that he meets the requirements listed in a job advertisement and whose application was rejected – to access information indicating whether the employer hired another applicant at the end of the recruitment process[24].

4. Vocational training

As with the job applicant who has no access to information about the person recruited by the employer, the applicant for vocational training has no access to information held by the course provider on the qualifications of the other applicants for the course in question. An applicant for vocational training who believes that his application has not been accepted because of an infringement of the principle of equal treatment is not entitled to information held by the course provider on the qualifications of the other applicants for the course in question for the purpose of establishing facts from which it may be presumed there has been direct or indirect discrimination[25].

Moreover, the Court interpreted Art. 4 of Directive 76/207 and Article 1(3) of Directive 2002/73 as meaning that they do not entitle an applicant for vocational training to information held by the course provider on the qualifications of the other applicants for the course in question, either because he believes that he has been denied access to vocational training on the basis of the same criteria as the other candidates and discriminated against on grounds of sex, referred to in

23 Opinion of the Advocate General in Judgement of 10 July 2008, Feryn (C-54/07, ECR 2008 p. I-5187).

24 Judgement of 19 April 2012, Meister (C-415/10).

25 Judgement of 21 July 2011, Kelly (C-104/10).

Article 4 of Directive 76/207, or because that applicant complains that he was discriminated against on the grounds of sex, referred to in Article 1(3) of Directive 2002/73, in terms of accessing that vocational training[26].

Another example in which the Court considered a case of discrimination on grounds of sex in access to training is the Schnorbus case. In this case, Julia Schnorbus had applied for practical legal training in order to obtain a post in the judicial service. Under national law, or in the higher civil service, a person must have passed the First State Examination in law, have undergone practical legal training and then have passed the Second State Examination. The plaintiff had passed the First State Examination in law, but her application to practical legal training was denied on grounds of no available training places. She argued that the selection procedure discriminated against women because preference was given to applicants who had completed compulsory military or civilian service, which only included men. National provisions governing the date of admission to the practical legal training which is a prerequisite of access to employment in the civil service fall within the scope of Council Directive 76/207 and such a delay may affect the career development of the people concerned. The Court held that the national provisions, which give men priority access to vocational training, constituted not direct but indirect discrimination on grounds of sex. Giving priority to applicants who have completed compulsory military or civilian service is evidence of indirect discrimination in favour of men, since – under the relevant national law – women are not required to do military or civilian service and therefore cannot benefit from the priority to applications in circumstances regarded as hardship cases[27].

5. Promotion

European legislation makes provision for measures to promote equal opportunity for men and women, in particular by removing existing inequalities which affect women's opportunities[28]. This provision is one of the allowed exceptions to the principle of equal treatment between men and women that is intended to eliminate or reduce actual instances of inequality which may exist in the reality of social life[29]. However, this exception should not be applied automatically

---

26 Idem.

27 Judgement of 7 December 2000, Schnorbus (C-79/99, ECR 2000 p. I-10997).

28 Art. 2 (4) of Directive 76/207.

29 Judgement of 25 October 1988, Commission/France (312/86, ECR 1988 p. 6315), Judgement of 17 October 1995, Kalanke/Freie Hansestadt Bremen (C-450/93, ECR 1995

since such a situation is contrary to the principle of equal treatment between men and women.

A national rule promoting equal opportunity for men and women breaches the principle of equal treatment if candidates of different sexes who are shortlisted for promotion are equally qualified, but priority is automatically given to women in sectors where they are under-represented. The court held that under-representation is deemed to exist when women do not make up at least half of the staff in the individual pay brackets in the relevant personnel group or in the function levels provided for in the organisation chart[30].

National rules that are designed to promote equal opportunities between men and women should give priority to promoting female candidates unless reasons specific to an individual male candidate tilt the balance in his favour[31].

A measure which is intended to give priority to promoting women in sectors of the public service where they are under-represented must be regarded as compatible with EU law if it does not automatically and unconditionally give priority to women when women and men are equally qualified, and the candidatures are the subject of an objective assessment which takes account of the specific personal situations of all candidates[32].

Therefore, Article 2(1) and (4) of the Directive does not preclude a national rule whereby priority is given to female candidates in sectors where women are under-represented, although the male and female candidates have equal qualifications, if this is necessary to ensure compliance with the objectives of the women's advancement plan, if no reasons of greater legal weight oppose such a prioritisation, and provided that the rule guarantees that candidatures are the subject of an objective assessment which takes account of the specific personal situations of all candidates[33].

Articles 2(1) and (4) of Council Directive 76/207 do not preclude a national rule relating to the composition of employees' representative bodies and administrative and supervisory bodies, but recommends that the legislative provisions adopted for its implementation take into account the objective that at least half the members of those bodies must be women[34].

---

p. I-3051), Judgement of 11 November 1997, Marschall/Land Nordrhein-Westfalen (C-409/95, ECR 1997 p. I-6363).

30 Judgement of 17 October 1995, Kalanke/Freie Hansestadt Bremen (C-450/93, ECR 1995 p. I-3051).

31 Judgement of 11 November 1997, Marschall/Land Nordrhein-Westfalen (C-409/95, ECR 1997 p. I-6363).

32 Judgement of 28 March 2000, Badeck and others (C-158/97, ECR 2000 p. I-1875).

33 Judgement of 28 March 2000, Badeck and others (C-158/97, ECR 2000 p. I-1875).

34 Idem.

6. Working conditions

Since Directive 76/207 does not contain any express provision on the measures taken on grounds of protecting national security or public order and, in particular, protecting public safety, the Court had to determine whether the Directive applies to such cases. The Court concluded that there is no general restriction to the application of the principle of equal treatment for men and women as regards measures taken in the interests of protecting public safety[35].

The EUCJ considered that the Directive provision does not allow women to be excluded from a certain type of employment on the grounds that public opinion demands women be given greater protection than men against risks which affect men and women in the same way and which are distinct from women's specific needs of protection, such as those expressly mentioned. Citing public safety as a reason for excluding women totally from such an occupational activity, owing to a general risk not specific to women, is not one of the differences in treatment that Article 2(3) of the Directive allows out of a concern to protect women[36].

7. Different treatment on grounds of gender reassignment

In the P. c. S. and Cornwall County Council case (C-13/94), the question that arises is whether the Art. 5(1) of Directive 76/207 on the implementation of the principle of equal treatment for men and women as regards access to employment, vocational training and promotion, and working conditions precludes the dismissal of a transsexual for a reason related to gender reassignment.

In the case in question, P. – a manager in an educational establishment operated at the time in question by Cornwall County Council – informed S. – the director of the establishment – of the intention to undergo gender reassignment. After undergoing minor surgical operations, P. was given notice of dismissal which took effect after the final surgical operation.

The principle of equal treatment covered by Directive 76/207 requires that there shall be no discrimination whatsoever on grounds of sex[37]. This is one of the general principles of EU law[38]. Furthermore, the right not to be discriminated against on grounds of sex is one of the fundamental human rights whose ob-

35 Judgement of 15 May 1986, Johnston/Chief Constable of the Royal Ulster Constabulary (222/84, ECR 1986 p. 1651).
36 Idem.
37 Art. 2 (1), Art. 3 (1), Art. 5 (1) of Directive 76/207.
38 Judgement of 30 April 1996, P/S and Cornwall County Council (C-13/94, ECR 1996 p. I-2143).

servance the Court has a duty to ensure[39]. The Court held that the scope of the Directive cannot be confined simply to discrimination based on the fact that a person is of one or other sex, but also to discrimination arising from gender reassignment[40]. This is because discrimination arising from gender reassignment is based on the gender of the person concerned.

In conclusion, the dismissal of a transsexual for a reason related to gender reassignment constitutes discrimination on grounds of sex[41], because he or she who is intending to undergo, or has undergone, gender reassignment is being treated unfavourably by comparison with persons of the sex to which he or she was deemed to belong before that operation.

The Court emphasises, in Richards case, that gender reassignment constitutes discrimination on grounds of sex.

Firstly, in the P. vs. S. and Cornwall County Council case, the Court ruled that different treatment for a reason related to gender reassignment constituted sex discrimination because it was based on the gender of the person concerned. In doing so,[42] the Court ruled that different treatment based on sexual orientation does not constitute sex discrimination. Since this judgement was mentioned in legislation, sexual orientation constitutes a distinct area of discrimination[43].

Discrimination on grounds of sex is different and does not cover discrimination on grounds of sexual orientation. The legislation on equality between men and women refers to discrimination on grounds of sex.

8. Maternity

Equality legislation must be without prejudice to provisions concerning the protection of women, particularly as regards pregnancy and maternity. Moreover, a refusal to employ a pregnant woman, or her dismissal because of her pregnancy is classed as direct discrimination based on sex.

---

39 Judgement of 30 April 1996, P/S and Cornwall County Council (C-13/94, ECR 1996 p. I-2143), Judgement of 15 June 1978, Defrenne/Sabena (149/77, ECR 1978 p. 1365), Judgement of 20 March 1984, Razzouk and others/Commission (75 and 117/82, ECR 1984 p. 1509) etc.

40 Judgement of 30 April 1996, P/S and Cornwall County Council (C-13/94, ECR 1996 p. I-2143).

41 Idem.

42 Judgement of 17 February 1998, Grant/South-West Trains (C-249/96, ECR 1998 p. I-621), Judgement of 31 May 2001, D and Sweden/Council (C-122/99 P and C-125/99 P, ECR 2001 p. I-4319).

43 For example in Article 21 of the Charter of Fundamental Rights of the European Union.

The Court of Justice has consistently[44] recognised the legitimacy of protecting a woman's biological condition during and after pregnancy. It has ruled that any unfavourable treatment of women related to pregnancy or maternity constitutes direct sex discrimination.

The Court of Justice was asked whether EU anti-discrimination legislation allows for parental leave, on expiry of the statutory protective period, be reserved to the mother to the exclusion of any other person. In the Hofmann case law[45], the Court considered that the maternity leave granted to a woman on expiry of the statutory protective period may legitimately be reserved to the mother to the exclusion of any other person, in view of the fact that it is only the mother who may find herself subject to undesirable pressure to return to work prematurely. The maternity leave granted to a woman on expiry of the statutory protective period takes into account at least two aspects:

- it is legitimate to ensure the protection of a woman's biological condition during pregnancy and thereafter until such time as her physiological and mental functions have returned to normal;
- it is legitimate to protect the special relationship between a woman and her child over the period which follows pregnancy and childbirth, by preventing that relationship from being disturbed by the multiple burdens which would result from the simultaneous pursuit of employment.

9. Burden of proof

Shifting the burden of proof is now expressly mentioned in EU legislation, but this principle was first mentioned in Court of Justice case law. Initially, the Court admitted the shift in the burden of proof when the employee had no possibility of proving he had been treated differently. Therefore, the Court states that it is up to the employer to prove equality is being respected, but that contrary behaviour may be justified by a legitimate aim.

In jurisprudence, shifting the burden of proof aimed to provide effective protection against discrimination. The burden shift is not automatic; as such, for an employee to claim he is being discriminated against is not enough; instead, the employee must prove the existence of facts which are alleged to be discriminatory.

44 For example Judgement of 8 November 1990, Dekker/Stichting Vormingscentrum voor Jong Volwassenen (177/88, ECR 1990 p. I-3941), Judgement of 3 February 2000, Mahlburg (C-207/98, ECR 2000 p. I-549).

45 Judgement of 12 July 1984, Hofmann/Barmer Ersatzkasse.

Art. 4(1) of Directive 97/80/CE is the relevant provision governing the burden of proof in cases of discrimination based on sex. Under that provision, when a person establishes facts from which direct or indirect discrimination may be presumed, it shall be up to the respondent to prove that there has been no breach of the principle of equal treatment. Consequently, where discrimination is apparent, the employer must show that this principle has not been not violated. In C-109/88, the Employees' Union (Handels-og Kontorfunktionarernes Forbund I Danmark) claimed that the Danfoss wages practice was discriminatory on grounds of sex. The Employees' Union wanted to prove the difference in pay using statistics relating to the wages paid to men and women, but the national court did not consider such evidence sufficient to prove discrimination. Therefore in C-109/88, the Court had to rule on the burden of proof in cases of equal pay[46]. Danfoss applied a system of individual supplements in such way that a woman was unable to identify why her pay differed from that of a man doing the same work, because the system of individual supplements was characterised by a total lack of transparency. In this situation, female workers were deprived of any effective means of enforcing the principle of equal pay before the national courts. In this instance, the employer must prove that his wage payment practice is not discriminatory. In the Enderby case[47], the Court also stated that if a company applies a system of pay which is wholly lacking in transparency, it is for the employer to prove that his wage payment practice is not discriminatory. So, where there is a prima facie case of discrimination, it is up to the employer to show that there are objective reasons for the difference in pay. In this case law, Pamela Mary Enderby was employed by the Frenchay Health Authority as a speech therapist, which is a female profession. Pamela Mary Enderby considered herself a victim of pay discrimination on grounds of sex due to the fact that at her level of responsibility she was less well paid than members of comparable professions in which there were more men than women.

Thus in a prima facie case of discrimination the employer must prove that there are objective reasons for the difference in treatment because employees were deprived of any effective means of enforcing the principle of equal pay before the national courts.

---

46 Judgement of 17 October 1989, Handels-og Kontorfunktionærernes Forbund i Danmark/Dansk Arbejdsgiverforening, acting on behalf of Danfoss (109/88, ECR 1989 p. 3199).

47 Judgement of 27 October 1993, Enderby/Frenchay Health Authority and Secretary of State for Health (C-127/92, ECR 1993 p. I-5535).

The obligation to adduce evidence in rebuttal which arises for the alleged perpetrator of the discrimination is a simple finding that a presumption of discrimination has arisen on the basis of established facts[48].

10. Remedies

EU Directives state that the sanctions imposed for breaches of national provisions adopted pursuant to European Directives on the prohibition of discrimination should be effective, proportionate and dissuasive, and may include the payment of compensation to the victim. EU Directives do not enforce a certain manner of sanction, instead leaving Member States free to choose how to penalise breaches of the prohibition.

Although it leaves the Member States free to choose between the different suitable solutions for achieving its objective, Directive 76/207 requires that, if Member states choose to penalise breaches of that prohibition by awarding compensation, then that compensation must be commensurate with the damage sustained in order to ensure it is effective and has a deterrent effect, and must therefore amount to more than purely nominal compensation such as, for example, the reimbursement only of the expenses incurred in connection with the application[49].

Member States are free to choose sanctions, but if they choose civil sanction this must, in itself, be sufficient to render the employer fully liable, without there being any possibility of invoking the grounds of exemption provided for by domestic law[50].

Directive 76/207 does not require discrimination on grounds of sex regarding access to employment to be made the subject of a sanction by way of an obligation imposed on the employer who is the author of the discrimination to conclude a contract of employment with the candidate discriminated against[51].

National legislation may prescribe an upper limit for the amount of compensation provided to a worker who has been the victim of sex discrimination, but

---

48 Judgement of 10 July 2008, Feryn (C-54/07, ECR 2008 p. I-5187).

49 Judgement of 10 April 1984, Von Colson and Kamann/Land Nordrhein-Westfalen (14/83, ECR 1984, p. 1891), Judgement of 10 April 1984, Harz/Deutsche Tradax (79/83, ECR 1984 p. 1921).

50 Judgement of 8 November 1990, Dekker/Stichting Vormingscentrum voor Jong Volwassenen (177/88, ECR 1990 p. I-3941), Judgement of 22 April 1997, Draehmpaehl/Urania Immobilienservice (C-180/95, ECR 1997 p. I-2195).

51 Judgement of 10 April 1984, Von Colson and Kamann/Land Nordrhein-Westfalen (14/83, ECR 1984 p. 1891), Judgement of 10 April 1984, Harz/Deutsche Tradax (79/83, ECR 1984 p. 1921).

may not impose a ceiling on the aggregate amount of compensation which several applicants claim[52].

Directive 76/207 must be interpreted as precluding that the reparation of the damage sustained by a person injured as a result of discriminatory dismissal may not be capped at an upper limit fixed a priori or by excluding an award of interest to compensate for the loss sustained by the recipient of the compensation as a result of the time that has passed until the capital sum awarded is actually paid[53].

In the Seymour-Smith and Perez case (C-167/97), the Court distinguished between the options open to an employee in the case of unfair dismissal: the right to compensation and the right to reinstatement or re-engagement. Only the conditions determining whether an employee who has been unfairly dismissed is entitled to reinstatement or re-engagement fall within the scope of Directive 76/207, the right to compensation falls within the scope of the principle of equal pay as laid down by the Treaty[54].

If a national court decides to award financial compensation in the case of unfair dismissal, this must be adequate to make up for the loss and damage actually sustained as a result of the discriminatory dismissal[55].

Even where there is no identifiable victim, the sanctions applicable to breaches of national provisions adopted in order to transpose the Directive must be effective, proportionate and dissuasive. If seemingly appropriate to the situation at issue in the main proceedings, these sanctions may, where necessary, include a finding of discrimination by the court or the competent administrative authority in conjunction with an adequate level of publicity, the cost of which is to be borne by the defendant. Sanctions may also take the form of a prohibitory injunction pursuant to national law, whereby the employer is ordered to cease the discriminatory practice, and, where appropriate, a fine is imposed. They may, moreover, take the form of damages awarded to the body bringing the proceedings[56].

Directive 92/85 on the introduction of measures to encourage improvements in the safety and health at work of pregnant workers and workers who have recently given birth or are breastfeeding must be interpreted as not precluding leg-

---

52 Judgement of 22 April 1997, Draehmpaehl/Urania Immobilienservice (C-180/95, ECR 1997 p. I-2195).

53 Judgement of 2 August 1993, Marshall/Southampton and South West Hampshire Area Health Authority (C-271/91, ECR 1993 p. I-4367).

54 Judgement of 9 February 1999, Seymour-Smith and Perez (C-167/97, ECR 1999 p. I-623).

55 Judgement of 2 August 1993, Marshall/Southampton and South West Hampshire Area Health Authority (C-271/91, ECR 1993 p. I-4367).

56 Judgement of 10 July 2008, Feryn (C-54/07, ECR 2008 p. I-5187).

islation by a Member State which provides a specific remedy concerning the prohibition of dismissal of pregnant workers or workers who have recently given birth or are breastfeeding, such specific remedy to be exercised according to procedural rules specific to that remedy. However, these rules should not be less favourable than those governing similar domestic actions (principle of equivalence) nor framed in such a way as to make it practically impossible to exercise the rights conferred by EU law (principle of effectiveness). The Court also ruled that a regulation denying a pregnant employee dismissed during her pregnancy the option to bring an action for damages was contrary to EU law[57], since such an action was available to any other employee who has been dismissed.

Bibliography

Handbook on European non-discrimination law, European Union Agency for Fundamental Rights, 2010.

Council Directive 76/207/EEC of 9 February 1976 on the implementation of the principle of equal treatment for men and women as regards access to employment, vocational training and promotion, and working conditions.

Council Directive 97/80/EC of 15 December 1997 on the burden of proof in cases of discrimination based on sex.

Judgement of 15 June 1978, Defrenne/Sabena (C-149/77, ECR 1978).

Judgement of 20 March 1984, Razzouk a.o./Commission (75 and 117/82, ECR 1984).

Judgement of 10 April 1984, Von Colson and Kamann/Land Nordrhein-Westfalen (14/83, ECR 1984).

Judgement of 10 April 1984, Harz/Deutsche Tradax (79/83, ECR 1984).

Judgement of 12 July 1984, Hofmann/Barmer Ersatzkasse (184/83, ECR 1984).

Judgement of 26 February 1986, Marshall/Southampton and South-West Hampshire Area Health Authority (152/84, ECR 1986).

Judgement of 15 May 1986, Johnston/Chief Constable of the Royal Ulster Constabulary (222/84, ECR 1986).

Judgement of 25 October 1988, Commission/France (312/86, ECR 1988).

Judgement of 30 June 1988, Commission/France (318/86, ECR 1988).

Judgement of 17 October 1989, Handels-og Kontorfunktionærernes Forbund i Danmark/Dansk Arbejdsgiverforening, acting on behalf of Danfoss (109/88, ECR 1989).

Judgement of 2 August 1993, Marshall/Southampton and South West Hampshire Area Health Authority (C-271/91, ECR 1993).

Judgement of 27 October 1993, Enderby/Frenchay Health Authority and Secretary of State for Health (C-127/92, ECR 1993).

Judgement of 17 October 1995, Kalanke/Freie Hansestadt Bremen (C-450/93, ECR 1995).

Judgement of 30 April 1996, P/S and Cornwall County Council (C-13/94, ECR 1996).

Judgement of 13 July 1995, Meyers/Adjudication Officer (C-116/94, ECR 1995).

57 Judgement of 29 October 2009, Pontin (C-63/08, ECR 2009 p. I-10467).

Judgement of 22 April 1997, Draehmpaehl/Urania Immobilienservice (C-180/95, ECR 1997).
Judgement of 11 November 1997, Marschall/Land Nordrhein-Westfalen (C-409/95, ECR 1997).
Judgement of 17 February 1998, Grant/South-West Trains (C-249/96, ECR 1998)6.
Judgement of 26 October 1999, Sirdar (C-273/97, ECR 1999).
Judgement of 28 March 2000, Badeck a. o. (C-158/97, ECR 2000).
Judgement of 3 February 2000, Mahlburg (C-207/98, ECR 2000).
Judgement of 11 January 2000, Kreil (C-285/98, ECR 2000).
Judgement of 7 December 2000, Schnorbus (C-79/99, ECR 2000).
Judgement of 31 May 2001, D and Sweden/Council (C-122/99 P and C-125/99 P, ECR 2001).
Judgement of 19 March 2002, Lommers (C-476/99, ECR 2002).
Judgement of 11 March 2003, Dory (C-186/01, ECR 2003).
Judgement of 10 July 2008, Feryn (C-54/07, ECR 2008).
Judgement of 29 October 2009, Pontin (C-63/08, ECR 2009).
Judgement of 21 July 2011, Kelly (C-104/10).
Judgement of 19 April 2012, Meister (C-415/10).

TRANSPOSITION OF EUROPEAN UNION DIRECTIVES INTO NATIONAL LAW

Implications of Discrimination on Economic Agents' Activity

PhD student Florina Mariana HOMEGHIU[1]
PhD student Mihaela CONSTANTINESCU[2]

Abstract

The paper approaches discrimination from two perspectives. On the one hand, it aims to present the types of discrimination to which economic agents are subjected and the measures that can be taken in order to eliminate their effects, and, on the other hand, the discrimination generated by economic agents and the sanctions that can be imposed. In this respect, we briefly present the authorities to whom the economic agents can appeal and the procedures they can follow. The paper cites national and international regulations in the field, and analyses and interprets the main provisions which have implications on economic agents. In order to understand their consequences, concrete situations are synthetised and identified from court jurisprudence and administrative authorities with jurisdictional role, without claiming to have exhausted all discrimination cases. Special attention was given to discrimination cases in the jurisprudence of the European Court of Justice and to the interpretation of Union treaties and other documents that are mandatory for the Romanian state.

Keywords: Discrimination, public acquisition, employee, sanctions, National Council for Discrimination Control, National Council for Litigations Settlement.

1. Types of discrimination and their legal regulation

According to Romanian legislation, discrimination is

> "any difference, exclusion, restriction or preference, based on race, nationality, ethnos, language, religion, social category, beliefs, sex, sexual orientation, age, disability, non-infectious chronic disease, HIV infection, affiliation to an under-privileged category, as well as any other criterion that has as purpose and effect the restriction, elimination of acknowledgement, use or exercise, under equal conditions, of the

---

1 Florina Mariana Homeghiu, National School of Political and Administrative Studies, Bucharest, Romania, Email: m_florinaolteanu@yahoo.com.

2 Mihaela Constantinescu, National School of Political and Administrative Studies, Bucharest, Romania, Email: mihaela.constrantinescu81@yahoo.com, beneficiary of the "Doctoral Scholarships for a Sustainable Society" project, co-financed by the European Union through the European Social Fund, Sectoral Operational Programme Human Resources and Development 2007-2013.

> human rights and fundamental freedoms or of the rights established by law, in the public, economic, social and cultural field or in any other field of public life"[3].

When first reading the legislative act, we tend to consider that the subjects of discrimination are natural persons as the only beings affected by the discrimination criteria expressly provided by law and enjoying the exercise of human rights and fundamental freedoms. Such an interpretation is also the result of the influence exerted by certain cases of discrimination that attracted public attention with their focus on natural persons, and especially employees. Yet, careful analysis of the law text prompts us to examine the extent to which legal persons – and especially economic agents – can be subject to discrimination. For example, the law allows any discrimination criterion which has as its purpose or effect the restriction, elimination of acknowledgement, use or exercise, under equal conditions not only of the human rights and his fundamental freedoms, but also

> "the rights established by law, in the political, economic, social and cultural field or in any other field of public life".

As a result, we observe that this provision does not exclude discrimination of legal persons; we can include their rights in the category of "rights established by law", especially as they benefit from rights in the "economic" field, which is the area where legal persons are active, or in "any other field of public life".

Discrimination against legal persons is explicitly provided by Government Emergency Ordinance no. 34/2006 regarding public acquisition contract awards, public works concession contracts and services concession contracts (hereinafter referred to as "GEO no. 34/2006"). Thus, the provisions of Art. 2, Para. 2 of GEO no. 34/2006 establish the fact that one of the fundamental principles for public acquisition contract award is that of non-discrimination. In order to observe this principle, a series of mandatory measures have been imposed through GEO no. 34/2006 that must be respected by the contracting parties[4]. The pur-

---

3 Art 2 of the Ordinance no. 137/2000 regarding prevention and sanctioning of discrimination deeds (hereinafter referred to as "Ordinance no. 137/2000").

4 We mention the following provisions of GEO no. 34/2006 regarding public acquisition contract awards, public works concession contracts and services concession contracts: according to Art. 85, Para. 2, when selecting candidates, the contracting authority is obligated to apply objective and non-discriminatory criteria, using only the selection criteria provided in the hiring announcement. Art. 101, Para. 2 has the same meaning. When preselecting the candidates, the contracting authority is obligated to apply objective and non-discriminatory criteria, using only the pre-selection criteria provided by the participation announcement. According to Art. 61- (1), the means of communication specified by the contracting authority must not restrict access of economic operators to the award

pose of most of these provisions is to prevent discrimination when establishing the criteria for candidate selection, and to define the criteria for preselecting candidates, the communication instruments specified by the contracting authority, and the information revealed to participants. The remaining provisions governing the non-discrimination of legal persons define the supervision modalities in case of discriminatory deeds, their sanctioning and the elimination of their effects.

Measures to protect legal persons against possible discrimination that can occur when developing relationships with the state are provided at international level, through *Directive 2004/18/CE of the European Parliament and of the Council of 31 March 2004 on the coordination of the procedures of adjudication of the public agreements of works, of supply and of services,* according to which contracts awarded in Member States on behalf of the state, of territorial communities and of public law bodies must respect the principles provided by the Treaty, especially the free circulation of goods, the principle of establishing freedom and the principle of freedom in providing services, as well as the principles derived from these, such as equal treatment, non-discrimination, mutual acknowledgement, proportionality and transparency.

Furthermore, *Directive 2004/17/CE of the European Parliament and of the Council of 31 March 2004 coordinating the procurement procedures of entities operating in the water, energy, transport and postal services sectors,* recommends the issuance at Community level of provisions governing the coordination of contracts, in order to guarantee the competitive freedom of public acquisition contracts awarded by entities operating in the water, energy, transport and postal services sectors. Such coordination is based on the principles of equal treatment, non-discrimination, mutual acknowledgement, proportionality and transparency.

---

procedure. (2) The instruments used in electronic communication, as well as their technical characteristics, must not be discriminatory, and must be easily available to any economic operator, and compatible with the usual technology used to provide information and to communicate. According to Art 106, Para. (2), the contracting authority is obligated to ensure the application of the equal treatment principle in its dialogue with all participants. In this respect, the contracting authority does not have the right to supply information in a discriminatory way which might give one/more participants an advantage over the others. According to Art. 120, Para. (2), which governs negotiations, the contracting authority is obligated to ensure the application of the principle of equal treatment to all candidates. In this respect, the contracting authority does not have the right to supply information in a discriminatory way that might give one/more participants an advantage over the others. According to Art. 137, Para. (1), the contracting authority has the right to preselect candidates using clear, objective, non-discriminatory criteria that have to be explicitly stipulated within the competition specifications.

As far as discrimination in labour relationships is concerned, we speak only of discrimination by legal persons, with employees as the passive subjects. Thus, the Labour Code only regulates discrimination on grounds of sex, sexual orientation, genetic features, age, nationality, race, colour, ethnos, religion, political orientation, social origin, disability, family situation or responsibility, union affiliation or union activity.

Moreover, *direct and indirect discrimination of employees by employers is discernible*. While direct discrimination is not particularly difficult to identify, certain situations occur in practice that may be indirectly discriminatory but hard to label as such. As a result, the victims of such discrimination hesitate to take the necessary steps to eliminate such discriminatory situations, and the employers are not fully aware of the discriminatory character of their own actions.

Bearing in mind the provisions of Art. 5 of the Labour Code, we could say that several conditions must be met to constitute direct discrimination:

- the occurrence of deeds and acts that exclude, differentiate, restrict or show preference;
- the effect of the employer's deeds and acts is to grant, restrict or exclude acknowledgement, use or exercise of the rights provided under labour legislation;
- the employer's acts and deeds are based on one or more of the following criteria: sex, sexual orientation, genetic features, age, nationality, race, colour, ethnos, religion, political orientation, social origin, disability, family situation or responsibility, union affiliation or union activity.

At the same time, the Council Directive of 27.11.2000 establishing the general framework for equal treatment in employment and occupation defines direct discrimination as a situation in which a person is treated less favourably than another is, has been or would be treated, on grounds of religion, belief, disability, age or sexual orientation, as regards employment and occupation.

In the case of *indirect discrimination*, the employer's acts and deeds are based, apparently, on criteria other than those of sex, sexual orientation, genetic features, age, nationality, race, colour, ethnos, religion, political orientation, social origin, disability, family situation or responsibility, union affiliation or union activity provided in the case of direct discrimination, but the effects are the same as those of direct discrimination.

According to the aforementioned Directive, indirect discrimination occurs when an apparently neutral provision, criterion or practice would put people with a particular religion or belief, a particular disability, a particular age, or a particular sexual orientation at a particular disadvantage. Furthermore, the Directive stipulates that there is no indirect discrimination when such a provision, criterion or practice is justified by a legitimate aim and the means of achieving that aim are appropriate and necessary, or in the case of persons with a particular disability, when the employer is obliged to take appropriate measures in order to eliminate disadvantages entailed by such provision, criterion or practice.

In addition to the legislative acts presented above, regulations exist in the field of discrimination, especially internationally, that are applicable to national law. These include: Council Directive 2000/43/EC of 29 June 2000 implementing the principle of equal treatment between persons irrespective of racial or ethnic origin, Council Directive 2000/78/EC of 27 November 2000 establishing a general framework for equal treatment in employment and occupation, the Universal Declaration of Human Rights, the International Covenant on Economic, Social and Cultural rights, the Convention on the Elimination of All Forms of Discrimination against women (CEDAW), the European Convention on Human Rights, and the European Social Charter, revised.

But if we try to identify provisions that regulate the discrimination of legal persons, we notice that internationally they are absent. All of the aforementioned Directives, Treaties and Agreements protect the rights of natural persons, not legal persons. Furthermore, not only do the abovementioned documents, not expressly contain regulations to protect legal persons against discrimination, they also do not allow the interpretation of terms such as "person" or "individual" to include legal persons. The lack of such regulation can create the premises for severe abuses in the context of economic globalisation, of the emergence of transnational companies which, in order to carry out their activity inevitably come into contact with the state: to obtain authorisations and licences, at least, if not to supply services and goods to state institutions. As a consequence, imposing certain criteria to prevent discrimination against companies, at least in their relationships with the state, can be beneficial to their functioning.

We find the principle of non-discrimination stipulated in the Treaty on European Union and the Treaty on the Functioning of the European Union, apparently referring to citizens' rights and freedoms. By extension, as we shall see, however, this principle is also applied by the European Court of Justice in decisions regarding legal persons[5]. Thus, in Article 2 of the Treaty on European Un-

5 According to Art. 2 of the Treaty on European Union, the Union is based on values such as respecting human dignity, freedom, democracy, equality, lawful state as well as respecting human rights, including minorities. These values are common to Member States in a society characterised by plurality, non-discrimination, tolerance, justice, solidarity and equality between men and women. According to Art. 10 of the Treaty on the Functioning of the European Union, in defining and applying its policies, the Union tries to fight any discrimination based on sex, race or ethnos, religion or belief, disability, age or

ion, non-discrimination is regarded as a general principle, as a basic value of the European Union, and consequently applicable to all persons.

2. Sanctions applicable for violation of provisions which regulate discrimination

Legislation has provided a different legal regime in the field for acts and deeds that are considered discriminatory. Thus, some of them are expressly enumerated by the law as contraventions for which fines are imposed by the body set up specifically for this task, the National Council for Discrimination Control, on request or ex officio, whereas no provisions exist for fining the other categories of acts and deeds that breach the provisions governing discrimination. In such cases, victims can only appeal either to the National Council for Discrimination Control or to the court in order to eliminate the consequences of discrimination and reinstate the prior situation.

An analysis of the criteria that define discrimination shows that only some of the deeds provided by the Labour Code constitute contraventions and have been adopted in Ordinance no. 137/2000 where they are punishable by fine.

But even if the remaining discriminatory acts and deeds are not provided explicitly as contraventions, employees can still cite the general provisions of Ordinance no. 137/2000 and request only the elimination of the consequences of the discriminatory deeds and reinstatement of the prior situation. Thus, we believe that the definition of discriminatory acts and deeds in Art. 2 of the Ordinance no. 137/2000 is not limitative; most of the time it includes differences, exclusions, restrictions or preferences based on

> "any other criterion that has as its purpose or effect the elimination of acknowledgement, use or exercise, under equal conditions, of the human rights and fundamental freedoms or of the rights established by law, in the public, economic, social and cultural field or in any other field of public life".

Thus, we believe that this definition includes discrimination criteria provided by the Labour Code that are not to be found among those expressly enumerated by Ordinance no. 137/2000, such as union activity or union affiliation. As a consequence, anyone who feels discriminated against on grounds of affiliation to a union can appeal to the National Council for Discrimination Control or the courts, although the deed is not expressly defined as a contravention.

---

sexual orientation. Furthermore, Art. 18 of the Treaty on the Functioning of the European Union forbids any discrimination based on citizenship or nationality.

Romanian legislation provides the following categories of contraventions in the field of labour relationships, which incur fines ranging from 400 lei to 4,000 lei if the discrimination relates to a natural person or from 600 lei to 8,000 lei if it relates to a group of people or a community:

- making a person's participation in an economic activity or the choice or exercise of a freelancer's activity conditional on his/her belonging to a certain race, nationality, ethnos, religion, social category, or on having certain beliefs, sex, sexual orientation, age or belonging to a disadvantaged minority.
- discrimination of a person on grounds of belonging to a certain race, nationality, ethnos, religion, social category, or of having certain beliefs, sex, sexual orientation, age or belonging to a disadvantaged minority within a labour relationship, manifested in the following fields:
  a) concluding, suspending, modifying or ceasing the labour relationship;
  b) establishment and modification of duties, place of work or wage;
  c) granting other social rights than those representing the wage;
  d) training, advanced training, and promotion;
  e) applying discriminatory measures;
  f) the right to join a union and access the facilities offered by it;
  g) any other conditions regarding work, according to the legislation in force.
- refusal by a legal or natural person to hire a person on the grounds that this person belongs to a certain race, nationality, ethnos, religion, social category or disadvantaged minority or because of his/her beliefs, age, sex or sexual orientation,
- making recruitment to a position that has been advertised or announced by the employer or its representative conditional on belonging to a certain race, nationality, ethnos, religion, social category or disadvantaged minority, age, sex or sexual orientation, or on the candidate's beliefs, except in situations where the public authorities or private-law legal persons favour a person, group or community with the aim of promoting their proper development and ensuring equal opportunity compared to other persons, groups or communities, and except for measures aimed at protecting disadvantaged minorities.
- discrimination of employees by employers, because of affiliation to a certain race, nationality, ethnos, religion, social category or disadvantaged minority, age, sex or sexual orientation, or of the employee's beliefs.

Fines for contraventions can be imposed on both legal persons who are guilty of breaching anti-discriminatory legal provisions and on natural persons operating within a legal person who is acting discriminatorily.

As a further consequence of discrimination, legal persons may be liable to pay compensation demanded by the victim or stipulated by the court if found guilty of breaching anti-discriminatory legal provisions.

Furthermore, the court can decide to rescind or suspend the official licence to operate issued to the legal person who has been found guilty of discrimination that has caused significant prejudice or who has repeatedly breached the provisions of Ordinance no. 137/2000.

The situation is different for legal persons who are victims of discrimination. Although they do not have the option of demanding sanctions against those guilty of discrimination, we believe that they can take advantage of the provisions of Art. 27 of Ordinance no. 137/2000, which do not limit the right to demand compensation to natural persons, and instead use the generic phrase of 'discriminated person' who is entitled to file for compensation[6].

Thus, any person – either legal or natural – who believes they are the victim of discrimination can appeal to the National Council for Discrimination Control to request elimination of the consequences of the discriminatory deeds and reinstatement of the prior situation. The decision issued by this body can subsequently be challenged in court.

As a result, victims of discrimination have the right to opt between the courts and the National Council for Discrimination Control. The latter is a jurisdictional body charged with resolving conflicts relating to discrimination and empowered to demand the elimination of the consequences of the discriminatory deeds and reinstatement of the prior situation but with no powers to grant compensation for prejudices caused by discriminatory deeds, as damages can only be awarded by the courts.

Although national provisions do permit discrimination to be interpreted as targeting both natural and legal persons, and allow decisions to be contested and challenged in court, in practice, petitioners are usually be natural persons and non-profit legal entities, since the jurisdictional authorities tend to reject contestations and challenges in court by firms.

Nevertheless, the phrase "discrimination of firms" is commonplace and frequently used both by businessmen and lawyers, especially when talking about public acquisition and state contract award procedures and referring to differential treatment in respect of fiscal measures. In the first instance, the alleged victims cite differential treatment in the execution of legal provisions or acquisition

---

6 According to Art. 27 Para. 1 of the Ordinance no. 137/2000: "the alleged victim of discrimination can request the court to order payment of damages and reinstatement of the previous situation or annulment of the situation caused by discrimination, according to common law. The request is exempt from paying any judicial tax and is conditional on the Council being informed".

procedures, whereas the second instance relates to discrimination based on the provisions of these legal acts. This very frequent use of the term discrimination of firms shows how deeply legal persons believe that they are the subjects of discrimination under certain circumstances, and that there is an urgent need for additional provisions to address these cases and for protection measures against abuse.

GEO no. 34/2006 regarding public acquisition contract awards, public works contract awards and services concession contracts provides measures that can be taken by legal persons who claim to be victims of discrimination in respect of public acquisition procedures. Victims can appeal to the National Council for Litigations Settlement or the competent court to annul the act and/or recognise the legal claim or legitimate interest. The Council examines the legality of the act in question and can order its partial or total annulment, or can order the authority to take action or any other measure it deems necessary to remedy the actions affecting the award procedure, including such actions to eliminate discriminatory situations. The Council can order the deletion of certain technical, economic or financial specifications from the request for quotation / invitation to tender, from the award documentation or from any other documents issued in respect of the award procedure. The interested party can object to the Council's decision and challenge it in the court. At the request of the interested party, the court can order deferment of execution of the contract that formed the basis of the public acquisition procedure that has been found to discriminate[7].

---

7 GEO no. 34/2006, Art. 285 - (1) The court admitting the complaint modifies the decision of the Council, by deciding, depending on the case

a) to annul entirely or partially the act of the contracting authority;

b) to oblige the contracting authority to take action;

c) to order the contracting authority to eliminate any discriminatory technical, economic or financial specifications in the request for quotation/invitation to tender, the tender documentation, award documentation or any other document issued in respect of the award procedure;

d) any other necessary measures to remedy the breach of the legal provisions in the field of public acquisition.

(2) If it admits a complaint filed against a decision of the National Council for Litigations Settlement, the court shall annul that decision, with explanation of its reasons for doing so.

(3) If the court admits the complaint, it modifies the decision of the Council and observes that the act of the contracting authority contravened legislation in the field of public acquisition, and the contract was concluded before the Council decision. As a result of this breach, the provisions of Art. 2563, Para. (3), Art. 28710, Para. (1), letter (b), Para. (2)-(6) or, depending on the case, Art. 28711 apply as appropriate.

(4) The court can reject the complaint.

The contracting authority that is guilty of breaching the non-discrimination principle when carrying out public acquisition procedures can be obliged to pay compensation. In case the harmed legal person wants to request compensation for discriminatory public acquisition contract award procedures, it should address the court directly as the National Council for Litigations Settlement is not empowered to award compensation[8].

3. Frequent cases of discrimination in goods and services acquisition procedures

The principle of non-discrimination is applicable to entities within the European Union as part of the procedures provided for the acquisition of goods and services. Some decisions by international courts are discussed below, and show that, over time, the non-discrimination principle has been breached by national bodies in public acquisition procedures.

For example, in Case T-461/08, Decision of 20 September 2011, Evropaïki Dynamiki – Proigmena Systimata Tilepikoinonion Pliroforikis kai Tilematikis AE vs. European Bank of Investments (EBI), referring to the establishment of certain non-discriminatory criteria for choosing the winners, the Court considered that choosing the economically most favourable offer leaves the contracting authorities free, not only to choose, the criteria for contract award, but also to determine relative ratios by which to theoretically evaluate the specified criteria in order to identify the economically most favourable offer. On the other hand, according to equal treatment and non-discrimination principles, relative ratios of different criteria and sub-criteria should not have been adopted by taking into consideration susceptible elements that might have a discriminatory effect on one of the offers. Furthermore, modifying relative ratios of the award criteria during the bid procedure undermines the principles of equal treatment and non-discrimination. As far as the alleged victim's claim for damages amounting to the sum they would have obtained if they had been awarded the acquisition, the Court argued that even if the plaintiff had been able to prove its rightful first place and that it should therefore have won the contract, the authority who was organising the bid procedure would not have been under any obligation to sign a framework agreement. Thus, neither the principle, nor the rule applicable to the tender procedure puts the authority under any obligation to enter into a contract

---

(5) The decision of the court is finite and irrevocable.

8 GEO no. 34/2006, Art. 287 - (1) damages for prejudice suffered in awards procedures can only be requested in court, under the provisions of Art. 2562 Para. (1) or by separate action.

regarding the public acquisition with the entity designated the winner as a result of the bidding process[9].

One example of the frequent practice of discrimination in public acquisition procedures when drawing up specifications and technical specifications is Case C-368/10 of 10 May 2012, the European Commission vs. The Netherlands, where the Court considered the presentation by the contracting authority of certain technical specifications that did not allow for precise determination of the contract object and, implicitly, the evaluation of the offer, to be discriminatory. Thus, the Court ruled that the principle of non-discrimination is vital as regards technical specifications, given the risks of discrimination inherent in the choice or formulation of the same. Thus, Art 23, Para. 2 and Para. 3 b) of Directive 2004/18 stipulate that technical specifications must allow equal access to bidders and must not pose unjustified obstacles to competing in public acquisition procedures, that they must be precise enough for bidders to determine the object of the contract and contracting parties to be able to award the contract, and that these specifications should be clear enough for all bidders to understand the criteria established by the contracting authority. Furthermore, compliance with the principles of equality, non-discrimination and transparency demands that the award criteria be objective in order to ensure objective bid comparison and evaluation, and, as a result, effective competition conditions[10].

In Case T-258/06, Federal Republic of Germany vs. European Commission, the Court confirmed the validity of the principle of non-discrimination on grounds of nationality for legal persons, as well, and its applicability in public acquisition procedures. In the Court's opinion, non-discrimination on grounds of nationality preconditions special measures, such as allowing a reasonable length of time for firms from Member States to evaluate the documentation and prepare their quotation, thus mitigating the risk of preferential treatment of national bidders or candidates which would breach the non-discrimination principle. At the same time, non-discrimination necessitates an objective and transparent approach to make sure all potential bidders are aware of the award criteria prior to submitting their quotations. These award criteria must guarantee the same chance to all potential bidders when drawing up their quotations or bids. The requirement of a non-discriminatory description of the contract object derives from the principle of equal treatment. According to the Court's considerations,

---

9 Case T-461/08, Evropaïki Dynamiki – Proigmena Systimata Tilepikoinonion Pliroforikis kai Tilematikis AE vs. European Investment Bank (EIB), available online http://eurlex.europa.eu/LexUriServ/LexUriServ.do?uri=CELEX:62008TJ0461:RO:HTML, accessed on 23.09.2012.

10 Case C-368/10, European Commission vs. Kingdom of the Netherlands, available online http://eurlex.europa.eu/LexUriServ/.RO.PDF, accessed on 23.09.2012.

the objective is to guarantee the economic agents, regardless of their origin, access to the same contract conditions derived from the principles of freedom of settlement, freedom to provide service, freedom of competition, especially by respecting the principle of equal treatment expressed in the form of non- discrimination on grounds of citizenship and nationality[11].

Furthermore, in order to respect the non-discrimination principle, the Court confirmed certain compulsory minimum requirements in respect of prior publication of the public acquisition procedure. Thus, the principles of equal treatment and non-discrimination on grounds of citizenship and nationality, as interpreted in the Court's jurisprudence, imply, among others, a transparent obligation for the authority granting the public concession to make sure these principles are observed. Consequently, when awarding public acquisition contracts, the Member States, and their contracting entities, must observe this transparency obligation by guaranteeing, in the interests of all potential bidders, an adequate level of publicity to ensure a competitive environment for public acquisition contracts and a means of controlling the impartiality of the award procedure. This obligation includes a means of publication prior to the award of the public acquisition contract, in other words advance publication before the award. Accordingly, *ex post* notification cannot guarantee adequate publicity[12].

Other frequently encountered cases where the principle of non-discrimination is breached when firms participate in public acquisition procedures involve the exclusion of corporate groups or member firms if the latter submit bids alongside other members of the group during the procedure, even if the bid of the aforementioned group has not been submitted on behalf of the name of this group of companies. Such exclusions of corporate groups are deemed contrary to international provisions. Such a measure can limit the freedom of settlement and free service provision guaranteed by the provisions of the Treaty. In this respect, a national provision that stipulates automatic exclusion of certain established groups and member companies of these groups can act as a deterrent for economic agents domiciled in other Member States and may result, on the one hand, in operators who wish to settle in that Member State through establishing a group, eventually setting up national and foreign firms and, on the other hand, those who wish to join such already existing groups in

11 Case T-258/06 Federal Republic of Germany vs. European Commission, available online http://curia.europa.eu/juris/document/document_print.jsf;jsessionid=9ea7d2dc30db4b0ad724952b4100ab9fec20ff0556f1.e34KaxiLc3qMb40Rch0SaxuKbx10?doclang=RO&text=&pageIndex=0&part=1&mode=DOC&docid=80961&occ=first&dir=&cid=411936, accessed on 23.09.2012.

12 Case T-258/06 Federal Republic of Germany vs. European Commission, available online http://eurlex.europa.eu/Result.do?idReq=9&page=4, accessed on 23.09.2012.

order to participate more easily in public acquisition contract award procedures initiated by contracting authorities of that Member State and to facilitate the provision of their services[13].

4. Frequently encountered cases of discrimination in employment relationships.

The most frequently encountered cases of discrimination in employment relationships and those deeds that constitute particularly novel forms of discrimination are discussed below by analysing both national and the European Court of Justice jurisprudence.

One of the most frequently encountered reasons for employee discrimination is age. The National Council for Discrimination Control has repeatedly imposed sanctions against economic agents for both direct and indirect age-related discrimination. In Decision no. 139/2008, for example, the Council decided that a recruitment advertisement that stipulated women aged between 25 and 50 and men between 30 and 54 was discriminatory. In this specific case, the firm's argument that it could not hire people above the mentioned ages because it would lose client contracts was overturned based on the nature of its activity and because the employer admitted to already employing people who were older than the age limits stated in the advertisement[14]. Furthermore, the length of service of at least 12 years was considered by the Council to be discriminatory. At the same time, the European Court of Justice, in Case C-132/11 Tyrolean Airways Tiroler Luftfahrt Gesellschaft mbH/Betriebsrat Bord der Tyrolean Airways Tiroler Luftfahrt Gesellschaft, considered that omitting to take the professional experience gained by an employee at another firm within the group into consideration did not constitute discrimination on age grounds. When determining salaries, an employer cannot be forced to take the professional experience gained by employees at other firms into consideration[15].

Directive 2000/78/EC on equal treatment in employment provides some exceptions to non-discrimination on age grounds. Accordingly, Member States can

---

13 Decision Serrantoni Srl and Consorzio stabile edili Scrl vs. Comune di Milano, Cauza C-376/08, available online http://www.europeana.ro/index.php/2011/04/13/c-37608-hotarare-2009-12-23-serrantoni, accessed on 27.09.2012.

14 Decision no. 139/2008, available online http://www.cncd.org.ro/hotarari/Domenii/Acces-angajare-si-profesie/HOT-NR-139-din-11-02-2008-121/, accessed on 19.09.2012.

15 Case C-132/11 Tyrolean Airways Tiroler Luftfahrt Gesellschaft mbH/Betriebsrat Bord der Tyrolean Airways Tiroler Luftfahrt Gesellschaft, available online http://curia.europa.eu/jcms/upload/docs/application/pdf/2012-06/cp120073en.pdf, accessed on 19.09.2012.

stipulate age-related conditions that do not constitute discrimination if it is justified objectively and reasonably, compliant with national law, and pursues a lawful objective, especially with regard to people connected to employment policy, the labour market and professional training, and provided that the means to achieve such an objective are adequate and necessary:

Differential treatment can apply specifically:

(a) when defining special conditions governing access to employment and professional training, and terms of dismissal and payment for younger or older workers and for those who support other people, in order to encourage their integration in the labour market or to protect them;

(b) when establishing conditions of minimum age, professional experience or length in service in order to gain access to employment or benefit from certain advantages connected to employment;

(c) when establishing the maximum age for employment, based on the necessary training for that position or on the need to ensure a reasonable length of service before retiring.

Furthermore, according to the aforementioned Directive, Member States can decide that defining an age criterion for professional social security regimes in respect of entitlements to pensions or invalidity benefits, or stipulating different ages for workers of categories of workers and using the age criteria as a basis for calculation does not constitute discrimination, as long as no discrimination on grounds of gender is present.

Sex is another criterion on which a large number of discrimination cases is based, where discrimination either occurs when hiring the employee, or during the employment relationship and mostly impacts the working conditions and the wage, or through unfair dismissal.

Discrimination of pregnant employees is one of the situations encountered among economic agents. By Decision of 14 July 1994, Carole Louise Webb vs. EMO Air Cargo (UK) Ltd., Case C-32/93, the European Court of Justice considered that dismissing a female worker on grounds of pregnancy constituted direct sexual discrimination. Reserving the right of Member States to uphold or introduce provisions aimed at protecting woman during "pregnancy and motherhood", Art. 2, Para. 3 of Directive 76/207 admits the legitimacy regarding the principle of equal treatment of the sexes, on the one hand, and of protecting the relationship between mother and child following pregnancy and birth. A pregnant woman on a permanent employment contract cannot be fired on grounds of her inability to perform the duties specified in her employment contract. While the availability of the employee is necessarily an essential condition for the employer to ensure proper execution of the employment contract, Community law guarantees the protection of women, both during pregnancy and after birth, regardless of the fact that the presence of the woman during motherhood, is indispensable to the welfare of the firm. A contrary interpretation would deprive the provisions of the Directive of their useful effect[16].

In Case C-271/91, D-l Helen Marchall vs. Southampton and South-West Hampshire Area Health Authority, Court Decision of 2 August 1993, the Court ruled that the plaintiff had been the victim of sex discrimination because she had been fired on reaching retirement age. Thus, a general policy of firing a woman merely because she is past retirement age, which differs from that of men pursuant to national legislation, constitutes sex discrimination, which is forbidden by Council Directive 76/207/EC of 9 February 1976 on equal treatment of men and women in employment, concerning the workplace and free access to employment, professional training and professional promotions[17].

In Case 237/85 Gisela Rummler vs. Dato-Druck GmbH, Decision of 1 July 1986, claiming sexual discrimination based on salary payment, the Court decided that establishing certain criteria when determining wages was not discriminatory. Wages should essentially be based on the actual tasks and not by taking into consideration the worker who performs that task. The non-discriminatory character should, indeed, be sought, not in each criterion separately but in the professional classification system overall. Furthermore, a system of professional classification should be based on common criteria for females and males and established in such a way as to exclude sexual discrimination[18].

Another frequently encountered discrimination criterion is *ethnos,* whereby gypsies are the most disadvantaged among employees. In order to eliminate such situations, the National Council for Discrimination Control has repeatedly imposed sanctions against employers. Thus, in its decisions, the Council decided that recruitment advertisements that excluded gypsies restricted their access to work. The Council decided that publishing job advertisements such as "I hire car mechanics with experience, aged 30-40 (except gypsies)", respectively "garment workers, tailors, except gypsies", constituted direct discrimination and imposed a fine of 2,000 lei on the hiring firm and a fine of 400 lei on the firm that owns

16 Decision Carole Louise Webb c. EMO Air Cargo (UK) Ltd., Case C-32/93, available online http://www.equalrightstrust.org/ertdocumentbank/Webb.pdf, accessed on 27.09. 2012.

17 Case C-271/91, D-l Helen Marchall vs. Southampton and South-West Hampshire Area Health Authority, Court Decision of 2 August 1993 available online http://www.ier.ro/documente/dct_fisiere/61991J0271.pdf, accessed on 27.09.2012.

18 Case 237/85 Gisela Rummler vs. Dato-Druck GmbH, Decision of 1 July 1986, available online http://www.costelgilca.ro/jurisprudenta/document/4515/, accessed on 26.09.2012.

the speciality site[19]. There were also cases in which the National Council for Discrimination Control has investigated job ads published in newspapers, which linked employment ethnicity. The Council considered that including publication on specialized sites of employment announcements stating the phrase "excluded Gypsies" constitutes discrimination. In all these cases, the Council decided that the advertisement constituted exclusion based on ethnic origin with the effect of restricting access to employment, and that its publication constituted active behaviour that, by dint of the effects it generates, unjustifiably discriminated against people from other ethnic groups[20].

Affiliation to a union can also be a reason for discrimination when it results in certain rights being granted or restricted. Thus, the National Council for Discrimination Control handled cases where sanctions were imposed against legal persons for conducting negotiations regarding collective wage agreements in the presence of the employer's representatives and of the union only, a fact that resulted in the newly negotiated collective wage agreement only granting payment to the representatives of the union for working extra hours. The Council considered that non-transparent and discretionary payment for the days when the union leader carries out union activities discriminates in effect against those union leaders who are not paid for the hours they spend on union activity and the members of these unions[21].

5. Conclusions

> "There is no doubt that specific and detailed legislation forbidding discrimination on the basis of several dimensions represents one of the first measures for fighting discrimination. In spite of this, anti-discrimination policy cannot be formulated and regulated solely in terms of judicial aspects; initiatives have signalled that the phenomenon is more complex, and has deep cultural, historical and sociological roots. From a political point of view, initiatives to spread information about anti-discrimination policies, to consolidate the social dialogue and to encourage social partners to promote equal treatment, especially in employment must be the first measures to take"[22].

---

19 Decision no. 97 of 17.05.2005, available online http://www.cncd.org.ro/files/file/Raport%20D43_2000_CNCD_final.pdf, accessed on 20.09.2012.

20 Decision no. 127 of 7 July 2010, available online http://www.cncd.org.ro/files/file/Raport%20D43_2000_CNCD_final.pdf, accessed on 20.09.2012.

21 Decision no. 132 of 11 April 2012 of the National Council for Discrimination Control.

22 Study carried out within the Sectoral Operational Programme for Human Resources Development 2007 – 2013. Title of the project: "Multi-regional network of counselling services against discrimination for social inclusion of the discriminated person". Diagnostic analysis in the field of equal opportunities and sexual equality in Romania: problems,

As the abovementioned elements show, a legal person can be both perpetrator and victim of discriminatory deeds. If legal persons discriminate against their employees through actions or inactions of themselves or their representatives, as employers, they can be fined by the authorities and ordered to pay damages to employees who have suffered discrimination. As such, the act of discrimination has financial implications for the legal person, as does the imposition by state authorities of certain conditions or limitations in public acquisition procedures or for obtaining special authorisation/licence to carry out these activities. If the tax on obtaining such a licence is too high, or a certain form of organisation is imposed, some legal persons will become victims of discrimination based on economic criteria and will not be able to apply for such a licence.

Acts of discrimination that infringe the rights of natural persons are more clearly defined, with clear legal provisions, authorities to apply them, and relevant court practices, whereas the situation is not as clear for legal persons, and necessitates the definition of discriminatory deeds, criteria for determining whether a deed is discriminatory, applicable sanctions, and the establishment of authorities with the powers to impose these sanctions.

The most effectively defended right of legal persons is that of not being discriminated, and the defence comes from the National Council for Litigations Settlement which is only empowered to rule on cases involving public acquisition contract awards. In the case of discrimination of natural persons, the competent administrative authority with the power to rule on claims of discrimination and to impose sanctions on legal persons found guilty of discrimination is the National Council for Discrimination Control. The courts are also empowered to rule on claims of discrimination, with different competences to those of the administrative authorities, and they can be approached by both natural and legal victims. Frequently, however, legal persons have to appeal to international courts to secure elimination of the abuse.

The provisions of the European Convention on Human Rights offer a means of fighting the discrimination of legal persons at international level by providing for appeals to the European Court for Human Rights. Article 14 of the European Convention on Human Rights stipulates that

> "exercise of the rights and freedoms recognised by the present Convention must be insured without any difference based, especially, on sex, race, colour, language, religion political opinions or any other opinions, national or social origin, belonging to a national minority, wealth, birth or any other situation".

---

needs, European solutions, p. 104, the document is available online http://www.nondiscriminare.ro/files/Studiu.pdf accessed on 10.09.2012.

Yet, this procedure implies the disadvantages of a lengthy period of time to appraise the case, and the impossibility of suspending discriminatory acts and deeds until the moment the Court decides. The easiest way to eliminate discrimination is to enact additional provisions in national law.

Businesses can, alternatively, appeal to the European Court of Justice if they feel discriminated by a law issued by the Romanian authorities that contradicts EU rules to protect against discrimination. Thus, they may refer to the European Court of Justice, through the national courts, for a preliminary ruling on the interpretation of Treaties and other acts taken by institutions, bodies, offices or agencies and on their consistency with national provisions. Legal persons who are the victims of discrimination may request the Court of Justice to order the suspension of acts that are damaging[23]. However, legal persons

> "may refer to the Court of Justice by way of direct actions claiming non-compliance with Community law of the conduct of states"[24].

Referring to the relationships within the European Union, we might say that

> "shaping equal opportunities for everyone, without discrimination, identifying ways of promptly reducing and eliminating any socio-economic discrepancies will increasingly take priority and become common action objectives."[25].

Such protection cannot be ensured if we lack the national and international legal regulations needed to reflect the present global economic context, in which cases of discrimination against legal persons are not only theoretical level; they are becoming more and more diverse, and are restraining their activities.

Bibliography

Manolache, Octavian: Tratat de drept comunitar, CH Beck, Bucharest, 2006.

National Council for Discrimination Control, Complementary system of protection of human rights and discrimination control in Romania, available online http://www.cncd.org.ro/publicatii/Carte-electronica-1/.

Study carried out within the Sectoral Operational Programme for Human Resources Development 2007 – 2013. Title of the project: "Multi-regional network of counselling services against discrimination for social inclusion of the discriminated person", Diagnostic analysis in the field of equal opportunities and sexual equality in Romania: problems,

23 Octavian Manolache, Tratat de drept comunitar, CH Beck, Bucharest, 2006, p.844.

24 Octavian Manolache, Tratat de drept comunitar, CH Beck, Bucharest, 2006, p.788.

25 National Council for Discrimination Control, Complementary system of protection of human rights and discrimination control in Romania, p. 6, available online http://www.cncd.org.ro/publicatii/Carte-electronica-1/, accessed on 20.09.2012.

needs, European solutions, the document is available online http://www.nondiscriminare.ro/files/Studiu.pdf.

Case T-461/08, Evropaïki Dynamiki – Proigmena Systimata Tilepikoinonion Pliroforikis kai Tilematikis AE vs. European Bank of Investments (BEI), of the European Court of Justice.

Case C-368/10 of 10 May 2012, European Commission vs. Kingdom of the Netherlands, of the European Court of Justice.

Case T-258/06, Federal Republic of Germany vs. European Commission, of the European Court of Justice.

Case C-376/08, Serrantoni Srl and Consorzio stabile edili Scrl vs. Comune di Milano, of the European Court of Justice.

Case C-132/11 Tyrolean Airways Tiroler Luftfahrt Gesellschaft mbH/Betriebsrat Bord der Tyrolean Airways Tiroler Luftfahrt Gesellschaft, of the European Court of Justice.

Case C-32/93 Carole Louise Webb vs. EMO Air Cargo (UK) Ltd, of the European Court of Justice.

Case C-271/91, D-l Helen Marchall vs. Southampton and South-West Hampshire Area Health Authority, of the European Court of Justice.

Case 237/85 Gisela Rummler vs. Dato-Druck GmbH, of the European Court of Justice.

Decision no. 139/2008 of the National Council for Discrimination Control.

Decision no. 97/2005 of the National Council for Discrimination Control.

Decision no. 190/2003 of the National Council for Discrimination Control.

Criminal Liability of the Legal Person and its Implications: a Case Study in Romania and the Czech Republic

Lecturer George GRUIA[1]
PhD student George Cristian GRUIA[2]

Abstract

In the third millennium and in the context of the current economic crisis, business law should, above all, concern itself with the commercial relations between individuals and/or legal persons. If commercial entities are to compete under the terms of competition law, but also under national, European and international law, they must abide by the law and to earn profits in accordance with the law without in any way affecting competition or the award of certain public or private auctions. Trade relations are carried out with the aim of earning profits, but at the same time the law must be respected because nobody is above the law[3], and both individuals and legal persons are subject to it. In this regard we intend to analyse peculiarities but also generalities among laws governing corporate criminal liability and prosecution in two different European countries: Romania and the Czech Republic.

Keywords: criminal liability, corporate, Romania, Czech Republic, particularities

1. History of the criminal liability of legal entities

The concept that not only individuals, but also, under certain conditions, legal persons should answer for behaviour defined as a criminal offence initially emerged in the United Kingdom in the 19th century[4]. In the case of Birmingham & Gloucester Railway Co. in 1842, the railway company was brought to trial and sentenced for disrupting public order through delays; it lost the right to acquire land for the construction of roads and bridges, which were necessary for the completion of the railway network construction.

In 1915, the House of Lords raised the issue in a civil case[5] of how the actions of a legal person should be judged, the driving principle of the mind (*the*

---

1 George Gruia, Spiru Haret University Bucharest, Romania, email: g.gruia@yahoo.com.

2 George Cristian Gruia, Czech Technical University in Prague, Czech Republic, email: georgecristian.gruia@fs.cvut.cz.

3 The Constitution of Romania, republished, Article 16, Para. 2.

4 COFFEE, J.C. Jr.: No Soul To Damn, No Body To Kick: An Unscandalized Inquiry into the Problem of Corporate Punishment, "Michigan Law Review", vol. 79, no. 3, p. 386, the document is available online at http://www.jstor.org/pss/1288201.

5 Lennard's Carrying Co. Ltd, 1915.

directing mind). According to this principle, important individuals (minds) must be identified within the legal person, whose actions and mental states are subsequently identified with the actions and mental state of the legal person, unlike the others (hands)[6]. This principle is described by Clarkson[7].

The downside is the cumbersome identification of individuals if the legal person has a complex or unclear leadership structure. The criminal prosecution is thus directed, most likely by the small legal entities by using them, the legal person was "directly" (and not through representatives) responsible[8] for offences. The principle of the red herring ("*red herring*")[9] had not yet been fully abandoned. A similar situation developed in Canada, as well.

Since the last quarter of the twentieth century, as the influence of legal persons in modern society has grown, European legislators have begun to react by implementing different models of making legal persons liable for offences committed, starting with the Netherlands in 1976. In 1988 the Council of Europe responded to

> "the growing number of offences committed in the context of commercial activities, which causes enormous damage to individuals and society".

Therefore, in order "to assign liability where criminal activities develop", the Council of Europe has adopted the recommendations by the Council of Ministers[10] on liability companies with legal personality \ subjectivity in respect of offences committed within the framework of their activities. This delinquent policy was manifested in other developed countries such as Norway (1991), France (1992), Denmark (1996) or Slovenia and Belgium (1999). Apart from the above mentioned countries and other members of the European Union, legal persons can also be held liable in some form for offences in countries such as South Korea, Japan, Chile, Mexico[11] (since 1999), Israel, China (since 1997) or New Zealand.

---

6 i.e. minds = "brains, people in positions of leadership", hands = "employees who carry out the company leadership's orders".

7 CLARKSON, C.M.V.: Kicking Corporate Bodies and Damning Their Souls, "The Modern Law Review Limited", 1996.

8 Tesco Supermarket Limited vs. Nattrass, 1972.

9 A red herring is a clue which is intentionally or unintentionally misleading or distracts from the actual issue.

10 Recommendations nos. 88, 18 approved by the Council of Ministers on 20 October 1998.

11 Chilean Law no 20393, which came into force at the end of 2009, establishes criminal liability for legal entities found guilty of corruption, money laundering and terrorist financing. The document is available online at http://www.oecd.org/dataoecd/60/12/442 54056.pdf for Chile and Para. no. 57 for Mexico at http://www.oecd.org/dataoecd/53/31/ 33 746033.pdf.

2. Case study: Romania vs. the Czech Republic

We performed a case study taking the same law from two countries with different historical and cultural backgrounds and tried to discover whether there are any similarities and differences.

Romanian legislation introduced the criminal liability of legal persons in 2006 through Law No. 278\2006, which amended and supplemented the Criminal Code, with the amendments and additions published in the Official Journal of Romania no. 601\2006 of 4 July 2006.

Criminal liability is a form of legal liability, which – according to Article 50 of the Criminal Code – entails public condemnation, in the name of the law, of criminal acts and of the persons who have committed them, whereby conviction may be preceded by compulsory measures prescribed by law. The categories of persons who can be held criminally liable are regulated in Article 21 of the Criminal Code, and can be both natural persons and legal entities in the cases covered by Article 21 Paras. 2, 3 and 4 of the Criminal Code.

The law on criminal liability of legal persons is legally based on Art. 191 Criminal Code which stipulates the following:

> "legal persons, except the State, public authorities and public institutions that are engaged in an activity that cannot be subject to private industry, are responsible for criminal offences perpetrated in accomplishing their task or object in the interest or on behalf of a legal person, if the deed was perpetrated with the form of guilt under the criminal law".

According to Article 531, Para. 3 of the Criminal Code, the penalties for legal persons found guilty in criminal cases can be main and complementary. The penalty is a fine of 2,500 lei to 2,000,000 lei (old), and the additional penalties are:

a) dissolution of the legal person;
b) suspension of legal activity for a period of 3 months to 1 year or suspension of one of the activities of the legal person in relation to which the offence was committed, for a period of 3 months to 3 years;
c) closing down offices of the legal person for a period of 3 months to 3 years;
d) ban on participation in procurement proceedings for a period of one to three years;
e) display or publication of the conviction.

The implementation and enforcement of complementary punishments for the legal entity are set out in Article 532 of the Criminal Code.

The Court can impose one or more additional punishments if it decides that such punishments are necessary, in light of the nature and gravity of the offence, as well as the circumstances in which it was committed.

One or more additional punishments must be imposed if stipulated by law. The additional penalties provided for in Article 531 Para. 3 lits. b) – e) can be imposed cumulatively.

According to Article 402 of the Criminal Code, the following situations constitute repeat offences by the legal person:

a) if, after final conviction, the legal person again wilfully commits a crime and the fine for the earlier offence was executed;
b) if, after final conviction, the legal person again wilfully commits a crime and the fine for the previous offence was executed or considered as executed.

If found guilty of a crime, a legal person is punishable up to imposition of a drastic fine of maximum 600,000 lei to 900,000 lei (old).

In addition to the main fine, the Court may impose one or more complementary penalties on the legal person according to Articles 712-716 of the Criminal Code, introduced by Law no. 278/2006.

The dissolution of the legal person is the most severe complementary punishment, which can be pronounced in the following situations:

a) if a legal person was constituted for the purpose of committing the offence or if the object of its activity was misused for this purpose;
b) in the case of default, one of the complementary penalties provided for in Article. 531 Para. 3 lits. b)-d) of the Criminal Code (suspension of legal activity of one of the activities of a legal person in respect of which the offence was committed, closure of some offices of the legal person, ban on participation in public procurement).

A complementary penalty of dissolution effectively winds up the legal person and a copy of the final conviction is sent to the competent civil court, which forwards it to the liquidator.

A copy of the final conviction is communicated to the body that authorised the establishment of the legal person and the body that registered the legal person so that they can take the necessary measures[12].

The dissolution of the legal person is not applicable for political parties, trade unions, employers' organisations and religious minorities formed according to the law, nor for legal entities engaged in press activities.

12 Article 479^{10}, Para. 2, Criminal Procedure Code of Romania, introduced by Law no. 356/2006.

The statutes of limitation for criminal liability of legal persons are:

a) 10 years, if the law provides for a prison sentence of life of more than ten years for the offence;
b) 5 years, if the law provides for a prison sentence of no more than ten years, or a fine, for the offence[13].

Prescription removes criminal liability except in the case of crimes against peace and humanity[14].

The suspension of activity or one of the activities of the legal person bans the legal person from pursuing all one of its activities, within the scope of which the offence was committed.

A suspension of activity or one of the activities of a legal person may be imposed for a period of 3 months to 3 years.

After the final decision, a copy of the conviction imposing this measure is communicated to the body that authorised the establishment of the legal person and the organ that registered the legal person, so that they can take the necessary measures[15].

Closing offices of the legal entity refers to the closure of one or more of the worksites where the legal person has been operating for profit and pursuing the activity within the scope of which the offence was committed. The measure may be imposed for a period from 3 months to 3 years. Such additional punishment cannot be imposed on legal persons that are financially engaged in press activity.

A ban on participation in public procurement procedures constitutes another additional punishment, forbidding the legal person, either directly or indirectly through agents, from participating in public procurement contract award procedures for a period of 1 to 3 years.

After the final decision, a copy of the conviction banning the legal person from participation in public procurement is communicated to the Trade Registry Office so that it can publish official notification in the trade registry, the Ministry of Justice so that it can publish official notification in National Register of Legal Persons without patrimonial purpose, and to other authorities responsible for maintaining the register of legal persons so that they can publish official notification[16].

Display or publication of the conviction negatively impacts the image of the brand, commercial reputation, and position of a legal person, leading to a loss of

---

13 New Criminal Code of Romania, General Part, Article 122, Para. 1.

14 New Criminal Code of Romania, General Part, Article 121.

15 Criminal Procedure Code, Article 479[11].

16 Criminal Procedure Code, Article 479[12], Para. 1.

clientele and diminishing its credibility. Potential victims of the legal person are therefore forewarned, and can exercise more caution when entering into contractual relations with the legal person concerned, or may turn to other partners.

Implementation of this additional punishment is carried out at the expense of the legal entity convicted.

The conviction is displayed in the form and places determined by the Court for a period of between one month and three months.

The publication can take the form of print or audio-visual notification, with the Court determining the number of occurrences, which may not be less than 10.

The convicted legal person is required to submit to the Court proof that it has displayed or, if applicable, published the conviction within 30 days from the date of communication of the decision.

After the final decision, a copy of the conviction is communicated to the body that authorised the establishment of the legal person and the organ that registered the legal person, so that they can take the necessary measures[17].

Establishing the criminal liability of a legal person does not exclude the liability of the natural person who contributed to committing the same crimes.

This regulation is legitimated by the social and economic reality of situations where legal persons have been created and used by individuals as instruments for committing crimes or to cover up economic crime, unfair competition, fraud, economic espionage at auctions, etc. Another reason for establishing the liability of a legal person derived from the conditions governing Romania's accession to the European Union, which demanded that all Member States draft and implement laws governing the criminal responsibility of legal persons.

In the Czech Republic, the law that establishes the criminal liability of legal persons is Law no. 418\2011 of the Code of Laws, which came into force on 1 January 2012.

When this law was submitted for the first time for approval, President Vaclav Klaus rejected it in Parliament, partly because it was not quite clear but also, according to the archives of the Presidency[18], for other reasons that we will present below.

The President said that:

> "the law of criminal liability of legal persons does not show a clear link between the offender and the punishment and is rather an example of an alibi instead of showing

---

17 Criminal Procedure Code, Article 479[14].

18 The point of view of the President of the Czech Republic on the law of criminal liability of legal persons according to the website of the Presidency http://www.hrad.cz/cs/ prezident-cr/rozhodnuti-prezidenta/vracene-zakony-parlamentu/15.shtml.

> an effort to punish the authors of the crime. Because the State is not able to find the main initiators and perpetrators of offences committed by legal persons, it has decided to accuse these legal persons instead. But a concrete person, not an institution, must be brought to justice for committing a crime. The law that was delivered to me for signature reinforces this way of action".

According to the President of the Czech Republic, the principle of individual criminal responsibility is derived from the historical development of law and forms part of the bedrock of continental law.

In his opinion:

> "modern tendency to invoke the criminal liability of legal entities is against the logical tendency to blame entire institutions collectively, instead of blaming someone else or apportioning the blame between a greater number of people ".

The President also recognises that certain facts that may be the subject of criminal charges take place in practice through legal persons, but

> "impeaching them does not resolve anything, and very likely only affects the innocent ones. The Parliament should try to seek a way to impeach effectively and considering these facts, even by upholding the principle of individual criminal responsibility, to thus find the true culprits".

Despite all these arguments voiced by the President against the law, it was finally passed by the Chamber of Deputies and the Czech Republic was compliant with the European Union's demand that all Member States enact such a law.

According to Law no. 418\2011 from the Code of Law, Article 8 – criminal liability of legal persons, provides that:

(1) a criminal offence committed by a legal person is an unlawful act committed by or on behalf or in the interest of its activities, if the perpetrator was acting:
   a) as the statutory body or a member of the statutory body or other person authorised to act on behalf of or as a legal person
   b) as the person who manages or controls the activities of the legal person even if it is not the person referred to in a),
   c) as the person who exerts a decisive influence on the management of a legal person, where his behaviour was at least one of the conditions for invoking the criminal liability of the legal person, or
   d) as an employee or person in a similar position (hereinafter "employee") performing their duties of employment, even if it is not the person referred to in a-c);

(2) the legal entity can be accused of committing a crime provided for in Art. 7, where it has been committed:

a) through the conduct of bodies of a legal person or persons referred to in (1) a)-c), or
b) by an employee referred to in (1) d) based on approval or instruction of the legal person or persons referred to in (1) a)-c) or if the bodies of a legal person or persons referred to in (1) a)-c) have failed to implement measures demanded by other legislation or legally required, and thus have failed to ensure the necessary or compulsory control over the activities of employees or other individuals in management positions, or have not taken the necessary measures to prevent or avoid the consequences of committing a criminal offence.

(3) the criminal liability of a legal person is not waived if the specific natural person who acted in one of the ways specified in (1) and (2) cannot be identified

(4) the provisions of (1) and (2) shall be applied, even if:
a) the facts referred to in (1) and (2) existed before the legal entity was established
b) the legal person is registered, but the Court subsequently declares it invalid
c) the act to establish legal authorisation to act as a legal person, is not valid or has not entered into force, or
d) the natural person in question is not responsible for the criminal offence.

The following punishments only can be imposed for crimes committed by a legal entity[19]:

a) dissolution of the legal person,
b) confiscation of property,
c) financial penalty,
d) confiscation of assets,
e) prohibition of activity,
f) ban on participation in public procurement contracts, participation in concession or public auction procedures,
g) prohibition to receive donations and grants,
h) publication of the judgement.

The seizure of property or other assets may prove necessary as a safeguard in the case of crimes committed by a legal entity[20].

The Court can impose these sanctions and protective measures separately or collectively, although fines cannot be imposed in addition to the confiscation of

19 Code of Laws, Law No. 418/2011, Article 15, Para. 1.
20 Code of Laws, Law No. 418/2011, Article 15, Para. 2.

assets, nor goods or other assets forfeited in addition to the seizure of the same goods or other assets[21].

In terms of financial punishment, the Court may impose a fine if the legal entity is condemned for a deliberate offence or on grounds of negligence. The imposition of a financial penalty does not affect the rights of the victim[22]. If a legal person is found guilty and sentenced to payment of financial penalties, it cannot raise the prices charged for certain individual services to cover any losses resulting from the loss of the case.

The per diem fine is CZK 1,000 minimum and 2,000,000 CZK maximum and is determined by the Court based on the financial situation of the legal person[23].

Thus, fines in Romania range from 2,500 lei to 2,000,000 lei up to a maximum of 2.900.000 lei (old), whereas fines in the Czech Republic are calculated per day, up to a maximum of 2,000,000 Czech Crowns per day, and can therefore total much higher amounts than in Romania, depending on how many days the Court specifies.

A penalty imposed on a legal person cannot be enforced after the expiry of the prescription, that is[24]:

a) thirty years, in the case of sentencing to a fine of at least 560 days, or a ban on activities or participation in public procurement contracts, concession procedures or public auctions, the prohibition to receive grants and donations;
b) twenty years, in the case of sentencing to a fine of at least 380 days;
c) ten years in the case of sentencing to a fine of at least 200 days;
d) five years after sentencing to another penalty.

3. Conclusions

If we compare the two laws, we can observe that there are a few differences between them, but the main idea remains the same, namely to establish the criminal liability and punishment of legal persons in the two countries. Although Romania passed its law in 2006, which means the legislation is more advanced than in the Czech Republic, but the changes are not significant.

---

21 Code of Laws, Law No 418/2011, Article 15, Para. 3.
22 Code of Laws, Law No 418/2011, Article 18, Para. 1.
23 Code of Laws, Law No 418/2011, Article 18, Para. 2.
24 Code of Laws, Law No 418/2011, Article 24.

Key differences include the differing levels of fines for legal persons, but also the prescription deadlines of the convictions. A fine is the amount of money the legal person is sentenced to pay for committing a crime.

A fine is a pecuniary penalty with a few advantages: it directly affects the property of a legal person, and – if tailored correctly to the individual case – ensures direct achievement of the aim of punishment.

Another peculiarity is that the law of the Czech Republic has certain substantive additions compared to Romania in that it focuses on individuals within the legal person and not necessarily upon the legal person as a whole, which we can see is the case in Romania. Questions can be raised regarding the interpretation of these laws if a lawsuit were to be filed against a legal person where Czech-Romanian shareholders each held a stake of 50-50%. To which of the two laws would the legal person be subject? The answer may depend on where the act was committed, which will play a decisive role in the court ruling, or the specific percentage stakes of the participating parties (partners) and who (the Romanian or Czech) holds the larger portion of the share capital, will dictate which law is applicable when judging the case. Or is the legal person subject to judgement according to the laws of the country where the registered office is located?

It is not enough for all countries simply to have the same laws, because problems may arise in their implementation in certain situations, such as the one described above. A single judicial entity with uniform and compact management at European level is necessary to prosecute crime at European level, but it must understand the needs of each country and pursue the common goals of eliminating corruption, money laundering and other criminal activities.

As pointed out in this article, the two laws issued in different countries do not have to remain the same forever. As generations change, so the laws must be amended and fine-tuned to respond to the conditions of the market economy and international European economy, which is heavily affected by the global crisis and which is still impacting the economies of the majority of European countries (apart from Germany which is registering the highest level of sustainable economic growth).

We recommend that the system of laws of each country of the European Union be comprehensively analysed to ultimately produce a European Criminal Code, Civil Code and European procedures for implementation at European level and not at the level of each country because – as stated above – the law is not clear in certain situations and can be subject to different interpretation, depending on the scene of the crime.

Bibliography

Coffee, J.C. Jr.: No Soul To Damn, No Body To Kick: An Unscandalized Inquiry into the Problem of Corporate Punishment, "Michigan Law Review", vol. 79, no. 3, the document is available online http://www.jstor.org/pss/1288201.

Clarkson, C.M.V.: Kicking Corporate Bodies and Damning Their Souls, "The Modern Law Review Limited", 1996.

Wagner, M.: Corporate Criminal Liability. National and International Response, The 13th International Conference "International Corporations for the Reform of Criminal Law", Malta, 8–12 July 1999, The International Centre for Criminal Law Reform and Criminal Justice Policy, Canada.

Law no. 418/2011, Code of Laws of the Czech Republic.

Chilean Law no. 20393. The document is available online: http://www.oecd.org/dataoecd /60 /12/44254056.pdf

The point of view of the President of the Czech Republic on the law of criminal liability of legal persons according to the website of the Presidency http://www.hrad.cz/cs/prezident-cr/rozhodnuti-prezidenta/vracene-zakony-parlamentu/15.shtml.

Constitution of Romania (republished in Official Gazette of Romania no. 767 of 31 October 2003).

Criminal Procedure Code of Romania (published in Official Gazette of Romania no. 78 of 30 April 1997, as amended).

Criminal Code of Romania, General Part (published in Official Gazette of Romania no. 65 of 16 April 1997, as amended).

Restrictions of Law Provided by the Jurisprudence of the Constitutional Court and the European Court of Human Rights

Associate professor Camelia Florentina STOICA[1]

Abstract

This article analyses the quality of legislation that is important for both business and other branches of law. The identification of solutions to such a problem is not easy; the adoption, amendment, abolition of normative acts, the association of these to the realities of permanent change; the context of general trends of globalisation, the permanent search for a balance between individual autonomy and civil solidarity is resulting in a real inflation of legislation.

Keywords: legislation, competent court, law, acts.

1. Introduction. Argument

The overall legislative instability which characterises the Romanian legal system, in general, and the multitude of legislative modifications in the fields concerning business law, in particular (a relevant example – the Fiscal Code which, since coming into force on 1 January 2004, has undergone more than 5,000 amendments and additions – according to some data quoted in a recent study[2]) prompted us to reflect on a problem which represents a direct consequence of such phenomena, namely the quality of legislation (or, rather, its lack of quality) which is important, obviously, both for business and other branches of law and, eventually, on the manner of perceiving and appreciating the state of law. As provided in juridical doctrine[3], which induces the idea of a real crisis of law in this context,

> "the first effect of incessant increasing the number of legal regulations is to decrease their quality. There is no rigorous programme for determining the need for new juridical regulations; frequently, the new laws derive from the political programmes of government, the law drafts are not substantiated or they pursue superficial purposes; contradictions appear between the old and new regulations, etc."

---

1 Camelia Florentina Stoica, Bucharest University of Economic Studies, Director of Law Department, Romania, cameliastoica@cig.ase.ro.

2 Mircea Ştefan Minea, Anca Mihaela Georoceanu, On some discrepancies of codification: lack of rigour and inconsistency in the use of specific terminology. Examples from the Fiscal Code and Code of Fiscal Procedure, www.ccr.ro.

3 Ioan Vida, Formal law, Lumina Lex, Bucharest, 2006, p.25.

The identification of solutions to such problems is not easy; the adoption, amendment, abolition of normative acts, the association of these to the social realities of permanent change in the context of general trends of globalisation, the permanent search for a balance between individual autonomy and civic solidarity4 is resulting in a real inflation of legislation. Is it possible to prevent such “inflation” or at least to submit it to some rigours to prevent it from influencing the addressees of juridical norms?

It is from the perspective of such difficulty, which is essentially caused by the complexity of law and the sphere of political actors that it involves, that we consider appreciable the fact that the lack of legislation quality is more and more frequently sanctioned by way of jurisprudence. We consider, in this context, mainly the jurisprudence of the Constitutional Court and, through its application of Art. 20 of the Constitution establishing the priority of international regulations in the field of human rights adopted by Romania in terms of national law, the jurisprudence of the European Court of Human Rights in respect of the application of the Convention for the protection of human rights and fundamental liberties.

The competence of the Constitutional Court in this field is determined by its role as "*guarantor of the supremacy of the Constitution*", provided by Art. 142 Para. (1) of Fundamental Law, to which Art. 1 Para. (2) of Law no. 24/2000 considering the norms of legislative technique for the elaboration of normative acts directly refers[5]:

> “Normative acts are initiated, elaborated, adopted and applied in conformity with the disposals of the Romanian Constitution, republished, and with the disposals of this law”.

According to Art. 3 Para. (1) of the same normative act,

> “(1)The norms of legislative technique are obligatory for elaborating law drafts by the government and legislative proposals from deputies, senators or citizens exercising their right to legislative initiative, as well as for elaborating and adopting government ordinances and decisions and normative acts of other authorities with such powers [...]”.

Legislative technique itself is defined by the same law in the disposals of Art. 2, according to which

4 Miguel Poiares Maduro, Global Governance and the Quest for Justice, vol. I – International and Regional Organisation, edited by Douglas Lewis, Hart Publishing, Oxford and Portland, Oregon, 2006, p. 238.

5 Published in the Official Gazette of Romania, Part I, no. 260, 31 April 2010.

> "(1) The legislative technique provides the systematisation, unification and coordination of legislation, as well as the juridical form and content relevant for each normative act.
>
> (2) The norms of legislative technique define the constitutive parts of normative acts, the structure, the form and the manner of systematisation of the content thereof, the technical procedures related to the amendment, completion, abolition, publication and republication of normative acts, as well as the language and style of normative acts".

Following the reference that the quoted texts make to the disposals of the Constitution, we observe that Art. 1 Para. (3) provides that

> "Romania is a state of law [...]",

and Art. 1 Para. (5), that

> "In Romania, the observance of the Constitution, its supremacy and of the laws is obligatory".

These constitutional and duly quoted disposals show that the elaboration of normative acts involving observance of the norms of legislative technique is subordinated to the disposals of the Constitution and constitutionally relevant, as the competence of the Constitutional Court for ensuring compliance in fulfilment by the legislator is circumvented. In the same respect, the Court has published several decisions, one example of which is *Decision no. 26/2012*[6] stipulating that

> "although the norms of legislative technique do not have constitutional value, [...] the legislator has, by stipulating them, imposed a range of obligatory criteria for the adoption of any normative act that must be observed in order to provide the systematisation, unification and coordination of legislation, as well as the content and relevant legal form for each normative act. Thus, the fulfilment of such norms contributes to the provision of a legislation that observes the principle of the security of juridical reports, with the necessary accuracy".

In addition, legality – including a transparent, responsible and democratic process for the adoption of law – and juridical certitude represent essential factors of the state of law, as also indicated in the *Report on the state of law* issued by the Venice Commission during its 86th plenary session[7], together with free access to justice, observance of human rights, non-discrimination and equality before the law. Consequently, the constitutional principle of the state of law, as stipulated by Art. 1 Para. (3) of the Constitution may be equally cited, together with Para. (5) of the same article, which is usually cited by the Court, as grounds

---

6 Published in the Official Gazette of Romania, Part I, no.116 of 15 February 2012.

7 Venice, 25 – 26 March 2011, www.venice.coe.int.

for examining the constitutionality of regulations which, by breaching the rules of legislative technique, influence the essential factors mentioned.

The examination of the jurisprudence of both the Constitutional Court and the European Court of Human Rights reveals the contribution by both bodies, within the limits of their competences, towards defining the exigencies of law in accordance with the pronounced principles of the state of law.

Considering the breadth of this subject, we shall refer to the relevant jurisprudence concerning the rules and principles stipulated by Law no. 24/2000 on the norms of legislative technique for the elaboration of normative acts, in the order that such law is ruling them. This will allow us, at the same time, to elaborate how such principles and rules became Art. 1 Para. (5) of the Constitution governing the standards for controlling constitutionality.

2. Exigencies of law

2.1. Fulfilment of the hierarchy of normative acts

According to Art. 4 Para. (3) of Law no. 24/2000,

> "The normative acts given in the execution of laws, ordinances or decisions of government are issued within the limits and according to the norms that rule them".

In its *Decision no. 298/2006*[8] concerning the unconstitutionality of the law governing healthcare reforms, where critics had claimed that such normative act contravened the obligation of observing the law – as registered as a general principle in Art. 1 Para. (5) with reference to Art. 34 Para. (3) of the Constitution – since a very large proportion of the entire law referred to norms and instructions to be elaborated by the Government, the Ministry of Public Health and other public administration authorities, the Court decided that the law had not been executed in accordance with the conditions of Art. 34 Para. (3) of the Constitution, but by ministerial and governmental norms and thus by administrative normative acts, stating that:

> "the criticised law texts stipulated the subsequent adoption of many governmental decisions, orders, instructions and other similar deeds of the heads of ministries and of other specialised central public administration bodies, for the approval of some rules, bylaws, methodologies or predominantly technical norms. However, the court considers that, according to Art. 108 Para. (2) of the Constitution and Art. 75 of Law no. 24/2000 [...], it is necessary that such regulations are issued only in terms of and

8 Published in the Official Gazette of Romania, Part I, no.372 of 28 April 2006.

with the enforcement of law. These regulations, being auxiliary norms issued for the application and enforcement of law, have to present a technical character".

2.2. Proper substantiation of legislative initiatives – preliminary evaluation of the impact of the new regulations

According to Art. 7 Para. (1)-(3) of Law no. 24/2000,

> "(1) The preliminary evaluation of the impact of law drafts, of legislative proposals and of the other drafts of normative acts represents a range of activities and procedures performed with a view to properly substantiating legislative initiatives. The preliminary evaluation of the impact involves the identification and analysis of the economic, social, environment, legislative and budgetary effects produced by the regulations proposed.
>
> (2) The preliminary evaluation of the impact of the drafts of normative acts is deemed to be the means of substantiating the legislative solutions proposed and must be completed before the adoption of normative acts.
>
> (3)The substantiation of the new regulation shall consider both the evaluation of the impact of specific legislation in force upon the elaboration of draft normative acts, and the evaluation of the impact of the political policies that the draft normative act is implementing".

With respect to the accomplishment of such exigencies, the Court passed, for instance, *Decision no. 666/2007*[9] concerning the constitutionality of the law to amend and supplement Law no. 128/1997 on the status of teaching staff. The Court noted that Art. 15 Para. (2) and (3) of Law no. 500/2002 on public finance, as amended by Law no. 314/2003, published in the Official Gazette of Romania, Part I, no. 506 of 14 July 2003, entitled "Limits on the reduction of incomes and increase of budgetary expenses", and stipulated that

> "(2) for the legislative proposals, the Government will submit to the Chamber of Deputies or to the Senate, as the case may be, the financial record stipulated in Para. (1), within 45 days pursuant to receiving the demand" and, "(3) Pursuant to submitting the draft annual budget law to Parliament, normative acts may only be approved under the conditions of the disposals of Para. (1), but stating the sources to cover the reduction of incomes or to increase the budgetary expenses, in respect of the budgetary exercise for which the budget was elaborated".

Since the criticised law was adopted "*without stating the financial sources of the measures stipulated therein*", the Court declared it unconstitutional.

Also, by *Decision no. 710/2009*[10], the Court determined the unconstitutionality of the law to amend and supplement Law no. 188/1999 on the status of

9 published in the Official Gazette of Romania, Part I, no. 514 of 31 July 2007.

10 published in the Official Gazette of Romania, Part I, no. 358 of 28 May 2009.

public officials. Analysing the recitals attached to the legislative proposal, the Court stated that

> "it is extremely brief, including only few generic mentions. The recitals do not include the motivation of any solution proposed, which is contrary to constitutional and legal disposals [...]". (i.e. see Art. 1 Para. 5 of the Constitution and Law no. 24/2000).

By *Decision no. 1658/2010*[11], the Court again addressed some criticisms voiced with respect to Art. 1 Para. (5) of the Constitution and the legal disposals quoted above. The authors claiming unconstitutionality with reference to the frame law on unit wages paid from public funds, overall, as well as specifically to Art. 1 Para. (2), Art. 4, Art. 10 Para. (1), Art. 14, Art. 22 Para. (1) and (2), Art. 33 Para. (1), Art. 37 Para. (1) and (3) of the law, stating that the Government, as initiator of the law draft, did not observe Art. 7 and 31 of Law no. 24/2000 concerning the norms of legislative technique for the elaboration of normative acts, since it did not perform a preliminary evaluation of the impact of such law on the social and economic budgets, which constituted a breach of Art. 1 Para. (5) of the Constitution. With respect to such critics, the Court considered that

> "the recitals of the criticised law, as presented to the Parliament, include references to the socio-economic nature of the draft normative act that are very brief indeed",

as well as that

> "the Government has fulfilled the obligation to evaluate the socio-economic impact of the criticised law, although the motivation is brief and lapidary. Consequently, the criticism of unconstitutionality is not substantiated, the breadth of the evaluation of socio-economic impact of the criticised law not being a constitutionally relevant subject that breaches the disposals of Art. 1 Para. (5) of the Constitution".

2.3. Approval of law drafts

According to Art. 9 Para. (1) and (2) of Law no. 24/2000,

> "In the cases stipulated by law, during the stage of elaboration of the drafts of normative acts, the initiator shall require the approval of the authorities interested in applying them, depending on the object of regulation. (2) Pursuant to their elaboration and conclusion of the approval procedure stipulated in Para. (1), the draft laws, the legislative proposals, as well as the drafts of ordinances and normative decisions of the Government are obligatorily submitted to the approval of the Legislative Council".

And, according to Art. 10 Para. (3) and (4) of the same normative act:

---

11 published in the Official Gazette of Romania, Part I, no. 44 of 18 January 2011.

> "The approval of the Legislative Council is a specialised approval and has a consulting character. (4) The observations and proposals of the Legislative Council related to the observance of the norms of legislative technique must be considered when finalising the draft normative act. Rejection of these must be substantiated in the presentation of the draft or in an attachment".

Examining the jurisprudence of the Constitutional Court in the field of approving normative acts, it has been established that it has constantly pronounced upon the obligation of requiring the approvals stipulated by law, even the obligation, as shall be noticed further on, to require new approval when the form of the act is different from that for which initial approval was awarded. The issuance of such normative acts is conditional upon asking for, not obtaining, approval.

Thus, by *Decision no. 710/2009*, which is mentioned above and determined the unconstitutionality of the criticised regulation, the Court, in its analysis of the issue, considered

> "that the approval awarded by the Legislative Council refers to the legislative proposal concerning some measures of public administration organisation, and that the draft law adopted by the Senate acquired a different form from that initially approved by the Council. In this situation, the fact that the amendments drawn up within the Committee [...] did not require consultation of the Legislative Council would have been appreciated".

By Decision no. 39/2008[12], the Court considered, with respect to the criticised regulation, that

> "the Government had the legal obligation to ask for the approval of C.S.A.T. [...] Pursuant to analysis of the disposals of Art. 119 of the Constitution, of the regulation of Art. 4 lit. d) of Law no. 415/2002 [...], there is no resulting obligation to obtain approval. No constitutional text refers to the notification of the normative acts initiated or issued by the Government, in the sense that issuance is conditional upon obtaining approval".

By *Decision no. 1658/2010* with respect to the assertions concerning the lack of approval by the Economic and Social Council, which is also mentioned above, the Court finds that

> "this request was submitted to the Ministry of Labour, Family and Social Protection no. 2.889/VM/19.11.2010. Although approval was not issued by the Economic and Social Council, the Court finds that, by requesting approval, the Government observed the constitutional disposals of Art. 141, respectively it considered the consulting character of such body".

12 Published in the Official Gazette of Romania, Part I, no. 122 dated 15 February 2008.

Although we agree with the Court in respect of the technical-juridical substantiation – namely that there is no explicit formulation that makes the issuance of such normative acts conditional upon such approval, we believe that the solution is disputable. The conduct of authorities with approval powers who, for different reasons, do not issue such approval (for instance, due to the lack of a quorum several times over in the case of the Economic and Social Council) is disputable, as is the transformation of the notification procedure of normative acts – whose motivation is too clear to need further explanation – within an absolutely formal procedure. These issues contribute to what we have called the lack of quality in law and should be sanctioned as such, whereby the mechanisms have to exist on the level of such institutions and authorities which are reduced, in terms of this aspect, to the same absolutely formal level.

2.4. The uniqueness of regulation in the field and avoidance of parallelisms

According to Art. 14 Para. (1) of Law no. 24/2000,

> "Regulations on the same level and with the same object are usually included within a sole normative act"

and according to Art.16:

> "(1) During the enactment process, it is forbidden to institute the same regulations within several articles or paragraphs of the same normative act or in two or more normative acts. The referral norm must be used to emphasise some legislative connections.
>
> (2) In case of parallelisms, they shall be abolished or amalgamated within one sole regulation.
>
> (3) Regulations governing the same issues in different laws will also be amalgamated into one regulation.
>
> (4) A normative act issued in terms of and for the enforcement of another, superior normative act shall not be used to reproduce some of the disposals from the superior act, and should preferably only indicate reference texts. In such cases, the adoption of some norms in the inferior act is only permissible for the purpose of developing or detailing the solutions from the basic act".

By reference to the disposals of Art. 1 Para. (5) of the Constitution, to such disposals, the Court established, by *Decision no. 415/2010*[13], the unconstitutionality of some disposals of Law no. 144/2007 concerning the incorporation, organisation and operation of the National Integrity Agency, considering, among others, that,

---

13 published in the Official Gazette of Romania, Part I, no. 294 of 5 May 2010.

> "parallel regulations exist to control the wealth acquired through the execution of mandates or the performance of certain public functions, including to verify conflicts of interests, namely, on the one hand, Law no. 115/1996 governing the declaration and control of the wealth of dignitaries, magistrates, other persons with managing and control positions and public officers, published in the Official Gazette of Romania, Part I, no. 263 of 28 October 1996, amended and supplemented by Law no. 161/2003 concerning some measures for ensuring transparency in public office, when exercising public functions, and in the business environment, and for preventing and punishing corruption, published in the Official Gazette of Romania, Part I, no. 279 of 21 April 2003, and, on the other hand, Law no. 144/2007 concerning the incorporation, organisation and functioning of National Integrity Agency, according to which this Agency is responsible for verifying any conflicts of interest and inconsistencies relating to the wealth acquired while exercising or performing public functions or offices, as the case may be".

Subsequently, by *Decision no. 1018/2010*[14], the law governing integrity in the exercise of public functions and offices, which amended and supplemented Law no. 144/2007 concerning the incorporation, organisation and functioning of the National Integrity Agency, as well as amending and supplementing other acts (namely the law adopted following the decision that the previous one was unconstitutional), the Court established that the overall normative act was unconstitutional, considering that it

> "does not observe the norms of legislative technique meant to provide the systematisation, unification and coordination of legislation, as well as of the content, legal form, language and style of the normative act. Thus, according to the disposals of Law no. 24/2000 on the norms of legislative technique for the elaboration of normative acts, republished, the legislative text shall be clear, fluent and intelligible, without syntactic difficulties and obscure and equivocal passages. The form and aesthetics of expression shall not influence the juridical style, the accuracy and clarity of disposals. Or, if the norms of legislative technique are obligatory upon the elaboration of draft laws by the Government and of legislative proposals by deputies and senators, the Court finds that the normative act was not properly systematised or drafted in a juridical language and style specific to the normative act, which must be succinct, clear and accurate, and must avoid any confusion".

Beyond the issues presented, this later decision addresses a serious problem concerning the certainty of juridical reports and principles of the state of law: disregard by the legislator of the decisions of the Constitutional Court, namely of the Constitution, which stipulates in Art. 147 Para. (4) the general character of such decisions. In this case, despite the Court ruling that some of the legislative decisions were unconstitutional (Decision 414/2010 mentioned above), a

---

14 published in the Official Gazette of Romania, Part I, no. 511 of 22 July 2010.

new law was adopted shortly after with practically the same content. This reveals deficiencies surrounding the entire enactment process – the legislative initiative, debate of law, adoption of it – in respect of the conduct of all public authorities involved in such process. The court censured such conduct and the act adopted, establishing the unconstitutionality of it and considering in this respect that

> "the adoption by the legislator of some norms contrary to those provided in a decision of the Constitutional Court breaches the fundamental law. Or, in a state of law, as Romania is proclaimed in Art. 1 Para. (3) in the Constitution, the public authorities do not have any autonomy in relation to the law, the Constitution stipulating in Art. 16 Para. (2) that no one is above the law, and in Art. 1 Para. (5) that the observance of the Constitution, of its supremacy and of laws is obligatory".

2.5. Form and style of drafting the normative acts: clarity, accuracy, expectancy and predictability

The ideas expressed above are equally emphasised by the jurisprudence of the Constitutional Court, the European Court of Human Rights, the Court of Justice of the European Union, and other Constitutional Courts, related to the concept of juridical certitude. The accessibility and predictability of legislation are frequently cited conditions in the decisions of all such Courts.

According to Art. 8 Para. (4) of Law no. 24/2000,

> "The legislative text shall be clear, fluent and intelligible, with no syntactic difficulties and obscure or equivocal passages. No affective term shall be used. The form and aesthetics of expression shall not prejudice the juridical style, the accuracy and the clarity of disposals",

and according to Art. 36 Para. (1) of the same law,

> "the normative acts be drafted in a juridically succinct, sober, clear and accurate language and style specific to normative acts, which shall exclude any ambiguities and shall strictly observe the rules of grammar and orthography".

By *Decision no. 418/2005*[15], which established the unconstitutionality of some disposals of the law governing healthy reproduction and medically assisted human reproduction, the Court considered, among others, that such law

> "contains contradictory and inaccurate disposals which do not fulfil the requirements of legislative technique imposed by the disposals of Art. 7 Para. (4) of Law no. 24/2000 [...]".

The Court also substantiated its assertions based on the jurisprudence of the European Court of Human Rights in this respect and, in its decision, identified four

---

15 published in the Official Gazette of Romania, Part I, no. 664 of 26 July 2005.

criteria to be observed in this respect during the enactment process. Thus, for instance, by *Decision no. 61/2007*[16], establishing the unconstitutionality of the disposals of Art. II Para. (1) and (3) of Law no. 249/2006 that amends and supplements Law no. 393/2004 concerning the status of local managers, the Court stated that

> "the poor elaboration of the legal disposals does not fulfil the exigencies of legislative technique specific to juridical norms. Or, with respect to such conditions, the European Court of Human Rights has pronounced constantly, stating that "a norm is «predictable» only when it is drafted accurately, so as to allow any person - who, if necessary, may resort to specialised consulting services – to amend their conduct" (Case Rotaru against Romania, 2000), and "[...] the citizen shall have enough information on the juridical norms applicable in a given case to be able to anticipate, to a reasonable extent, the consequences that may result from a determined act. Briefly, the law has to be simultaneously accessible and predictable" (Case Sunday Times against United Kingdom, 1979).

Or, in this case, the Court stated,

> "the legal texts examined do not meet *the four criteria of clarity, accuracy, expectancy and predictability* for the subject of law concerned to be able to adjust its conduct, so as to avoid the consequences of breaching the law".

Also, by *Decision no. 604/2008*[17], establishing the unconstitutionality of Art. 121 Para. (1) of Law no. 122/2006 governing asylum in Romania, the Court considered that the disposal included in this text providing for complaints to be submitted within two days after receiving the communication of decision is inaccurate,

> "since the moment when this term starts to elapse cannot be known by the solicitor, who does not have the possibility to know when such evidence reaches the Romanian Immigrations Office".

Thus, by *Decision no. 26/2012*, the Court, analysing the disposals of the Law on authorising the location and means of advertising, noted that, according to Art. 52 of this Law, the local public administration authorities were obliged to elaborate on, or, if appropriate, update local regulations with respect to the location of the advertising means within 60 days after application. Also, according to Art. 54 and 55 of the criticised law, the authorities of local public administration should identify and notify the owners of the advertising means whose location no longer corresponds to the new regulations for decommissioning. The court considered that

---

16 published in the Official Gazette of Romania, Part I, no. 116 of 15 February 2007.

17 published in the Official Gazette of Romania, Part I, no. 469 of 25 June 2008.

> “the corroborated interpretation of such law disposals induces the idea of regulation of a term during which the persons to whom the law applies could amend their conduct by fulfilling all of the obligations imposed by the new disposals”.

Reiterating the four criteria mentioned above - clarity, accuracy, expectancy and predictability – that a law text shall observe, and invoking the decisions by the European Court of Human Rights in this field - (Decision dated 29 March 2000 in the case *Rotaru against Romania*, Decision dated 23 September 1998 in *Petra against Romania*), the Court reminded that

> “the legislative authority, the parliament or the government as the case may be, has the obligation to edict norms that shall meet the foregoing characteristics”,

stating, as well, that

> “the existence of a contradictory legislative solution and the annulment of some law disposals by other disposals included in the same normative act leads to the breach of the principle of security of juridical reports, pursuant to the lack of clarity and predictability of the norm”.

Thus, the Court established that the criticised regulation

> “by breaching the norms of legislative technique, entails the appearance of some incoherent and instable situations, which is contrary to the principle of the security of juridical reports with respect to the clarity and predictability of law”.

Maybe the best-known decision of the Constitutional Court in this respect is *Decision no. 1258/2009*[18] by which it established the unconstitutionality of the disposals of Law no. 298/2008 concerning the maintenance of the data generated or processed by suppliers of electronic communication services supplied to the public or by the public communication networks, as well as amending Law no. 506/2004 on the processing of personal data and protection of privacy in the field of electronic communications, which transposed into national law Directive 2006/24/EC of the European Parliament and Council of the European Union. The Court considered that

> “the absence of an accurate legal regulation, which may determine exactly the scope of such data needed to identify users - natural or legal persons – provides for possible abuse in maintaining, processing and using the data stored by the suppliers of electronic communication services or public communication networks. The limitation on exercising the right to privacy and mail secrecy and freedom of expression, [...] has to be clear, predictable and with no ambiguity, so as to preclude the incidence or abuse by the relevant authorities wherever possible. The addressees of the juridical norm [...] shall have a clear representation of the applicable juridical norms so as to adjust their conduct and to anticipate the consequences resulting from the breach of them”.

---

18 published in the Official Gazette of Romania, Part I, no. 798 of 23 November 2009.

The Constitutional Court also noted

> "the same ambiguous manner of drafting, which does not conform with the norms of legislative technique, in terms of the disposals of Art. 20 of Law no. 298/2008, according to which,
>
> "In order to prevent and avert threats against national security, the state bodies empowered to act in this field may access the data collected by electronic communication service providers and public communication networks under the conditions determined in the normative acts that regulate the performance of national security".

The legislator does not define what it is understood by "threats against national security", thus – in the absence of some accurate criteria of delimitation – different actions, information or usual, routine activities of the natural or legal persons may be regarded arbitrarily and abusively as threats. The addressees of the law may be categorised as suspicious without being aware of this or able to prevent, by their conduct, the consequences of applying the rigours of law. Also, the use of the syntagma "may access" suggests the idea that the data to which Law no. 298/2008 refers are not maintained for the exclusive purpose of being used only by state bodies with specific responsibility for protecting national security and public order but by other persons or entities as well, since they "may", and do not "have" access to such data.

Ultimately, the Court considered that

> "observance of the norms of legislative technique, within the complex of rules specific to the activity of enactment, represents an essential factor in transposing the will of the legislator to ensure that the normative act adopted fulfils the exigencies imposed by the need to observe fundamental human rights. [....] As accurate as possible a regulation of the field of application of Law no. 298/2008 is crucial, considering mainly the complex nature of the rights, as well as the consequences that potential abuse by the public authorities may have on the private life of its addressee [...]".

The Constitutional Court thus draws attention to the need to define accurately the field of application of regulations, referring mainly to the "scope *of the data needed to identify users – natural or legal persons*", as well as the conditions for using such data, mainly situations that the legislator, respectively the state bodies that have access to the stored data, consider to be "*threats against national security*". One has to observe in this respect the standards of the European Court of Human Rights that has constantly stated that

> "[...] the citizen has to hold enough information on the legal norms applicable in a given case and to be able to anticipate reasonably the consequences that may be generated by a certain act". (*Sunday Times vs. United Kingdom, 1979);*

> "a norm is «predictable» only when it is drafted accurately, so as to permit any other person - who, if necessary, may resort to specialised consulting - to amend their conduct" (*Rotaru vs. Romania, 2000)*.

Resuming the aforementioned in a study dedicated to this decision[19], we outline in this context as well the constant jurisprudence of the Court of Justice of the European Union, stating that

> "each Member State has the obligation to enforce the disposals of directives so as to fully satisfy the clarity and certitude conditions in the legal situations imposed by the communitarian legislative in the interest of such persons established in the Member States. In this respect, such disposals have to be enforced with an incontestable juridical certitude and with the specificity, accuracy and clarity necessary"[20].

Juridical certitude

> "imposes that the effects of communitarian legislation are clear and predictable, the purpose of such requisite being that of assuring that the juridical reports governed by communitarian law remain predictable[21].
>
> The Member States have to provide an accurate legal frame in such field by adopting rules of law able to create a clear, accurate and transparent situation, enough to allow the persons to know their rights and to claim them before national courts"[22].

2.6. Elaboration of codes and complex laws

Law no. 24/2000 dedicates an entire Section to such object of regulation, considering its complexity. Unfortunately, in recent years the government has avoided this regulation, using assumption of responsibility on a draft law in Parliament namely by a fast procedure, without parliamentary debates - and not by a common procedure of enactment regulated by Law no. 24/2000.

We criticise this means of enactment, since it breaches, in our opinion, both the norms of legislative technique and the disposals of Art. 61 of the Constitution governing the role of Parliament. In consequence, codes could not be enforced immediately, although adopted, or, once enacted, they required, and still

---

19 Camelia Stoica, Marieta Safta: Transposition of Directive 2006/24/EC of the European Parliament and Council of the European Union concerning the provision of electronic communication services to the public or to public communication networks into Romanian legislation, Judicial Courier no. 5/2010.

20 C 354/99, Comisia vs. Irlandei, 18 Oct.2001, Para. 27.

21 Takis Tridimas, The General Principles of EU Law, Oxford EC LAW Library, p. 244.

22 C.220/94, Commission vs. Luxembourg, decision dated 15 June 1995, Para. 9-10, in ECR, 1995-6 (I), 1606-7.

require, amendments and supplements, which renders risible the idea of codification.

Although the criteria that the adoption of a normative act by way of assumption of responsibility on a draft law in Parliament may be observed when adopting a Code, its complexity recommends the use of common enactment procedure, which involves the analysis of texts by the parliamentary committee and parliamentary debates. We state these criteria determined by the Constitutional Court by way of jurisprudence (*Decision no. 1655/2010*[23]), in the attempt of stopping the enactment by this way, derived from Art. 114 of the Constitution:

> "existence of an emergency in adopting the measures; the need that such regulation shall be adopted with maximum celerity; importance of the field regulated; immediate application of such law".

We consider applicable *mutatis mutandis*, and in terms of the adoption of Codes by such procedure, the disposals of *Decision no. 51/2012*[24] by which the Constitutional Court established, for other reasons however, the unconstitutionality of the law concerning the organisation and development of elections for local public administration authorities and of elections for the Chamber of Deputies and the Senate from 2012, as well as amending and supplementing title I of Law no. 35/2008 governing elections of the Chamber of Deputies and the Senate and amending and supplementing Law no. 67/2004 on elections of local public administration authorities, Law no. 215/2001 governing local public administration and Law no. 393/2004 on the status of local officers. The Court considered in this respect the following:

> "the criticised law rules within a field - namely the field of elections – which is the essence of any democratic politic regime. [...]. A democratic and stable electoral system, inspired by a real will of those who, according to Art. 2 of the Constitution, are the holders of national suzerainty, is liable to determine a perception and a civic proper attitude of citizens and, at the same time, it may impose proper conduct on electoral competitors. Or, according to Art. 2 of the Constitution, the national suzerainty is exercised by the representative bodies of the Romanian people and by referendum, and according to Art. 61 Para. (1) of the Constitution, "The Parliament is the supreme representative body of the Romanian people and the unique legislative authority of state". On the other hand, according to Art. 73 Para. (3) lit. a) of Fundamental Law, the electoral system is regulated by organic law. These considerations recommend that regulations in the field of elections shall be debated in Parliament and not adopted by an exception procedure, by which Parliament is avoided, but compelled to a tacit vote on the normative content at the almost exclusive discretion of Government. The mechanism of censure motion, ruled by Art. 114 of the

23 Published in the Official Gazette of Romania, Part I, no. 51 of 20 January 2011.

24 Published in the Official Gazette of Romania, Part I, no. 90 of 3 February 2012.

> Constitution, may have an illusionary character when the Government holds a certain majority in Parliament, the adoption of the law on which the Government assumes responsibility in Parliament becoming a pure formality under such conditions".

2.7. *Enactment of normative acts*

According to Art. 12 of Law no. 24/2000,

> "(1) The laws and ordinance issued by government in terms of a special law of authorisation come into force three days after the date of publication in the Official Gazette of Romania, Part I, or to a subsequent date stipulated therein. The 3-day term is calculated based on calendar days, starting with the date of publication in the Official Gazette of Romania and expires at midnight on the third day of publication.
>
> (2) The emergency ordinances of government come into force on the date of publication in the Official Gazette of Romania, Part I, on condition that they have been previously submitted to the relevant Chamber in order to be notified if a subsequent date is not stipulated therein.
>
> (3) The normative acts stipulated in Art. 11 Para. (1), except for the laws and ordinances, come into force on the date of publication in the Official Gazette of Romania, Part I, if a subsequent date is not stipulated therein. If enforcement is not stipulated on the date of publication, such normative deeds shall provide a subsequent date of enforcement".

But situations occurred whereby shortcomings in the norm either produced delays or a lack of correlation, resulting in publication in the Official Gazette after the date set for enactment, or in two different dates for the enactment of the same provisions. When informed about such cases, the Constitutional Court found such rules to be unconstitutional.

Thus, by *Decision no. 7/2002*[25] the Court found unconstitutional the provisions of Article 87 of Law no. 164/2001 on state military pensions, which was published in the Official Gazette, Part I, no. 183 of 10 April 2001, and according to which "This law comes into force on 1 April 2001", taking into consideration that,

> "without prejudice to the principle of non-retroactivity of law, unless criminal law is more favourable, as stipulated in Article 15 Para. (2) of the Constitution, no law can provide in its text, for its entry into force, a date previous to the one when it is published in the Official Gazette in Romania".

Also, by *Decision no. 185/2009*[26] concerning the objection of unconstitutionality of the provisions of Art. XIII of Law no. 251/2006 amending and supplementing

25 Published in the Official Gazette of Romania, Part I, no. 220 of 2 April 2002.

26 Published in the Official Gazette of Romania, Part I, no. 187 of 25 March 2009.

Law no. 188/1999 on the status of civil servants with regard to the entry into force on 1 January 2007 of Art. 29 of Law no. 188/1999, republished, as subsequently amended and supplemented by Law no. 251 / 2006, the Court admitted this exception, stating that

> "the reference, by Art. XIII of Law no. 251/2006, to the entire Article 29 of Law no. 188/1999, and not only to Para. (1). d) thereof, which was amended by this Law, concerning its entry into force on 1 January 2007, is unconstitutional and does not meet the requirements of legislative technique. The legislature cannot regulate by two successive normative acts, two different times of entry into force of the same provisions of law, without conflicting with Art. 78, according to which "the Law is published in the Official Gazette of Romania and shall come into force 3 days after publication or on a later date provided in its text". Or, in this case, the same provisions of law entered into force by the effect of two different laws: first, the entry into force of Law no. 161/2003 and then as effect of Art. XIII of Law no. 251/2006. However, the setting of a new date of entry into force of the legal texts mentioned, which, as shown, were already in force and were applicable and produced legal effects for a short period, violates Art. 15 Para. (2) of the Fundamental Law on the principle of non-retroactivity of law since the new date of entry into force affects the legal situation arisen before".

2.8. Modification, addition, abrogation and other legislative events

According to Para. 58. (1) of Law no. 24/2000,

> "After the entry into force of a bill, various legislative events, such as modification, addition, abrogation, republishing, suspension or the like may take place during its existence".

But there were situations when the Romanian legislature made changes to some bills after their abrogation.

Thus, *Decision no. 1595/2011*[27] constituted the Court's pronouncement concerning the Law for completion of Education Law no. 84/1995. In its examination of the voiced criticisms, the Court took into consideration that

> "Education Law no. 84/1995, republished in the Official Gazette of Romania, Part I, no. 606 of 10 December 1999, with subsequent amendments and integrations, was abrogated by the provisions of Art. 361, Paragraph (2) of the National Education Law no. 1/2011, published in the Official Gazette of Romania, Part I, no. 18 of 10 January 2011. [...] In this case, the criticised law, which aims to intervene on a bill abrogated, [...] is contrary to Art. 62 of Law no. 24/2000 on technical legislative rules for legislative drafting, republished in the Official Gazette of Romania, Part I, no. 260 of 21 April 2010, as subsequently amended and integrated, according to which "the provisions for amendments and additions shall be incorporated, from

27 Published in the Official Gazette of Romania, Part I, no. 924 of 27 December 2011.

their entry into force, in the basic act, identifying with it. Subsequent interventions for amendments or additions of the same shall be referred also to the basic act".

3. Conclusions

The examples show only some of the flaws in the legislative instrument:

- Highly complex laws adopted practically without parliamentary debate;
- Bills lacking the authorisations provided by law although they were requested;
- Amendments and supplements to some bills that have already been abrogated;
- Definition of different dates for the entry into force of the same legal rules or of a date of entry into force of the same that is prior to publication in the Official Gazette;
- The existence of legislative parallelisms;
- The existence of legislative mismatches;
- Dense and confusing legislation;
- Transposition of European acts into national law by simply copying, without performing the necessary adaptations to specific national realities.

In most cases that we referred to, the Constitutional Court mostly censured laws, finding them to be unconstitutional. .Pursuant to Article 147 of the Constitution, legal rules affected by flaws of unconstitutionality become ineffective (in case of *a posteriori* control), respectively, in case of *a priori* control, the Parliament is bound to reconsider the provisions in question for their implementation in accordance with the decision of the Court.

Constitutional control is achieved, but only upon referral by people endowed with special rights, and it is limited by law. Therefore, we believe that this control should be complemented by efforts of the authorities involved in the legislative act.

Bibliography

Vida, Ioan: Formal law, Lumina Lex, Bucharest, 2006.

Maduro, Miguel Poiares: Global Governance and the Quest for Justice, vol. I – International and Regional Organisation, edited by Douglas Lewis, Hart Publishing, Oxford and Portland, Oregon, 2006.

Stoica, Camelia, Safta, Marieta: Transposition of Directive 2006/24/EC of the European Parliament and Council of the European Union concerning the provision of electronic com-

munication services to the public or to public communication networks into Romanian legislation, Judicial Courier no. 5/2010.
Tridimas, Takis: The General Principles of EU Law, Oxford EC LAW Library.
www.ccr.ro.

Protection against Gender Discrimination and Equal Treatment in the Legal Framework of Romania

Lecturer Mihaela TOFAN[1]

Abstract

In the past two decades, important changes have been made in Romania's legal framework. Concepts such as liberty, equality and equity have evolved from declarations into effective values, applied into reality. Fundamental principles, such as non-discrimination, equal treatment and equality between all individuals have been ruled and are in force, as they are included in constitutional texts, laws, ordinances and regulations. The constant, systematic and concentrated promotion of the equal opportunity principle for men and women, as it is known today, represents a relatively new concern for the international community, even though legal aspects about equality between men and women have been evoked since 1948 (the Universal Declaration of Human Rights). In the European Union, the principle was officially recognised starting with the European Treaty from Maastricht (1993), then Directives were adopted for this purpose and the jurisprudence of Luxembourg's Court of Law reinforced it. On an institutional level, private and public bodies have been founded to carry out the mission of protecting the equal treatment and non-discrimination principles. An important role is reserved to judges, but a large number of citizens have appealed to the European Court of Human Right to find justice.

Keywords: non-discrimination, gender equality, institutional mechanism.

1. Introduction

Principles of law are fundamental precepts imposed over time due to their large degree of generality and because of their widespread effect. Due to their force and meaning of higher standards, legal principles are general texts that may be included in normative acts, usually in the constitutions. If the principles are not formulated specifically in legislation, they are deducted in the light of promoting social values. Some of them are in the form of *maxima* or *adagios*, especially those drawn from ancient Roman rules of law[2].

---

1 Mihaela Tofan, «Alexandru Ioan Cuza» University of Iasi, Romania, Email: mtofan@uaic.ro.

2 Ion Craiovan, "Tratat elementar de teoria generala a dreptului", All Beck Publishing House, Bucharest, 2001, p. 208.

The Explanatory Dictionary of the Romanian language defines the legal principles as the fundamental element, the idea or the basic norm that supports a scientific theory, a basic law or a concept for scientific disciplines[3].

General principles of law have an important and constructive role for the value of the legal system, meaning that they establish the objective requirements for human activities, but they also play an important role in understanding the proper meaning of the law and ensuring its correct application[4].

Although the concept is widely recognised and accepted today, the legal principles have not always had equal significance and importance for different legal systems. Today, all civilised states recognise the principles of law and claim that their legal systems comply with these fundamental rules of law.

Equality and non-discrimination are pair values; affirmation and recognition of one of these concepts is always directly related to the analysis of the other. However, we consider that equality as a principle of law has a broader coverage range. This concept is not subject to collateral arguments, because individuals have equal rights regardless of any other criteria that could be brought into question. The principle of equality is the product of the evolution of law in general, due to changes in how individuals perceive their fellows. On the contrary, the problem that always arises regarding discrimination is the criteria that are considered when the discriminatory act is analysed. This criterion or these criteria should make the difference between two similar situations, otherwise discrimination is not proved.

2. The concept of equality among people on an international level

Even if there is not a specific date when the idea of equality among people emerged, it is however certain that applications of this concept have become more diversified, and that it evolved simultaneously with the evolution of society as a whole. We note the social implications of the relationship of equality in rights, freedoms and obligations of citizenship. From one place to another in Europe and from one historical stage to another, the social concerns surrounding the protection of certain civil rights and their recognition for large groups of people also represented the starting point for the idea of equality.

The French Revolution from 1789 is the historic event merited with drafting and prompting the adoption of the first legally binding document defining hu-

---

3 http://dexonline.ro/search.php?cuv=principiu, viewed on 25 September 2012.

4 Ion Dogaru, "Teoria generală a dreptului", Universitaria Publishing House, Craiova, 1996, p. 114.

man rights in Europe[5]. This made 1789 a crucial year in the evolution of the concept of "human rights" or "freedom" at European and even global level, starting from the premise of equality. The French Revolution gave the first official explanation of equality, stating that individuals are born and die equal, they have equal rights and the social differences are permitted under common criteria[6].

In the United States of America, the first recorded mention of the word "discrimination" is in a speech by President Andrew Johnson in 1866, when he vetoed a law on civil rights[7]. Congress declared that African Americans were citizens like any other Americans and should enjoy the same rights arising from such citizenship. The citizenship was the source of discrimination in the U.S., but the legal concept of discrimination occurred much later[8]. At the end of the 19th century, theoreticians of law discussed discrimination solely with reference to the criterion of race.

It can be said that legal recognition and the attempt to protect women's rights debuted internationally in 1919, when the Convention on Maternity Protection was adopted. This act made the International Labour Organisation the first international institution to accept legally binding rules for women's rights and, consequently, for equal opportunities between women and men. The Convention on Maternity Protection, revised at Geneva on 28 June 1952, refers specifically to the granting of maternity leave, the entitlement to maternity leave and medical pecuniary benefits, the right to stop working when nursing a child, and the ban on sacking women on maternity leave.

Perhaps the first occasion on which the term was used more generally in a legal act is in 1958, when the Convention on Discrimination issued by the International Labour Organisation defined discrimination as

> "any distinction, exclusion or preference made on the basis of race, colour, sex, religion, political opinion, national or social origin".

This document also has normative value as the first document to use the term "equal opportunities"[9].

---

5 Albert Soboul, „L'an un de la liberte – etude historique, texts originaux", Paris, 1973, p. 242-244.

6 "Les hommes naissent et demeurent libres et egaux en droit. Les distinctions sociales ne peuvent etre fondees que sur l`utilite commune".

7 "Congress can repeal all States' laws which discriminate between blacks and whites in matters governed by this law".

8 Banton Michael, "Discriminarea", Du Style Publishing House, Bucharest, 1998, p. 26.

9 Idem, p. 27.

Protection of fundamental rights for European citizens and third countries' residents was a constitutive element of European construction from the very beginning. The non-discrimination plan, as presented in Article 12 (ex Art. 6) of the EC Treaty (1957), aimed to condemn any discrimination based on citizens' nationalities. This article was not considered sufficient to provide effective protection in the fight against discrimination, so its power was enforced with other legal texts.

The construction of the principle of equality in the Community consists of three stages, each one referring to the adoption of directives: 1970 (Directive on Gender Equality), 1990 (Directive on Nationality) and 2000 (Directive on New Grounds of Discrimination). Thus, the Council adopted in 1975 the Directive on Equal Pay (75/117/EEC) amending the rules relating to the principle of equal pay for workers. This adds the principle of equal remuneration to the principle of equal treatment between women and men, both in terms of access to employment, and training and other working conditions. These directives prohibit any discrimination on grounds of sex, either directly or indirectly, protect women, especially in cases of pregnancy and maternity, promote equal opportunities between men and women, and implement the principle of equal treatment between men and women in social protection.

The Maastricht Treaty on European Union gave a new impulse to the principle of equality and non-discrimination regulations by establishing European citizenship. In consideration of the concept of European citizenship, the European Court of Justice has extended its competence *rationae personae* from the narrow "workers" to the more general "European citizens lawfully resident in another Member State"[10].

Following adjustments in the Amsterdam Treaty, Article 13 from TEU has extended the principle stating

> "without prejudice to this Treaty and within the powers conferred by the European Community, the Council, acting unanimously on a proposal from the Commission and after consulting the European Parliament, may take appropriate action to combat discrimination based on sex, race or ethnic origin, religion or belief, disability, age or sexual orientation"[11].

As is clearly stated in the Treaty, Art. 13 is looming as a more precise legal basis. Besides this article there are other key previsions that support the fight against discrimination, such are Article 3, Para. 2 (which focuses not only on

10 Emanuela Ignatoiu-Sora, "Egalitate şi nondiscriminare în jurisprudenţa Curţii Europene de Justiţie", C.H.Beck Publishing House, Bucharest, 2008, p. 19.

11 "Documente de bază ale Comunităţii şi Uniunii Europene", third edition, Polirom Publishing House, Iaşi, 2002, p. 22.

eliminating inequalities, but also on promoting equality between women and men), Articles 136 and 137 (which especially fights exclusion), Article 141 (addressing gender equality in active life), Declaration no. 22 of the Final Act of the Treaty of Amsterdam (which rules equal opportunities for disabled people).

Discrimination should be seen also as an obstacle to the economic and social cohesion of the European Union[12]. The social cost is obvious, since these practices are exercised against one or more persons because of their belonging to one group or another. They are even more intolerable when they concern people who require assistance, for example, the disabled or elderly. On the other hand, it is totally legitimate for the EU to be concerned with, and to supervise the respect of human rights in its treaties. Discrimination is an obstacle to the four freedoms of the European Economic Community, and mainly for the free movement of persons, representing an important barrier to the smooth functioning of the internal market.

Neither the term "discrimination" nor related concepts are defined in the Treaty; therefore it is necessary to examine the European Court of Justice, which has gradually built a definition of this term. In its opinion, discrimination is

> "the application of different rules to comparable situations or the same regulations to different situations".

Thus, the European court not only holds the case of voluntary discrimination but also disguised/indirect discrimination and both are punishable.

Grounds for discrimination are varied enough to provide a wide range of these practices, being based on race or ethnic origin, disability, age, sexual orientation, gender, religion or belief, touching virtually every aspect of daily life. Thus, different practices can be found, for example, in cases such as: aging workforce management, the transition from working life to retirement, employability of disabled people, reconciliation between working life and family, and access to training opportunities, social protection, education and culture, access to goods and services etc.

During the Intergovernmental Conference held in Nice in December 2000, the Member States decided to add a new paragraph to Article 13 from the TEU. Since the entry into force of the Treaty, the Council may adopt the procedure established by Article 251 of the EC Treaty, encouraging measures to support actions by Member States to combat all forms of discrimination.

Council Directive 2000/43/EC on equal treatment of people irrespective of their racial or ethnic origin, and Council Directive 2000/78/EC established a

---

12 http://www.europa.eu.int/scadplus/leg/fr/lvb/l33112.htm.

general framework for respecting equal treatment in employment, prohibiting both direct and indirect discrimination[13].

Article 3 of the Directive on Labour Relations (2000/78/EC) aims to protect access to employment, self-employment and occupation (including promotion), access to counselling and vocational training, labour relations and working conditions, including dismissal and pay, membership of trade unions and employers.

The Race Directive (2000/43/EC) pays more attention to protection against discrimination, including areas such as education, social protection, including social security and health care, social advantages, and access to goods and services, including housing.

Among the legal instruments that promote the principle of equal rights for women and men throughout Europe can be mentioned: European Convention on Human Rights and Fundamental Freedoms (Rome, 1950) and its additional protocols, European Social Charter (1961) and Revised European Social Charter (1996). The charter marks another important step in the construction of the Community law principle of equality and discrimination. Article 20 refers to the principle of equality, as "all persons are equal in rights". The Charter explicitly states (Article II-83) that

> "equality between men and women must be ensured in all areas, including the access to employment, working conditions and remuneration".

The right not to be the victim of discrimination is clearly stated in the general principle that asserts the equality of all human beings. The principle appears in Art. 14 of the European Convention on Human Rights. The non-discrimination principle is not exhaustive, but illustrative. In fact, relatively recently the European Court of Human Rights has ruled that this principle also applies to discrimination based on sexual orientation.

In terms of terminology, it should be noted that, according to the translation from English[14], the principle does not relate to any kind of discrimination, but only those which are arbitrary. In fact, however, discrimination is prohibited, regardless of its foundation. Article 14 applies by extension to social rights, according to a large number of European decisions, such as differences in tax treatment between residents and non-residents. So, it is also used to justify the difference in treatment between adults and minors in detention[15].

---

13 Emanuela Ignatoiu-Sora, "Egalitate şi nondiscriminare în jurisprudenţa Curţii Europene de Justiţie", C.H.Beck Publishing House, Bucharest, 2008, p. 21.

14 Jean François Renucci, Droit européen des droits de l'homme, Librairie Générale de Droit et de Jurisprudence, EJA, 2002, Paris, p. 108.

15 Idem, p. 109.

Under the European Convention, Article 14 has no independent existence: discrimination is banned only if it occurs in respect of a right or a freedom enshrined in the Convention text. Thus, Article 14 aims to strengthen the guarantee of rights and freedoms provided for by the Convention. However, independent application cannot be prevented, which means that Article 14 is not necessarily in conjunction with the impairment of a right protected by the Convention and therefore if the right is violated, Article 14 can be invoked.

Non-discrimination was regulated by Protocol no. 12 at the European Convention on Human Rights. The aim was to provide a broad framework to ensure equal treatment, as Article 14 covers non-discrimination with respect to the rights expressly covered by the Convention.

The Treaty of Lisbon constituted a thorough reform and transformed non-discrimination into a specific purpose of the entire activities of the European Union. Thus, Article 2 of the Treaty states that the Union is founded on values of respect for human dignity, freedom, democracy, equality, rule of law and respect for human rights, including the rights of persons belonging to minorities. These values are common to all the Member States in a society characterised by pluralism, non-discrimination, tolerance, justice, solidarity and equality between women and men. According to Article 10, in the definition and implementation of policies and activities, the Union shall aim to combat discrimination based on sex, race or ethnic origin, religion or belief, disability, age or sexual orientation.

In Title II of the EU Treaty, as amended by the Treaty of Lisbon, the second part, called "Non-discrimination and citizens" explicitly states the protection against any discrimination on grounds of nationality in Article 18 (ex Article 12 TEU) as the scope of the Treaties and without prejudice to any special provisions contained therein. Mandatory rules on the protection of equal treatment and discrimination are found throughout the common market regulations to protect free trade and traders' activity.

The Lisbon Treaty rules on non-discrimination go deeper, touching areas of detail such as equal pay for equal work. Thus, Article 157 (ex Article 141 TEU) provides that each Member State shall ensure the principle of equal pay for all genders.

Sex discrimination is relatively self-explanatory, as it refers to discrimination that is based on the fact that an individual is either a woman or a man. This is the most highly developed aspect of EU social policy and has long been considered a core right. The development of the protection on this ground served a dual purpose: firstly, it served an economic purpose in that it helped to eliminate competitive distortions in a market that had grown ever more integrated, and; secondly, on a political level, it provided the Community with a facet aimed at social progress and the improvement of living and working conditions. Consequently, protection against discrimination on the grounds of sex has been, and remains, a fundamental function of the European Union. The acceptance of the social and economic importance of ensuring equality of treatment was further crystallised by the central position it was given in the Charter of Fundamental Rights. Similarly, under the ECHR, protection against discrimination on the grounds of sex is well developed. While cases of sex discrimination typically involve women receiving less favourable treatment than men, this is not exclusively the case[16].

Considering the lessons learned from cases already resolved, the court decided to publish an official text, a synthesis of the non-discrimination cases that had already been resolved. The Handbook on European Non-discrimination Law, published online[17] is the result of joint efforts by the specialists from the European Court of Human Rights and the European Union Agency for Fundamental Rights. The handbook marked the 60th anniversary of the European Convention on Human Rights in 2010 and the 10th anniversary of the adoption of two fundamental texts into European law in the fight against discrimination at EU level – the Racial Equality and Employment Equality Directives.

3. The Romanian legal framework for equality and non-discrimination

The legal framework in Romania puts into practice all the relevant rules adopted by the International Labour Organisation (ILO), as Romania is party to the convention and has to align its national legal framework to the *acquis communautaire* in the field of equal opportunities and treatment. These international provisions are implemented in domestic regulations in the following acts: the Romanian Constitution, Government Ordinance no. 137/2000 with subsequent amendments, the Labour Code, Law no. 54/1991 on employees' unions, Law no. 202/2002 on equal opportunities between women and men.

Equality of rights in the Romanian legal system is a principle with constitutional value. Article 16 of the Constitution, adopted in 1991 and partially revised in 2003, provides that

> "all citizens are equal before the law and public authorities, no one is above the law".

16 http://www.echr.coe.int/NR/rdonlyres/DACA17B3-921E4C7C-A2EE3CD B68B0133E/0 /182601_FRA_CASE_ LAW_HANDBOOK_EN.pdf, p. 90, viewed on 10 September 2012.

17 http://www.echr.coe.int/ECHR/EN/Header/Case-Law/Case-law+analysis/Handbook+on+non-discrimination/, accessed on 6 September, 2012.

The Romanian state shall guarantee equal opportunities between women and men, in both public and civil service jobs.

At constitutional level, Parliament has complete legislative power in Romania. Yet the Government has the power to adopt ordinances, if Parliament is not able to act. Unfortunately, the process of ruling through ordinances became the prior method and not the exception, as it should be. As a result, equal treatment and non-discrimination principles are ensured by ordinance, and many of the aspects are criticised.

Government Ordinance no. 137/2000, adopted with amendments by Law No. 48/2002 and supplemented by Law no. 324/2006, transferred the international regulatory requirements to domestic level. Any form of discrimination by public authorities on grounds of race, nationality, ethnic origin, religion, language, gender or sexual orientation is forbidden, protecting every private legal person or individual[18].

The first chapter of Law no. 48 of 2002 presents the principles governing the exercising of citizens' rights that are guaranteed by law. Chapter II details the objectives of the law and the third chapter establishes penalties. According to Article 1 of Ordinance 137/2000, in Romania, the rule of law, democratic and social, human dignity, rights and freedoms, and the free development of human personality are supreme values and are guaranteed by law. The principle of equality among citizens, the exclusion of privileges and discrimination are guaranteed in particular when exercising the following rights:

- The right to equal treatment before the courts and any other judicial body;
- The right to personal security and to obtain state protection against violence or ill-treatment from any individual, group or institution;
- Political rights, namely election rights, right to participate in public life and access to public office and titles;
- Civil rights, especially the freedom of movement and choice of residence, the right to leave and return to the country, the right to obtain and give up Romanian citizenship, the right to marry and to choose their partner, property, the right of inheritance, freedom of thought, conscience and religion, freedom of opinion and expression, freedom of assembly and association, the right to petition;
- Economic, social and cultural rights, particularly the right to work, to free choice of employment, to just and favourable working conditions, protection against unemployment, to equal pay for equal work, to just and favourable

18 Gergely Dezideriu, "Practici pozitive: mecanisme specializate în combaterea discriminării", E.C.A Publishing House, Bucharest, 2003, p. 72.

remuneration, the right to form unions and to join unions, the right to housing, the right to health, medical care, social security and social services, the right to education and training;

- Access to all places and services for public use.

According to Government Ordinance no. 137/2000, discrimination is any distinction, exclusion, restriction or preference based on race, nationality, ethnicity, language, religion, social status, belief, sex, sexual orientation, age, disability, non-contagious chronic disease, HIV infection, belonging to a disadvantaged category, and any other criterion which has as its purpose or effect the restriction, elimination of recognition, use or exercise, on equal footing, of human rights and liberties, fundamental freedoms and rights recognised by law in the political, economic, social, cultural or any other areas of public life.

Article 1 Para. 3 of Government Ordinance 137/2000 states that provisions, criteria or practices are discriminatory if they disadvantage certain people, even if the criteria or practices are objectively justified by a legitimate aim, and the methods of achieving that aim are appropriate and necessary.

In accordance with the European fight against all forms of discrimination, Para. 2 from Article 5 of the Romanian Labour Code provides that any direct or indirect discrimination against an employee based on gender, sexual orientation, genetic characteristics, age, national affiliation, race, colour, religion, political option, social origin, disability, situation or family responsibilities, trade union membership or activity is prohibited. In addition, the code punishes direct discrimination and acts of exclusion, distinction, restriction or preference based on one or more of the criteria detailed above, which have the purpose or effect of denial, restriction or elimination of recognition, use or exercise of rights under the labour laws. Even actions based on criteria other than those above are considered direct discrimination if their effects are directly discriminatory.

According to Article 5.4 from the same Labour Code, indirect discrimination is prohibited.

We may distinguish two main types of discrimination: the first related to the moral identity of the person and second to the person's physical identity. Physical identity is directly related to attributes such as sex, race and health. These elements are easily identified by the author of discrimination[19]. The moral identity of a person is directly connected to criteria such as family situation, manners, religious and political beliefs. None of these criteria should be reasons for exclusion or removal of a person. Of course, the law still allows justifiable dis-

19 Dan Ţop, Marie Richevaux, "Marile principii ale dreptului comunitar al muncii", Lumina Lex Publishing House, Bucharest, 2006, p. 42.

tinctions, such as preferring women candidates (or men, if applicable) for a fashion show, depending on the type of presentation.

Although it seems to comply with international provisions, the regulation of equal treatment and non-discrimination in Romanian law is not effective in all situations. Limitations on the principle of non-discrimination and equal treatment may be observed by analysing the effects they produce in practice. Based as it is on the Roman-Germanic legal system, the Romanian legal system does not use legal practice as a source of law, its value being only interpretive. There are, however, two important exceptions, namely the jurisprudence of the European Court of Human Rights and the European Court of Justice. Consequently, in the event of different rulings by Romanian judges for similar cases based on equality, the only possible path is to appeal to the ECHR, citing violation of Protocol 12 to the Convention, which governs, in general terms, the principle of non-discrimination and equal treatment.

The issue remains a limitation on the principle of equal opportunities and treatment in Romanian legislation, a problem for which the solution would be recognition of the legal force of law for solutions already pronounced by judges in similar cases, at least in relation to disputes concerning sex discrimination.

4. The legal and institutional framework to protect gender equality

In the field of equality between women and men, the provisions of Law no. 202/2002, as amended by Ordinance no. 84/2004 are applicable. The law is meant to regulate measures to promote equal opportunities between women and men, in order to eliminate direct and indirect discrimination on the criterion of sex in all spheres of public life in Romania, meaning labour, education, health, culture and information, participation in elections and in other areas governed by special laws. Under this regulation discrimination is not allowed in religious activities or in the private and intimate lives of the individuals[20].

An analysis of the regulations of Law no. 202/2002reveals different sections that govern equal opportunities and treatment in employment, in access to education, health, culture and information. Article 7.1 states that the equality of opportunity and treatment between men and women in labour relations means non-discriminatory access to the choice and free exercise of a profession or craft, employment, equal remuneration, promotion, equal working conditions, and benefits. In labour relations, employers are obliged to ensure equal opportunities

20 Cornel Răduş, "Egalitate şi nediscriminare", Universitaria Publishing House, Craiova, 2006, p. 32.

and treatment of employees, women and men, including the introduction of provisions prohibiting discrimination in the organisation. Employers should systematically inform their employees of their right to equal opportunities and treatment in relationships between men and women by visibly displaying the legal information. Article 10 of the law governing the protection of women in employment during maternity and Art. 11 provides that any unwanted behaviour, defined as sexual harassment, is considered direct discrimination on grounds of sex, if it leads or may lead to one or more of the following purposes or effects:

- To create a workplace atmosphere of intimidation, hostility or discouragement for the person affected
- To negatively influence the situation of the employee in terms of promotion, remuneration or income of any kind, or access to training and professional development, because of his or her refusal to accept unwanted conduct related to his or her sex life.

Since motherhood may be a reason for discrimination, requiring candidates to take a pregnancy test is prohibited. Pregnant women are entitled to a lighter work schedule, if they request it and provide a certificate from the doctor to prove the need for particular working conditions.

The first thing the pregnant employee must do is to notify the supervisor responsible in writing that she is pregnant, in order to claim and to be granted all the rights arising from this situation. The employer is obliged to maintain confidentiality and to comply with the request to improved working conditions. The law in force prohibits the dismissal of women during pregnancy, maternity leave, prenatal or illness, and the period for these privileges is determined by national legislation. She must have assurance that when she returns to work at the end of maternity leave she may return to the same or an equivalent position, and be paid at the same level.

In Romania, specialised institutions that fight discrimination are the National Council for Combating Discrimination and the National Agency for Equal Opportunities between Women and Men. These governmental institutions are joined by numerous non-profit organisations that advise and support victims of discrimination and violation of equal treatment.

The National Council for Combating Discrimination (CNCD) is the central public authority – a legal personality that is subject to parliamentary control – which watches over compliance with the principles of non-discrimination and equal treatment. It is an executive structure, answerable to the government, whose main task is to propose new legal documents, to cooperate with other public equal treatment authorities, to elaborate studies and research reports. It also takes on petitions and claims from victims of unequal treatment or discriminatory actions[21].

The Council works independently, without any influences or pressure from any institution or public authority. The president, the vice-president and the board manage the Council for a 5-year period. The president is the person who signs the activity report of the council and presents the report for the previous year to Parliament by 15 April. The main tasks of the Council are: to prevent discriminatory actions, to mediate in discrimination conflicts, to investigate suspicions of discrimination, to monitor the public strategy in its area of competence, and to assist and support victims of discrimination.

According to Article 24 of Law no. 202/2002, the National Agency for Equal Opportunities is the central public administration organ that is responsible for implementing the principle of gender equality.

In spite of the important mission entrusted to these two public institutions by regulatory act, some claim they are inefficient and do not produce satisfactory results[22]. Indeed, the number of petitions that CNCD resolved during the period of one year (from the total of 836 petitions in 2007, only 546 were resolved in the same year[23]) may seem too few for a country that claims to take a strong stance against discrimination on grounds such as minority, gender and ethnic membership. Transparency is also a negative issue. Finding information on the activity of these authorities on their websites is difficult, although the media does comment on them in depth.

Furthermore, in the context of the global financial crises and considering the lack of funds in the Romanian budget, the Romanian Government decided to dissolve ANES in 2010. Of course, the activities of this agency were moved to the responsibility of another central public authority (the Labour Minister), but they are obviously being neglected. Civil society has been struggling to find a solution for rebuilding this institution, but has so far not succeeded.

Today, the institutional public system in Romania is not able to uphold the principle of non-discrimination and gender equality, so victims may ultimately have to appeal to the European Court of Human Rights (ECHR). Victims can, however, only resort to this option once the national judicial system has failed to rule in favour of their petition by which time the victims' financial resources and patience have often been exhausted.

---

21 Cristian Jura: "Complementary system of protection of human rights and combating discrimination", Universal Publishing House, Bucharest, 2004, p. 29.

22 http://romaniatotalitara.wordpress.com/2007/10/01/, viewed on 20 September 2012.

23 http://www.telegrafonline.ro/1220562000/articol/64017/cele_mai_8222tari8221_motive _ de _discriminare_hivsida_handicapul_si_homosexualitatea.html.

Romanian's accession to the convention was signed on 7 October 1993 and ratified on 20 June 1994. Statistics on Romanian court cases between then and 1 January 2011 show:

Total number of judgements	791
Violation judgements	719
No violation judgements	21
Other judgements	51
Inadmissibility decisions	22567
Pending applications	11950

Violations of the rule protecting the prohibition of discrimination by Romania were the subject of discussion in 22 court cases[24].

5. Romania's public administration strategy to protect equality between women and men

In Romania, even though civil society and non-governmental organisations that militate for women rights have repeatedly pinpointed the existing inequities between men and women, the public and political institutions have shown only formal interest in the matter, being constrained by the accession to the EU, which at the time was conditioned by the standards in the field.

In the legislative sector, Romania was slow to apply the community's acquis regarding gender equality. The 2001 national report of the European Commission pointed out that the National Action Plan had not materialised into any concrete action, with the legal project regarding sexual equality spending longer in debate in Parliament than was reasonable. Also, in 2001, when Romania assumed some serious commitments with the European Community, it took first measures to implement the community's acquis, measures that were of an institutional nature. But what was missing in those newly created institutions was a central body for watching over the implementation of equal opportunities and an adequate system for financing the measures and efforts of these institutions.

The National Strategy aimed at protecting equality between men and women in the period 2006-2009 was structured in intervention areas, with specific objectives defined for each area. Thus, the main objectives of the institutional area were enforcement of the institutional capacity, specialisation of the relevant staff in the field of equal opportunities and improvement of communications with international organisations in the sector. The second objective is considered to be

24 http://www.echr.coe.int/NR/rdonlyres/ACD46A0F-615A-48B9-89D6-8480AFCC29FD/0/FactsAndFigures_EN.pdf, p. 15, viewed on 6 September 2012.

the most important as it promotes the exchange of expertise between states. The national governmental and non-governmental organisations were omitted from the Public Administration Strategy or not given much importance. Good cooperation between, and a public financing system for, such organisations could have created a series of projects to support the application of the strategy. Non-reimbursable European funds have always been available to citizens and, implicitly to such organisations, social protection institutions and a country's employment organisations, but they are misused.

The main objective of the business area is to support equal access for women on the labour market. Salaries are the most contested factor. Although the law prescribes similar salary levels for equal positions and jobs, discrepancies arise when jobs and working conditions are not similar or when specifically female-related factors, like maternity leave, are taken into consideration. According to the Public Administration strategy, this period is to be blamed for the lack of progress, mostly at professional development level.

Equal opportunities for men and women became a necessity when differences at both European and national level were revealed in working conditions, wage levels, employment and unemployment rates, and especially when the figures were broken down by gender. Equal opportunities and treatment in employment mean equal access to choosing a profession, when applying for a job and being selected for that particular job, to equal remuneration, promotion, equal working conditions, equal benefits and equal social services.

When talking about solutions, the Public Administration strategy offers the implementation of certain professional retraining programmes and the stimulation of interest in continuous professional training aimed ultimately at facilitating access to all areas of the economy. The Public Administration authorities saw the above strategy as playing a very important role, but only for some of this area's objectives, such as sustaining measures for preventing and fighting female trafficking and violence against women. When striving to promote equality between men and women in the community, it is not the legal framework where the links are missing; it is each nation's mentality and education. Measures for achieving these goals should be aimed more towards convincing citizens and changing perceptions and values, and less towards changing laws.

The participation of men and women in decisions relating to all aspects of social, business and political life is an elementary part of the strategy that also reflects the past and the history of the nation. As the strategy mentions, equal participation in decision making processes would be clear proof of democracy, but only time will underline the truthfulness of these values in the Romanian conscience. The assurance of equal representation of men and women in the decision-making process can be achieved through mass media and through mobilising civil society, and less by interfering with legislation, because "according to the law, the majority decides", and the number of positions held by females increases noticeably as the level of decision decreases.

Chart 1 and 2. The percentage of females in the decision-making process at governmental level in Romania and in the EU[25].

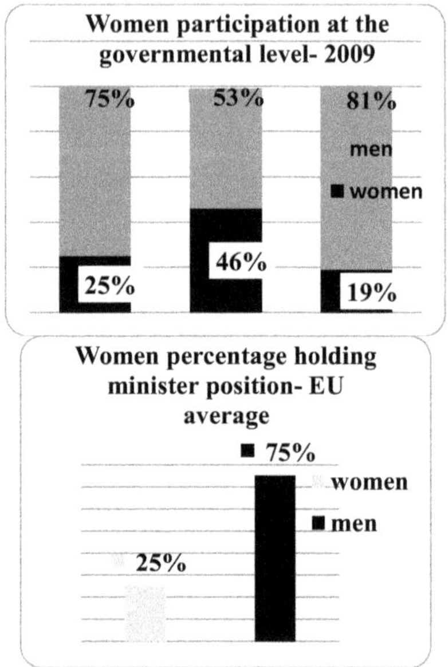

We believe that Romania has understood that adopting a strategy and an action plan at national level is not enough. Educating – especially women – about the options for taking action against discrimination, and a long-term programme aimed at raising social awareness could play an important role in implementing European law and for the development of the national economy. Until now, discrimination cases have seldom turned into trials and those that did were not publicised enough to produce changes in the mentality and behaviour of the Romanian people.

The basic goal of the EU objective – equal opportunities for men and women – can only be achieved if all Member States make the necessary efforts to promote this principle and if social policy in this direction does not remain at a theoretical level, but is put into practice. In policies aimed at full employment,

25 http://www.anes.ro/, viewed on 14 December 2010.

the objectives of equal opportunities have to be correlated with the objectives of the national economy and with the plans for securing long-term development.

6. Conclusion

In preparing for accession to the EU, Romania thoroughly modified its national legal rules, including the framework governing the principles of equality and non-discrimination, although the process is not yet finished.

Regarding positive discrimination in the Romanian context, we conclude that the legal texts in force today may generate more discrimination actions. It is possible to respect positive discrimination if we do not fail to create equal opportunities. Although morally justified, positive discrimination may create negative discrimination for the majority. This is neither the spirit nor the intention of the principle of equality and equal treatment as it is regulated in international and European law. The role of the rule of law in the fight against discriminatory behaviour is to punish discriminating acts, which is not achieved if the adopted methods generate further discriminatory conduct.

Continuing the European model, a handbook of best practices on combating discrimination could be a way to contribute to the success of prevention initiatives that state authorities and civil society might take in future. Continuous professional training of all social actors that may be involved in the phenomenon of discrimination is mandatory. Such an approach could be initiated by the National Council for Combating Discrimination and continued together with NGOs with experience in the field. It is regrettable that the only central public administration agency that acted as the gender equality watchdog was dissolved.

We must admit that Romanian society is very "tolerant" towards discrimination, and the educative role of the media remains negligible. Civil society does not take a firm stance against discriminatory conduct. The education system could make a difference by promoting understanding and respect for these values. In such a social environment, the authorities have to stand firm against discrimination. Regulations should respond to social needs and, in turn, lead to new social behaviour. From this point of view, the existence of proper legislation and specialised institutions to combat discrimination should be embraced.

Bibliography

Chinole, Cristina; Ţiriac, Alina: Ethnographic research on multiple discrimination, Bucharest, 2007.

Craiovan, Ion: Treaty elementary general Theory of Law, Bucharest, 2001.

Dezideriu, Gergely: Positive practice: specialised mechanisms to combat discrimination, Bucharest, 2003.
Djuvara, Mircea: Law and sociology, Bucharest, 1936.
Ignatoiu-Sora, Emanuela: Equality and non-discrimination in the European Court of Justice, Bucharest, 2008.
Jura, Cristian: Complementary system of protection of human rights and combating discrimination, Bucharest, 2004.
Manolache, Octavian: Community Law, Craiova, 1996.
Prisecariu, Petru: The Common European Union, Bucharest, 2004;
Profiroiu, Marius; Profiroiu, Alina, Popescu, Irina: Institution and Policies, Bucharest, 2008.
Răduş, Cornel: Equality and non-discrimination, Craiova, 2006.
Ţop, Dan; Richevaux, Marie: The great principle of community law work, Bucharest, 2006.
Report by the Council of the European Commission, European Parliament, the Economic and Social Committee, Equality between women and men, Brussels, 18 February 2009.
National Report on Equality between Women and Men, Bucharest, 6 March 2002.

Brief Analysis of Fiscal Measures in a Time of Crisis

Vincenzo CARBONE[1]

Abstract

Different productive and financial innovations have historically played a key role in the origin of any economic crisis. The special feature of the present one is no doubt its magnitude. Many measures have been taken by various European Governments to tackle the crisis. All aim to curtail tax reliefs and raise taxes. Can these measures succeed in helping the various states to recover from the current economic situation? The present study critically examines the measures taken by Italy and Romania, and proposes some alternative measures.

Keywords: Italy, Romania, Tax reliefs, Tax shield, Tax evasion, Crisis.

1. Introduction

Different productive and financial innovations have historically played a key role in the origin of any economic crisis. The special feature of the present one is no doubt its magnitude. Indeed, it's becoming a real economic crisis without precedent.

Among the various causes, as highlighted and discussed by scholars, the economic growth in the early 90s based on over-indebtedness of both citizens and states seems to rank as the most significant. This crisis has fuelled speculation of various kinds ranging from real estate to purely financial.

2. The anti-crisis measures

Several measures are being taken by European countries to tackle the crisis. Romania, with Government Emergency Ordinance no. 58 of 26 June 2010, has adopted a series of fiscal measures. From 1 July 2010 the ordinary VAT rate was raised from 19 to 24%[2], conditions that qualify the nature of employment have been restated, the share of expenditure deductions for dependent income was reduced from 40 to 20% of the taxable base[3].

At the same time, tax reliefs were abolished for micro-enterprises, i.e. companies (for whom activities other than consultancy and management account for

---

1 Vincenzo Carbone, Lawyer, Bar of Lecce, Italy, Email: vincenzo-carbone@hotmail.it.

2 Causing, in the opinion of the writer, a contraction in consumption.

3 See the website www.fiscooggi.it.

more than 50% of their operations) with less than 100 thousand euros in turnover and fewer than 9 employees during the fiscal year[4]. Until 31 December 2009, they enjoyed a tax rate that was reduced by as much as 3% (was 2% in 2007 and 2.5% in 2009) whereas a standard tax rate of 16% has been applicable since 1 January 2010[5].

The Italian government has also tried to solve the particular economic situation that characterises "the boot" by adopting stringent fiscal measures.

The Secretary of the Treasury has, in fact, proposed higher taxation of financial income (up to 20%), albeit with a reduction of the tax on postal deposits (from 27% to 20%). And again, cutting civil servants' salaries; amending Article 81 of the Constitution (which governs the rules of the state budget); cutting old-age pensions and those of women in the private sector.

According to Premier Monti, the interventions outlined above were suggested in a letter sent by the ECB to Italy. Not only that, the European Central Bank also advocated the right for companies to dismiss employees (albeit compensated by insurance mechanisms); the liberalisation of public and professional services, and the large-scale privatisation of local public services.

3. Hypothesis of resolutive manoeuvres

Are the measures taken by European governments really effective? Are the tax increases and drastic reduction in tax relief capable of reviving the country's economy?

Increasing the tax burden undoubtedly raises the tax revenues that enrich the state coffers, at least theoretically. Such manoeuvres, however, inevitably lead to a contraction in consumption, thus reducing GDP[6]. The increase in the tax burden also increases the mistrust that the people nurture for the government, encouraging tax evasion.

Manoeuvres in this sense, therefore, run the risk of aggravating the economic situation, plunging the nations into the abyss.

---

4 See Clujescu C., Impactul eliminării impozitului minim, in Curierul Fiscal no. 10/2010, p. 15.

5 With the income tax reform of 2005, the Romanian tax system adopted a single tax rate of 16%, the so-called flat tax. In addition, some components of income became subject to withholding tax, always at a rate of 16%.

6 Gross domestic product is called Prodotto Interno Lordo (PIL) in Italy, and "Produsul Intern Brut (PIB)" in Romania.

In the opinion of the writer, wise and decisive action would be to focus on three fundamental aspects:

- increasing tax breaks to guide the behaviour of taxpayers, concentrating capital in certain geographical areas;
- implementing a tax shield to allow the repatriation of foreign capital without imposing particular sanctions;
- combating tax evasion.

3.1. The role of tax relief in a time of crisis

As is well known, the aims pursued by tax relief are manifold. In fact, they can bridge a pre-existing disadvantage, for example, tax relief for people with disabilities. Or they may induce taxpayers to take a certain action, through the provision of incentives.

At this particular juncture, incentives aimed at developing specific geographic areas seem to be extremely attractive.

These incentives can promote the economic and social development of neighbourhoods and urban areas that are characterised by social unrest, and demonstrate economic, employment and development potential.

Although legal doctrine denies similar forms of incentive, considering the latter an obstacle to the Community authorities since they are able to generate phenomena of harmful tax competition, the Hökmark Report, approved by Parliament on 14 February 2006, provides for states to

> "introduce favourable tax conditions for transition periods not exceeding five years [...] provided that the aid does not generate an added value that could be achieved with any other policy measure".

This report authorised forms of tax concessions for certain areas, including within a given territory, as long as they comply with Community rules on competition policy.

As a result, aid, even if granted in the form of tax relief, may be considered acceptable if, in the first place, it is proportionate to the aim that we want to achieve, and secondly it is granted in descending order and able to achieve lasting effects even after cessation.

In Italy, the proposal to establish the so-called Zone Franche Urbane (Free Trade Zone), consisting of a series of tax breaks to facilitate and initiate local development policies, found initial confirmation in the Budget Law for 2007 (Law no. 296/2006)[7].

Para. 340 et seq. of Article 1 of the mentioned Law established a fund at the Ministry of Economic Development for setting up free trade zones (ZFU)

> "in order to promote the economic and social development, including through restoration of urban areas and slums, in the cities of the South".

The new provisions, however, in accordance with Community rules on state aid for regional purposes for the 2007-2013 period have eliminated all references related to the South, extending to all ZFU territories in derogation of Art. 87, Para. 3, lit. a) and c). It follows that the ZFU currently include the central and northern areas, as defined by the new Charter of regional aid. Currently there are 22 ZFU, selected based on a series of socio-economic distress indicators[8].

Under the new law, beneficiaries of such facilities shall only be microenterprises[9], with the exception of those operating in the so-called sensitive sectors[10].

As in France, this system only and exclusively applies for companies that started a new business in the period between 1 January 2008 and 31 December 2012 in a given ZFU.

The scheme just outlined is compatible with the rules of the Treaty because, according to the Commission: a) it aims to achieve a Community objective, namely the economic and social cohesion imposed by Art. 2 and 3 of the Treaty itself, b) it is necessary and proportionate to the objective, as it affects only 2.6% of the total population and the areas are selected through systematic indices. For these reasons, the European Commission has approved the above help with note C-2009-8126 of 28 October 2009[11].

---

7 As you can see from the website of the Ministry of Economic Development, the initiative comes from the French Zones Franches Urbaines, launched in 1996 and now active in more than 100 districts. See www.dps.tesoro.it.

8 They are: Catania, Gela, Erice in Sicilia; Crotone, Rossano and Lamezia Terme in Calabria; Matera in Basilicata; Taranto, Lecce and Andria in Puglia; Napoli, Torre Annunziata and Mondragone in Campania; Campobasso in Molise; Cagliari, Quartu Sant'Elena and Iglesias in Sardegna; Velletri and Sora in Lazio; Pescara in Abruzzo; Massa Carrara in Toscana and Ventimiglia in Liguria.

9 For the definition of microenterprise, see European Commission Recommendation, 6 May 2003, GU L 124 of 20.05.2003.

10 The sensitive sectors are the sectors of metallurgy, shipbuilding, synthetic fibre production, automobile manufacturing and road haulage.

11 On 11 June 2009, the DPS initiated the procedure for notification of the aid scheme, N346/2009 registered at the competent services of DG Competition of the European Commission. By letters dated 15.07.2009 (D/53152) and 08.28.2009 (D/53666), the European Commission has requested additional information. The Italian authorities have

These forms of tax relief are one of many examples to help you understand how these institutes can have a positive impact on the national economy. Romania is familiar with these types of institutes too. The Facilitate pentru zone defavorizate, in fact, are the Romanian version of the facilities in question. However, they were banned by the European Community as they did not meet certain parameters, such as duration.

From my humble point of view, Romania could, or should accomplish and re-implement similar tax reliefs.

3.2. The tax shield and the fight against tax evasion

A manoeuvre that focuses only on tax breaks is, surely, insufficient. Measures are required to increase the economic budget. But what measures can increase tax revenues without raiding the wallets of citizens? The answer, which might not be too obvious, is: the tax shield.

Tax shields address the illegal or irregular production and possession of capital abroad by taxpayers who have not declared their income, allowing them to rectify the situation through a one-off payment of tax at a flat rate that is less than the normal tax rates.

Decree-Law 194/2009, the so-called "thousand extensions", introduced a so-called tax shield Ter in Italy[12]. It has resulted in the repatriation of about 300 billion euros, which have produced tax revenues of 5 billion euros.

Another method of increasing the financial resources without burdening citizens who regularly pay their taxes is to combat tax evasion. If everyone paid correctly, everyone would pay less.

A possible solution to the problem of tax evasion is offered by the U.S. model.

In Italy, consumers are not allowed to deduct family expenses and consumption from their taxes.

So obviously, if someone asks "do you want a receipt?" or "do you want the invoice?" a consumer will respond with appropriate disinterest, perhaps trying to exploit the situation to tweak a small discount on the selling price.

If consumers could deduct 10-15% of the costs incurred for the purchase of consumer goods from their taxes, they would be more insistent on being given the receipt or invoice.

---

provided such information by electronic mail dated 07.20.2009 (A/16932) and 09.09.2009 (A/19466). On 28 October 2009, the Commission authorised the ZFU with note C-2009-8126. In relation to the suitability of urban zones, see Boria P., Diritto tributario europeo, 2010, Milan, p. 231.

12 Indeed, this was the third time that it was called the shield.

Tax evasion would be reduced drastically and in a natural way. The political class (of all colours) seems to reject the US solution, claiming that this method would force consumers to fill out complex tax returns and to retain receipts and invoices.

However, consumers would be happy to keep some more paperwork in return for being allowed to reduce their tax burden, while tax evasion in Italy would receive a blow without increasing the cost of controls and verification costs.

4. Conclusion

At a time of global crisis, tax breaks must be stimulated and evasion combated through natural methods and inexpensively in order to boost the economy.

Tax increases inevitably impoverish the population who will lose more and more confidence in the state.

Certainly we cannot say that the measures analysed in this work are the only ones likely to heal the pitiful economic situation. However, as shown, even if they increase revenue to the Treasury, they don't raid the wallets of the citizens, because, in the opinion of the writer, exaggerating the tax burden will increase tax evasion.

Bibliography

Clujescu, C.: Impactul eliminării impozitului minim, in Curierul Fiscal no. 10/2010.
Boria, P.: Diritto tributario europeo, Milan, 2010.
www.fiscooggi.it.
www.dps.tesoro.it.

Legal Regime Applicable to Non-Refundable Financing Contracts within the Sectoral Operational Programme "Human Resources Development 2007-2013 (Sop Hrd)"

PhD student Mihaela AIRINEI[1]

Abstract

The administration of non-refundable European funds represents a new challenge for public administration bodies. Presumably, this new function by the public administration requires the organisation and action of a management and control system that is able to efficiently administer the funds assigned to Romania for 2007-2013. Structural changes achieved within public administration have produced new legal constructions, among which we can mention the non-refundable financing contract. By analysing the characteristics of non-refundable financing contracts we shall attempt to enclose this type of contract within the category of administrative contracts. Specific to establishing the judicial regime applicable to this contract shall be the appraisal of the private or public interest pursued by the public authority when concluding such a contract. Furthermore, we have to mention that in the case of European fund administration, the efficacy of the public administration bodies is reflected by the absorption degree of these European funds and, without clear regulation in this field, we cannot claim efficient functioning of the management and control system.

Keywords: non-refundable financing contract; public administration; public interest; private interest; European funds;

1. Introduction

> "Reality acknowledges that the border line between public and private law has become, sometimes, unrecognisable, not due to the fact that separation is in the pipeline anymore, but because new legal persons appear all the time, persons that complicate the public-private separation by the celerity of structural changes, thus introducing an uncertainty and random element within judicial constructions, where certain reliability was maintained"[2].

---

1 Mihaela Airinei, National School of Political and Administrative Studies, Bucharest, Romania, Email: elladaraban@yahoo.com, beneficiary of the "Doctoral Scholarships for a Sustainable Society" project, co-financed by the European Union through the European Social Fund, Sectoral Operational Programme Human Resources and Development 2007 -2013.

2 J. Caillosse, J. Hardy, Droit et modernisation administrative, Paris, 2000, La Documentation Française, p. 32.

Hereinafter, we propose analysing a new type of contract that has emerged in the area of public administration following structural changes achieved in order to administer European funds, namely the non-refundable financing contract concluded between the Management Authority and any other legal entity under private or public law. As we know, since becoming an EU Member State, Romania benefits from structural tools amounting to 19.7 billion euros for use in operational programmes from 2007-2013.

For 2007-2013, Romania has drawn up 7 operational programmes under the objective of convergence and cohesion policy, which focus on fostering:

a) Human resources development
b) Competitive economic growth
c) Transport
d) Environment
e) Administrative capacity development
f) Regional development
g) Technical assistance[3]

The operational programme is a document presented by a Member State and adopted by the Commission, which defines the development strategy according to a coherent set of priorities, in order to obtain funding[4].

Operational programmes contain a large number of priority axes, within which there are several major intervention fields. The eligible beneficiaries, eligible activities, eligible expenses, etc., have been established for each major intervention field within the priority axes, to determine who receives financing by structural tools.

Each operational programme is financed by one of the following funds: European Social Fund, European Regional Development Fund and Cohesion Fund, the exceptions being operational programmes for the environment and transport, which are financed by European Regional Development Fund and Cohesion Fund.

The administration of non-refundable European funds by a Member State necessitates certain changes within the public administration system. In order to ensure strict and efficient management of these funds, the European Commission has developed a set of rules and conditions meant to ensure good administration at the level of each Member State. The action of the European Union in this field is justified by applying the subsidiarity principle[5] and by a shared ad-

---

3 National Strategic Reference Framework 2007-2013.

4 The document is available online: www.fonduri-ue.ro, 10.09.2012.

5 Except for the fields under the exclusive competence of the European Community, the subsidiarity principle stipulates, on the one hand, the protection of the decision and ac-

ministration mechanism through which the European Commission delegates certain budgetary execution tasks to the Member States responsible for the administration and application of non-refundable external funds, while the European Union Commission acts as the monitoring authority within the shared administration. Thus, the national public administration takes on an intermediary role between the European Union and the beneficiary within the scheme of non-refundable European funds allotment.

In order to accomplish this new role in public administration, the provisions of Art. 59 of European Regulation no. 1083/2006 stipulate that each Member State must designate the following for each operational programme financed by European Funds:

- Management Authority: a public authority or a national public or private body, regional or local, appointed by the Member State to administer the operational programme;
- Certification Authority: a public authority or a national public or private body, regional or local, appointed by the Member State to certify the expenses and payment requests before sending them to the Commission;
- Audit Authority: a public authority or a national public or private body, regional or local, independent of the Management Authority and Certification Authority from a functional point of view, appointed by the Member State for each operational programme and charged with checking the efficient functioning of the management and control system.

The Member State can designate one or more intermediate bodies to wholly or partially assume the responsibilities of the Management Authority or of the Certification Authority under the supervision of the respective Authority.

The Member State shall stipulate the regulations governing its relations with those authorities that are responsible for administering European funds and their relations with the Commission. Thus, the European Commission will not approve the launch of a programme financed by European funds for a Member State if the functions through which the national institutions ensure the coordination and administration of the funds are not in place: the management authority, certification authority, intermediary body, and audit authority functions.

---

tion capacity of the Member States and, on the other hand, it justifies the intervention of the Community in case the objectives of an action cannot be accomplished satisfactorily by the Member States "due to the dimensions and effects of the planned action". Introducing this principle within European treaties aims to bring competencies as close to the citizens as possible.

Through Government Decision no. 457/2008 regarding the institutional framework for coordination and administration of structural tools, new structures have been implemented in the Romanian administrative system to ensure the necessary functions in order to administer the allotted non-refundable European funds[6]:

The Ministry of Public Finance performs the function of Structural Coordination Authority (ACIS), which is responsible for coordination, preparation, development, harmonisation and functioning of the legislative, institutional, procedural and programmatic framework in order to administer structural instruments.

The function of Management Authority (MA), which is responsible for administering and implementing the non-refundable financial assistance allotted to the administered programme, is performed as follows:

- for the Regional Operational Programme, by the Ministry of Regional Development and Tourism;
- for the Sectoral Operational Programme "Increase of economic competitiveness", by the Ministry of Economy;
- for the Sectoral Operational Programme "Transport", by the Ministry of Transport and Infrastructure;
- for the Sectoral Operational Programme "Environment", by the Ministry of Environment and Forests;
- for the Sectoral Operational Programme "Human Resources Development", by the Ministry of Labour, Family and Social Protection;
- for the Operational Programme "Administrative Capacity Development", by the Ministry of Administration and Internal Affairs;
- for the Operational Programme "Technical Assistance", by the Ministry of Public Finance;
- for the Romanian-Bulgarian Cross-border Cooperation Programme 2007-2013 and for the Romanian-Serbian Cross-border Cooperation Programme, for the common Operational Programme of cooperation in the Black Sea region (as the common management authority) and for the common Operational Programme Romania-Ukraine-Republic of Moldova (as the common management authority), by the Ministry of Regional Development and Tourism.

The Ministry of Public Finance performs the function of Certifying and Payment Authority (CPA) for operational programmes financed through structural instruments, respectively through the instrument for pre-accession assistance (IPA).

6 We have used the updated names of the authorities.

The Audit Authority (AA) performs a self-explanatory function in conjunction with Romania's Audit Court.

The function of Intermediary Body (IB), which is responsible for performing tasks delegated by the Management Authority responsible for administering the operational programme, is performed as follows:

- for the Regional Operational Programme, by Regional Development Agencies and by the Direction of Community Funds Administration for SMEs;
- for the Sectoral Operational Programme "Increase of economic competitiveness", by the Direction of Community Funds Administration for SMEs, National Authority for Scientific Research; Ministry of Communications and Information Society and the Ministry of the Economy, General Direction Energy, Petroleum and Gas;
- for the Sectoral Operational Programme "Environment", by the Ministry of the Environment, through structures under its orders that do not constitute legal entities and are organised at the level of the 8 development areas established by Law no. 315/2004 regarding regional development in Romania, with subsequent amendments and supplements;
- for the Sectoral Operational Programme "Human Resources Development", by the Ministry of Education, Research, Youth and Sports, National Agency of Employment, National Centre of Vocational and Technical Tuition Development and the Ministry of Labour, Family and Social Protection, through the 8 structures under its orders that do not constitute legal entities and are organised at the level of the 8 development areas established by Law no. 315 of 28 June 2004 regarding regional development in Romania, with subsequent amendments and supplements.
- the functions of ACIS, MA, ACPA, IB and AA are organised as separate structures (general direction, direction or department) within the designated institutions.

2. Non-refundable financing contracts - a new legal means by which the public administration performs its functions

All these new structures, set up within the Member State, have the role of ensuring the proper functioning of the mechanisms for managing and controlling the European funds, under the supervision of the European Commission. Furthermore, the emergence of these mechanisms in public administration has produced changes in how the administration functions and has proliferated new judicial instruments.

Access to non-refundable European funds is organised on the basis of competitions, projects organised by Management Authorities, in which legal entities can take part if they meet the eligibility criteria. Following assessment of the projects, the Management Authority notifies the winning legal entities and invites them to sign a non-refundable financing contract.

The provisions of non-refundable financing contracts differ from one Management Authority to another. In this paper, we analyse the characteristics of the non-refundable financing contracts used for the Sectoral Operational Programme "Human Resources Development 2007-2013 (SOP HRD)".

The framework model of the financing programme for the Sectoral Operational Programme "Human Resources Development 2007-2013" was approved, for the first time, by the Secretary of State for Labour, Family and Equal Opportunities, in Order no. 499/2008 of 11 August 2008. We have to mention that the framework model of the financing contract was subsequently modified through Secretary of State Order as well.

According to Art.1 of Government Decision no. 759/2007, with subsequent amendments and supplements, the financing contract

> "represents the legal document through which non-refundable financing assistance associated with operations (projects) is granted in order to achieve the priority axis objectives of an operational programme and it sets up the rights and obligations of the parties".

The financing programme is concluded between the Management Authority, hereinafter MA SOP HRD[7] and a public or private law legal entity, which is the beneficiary of the non-refundable financing, hereinafter called the Beneficiary.

In the case of the Sectoral Operational Programme "Human Resources Development 2007-2013", for whose implementation Intermediary Bodies have been designated in order to perform the tasks delegated by the Management Authority, the non-refundable financing contracts are tripartite. In this case, the parties are the Management Authority SOP HRD, the Intermediary Body for SOP HRD, delegated according to the Functions Delegation Agreement and the Beneficiary of the financing.

This delegation of functions between the MA SOP HRD and the Intermediary Body SOP HRD is based on the provisions of OMMFPS Order no. 600/2008 which approves the delegation of certain functions in respect of SOP HRD implementation. According to the legal provisions, MA SOP HRD can delegate some of its responsibilities, competences, commitments, obligations and/or rights from the financing contract to the delegated Intermediary Bodies SOP

7 Management Authority for the Sectoral Operational Programme "Human Resources Development 2007-2013".

HRD. Thus, the delegated Intermediary Body assumes some of the responsibilities, competences, commitments, obligations and/or rights provided by the financing contract regarding the modification, severance, monitoring and execution of the contract.

Starting from the idea that this financing contract falls into the category of "configurations of public administration activities that produce legal effects"[8], we shall try to see if it falls entirely under the regime of public law or under the regulations of the private law.

As we know, the public administration acts through administrative documents (unilateral manifestation of legal will on behalf of the public authorities) and administration documents, which include: administrative contracts, civil contracts, commercial contracts, etc. The difference between these types of contracts is dictated by the judicial regime governing them; thus, administrative contracts are subject to public law regulations whereas the other categories of contracts are governed by common law regulations.

In the doctrine of speciality[9], administrative contracts have been defined in different ways.

J. M. Auby defines the administrative contract as

> "the contract concluded by one or more public entities and that falls under the judicial regime of the public law".

G. Costi defines the administrative contract as

> "the consensus manifested through a certain form and concluded between qualified representatives of administrative authorities and private entities or public administration agencies, regarding determined objects, with the purpose of producing legal effects necessary to satisfy the general interest".

Administrative contracts are defined as

> "bilateral or multilateral judicial documents concluded by structures of the public administration with the administered bodies, documents which contain a will agreement producing rights and obligations for the contracting parties, falling under the regulations of public law, part of the judicial administrative regime"[10].

Ioan Alexandru defines administrative contracts as representing

> "the agreement of will with bilateral or multilateral character, between an administrative authority and one or more legal or natural persons through which a general

8 Emil Bălan, "Instituții administrative" (Administrative institutions), C.H. Beck Publishing House, Bucharest, 2008, p. 159.

9 See Cătălin-Silviu Săraru, "Contractele administrative. Reglementare. Doctrină. Jurisprudență" (Administrative contracts. Regulation. Doctrine. Jurisprudence), C.H. Beck Publishing House, Bucharest, 2009, p. 22-47.

10 Emil Bălan, cited work, 2008, p. 159.

> interest is pursued and which has as an object carrying out public works, valorisation of an asset publicly or privately owned by the state or by a territorial and administrative division or carrying out public acquisitions".

According to speciality literature, certain specific features distinguish administrative contracts from other contracts. By trying to establish the judicial regime applicable to the financing contract, we shall analyse whether features of the administrative judicial regime are to be found in this new type of contract. In doing so, we are trying to analyse whether the financing contract falls under the category of administrative contracts, making it subject to the public law regime, or the category of contracts concluded by public administrative authorities with the administered parties, which makes it subject to common law provisions.

Speciality literature distinguishes the following characteristic features of administrative contracts:

- Judicial inequality of the parties.

> "The consensus appears as a result of an inequality between the contract parties, resulting from the superiority of the public authority. Intervention, as a contract party, of the public administration body is justified by the law execution activity according to competences conferred by judicial regulations in order to achieve a public interest or to make use of the public domain"[11].

According to Art. 13, of the framework model of the financing contract within SOP HRD 2007-2013, approved by Order of the Ministry of Labour, Family and Social Protection no. 1184 on 29 March 2011,

> "any amendment to the Contract shall be made by both parties' agreement, by approving a notification or by concluding an additional document, except for amendments prompted by changes in national and European legislation which shall come into force on the date stipulated in the respective regulatory document, without the prior agreement of the Beneficiary".

Until the 29 March 2011 update of the framework model of the financing contract, contract provisions regarding modifications were much more intransigent, emphasising the superiority position of the public authority, in such a way that

> "amendments prompted by changes in national and European legislation shall be carried out by the Management Authority SOP HRD without the prior agreement of the beneficiary".

Furthermore, in the case of administrative contracts

---

11 Ioan Alexandru, "Drept administrativ" (Administrative Law), Lumina Lex Publishing House, Bucharest, 2005, p. 412.

> "the administration reserves the right to unilaterally or judicially void the contract, if required in the general interest or if the natural person has failed to honour their contractual obligations"[12].

Thus, according to the financing contract provisions within SOP HRD, it can be terminated by the public authority (MA SOP HRD) de jure without court intervention and without the need for any formalities, other than simply informing the Beneficiary in the event of the latter's failure to observe contract provisions.

- One contract party always exercises public authority.

> "One of the parties must be a public institution, a public administration body which acts on the basis of the competence invested by law to achieve a public interest, the other party - a particular, natural or legal person from outside the public administration system"[13].

If both parties are legal persons under public law,

> "the contract is in principle an administrative contract"[14].

There is also an exception, according to which

> "if two public persons conclude a contract, it is in principle administrative, unless it produces judicial relationships of a private law nature"[15].

As we saw in the first part of this paper, the non-refundable financing contract within SOP HRD was concluded between the Management Authority, Intermediary Body and the Beneficiary. The Beneficiary of the financing contract can be a legal person under private law (firms, associations, foundations, etc.) or a legal person under public law (ministries, agencies, education inspectorates, city halls, etc.). Thus, the condition that at least one of the parties must be a public institution is observed, but it cannot be defining when establishing the judicial regime that is applicable to such a contract. In this respect, the distinction between the judicial regimes under public law and private law depends on the interest being promoted: public (general) or private. We consider defining the establishment of the interest pursued by the public administration through the financing contract. In this case, the question is whether the non-refundable financing contract pursues a general (public) interest or if it is only a new judicial form through which the national public administration exerts its intermediary role of

---

12 Emil Bălan, cited work, 2008, p. 160.

13 Ioan Alexandru, cited work, 2005, p. 412; Cătălin-Silviu Săraru, cited work, 2009, p. 185.

14 Ioan Alexandru, cited work, 2005, p. 413.

15 Eugen Popa, "Administrative Law", Bucharest, 2000, p.139.

administering European funds between the European Commission and the Beneficiary.

The object of the financing contract within SOP HRD is the approval of non-refundable financing by the MA SOP HRD /IB SOP HRD to the Beneficiary in order to implement the selected Programme as it is described in the Financing Request, submitted during the projects bid launching process. The Beneficiary is granted non-refundable financing under the terms and conditions established through the contract and its addenda. By signing the contract, the Beneficiary can accept the non-refundable financing and commits to implementing the project at its own risk, according to the provisions of the contract, and to Community and national legislation. At first sight of the above mentioned provisions, we can conclude that the public authority (MA SOP HRD / IB SOP HRD), by concluding the financing contract, does not directly pursue the general interest of those under its administration, but it has the role of ensuring that the amounts from non-refundable European funds are spent according to Community and national legislation. But if we analyse Community legislation as regards European Union cohesion policy, which is the basis for issuing documents relating to the structural programmes (European Social Fund, Cohesion Fund and European Regional Development Fund) allotted to Romania for 2007-2013, the financing contract does not only comprise a judicial instrument through which amounts of money from European funds are transferred to beneficiaries. The Beneficiary – by signing the contract – commits to implementing the financed project in order to achieve the objectives of the priority axis[16] established within the Operational Programme which results from the general objective of European Union cohesion policy, whose aim is

> "reducing existing discrepancies between different regions of Europe by using the financial resources redistribution mechanism within the Union"

in order to promote harmonious development of the entire Union. The existence of the financial resources redistribution mechanism within the European Union is justified-by promoting the general interest of the EU of

> "harmonious, balanced and durable development of the Community".

By signing the financing contract, the Beneficiary contributes to project implementation and to promoting the general interest of the EU, while the goal of the public authority is to ensure that the Beneficiary acts to promote the public interest pursued through the project.

---

16 According to European Regulation 1083/2006, the priority axis represents "one of the priorities of the strategy in an operational programme comprising a group of operations which are related and have specific measurable goals".

Furthermore, European regulations explicitly state that the funds were created to support Member States' policies. The European Social Fund, which finances the projects within SOP HRD, supports

> "Member States' policies aiming to achieve full employment and quality and productivity at work, promote social inclusion, including the access of disadvantaged people to employment, and reduce national, regional and local employment disparities"[17].

In our opinion, the public national administration, by concluding the financing contract within SOP HRD, undertakes to act as intermediary between the European Commission and the Beneficiary in order to oversee the accomplishment of general (public) interest activities by legal persons under private or public law.

The non-refundable financing contract seems to be a genuine administrative contract, governed in principle by the public law regime, bearing in mind that:

a) one contract party always exercises public authority: Management Authority/ Intermediary Body;

b) the Management Authority/ Intermediary Body act as owners of public authority stemming from the general interest they are promoting, and reserve the right to impose the superiority of their position through contract clauses;

c) the authority of the Management Authority/ IB to conclude financing contracts with beneficiaries is provided by law;

d) the object of the financing contract is to grant non-refundable financing in order to implement a project by legal persons under public or private law that promotes the public interest; thus

> "the general theory of why the public administration exists – to serve the general interest".

We have to mention that the projects implemented within SOP HRD do not always generate income

e) financing contract clauses are pre-established through Order by the Secretary of State, the Beneficiary only has the possibility to adhere to them. Contractual freedom is subordinated to the public interest principle;

f) the Management Authority/ IB has the right to take unilateral, executory measures. The Authority can modify or terminate the contract if required in the public interest without addressing the courts.

g) the non-refundable financing contract is concluded for a limited period. Thus, depending on the type of strategic project or on the grant, the financing contract can be concluded for a period of maximum 3 years, in the case of strategic projects, or maximum 2 years, in the case of grants.

---

17 Art. 2 of European Regulation 1081/2006.

We have to mention that, as far as both the non-refundable financing contract within SOP HRD and the vast majority of administrative contracts are concerned, breaches by the public authority of its assumed obligations do not invoke sanctions. According to the financing contract, MA SOP HRD / IB SOP HRD commit to reimbursing expenses on request by the Beneficiary within maximum 30 (thirty) calendar days of submission of the request. According to the list of payments made by MA SOP HRD between 29 June and 18 July 2012[18], payments to Beneficiaries were delayed by at least 6 months. The length of delay depends on who submits the reimbursement request. For example, in the case of the project implemented by SC Acz Consulting Ltd, expenses submitted by the Regional Intermediary Body SV for SOP HRD on 30 January 2012 were reimbursed on 2 July 2012[19]. The reimbursement request submitted by Forensics Institute in Iasi on 11 May 2011 to the Intermediary Body SOP HRD -MECTS was paid on 4 July 2012.

The provisions of the financing contract do not mention any sanctions for breaches of contract terms by the public administration. The only option open to the Beneficiary is to instigate court proceedings. In our opinion, the financing contract should contain provisions that impose financial penalties on the public authority MA/IB SOP HRD for delays in reimbursing expenses to Beneficiaries.

The inequality of the parties to the non-refundable financing contract for SOP HRD is also reflected by the provisions of Art. 9 (A), according to which the Beneficiary is obligated to request the conclusion of an additional contract by MA SOP HRD or by IB SOP HRD, under the following conditions:

> "(...) on explicit request, in written form, submitted on behalf of MA SOP HRD /IB SOP HRD delegate.
>
> MA SOP HRD/IB SOP HRD reserves the right to amend the contract clauses by forcing the beneficiary to request the amendment through Additional Act".

In July 2012, MA SOP HRD requested the Beneficiaries, on the basis of Art. 9 A of the financing contract and on the provisions of Order MMFPS no. 882/25.05.2012, to approve additional acts to the agreements governing the delegation of functions related to the implementation of the Sectoral Operational Programme "Human Resources Development 2007-2013", and to initiate an Additional Act to amend the financing contract in respect of the contract parties. Thus, certain financing contracts concluded by MA SOP HRD have been taken

18 Document available online: http://www.fseromania.ro/index.php/implementeaza/plati, date of last access: 10 September 2012.

19 Document available online: http://www.fseromania.ro/index.php/implementeaza/plati, List of payments made by MA SOP HRD between 29 June and 18 July 2012, date of last access 10 September 2012.

over by Regional Intermediary Bodies SOP HRD. The Beneficiaries found themselves in the situation of having to request amendment of the contract provisions based on which their project, which was administered by MA SOP HRD until the date of approval of the Additional Act, was taken over by an IB SOP HRD.

3. Conclusions

The development of a management and control system that is able to administer non-refundable European funds allotted to Romania represents a challenge for the public administration. After a period of about 4 years, the functional performance of such a system is being questioned, the staff at the authorities responsible for administering funds complain of being overworked, and beneficiaries are unsatisfied with the abuse of power by the administration. The main causes are: lack of transparency, excessive regulation and changing the "rules during the game" by the public administration, without first consulting the beneficiaries.

By analysing the features of the non-refundable financing contract within SOP HRD 2007-2013, we can observe that the public administration is in a superior position to that of the Beneficiary. As a framework contract, with no possibility to negotiate any of the clauses, the public administration reserves the right to amend contract clauses during project implementation without first consulting the Beneficiaries through additional acts, notifications of contract amendments or mere instructions issued by the manager of the Management Authority. Most of the time, these amendments occur very close to the end of the project implementation period, and the Beneficiaries are forced to tacitly accept the amendments or withdraw from the contract. Breaches by the Beneficiary of the "execution terms" of the financing contract, such as submitting pre-financing or reimbursement requests, can result in sanctions being applied by the public authority, including the unilateral termination of the financing contract. On the other hand, breaches by the public administration of its obligations, such as approving notifications by beneficiaries within 15 days and honouring reimbursement requests within 45 days as long as they were submitted according to the contract clauses and compliant with legislation, do not incur any sanctions or delay penalties. Indeed, the inequality of the parties in the case of administrative contracts is justified through

> "administration activity of organising law enforcement according to the competence conferred by judicial regulations in order to accomplish the general interest"[20].

---

20 Ioan Alexandru, cited work, 2005, p. 412.

But, we should not lose sight of the fact that this type of contract is not an authentic administrative contract.

The non-refundable financing contract seems to be a new judicial mechanism, in the context in which the public administration takes on a new role as intermediary between the European Commission and the Beneficiary, in order to accomplish the general interest of the European Union which is the

"harmonious, balanced and durable development of the Community".

BIBLIOGRAPHY

Alexandru, Ioan: Drept administrativ (Administrative Law), Lumina Lex Publishing House, Bucharest, 2005.

Bălan, Emil: Instituţii administrative (Administrative institutions), C.H. Beck Publishing House, Bucharest, 2008.

Caillosse, J.; Hardy, J. : Droit et modernisation administrative, La Documentation Française, Paris, 2000

Săraru, Cătălin-Silviu : Contractele administrative. Reglementare. Doctrină. Jurisprudenţă (Administrative contracts. Regulation. Doctrine. Jurisprudence), C.H. Beck Publishing House, Bucharest, 2009.

Popa, Eugen: Administrative Law, Bucharest, 2000.

Regulation of the Parliament and European Union Council no. 1083/2006 laying down general provisions on the European Regional Development Fund, the European Social Fund and the Cohesion Fund.

Regulation of the Parliament and European Union Council no. 1080/2006 on the European Regional Development Fund.

Regulation of the Parliament and European Union Council no. 1084/2006 on the Cohesion Fund.

Regulation of the Parliament and European Union Council no. 1081/2006 on the European Social Fund.

Regulation of the Parliament and European Union Council no 1828/2006 establishing rules for implementing Council Regulation no. 1083/2006 laying down general provisions on the European Regional Development Fund, the European Social Fund and the Cohesion Fund.

Analysis of the Sanctions Applicable to Unfair Contract Terms under Romanian Law

PhD student Liviu Titus PAVELIU[1]

Abstract

This paper presents the arguments supporting the idea, from the author's standpoint, that the sanction for unfair contract terms proposed by scholars and applied in practice is neither entirely efficient nor exact from a theoretical standpoint due to the recent changes brought to the Romanian Civil Code. As a result of the current legal frame, the author presents the case that deeming an unfair contract term not written is the best alternative to the established majority opinion that unfair contract terms should be rendered void.

Keywords: unfair contract terms, annulment, terms deemed not written.

1. Preliminary ideas. The usefulness of analysing unfair contract terms

The sanction applicable to unfair contract terms has been subject to an extended debate among scholars during the past decade. The recent changes made in Romanian legislation, primarily due to the recent enactment of the Civil Code[2], have determined the necessity to reopen the aforementioned debate.

Romanian legislation regarding unfair contract terms is not very clear or exact, mainly due to the relatively deficient implementation of the European provisions regarding unfair contract terms. As a result, the Romanian doctrine treated this conundrum by suggesting various sanctions which would correspond to the theoretical and practical standards to be met so that the problem of unfair contract terms may be dealt with in a compelling and constant manner from a legal standpoint. The majority opinion of the Romanian doctrine advocated that absolute nullity is the best solution in this regard.

One of the new institutions brought by the Civil Code is the sanction through which a contract clause is deemed not written. Although absolute nullity is a correct solution in terms of correlating other established institutions, such as vices of consent or cause of the contract, we can consider that, given recent European case law[3], deeming a contract term not written may have been the solu-

---

1 Liviu Titus Paveliu, Bucharest University of Economic Studies, Romania, titus.paveliu@gmail.com.

2 Law no. 287/2009, published in Official Journal no. 505, 15 July 2011.

3 Case C-453/10 Perenicova and Perenic against SOS finance.

tion which the EU lawmakers had in mind when drafting the directive regarding unfair contract terms.

Until recently, deeming a contract term not written was considered to be an innovative solution, accepted only by a small group of scholars. However, given that this sanction now benefits from being regulated in the Civil Code, we consider this solution to be a real alternative against unfair contract terms. In the following sections we will present the arguments in favour of deeming contract terms not written as the proper solution against unfair contract terms and we will highlight the advantages of it in relation to other remedies present in current Romanian legislation.

2. European requirements and provisions in relation to unfair contract terms

2.1. Legal background and context of the Directive

In European law the main legal source for this matter is Directive 93/13/EEC regarding unfair terms in consumer contracts[4]. Aside from the European provisions, Romanian legislation has managed to assure a minimal level of protection for consumers, but nothing more.

It's a known fact that the Directive has ambiguities[5] and gaps[6], which is however understandable, given that the scope of the directive is to establish principles and ways of thought, and subsequently the Member States would have to solve the ambiguities and gaps with proper legislation in order to establish a protection mechanism with wide array of application.

According to a study made by the European Commission[7], there are two theories regarding the evaluation of contract terms.

The first theory is based on the evaluation of the transaction cost. In a contract where a party offers a set of predetermined contract terms, it is reasonable to assume that the given party has a better understanding of the content and practical implications of the terms. In relation to accession contracts, given that

4 Published in the Official Journal of the EC no. 95 dated 21 April 1993.

5 In this regard, the essential notions for the implementation of the directive provisions are not clearly stipulated. Thus, it's not clear if a significant imbalance must be caused by a breach of good faith, or if this is a separate condition, in which case both conditions should be met for the application of the provision, see Art. 3(1) of the directive.

6 The Directive does not offer criteria to assess if an imbalance is significant or not.

7 Martin Ebers, Comparative analysis. C. Unfair contract terms directive (93/13), in Consumer Law Compendium, p.354.

a professional uses the same terms in several other contracts he saves money which otherwise would have been spent on legal costs associated with the negotiation and review of the contract terms. Thus, prior to concluding an accession contract with a professional, it is very likely that the consumer does not have the necessary funds in order to seek proper legal advice in order to negotiate and understand the content of the contract. Aside from the field of consumer protection, the same discrepancy from a financial standpoint, which would be reflected in a lack of negotiating power and diminished access to top legal advice, may occur even between professionals. In order to avoid such imbalances, countries such as Germany and Holland[8] have extended the unfair terms theory in order for it to apply to contracts concluded among private persons and professionals, not just in relation to consumers.

The second theory is predicated on the abuse theory, according to which unfair terms are mainly used against weaker contracting parties. The base of this theory does not rely on accession contracts, rather the superior economic, social, intellectual and psychological stature of the professional which leads the consumer to accept the contract as a 'given' with no option to negotiate. In order to remedy this situation, the validity of the contract will be interpreted while taking into account the imbalance in power and knowledge[9]. Basically, this theory focuses on protecting the weaker party regardless of whether the professional uses an accession contract or contracts negotiated formally with the consumer.

In light of the aforementioned theories, Romania has set out a system similar to the one based on the abuse theory, thus placing it in the group of Member States which resumed their legislation only to B2C (business to consumer) contracts and only in regard to negotiated terms.

2.2. Provisions of the European legislation

The primary norm which grants protection to the consumer in contractual matters is regulated by Article 6 Para. 1 of Directive 93/13/EEC according to which

> "Member States shall lay down that unfair terms used in a contract concluded with a consumer by a seller or supplier shall, as provided for under their national law, not be binding on the consumer and that the contract shall continue to bind the parties upon those terms if it is capable of continuing in existence without the unfair terms".

Given that unfair terms have been regulated through a Directive, it was up to the national lawmakers to choose and implement the legal institutions which they considered adequate to protect the consumer, while also respecting the European

8 Ibidem, p. 351.
9 Ibidem, p. 352.

provisions. To a large extent, the Romanian law represents a copy of the European provisions. This approach was criticised heavily, but it was also defensible on the grounds of harmonisation of the legal provisions as stated in the preamble of the Directive, according to which,

> "in particular the laws of Member States relating to unfair terms in consumer contracts show marked divergences".

Judging from the wording used in the Directive, namely that unfair terms will *not be binding on the consumer* we can affirm that the sanction is very vague.

Recent case law[10] of the European Union Court of Justice indirectly supported this opened approach by (i) imposing a cap regarding consumer protection and (ii) by invoking contractual balance, as being the criteria which will be taken into account when assessing the unfair nature of a contract term. These arguments highlight the fact that the national mechanism against unfair terms shall not be strict, but rather susceptible to nuances, which will come by way of case law. This approach proves conflicting points with the well-established and strict legal regime of nullity. As a result, this leads us to believe that the intention of the Directive and case law is to open the door for modern and innovative sanctions, such as deeming a terms not written.

3. Solution chosen by Romanian lawmakers.

3.1. National law provisions

According to Art. 4 Para. 1 of Law no. 193/2000 regarding unfair terms in contracts concluded between consumers and professionals[11]

> "a contract term which has not been directly negotiated between the consumer and the professional will be deemed as unfair if the term, in contradiction with good faith to the prejudice of the consumer, by itself has created an imbalance between the rights and obligations of the parties".

These provisions are not very strict from a legal standpoint[12], thus in case of a dispute the judge has a lot of leeway in assessing if a term is unfair.

---

10 Case C-453/10 Perenicova and Perenic against SOS finance.

11 Published in Official Journal no. 305, 18 April 2008.

12 Dumba, D., Unele considerații critice în legatură cu Legea nr. 193/2000 privind clauzele abuzive din contractele încheiate între comercianți și consumatori, precum și cu modificările aduse acesteia prin Legea nr. 65/2002, in "Dreptul" no. 6/2002, p.72, in the au-

It should be noted that the term "*abuziv*" in Romanian is not adequate from a legal terminology standpoint, because this word is mainly associated with abuse of power or abuse of a right[13].

An unfair term as defined by the law does not take into account the pre-existent financial imbalance, the privileged position or the monopoly of a party (which is often the reason for specific price policies)[14]. The purpose of the legal provision is to raise consumer awareness and knowledge regarding their rights and obligations in the contract so that they can take a well-informed decision in relation to the risk they are undertaking.

Thus, we figure that it's advisable and better to use terminology closer to that used in the English and German translation, meaning "unfair" and "miss-bräuchlich".

The recommended translation of the respective terms would be "*clauză neloială*", "*necinstită*", "*nedreaptă*" or "*injustă*" (meaning in English unfaithful, misleading, dishonest and unjust). Although these Romanian terms are not well established in the field of legal terminology, they prove to be more compatible with the notion of good faith in relation to its roles as (i) a code of conduct (loyalty), (ii) a requirement when executing obligations[15] according to Art. 14 Civil Code and (iii) a factor in evaluating the contractual balance between the parties involved. These correlations regarding good faith present relevance in our research given that good faith is at the core of consumer protection in contracts, as set out by the law and the Directive.

Another advantage brought to consumer protection is set out by Article 6 of law 193/2000, according to which,

> "unfair contract terms challenged personally, or by the competent authorities, will not have any effects on the consumer and the contract will continue to be executed, with the consent of the consumer, if the contract can still exist after the removal of the unfair terms".

---

thor's opinion, the use of subjective concepts, such as good faith and contractual balance, is likely to lead to practical difficulties in applying the law.

13 Turcu, I., Noul Cod civil republicat. Cartea a V-a. Comentarii şi explicaţii. Second edition, CH Beck Publishing House, Bucharest, 2011, p. 320: "Although the text uses the phrasing 'unfair terms', it's clear that in fact it refers to clauses, which given their abusive nature, should be deemed unwritten".

14 See also Art.4 (6) of the law: "The assessment of the unfair nature of the terms will not be based on the object of the contract, nor on the price and the goods and services offered in return, but on the extent to which the terms are expressed in an understandable language".

15 In the field of consumer legislation, the aforementioned obligation refers to the requirement that the professional should inform the consumer about the content of the pre-formulated terms.

Thus, we consider it necessary to highlight preferential treatment, exaggerated even by consumer standards, by which the faith of the contract is dependent upon the consumer's desire. This option granted to the consumer clearly bears no resemblance to the philosophy intended by the lawmakers.

3.2. Thoughts regarding Romanian legislation

In Article 7 of Law 193/2000 the lawmaker decided to implement the institution of severance (in Romanian "reziliere") in case the contract cannot exist without the unfair terms. This way of action has been heavily critiqued by scholars[16], given that there are practical and theoretical arguments against it.

Firstly, severance occurs if a party does not fulfil its obligation in a contract which is executed over a period of time. Although contracts concluded between professionals and consumers are usually of this nature, if severance is the only sanction imposed by the law this would leave *uno ictu* contracts without a real remedy. As a solution, future enactments of the law should consist of severance and termination (specific to *uno ictu* contracts, in Romanian "rezoluțiune").

Secondly, the law provides that specialised public authorities may challenge in court the contract containing unfair terms. Thus, given the right granted to the authorities and the right of the judge to invoke absolute nullity ex officio, legal doctrine[17] has highlighted the fact that severance does not comply from a theoretical standpoint with the practical ways to combat unfair terms. Furthermore, severance as a sanction would also limit the number of people who can invoke it, i.e. other than the consumer, only the consumers' creditors may take the course of legal action.

Thirdly, severance represents a cause of contract ineffectiveness which occurs after the signing of the contract[18], whereas the occurrence of unfair terms implies two events that take place before conclusion of the contract, namely the lack of negotiations and failure to comply with the obligation to inform the consumer.

---

16 Popa, I. Fl., Reprimarea clauzelor abuzive, in P.R. n. 2/2004, p. 215; Toader, C., Ciobanu, A., Un pas important spre integrarea europeană: Legea nr. 193/2000 privind clauzele abuzive, Ordonanța Guvernului nr. 87/2000 privind răspunderea producătorilor şi Ordonanţa Guvernului nr. 130/2000 privind contractele la distanţă, in R.D.C. n. 3/2001 p. 77; Dumba, D., cited work, p. 73; Belu Magdo, M.-L., Clauzele abuzive în contractele incheiate intre comercianţi şi consumatori, in R.D.C. n. 12/2006 p.12.

17 Belu Magdo, M.-L., cited work, p.13.

18 Stoica, V., Rezoluțiunea şi rezilierea contractelor civile, All Educational Publishing House, Bucharest, 1997, p. 57-59.

Lastly, severance and termination as regulated by law 193/2000 do not comply with the provisions of the Civil Code for the same institutions, in that only one party may invoke them. In the case of unfair terms, severance is the result of actions which do not comply with obligations stated by law[19], as opposed to the general rule, according to which severance occurs in case a contractual obligation is not fulfilled.

Apparently unjust, the sanction to terminate the contract has been backed up by the European Union Court of Justice in case C-453/10 according to which the protection and legal frame granted to consumer contracts must not lead to an imbalance in the consumers' favour, so that saving the fate of the contract should not lead to extremes and ultimately lead to it being ineffective.

Thus, the best course of action is for the consumer to unilaterally terminate the contract if the contract may not continue to be effective and both parties are not inclined to modify the content of the unfair terms[20].

3.3. Analysing the past arguments of the legal doctrine

The phrasing "the terms will not produce effects" outlines the results of several civil sanctions which may apply to the validity of a contract. In this regard, legal doctrine[21] has presented a series of arguments in order to establish the proper interpretation of this text, from a theoretical standpoint.

Some authors[22] expressed their opinion that either relative nullity is the proper sanction, given its close ties with vices of consent, or absolute nullity, based on the lack of cause[23].

It is generally accepted that a professional's goal is to maximise its profits as a result of the contracts it concludes with consumers, but not in prejudice or at the expense of the consumer. This goal in and of itself is not enough in order to qualify the actions and intentions of the professional as being unlawful, or to be viewed as a breach of good faith in the relation with the consumer.

---

19 Popa, I. Fl., cited work, p.215.

20 After systematic interpretation, it can be found that – although unilateral termination was the envisioned applicable institution –the lawmakers chose to use severance/termination.

21 Popa, I. Fl., cited work, p.213; Toader, C., Ciobanu, cited work, p.78; Belu Magdo, M-L, cited work, p.12.

22 Dumba, D, cited work, p.73.

23 Popa, F., Eficacitatea sancţiunilor contractuale în materia viciilor de consimţământ, Revista de Ştiinţe Juridice, n. 1/2006 p. 80, footnote 12. The author indicates French doctrine in order to show that an unfair term can be founded on the lack of cause, in which case absolute nullity would be applicable.

Error on behalf of the consumer is not technically possible given the professional's obligation to inform the consumer of their rights and obligations. Moreover, the Civil Code states that the party opposed to the one who proposed the terms is obligated to initial each page of the contract in order to avoid the presumption of unacquaintance with the contract terms.

Added to which, for a term to be deemed unfair, it is necessary for that term to not have been directly negotiated with the consumer, which implies lack of negotiation. Thus error on behalf of the consumer cannot be applicable because it implies a false understanding of the contract, whereas in case of a non-negotiated term they have no knowledge whatsoever of it.

Misleading and error as vices of consent do not apply in the field of unfair terms, because the latter deals with the substance and identity of the contract, whereas the former strictly applies to cooperation between the parties and execution of the contract in good faith.

4. Arguments for deeming a contract term not written to be the best solution against unfair contract terms

4.1. Hypothesis

We cannot deny the fact that absolute nullity covers a lot of the gaps in legislation, however in the following we will present the arguments supporting a newly regulated sanction in the Civil Code, namely deeming a contract term not written, as being a valid alternative in dealing with unfair contract terms.

This sanction is not new to Romanian doctrine; until recently it was viewed as *unspecific* for Romanian law, and that the range of sanctions offered by national law was enough to meet the Directive's standards for eliminating unfair terms.

The counter-arguments brought by well-established scholars in the field of consumer protection[24] were that none of the sanctions used in consumer law were specific from the point of view of conservative national law. This theory exists and is supported in several countries, and its success has mainly been driven by the efforts of the scholars and case law.

24 Goicovici, J., Riscul de dezvoltare, in "Dreptul" no. 9 / 2004, p. 13-46, Popa, F., cited work, p. 82.

A similar situation regarding the origin of foreign induced legal notions has been presented by foreign authors[25] in relation to good faith. They highlighted the lack of flexibility in national legislations.

4.2. Enactment of deeming a term not written in the context of the Civil Code

With the enactment of the new Civil Code, nullity has benefited from a detailed approach in comparison with the previous legislation. Related to this institution are the contract terms deemed not written which represent a different sanction from that of nullity, although both demonstrate several similarities, which will be detailed in the following paragraphs.

The main provision for deeming a terms not written is Art. 1255 Civil Code which defines partial nullity. By interpreting *per a contrario* the conditions required to apply partial nullity, we can reveal the situations in which deeming a term not written applies. According to Article 1255 (1) Civil Code

> "A sanction of total nullity will be imposed on contract terms that are contrary to law, public order or morale, and which are not deemed not written, only if – according to their nature – the terms are essential, and in their absence the contract would not have been concluded".

An interpretation of this Article reveals that partial nullity is different from terms deemed not written, and that they do not refer to terms which are essential to the contract.

By using the phrase "will not have effects on the consumer" in Article 6 of law 193/2000, the lawmaker practically avoided pinpointing the applicable solution. The lack of precise regulation of this provision presents a current counterargument to the sanction of deeming terms not written, however it cannot be denied that at least as lex ferenda, not written contract terms respond in an effective[26] manner to the problem of unfair contract terms.

Furthermore, by correlating the provisions of Art. 1255 (1) and (3) we consider that – given that the contract terms are not essential – they are secondary/accessory terms. Thus, limiting the field of application for this prominent

---

25 Zimmerman, R. Introduction to European contract law, 2001, p.23.

26 Popa, F., cited work, p.79, "The effectiveness of sanctions in altering consent, regardless of whether they are preventive or restorative, depends, on the one hand, on their effectiveness, and on the other hand the capacity to adapt to the effects of the aims of sanctions".

sanction, we find this approach to be geared towards assuring the stability of the civil contract by way of trying to save the existence of the affected contract[27].

Given the importance of the terms to which they apply, we support the idea that partial nullity and deeming not written represent more practical sanctions than relative and absolute nullity when the salvation of the contract is in discussion.

4.3. Legal regime of terms deemed not written and differences relating to nullity

As a rule, we consider unfair contract terms to be a cause of contractual imbalance, which in principle is remediable, but by no means grounds for terminating a contract. From our standpoint, the legal regime of unfair contract terms is designed to salvage contracts, albeit with exceptions, such as when a contract has too many unfair contract terms which, if removed, would make the contract ineffective from a legal standpoint.

The Directive and the Romanian law contain an appendix, otherwise known as "black list", where several terms are designated unfair regardless of the context. An analysis of this list leads to the conclusion that none of the terms are related to the main and specific clauses agreed upon in a contract between a consumer and a professional.

A key difference between the terms nullity and not written is that the former relates to secondary terms, whereas the latter may apply to any type of term. Thus, scholars have used this broader application to argue in favour of nullity being the sanction for unfair terms.

However, our opinion is supported by arguments used by the European Union Court of Justice[28], according to which

> "national courts are required solely to exclude the application of such a term in order that it does not produce binding effects with regard to the consumer, without having the power to revise the content of that term".

As a result, if a judge rules that a term is unfair, he will not have the competence to review the content of the term, consequently he will not be able to rule in relation to the parties' will in respect of the contract. However, regardless of the nature of the claim, the judge may determine that a term is void ex officio if the case may be.

---

27 Baias, F.A., Constantinovici, R., Chelaru, E., Macovei, I. Noul Cod civil. Comentariu pe articole Art. 1 – 2664, CH Beck Publishing House, Bucharest, 2012, p.1315.

28 Case C-618/10 Banco Espanol de Credito SA vs. Joaqin Calderon Camino.

In practical terms, filing a claim to determine the existence of unfair terms in a contract can re-establish the contractual balance rather than leading to annulment of the contract.

Another practical consequence is that, by filing a claim to determine the existence of unfair terms, the given terms will be not analysed in substance, but rather in how they became part of the contract. In this regard, the law[29] imposes a relative presumption that the professional has not negotiated with the consumer. This presumption creates a great advantage for consumers who only have to prove the existence of the clause in the contract[30], whereas professionals face the more difficult task of proving that they negotiated directly, and not just formally[31], with the consumers[32].

The nature of deeming a term not written is very controversial, mainly because some consider it to be a type of nullity with the extra quality of being effective by virtue of the law[33], which is similar to de jure nullities, but nowadays distinct from them. The reason for associating not written terms closely with partial nullity clauses is mainly due to the almost identical effects they produce[34].

5. Conclusions

Directive 93/13/EEC and Law 193/2000 have managed to impose a minimum protection mechanism for consumers in contractual matters, which have been confirmed in practice by legal disputes won by consumers. Although Romanian lawmakers failed to eliminate the ambiguities of the Directive, this problem has been solved through national doctrine and the case law of the European Union Court of Justice. However, we are of the opinion that – in order to understand the law and to avoid legal standstills –lawmakers must strive to enact proper and complete legislation.

---

29 See Art. 4 (3) Law 193/2000: if a professional claims that a pre-formulated term has been negotiated with the consumer, it is his duty to provide evidence in this regard.

30 Goicovici, J., cited work, p. 43.

31 See Art. 4 (3) of the law, "The fact that certain contract terms, or just a few, have been directly negotiated with the consumer, does not exempt the application of this law to the rest of the contract, which would require a global evaluation of the contract in order to assess if the terms were unilaterally imposed by the professional".

32 See Art. 3 (2) Directive 93/13/EEC.

33 Boroi, G, Carla, C.A. Curs de drept civil. Partea generala, Hamangiu Publishing House, Bucharest, 2011.

34 Baias, F.A., Constantinovici, R., Chelaru, E., Macovei, I., cited work, p.1315.

At present, given the institutions and provisions of the Romanian Civil Code, we support the idea that the proper remedy against unfair contract terms is deeming them not written. In this regard, a not written contract represents a means of salvaging a contract, and also highlights the arguments and principles used in recent cases by the European Union Court of Justice. Thus, in order to promote certainty in legal relationships and to improve the protection mechanism against unfair contract terms, we propose that deeming a clause not written should be expressly stated as the sanction for unfair contract terms.

Bibliography

Apan, R. D.: Protecţia juridică a consumatorilor – Creditul destinat consumului şi domeniile conexe, Sfera Juridică Publishing House, Cluj Napoca, 2007.

Baias, F.A., Constantinovici, R., Chelaru, E., Macovei, I.: Noul Cod civil. Comentariu pe articole. Art. 1 – 2664, CH Beck Publishing House, Bucharest, 2012.

Belu Magdo, M.-L.: Clauzele abuzive în contractele încheiate între comercianţi şi consumatori, in R.D.C. n. 12/2006.

Boroi, G, Carla, C.A.: Curs de drept civil. Partea generală, Hamangiu Publishing House, Bucharest, 2011.

Bălan, I.: Clauzele abuzive din contractele încheiate între comercianţi şi consumatori, in "Dreptul" no. 6/2001.

Dumba, D., Unele consideraţii critice în legătură cu Legea nr. 193/2000 privind clauzele abuzive din contractele încheiate între comercianţi şi consumatori, precum şi cu modificările aduse acesteia prin Legea nr. 65/2002, in "Dreptul" no. 6/2002.

Ebers. M.: Comparative analysis. C. Unfair contract terms directive (93/13), in Consumer Law Compendium, (http://www.eu-consumerlaw.org/consumerstudy_part2c_en.pdf found on 30.07.2012).

Goicovici, J.: Riscul de dezvoltare, in "Dreptul" no. 9 / 2004.

Popa, I. Fl.: Reprimarea clauzelor abuzive, in P.R. no. 2/2004.

Popa, F.: Eficacitatea sancţiunilor contractuale în materia viciilor de consimţământ, Revista de Ştiinţe Juridice, no.1/2006.

Stoica, V.: Rezolutiunea şi rezilierea contractelor civile, All Educational Publishing House, Bucharest, 1997.

Toader, C., Ciobanu, A.: Un pas important spre integrarea europeană: Legea nr. 193/2000 privind clauzele abuzive, Ordonanţa Guvernului nr. 87/2000 privind răspunderea producătorilor şi Ordonanţa Guvernului nr. 130/2000 privind contractele la distanţă, in R.D.C. no. 3/2001.

Turcu, I.: Noul Cod civil republicat. Cartea a V-a. Comentarii şi explicatii. Second edition, CH Beck Publishing House, Bucharest, 2011.

Zimmerman, R.: Introduction to European contract law, 2001.

European Works Council

PhD student Iulia BĂDOI[1]

Abstract

Without aiming to entirely cover the subject related to the establishment of a European Works Council or a procedure in Community-scale undertakings and Community-scale groups of undertakings for the purposes of informing and consulting employees, the present article's purpose is to assess some of the aspects concerning regulation at European level and the means of implementing Community provisions within national legislation. The need for legislative regulation within the above mentioned domain was emphasised by the recitals of Council Directive 94/45/EC. The constant social, economic and legislative changes, both at European and national level, have, over time, made it necessary to revise, modify and update the provisions of Council Directive 94/45/EC. The most recent amendment of Directive 94/45/EC led to the adoption of Directive 2009/38/EC of the European Parliament and of the Council, with some amendments mainly suggested by the European social partners.

Key words: European Works Council, employees' representatives, information, consultation, transnational.

1. Legal framework

1.1. Community legislation

The legislative framework for the European Works Council dates back to 1994 when Directive 94/45/EC/22.09.1994[2] on the establishment of a European Works Council or a procedure in Community-scale undertakings and Community-scale groups of undertakings for the purposes of informing and consulting employees was adopted by the EU Council based on Protocol No. 14 on social politics, annexed to the Maastricht Treaty from 1992, which obliged the Member States to implement the Community's regulations within the social domain. The agreement on social politics, annexed to Protocol No. 14, imposed the social dialogue in Article 3. The 1997 Amsterdam Treaty integrated Protocol No.

---

1 Iulia Bădoi, Bucharest University of Economic Studies, Romania, Email: iulia.badoi@yahoo.com.

2 Published in the EU's Official Journal L254/30.09.1994, modified by Directive 97/74/EC, published in the EU's Official Journal L10/16.01.1998, modified by Directive 2006/109/EC, published in the EU's Official Journal L363/20.12.2006, abrogated by Directive 2009/38/EC, published in the EU's Official Journal L 122/28/16.05.2009.

14 to the Community's acquis such that Art. 137 Para. no. 137, letter E of the EU Treaty, amended by the 2001 Nice Treaty, provides the obligation of the European Commission to support and to complete the Member States' actions in respect of informing and consulting employees[3].

The legal framework needed to be adapted to the evolution of the legislative, economic and social environment, and to become clearer. After consulting the European social partners and carrying out an impact assessment, the Commission submitted in 2008 a proposal to recast the Directive. This new Directive was adopted in 2009 by the European Parliament and the Council, with some amendments mainly suggested by the European social partners.

Building on the results of the existing legal framework, recast Directive 2009/38/EC aims, in particular, to ensure the effectiveness of employees' transnational information and consultation rights, to promote the creation of new European Works Councils and to assure legal certainty in their establishment and operation[4].

As presented in the recitals of Directive 2009/38/EC, Community legislation on transnational employee information and consultation needs to be modernised with a view to ensuring the effectiveness of employees' transnational information and consultation rights, increasing the proportion of European Works Councils established while enabling the continuous functioning of existing agreements, resolving the problems encountered in the practical application of Directive 94/45/EC, and remedying the lack of legal certainty resulting from some of its provisions or the absence of certain provisions, and ensuring that Community legislative instruments on employee information and consultation are better linked[5].

Directive 2009/38/EC had to be transposed by Member States before 6 June 2011. On that date, the existing Directive 94/45/EC (as amended by Directive 97/74/ EC and Directive 2006/109/EC) was repealed and replaced with Directive 2009/38/EC.

National implementing measures for the repealed Directives were, however, maintained after 6 June 2011 in order to cover the cases where the new obligations introduced by Directive 2009/38/EC do not apply.

A window of opportunity of two years is provided by Directive 2009/38/EC for companies whereby agreements to establish new European Works Council are concluded between 5 June 2009 and 5 June 2011 or whereby existing

---

3 Ovidiu, Ţinca, Observaţii referitoare la Legea no. 217/2005 privind instituirea comitetului european de întreprindere, Revista de Drept Comercial, no. 2/2008, p. 25.

4 http://ec.europa.eu/social/, last accessed on 07.10.2012.

5 Recitals of the Directive 2009/38/EC, Para. 7.

agreements revised during this period are not bound by the new obligations introduced by Directive 2009/38/EC[6].

1.2. National legislation

During the process of assimilating the Community acquis, which became mandatory for Romania upon joining the EU, Law no. 217/2005[7] integrated the concept of the European Works Council into national labour legislation[8].

Law no. 217/2005 on the establishment, organisation and functioning of a European Works Council transposed Directive 94/45/EC into national legislation, and became binding when Romania became an EU Member State[9].

Following amendments to the above mentioned Directive, it became necessary to also update Law no. 217/2005 which was adapted to the Community provisions in the domain by regulatory acts adopted at national level as follows: Law no. 217/2005 was updated by Government Ordinance no. 48/2006, published in the Romanian Official Journal, Part I, no. 1.028/ 27 December 2006, by Law no. 186/2011, published in the Romanian Official Journal, Part I, no. 763/28 October 2011.

When the new Directive 2009/38/EC was adopted, Law no. 217/2005 was republished in the Romanian Official Journal, Part I, no. 889/15.12.2011, when it also become binding.

The law transposed into national legislation the recast Directive 2009/38/EC of the European Parliament and of the Council of 6 May 2009 on the establishment of a European Works Council or a procedure in Community-scale undertakings and Community-scale groups of undertakings for the purposes of informing and consulting employees[10].

2. Principles

The establishment of a European Works Council or a procedure in Community-scale undertakings and Community-scale groups of undertakings for the purposes of informing and consulting employees is set up on the basis of the Commu-

6 http://ec.europa.eu/social/, last accessed on 07.10.2012.

7 Law no. 217/05.07.2005, published in the Romanian Official Journal, Part I, no. 628/19.07.2005.

8 Ovidiu, Ţinca, Observaţii referitoare la Legea no. 217/2005 privind instituirea comitetului european de întreprindere, Revista de Drept Comercial, no. 2/2008, p. 25.

9 Law no. 217/2005, Art. 51.

10 www.juridice.ro, last accessed on 07.10.2012.

nity general principles and based on the principles developed by the recast Directive, which were also transposed into national legislation.

A) The principle of effectiveness

The arrangements for informing and consulting employees need to be defined and implemented in such a way as to ensure their effectiveness with regard to the provisions of this Directive. To that end, informing and consulting the European Works Council should make it possible for it to give an opinion to the undertaking in a timely fashion, without calling into question the ability of undertakings to adapt. Only dialogue at the level where directions are prepared and effective involvement of employees' representatives make it possible to anticipate and manage change[11].

This principle was also integrated into Law no. 217/2005, whose Art. 2 Para. 2 provides that the means of informing and consulting the employees as they were presented in the first paragraph are defined and are being applied based of the principle of effectiveness, so as to ensure that employees can effectively exercise their right to transnational information and consultation and to allow the Community-scale undertakings and Community-scale groups of undertakings to take efficient decisions.

Based on the effectiveness principle, it is necessary to clarify the concepts of employee information and consultation, with the objectives of reinforcing the effectiveness of dialogue at transnational level, permitting suitable linkage between the national and transnational levels of dialogue and ensuring the legal certainty required for the application of this Directive[12].

B) The principle of autonomy of the parties

In accordance with the principle of autonomy of the parties, it is for the representatives of employees and the management of the undertaking or the group's controlling undertaking to determine by agreement the nature, composition, the function, mode of operation, procedures and financial resources of European Works Councils or other information and consultation procedures so as to suit their own particular circumstances[13].

C) The principle of subsidiary

In accordance with the principle of subsidiary, it is for the Member States to determine who the employees' representatives are and in particular to provide, if they consider appropriate, for a balanced representation of different categories of employees[14].

---

11 Recitals of Directive 2009/38/EC, Para. 14.

12 Ibidem, Para. 21.

13 Ibidem, Para. 19.

14 Ibidem, Para. 20.

Compliance with the principle of subsidiary is also assured in cases where the Community adopts measures to ensure the fulfilment of the recast Directive's objective, when respecting the right to information and consultation of the employees in Community-scale undertakings and Community-scale groups of undertakings cannot be sufficiently achieved by the Member States and can therefore be better achieved at Community level[15].

D) The principle of efficiency

The arrangements for informing and consulting employees shall be defined and implemented in such a way as to ensure their effectiveness and to enable the undertaking or group of undertakings to take decisions effectively[16].

Thus, information and consultation of employees must occur at the relevant level of management and representation, according to the subject under discussion. To achieve that, the competence of the European Works Council and the scope of the information and consultation procedure for employees governed by this Directive shall be limited to transnational issues[17].

The definitions of "information" and "consultation" need to take account of the goal of allowing employees representatives to carry out an appropriate examination and of allowing for the expression of an opinion that will be useful to the decision-making process, which implies that the information be provided at such time, in such fashion and with such content as are appropriate without slowing down the decision-making process in undertakings[18].

E) The principle of proportionality

In compliance with the principle of proportionality the Directive does not go beyond what is necessary in order to achieve that objective[19].

F) The principle of cooperation/collaboration

Art. 9 of the recast Directive underlines that the relations between the central management and the European Works Council shall be governed in a spirit of cooperation with due regard to their reciprocal rights and obligations. The same obligation was transposed in the national legislation, with Art. 9 of republished Law no. 217/2005 mentioning that

> "the relations between the central management from Romania and the European Works Council are based on the principle of collaboration with due regard to their reciprocal rights and obligations".

---

15 Ibidem, Para. 45.

16 Directive 2009/38/EC, Art. 2 and 3.

17 Directive 2009/38/ EC, Art. 3 and republished Law no. 217/2005, Art. 3.

18 Recitals of Directive 2009/38/EC, Paras. 22 and 23.

19 Ibidem, Para. 45

By transposing the Community regulation, Law no. 217/2005 provides that this principle is also extended to the procedure of information and consultation of the employees:

> "the collaboration between the central management and the employees' representatives is also necessary within the procedure of informing and consulting employees".

G) The principle of confidentiality

Member States shall provide that members of special negotiating bodies or of European Works Councils and any experts who assist them are not authorised to reveal any information which has expressly been provided to them in confidence[20].

3. Recitals

The essential premises of the regulation governing European Works Councils and procedure in Community-scale undertakings and Community-scale groups of undertakings for the purposes of informing and consulting employees are presented in the recitals of Directive 94/45/EC and partially assumed, with the amendments imposed by the legislative, economic and social changes, by Directive 2009/38/EC which rendered the first mentioned Directive obsolete.

Thus, Directive 94/45/EC highlighted the reasons for needing a legal framework in the domain, as follows:

- The functioning of the internal market involves a process of concentrations of undertakings, cross-border mergers, take-overs, joint ventures and, consequently, a transnationalisation of undertakings and groups of undertakings. If economic activities are to develop in a harmonious fashion, undertakings and groups of undertakings operating in two or more Member States must inform and consult the representatives of those of their employees who are affected by their decisions[21].
- Otherwise, in the absence of a regulation that has to be transposed into the national legislation of the Member States, the effect could be the existence of an unequal treatment for the employees from the same undertakings and groups of undertakings[22].

---

20 Directive 2009/38/EC, Art. 8.

21 Recitals of Directive 94/45/EC, Para. 9.

22 Ion Traian Ştefănescu, Tratat teoretic şi practic de drept al muncii, Universul Juridic Publishing House, Bucharest, 2010, p. 131.

Although Directive 94/45/EC was abrogated by Directive 2009/38/EC, the above-mentioned recitals were also included in the recast Directive. The recitals of Directive 2009/38/EC also indicate the reasons that led to the recast of the Directive 94/45/EC:

> "In the interests of clarity, that Directive should be recast"[23].

The novelties inserted by the recast Directive on the establishment of a European Works Council or a procedure in Community-scale undertakings and Community-scale groups of undertakings for the purposes of informing and consulting employees mainly envisage the following:

- The definition and applicability of the means of information and consultation of the employees based on the efficiency principle, at the relevant level of management and representation;
- The delimitation between the competencies and the domain of intervention for the European Works Council and the national representation organisms;
- The limitation of the domain of intervention for the European Works Council to transnational matters. Directive 94/45/EC and the recast Directive mention this limitation in respect of the procedure of employee information and consultation. According to Art. 6[24] on the content of the agreement between the central management and the special negotiating body concerning the means of ensuring employee information and consultation, information refers mainly to transnational matters that seriously affect the employees' interests. What is new about the recast Directive 2009/38/EC is that the recitals show the necessity of restraining the domain of intervention of the European Works Council and establishing the transnational nature of a matter by taking account of both the scope of its potential effects, and the level of management and representation that it involves[25];
- The definition of the terms "information", "consultation", "transnational";
- The regulation of the obligation for the management of each undertaking from the undertakings group, as defined by Directive 2009/38/EC[26] and by republished Law no. 217/2005[27], to obtain and to transmit to the interested parties the necessary information in order to initiate the negotiations for establishing a European Works Council or a procedure on informing and consulting the employees;

23 Recitals of Directive 2009/38/EC, Para. 1.
24 Directive 94/45/EC.
25 Recitals of Directive 2009/38/EC, Para. 16.
26 Art. 4 Para. 4.
27 Art. 10.

- The amendment of the provisions related to the organisation of the European Works Council, to the establishment and operation of a select committee, to the meetings, to the content of the information and consultation[28];
- The regulation of the situation where the structure of the undertaking or group of undertakings changes significantly, in the absence of some provisions within the acting agreements or in the presence of some conflicts between the provisions of two or more applicable agreements[29];
- The recognition of the unions' organisational role in respect of the negotiation or renegotiation of agreements on establishing the European Works Council, by supporting employees' representatives who need such support[30];
- The insertion of provisions related to training the employees' representatives to enable them to perform their tasks[31]. The republished Law no. 217/2005 transposed the provision of the recast Directive by mentioning that training courses must be made available for the members of the special negotiating body and of the European Works Council[32].

4. Terms and definitions - novelties

With a view to accomplishing the objectives outlined by the recitals of the recast Directive and in the spirit of Art. 1 of the same Directive, it was necessary to define some terms and notions[33].

A new element is represented by the definition of the term *"transnational"*. A matter is considered to be transnational when, regardless of the number of Member States involved, it is important for the European workforce in terms of the scope of its potential effects or involves transfers of activities between Member States.

At the same time, a definition of the notion of "information" and redefinition of the term "consultation" were required.

In the spirit of the recast Directive *"information"* means the transmission of data by the employer to the employees' representatives in order to enable them to acquaint themselves with the subject matter and to examine it; information shall be given at such time, in such fashion and with such content as are appropriate to enable employees' representatives to undertake an in-depth assessment of the possible impact and, where appropriate, prepare for consultations with the

28 Directive 2009/38/EC, Art. 5, republished Law no. 217/2005, Chapter 3.

29 Republished Law no. 217/2005, Art. 25 and Recitals of Directive 2009/38/EC, Para. 40.

30 Directive 2009/38/EC, Art. 4 Para. 4.

31 Recitals of Directive 2009/38/EC, Para. 33.

32 Art. 48.

33 Directive 2009/38/EC, Art. 2.

competent organ of the Community-scale undertaking or Community-scale group of undertakings.

"Consultation" consists of the establishment of dialogue and exchange of views between employees' representatives and central management or any more appropriate level of management, at such time, in such fashion and with such content as enables employees' representatives to express an opinion on the basis of the information provided about the proposed measures to which the consultation is related, without prejudice to the responsibilities of the management, and within a reasonable time, which may be taken into account within the Community-scale undertaking or Community-scale group of undertakings. The term consultation was redefined in the spirit of the principles of efficiency and effectiveness.

The recast Directive maintained the other definitions previously used in Directive 94/45/EC with its amendments. These definitions relate to the terms: Community-scale undertaking, group of undertakings, Community-scale group of undertakings, employees' representatives, central management, European Works Council, special negotiating body, controlling undertaking.

5. Applicability of the provisions of the recast Directive 2009/38/EC

Directive 2009/38/EC applies to Community-Scale undertakings and Community-scale groups of undertakings in order to improve employees' rights to information and consultation[34]. In the spirit of the recast Directive, *"Community-scale undertaking"* means any undertaking with at least 1 000 employees within the Member States and at least 150 employees in each of at least two Member States.

"Group of undertakings" was defined as being a group composed by a controlling undertaking and its controlled undertakings.

In order for a *"group of undertakings"* to be considered of *"Community-scale"* it must:

- have at least 1 000 employees within the Member States;
- comprise at least two group undertakings in different Member States;
- comply with the rule of having at least one group undertaking with at least 150 employees in one Member State and at least one other group undertaking with at least 150 employees in another Member State.

34 Directive 2009/38/EC, Art. 1.

As from 6 June 2011, European Works Councils must be established and operate within the framework of recast Directive 2009/38/EC through its implementing provisions in the Member States[35].

The obligations arising from this Directive shall not apply to Community-scale undertakings or Community-scale groups of undertakings in which either an agreement or agreements covering the entire workforce and providing for the transnational information and consultation of employees have been concluded pursuant to Article 13(1) of Directive 94/45/EC or Article 3(1) of Directive 97/74/EC, or where such agreements are adjusted because of changes in the structure of the undertakings or groups of undertakings; or an agreement concluded pursuant to Article 6 of Directive 94/45/EC is signed or revised between 5 June 2009 and 5 June 2011[36].

There is no general obligation to renegotiate the agreements establishing European Works Councils in the new directive. In addition, since the first directive, an incentive has been given for early establishment of European Works Councils, in advance of the legal requirements. Those companies which had agreements in place providing for the transnational information and consultation of their entire workforce when the directive first took effect in 1996 are not subject to the obligations arising from the new directive. The same applies in relation to the extension of the directive to the UK in 1999. The continuity of such agreements is ensured by Directive 2009/38/EC[37].

6. The role of the European Works Council

The recast Directive foresees three means of accomplishing the established objective[38]:

- The negotiation of an agreement between the central management and the special negotiating body in order to establish a European Works Council;
- The central management and the special negotiation body don't set up a European Works Council, but conclude a written agreement by which they establish the initiation of one or more procedures on informing and consulting the employees;

35 Directive 2009/38/EC, Art. 17.

36 Directive 2009/38/EC, Art. 14.

37 http://ec.europa.eu/social/, last accessed on 07.10.2012.

38 Ovidiu, Ţinca, Observaţii referitoare la Legea no. 217/2005 privind instituirea comitetului european de întreprindere, Revista de Drept Comercial, Anul XVIII, no. 2/2008, p. 35

- The European Works Council may be constituted, without the negotiation of an agreement, based on the subsidiary requirements of Art. 7 of the Directive 2009/38/EC and the provisions of the directive's annexes.

European Works Councils are bodies representing the European employees of a company. Through them, workers are informed and consulted at transnational level by management on the progress of the business and any significant decision that could affect them.

The right to establish European Works Councils was introduced by Directive 94/45/EC for undertakings or groups of undertakings employing at least 1000 employees in the European Union and the other countries of the European Economic Area (Iceland, Liechtenstein and Norway) with at least 150 employees in each of two Member States. Some 970 European Works Councils represent over 15 million employees, encouraging social dialogue and anticipation of change in transnational companies[39].

The central management shall be responsible for creating the conditions and means necessary to set up a European Works Council or an information and consultation procedure, as provided for in Article 1(2), in a Community-scale undertaking and a Community-scale group of undertakings[40].

Central management means the central management of the Community-scale undertaking or, in the case of a Community-scale group of undertakings, of the controlling undertaking. Art. 3 of the recast Directive and Art. 6 Para. 6 of Romanian Law no. 217/2005 establish the conditions under which an undertaking is considered to be the controlling undertaking.

The special negotiating body which represents the employees in the negotiations aiming at concluding an agreement on a European Works Council is composed of one representative for each 10 % of the employees in a Member State. It has the right to meet alone before and after any meeting with the central management[41].

The competent European trade union and employers' organisations are to be informed of the start of negotiations to enable them to monitor the establishment of new European Works Councils and promote best practice[42]. Trade unions are also among the experts on whom the special negotiating body may call for assistance in the negotiations[43].

---

39 http://ec.europa.eu/social/, last accessed on 07.10.2012.

40 Directive 2009/38/EC, Art. 4 Para. 1 and republished Law no. 217/2005, Art. 9.

41 http://ec.europa.eu/social/, last accessed on 07.10.2012.

42 Recitals of Directive 2009/38/EC, Para. 27.

43 http://ec.europa.eu/social/, last accessed on 07.10.2012, Directive 2009/38/EC, Art. 4 Para. 4.

The central management and the special negotiating body must negotiate in a spirit of cooperation with a view to reaching an agreement on the detailed arrangements for implementing the information and consultation of employees.

Without prejudice to the autonomy of the parties, the agreement referred to in Para. 1 and effected in writing between the central management and the special negotiating body shall determine:

- the undertakings of the Community-scale group of undertakings or the establishments of the Community-scale undertaking which are covered by the agreement;
- the composition of the European Works Council, the number of members, the allocation of seats, taking into account where possible the need for balanced representation of employees with regard to their activities, category and gender, and the term of office;
- the functions and the procedure for information and consultation of the European Works Council and the arrangements for linking information and consultation of the European Works Council and national employee representation bodies, in accordance with the principles set out in Article 1(3);
- the venue, frequency and duration of meetings of the European Works Council;
- where necessary, the composition, the appointment procedure, the functions and the procedural rules of the select committee set up within the European Works Council;
- the financial and material resources to be allocated to the European Works Council;
- the date of entry into force of the agreement and its duration, the arrangements for amending or terminating the agreement and the cases in which the agreement shall be renegotiated and the procedure for its renegotiation, including, where necessary, where the structure of the Community-scale undertaking or Community-scale group of undertakings changes[44].

If the central management and the special negotiating body are unable to reach agreement, they can either apply the provisions of the subsidiary requirements or initiate a procedure on informing and consulting the employees as regulated by Directive 2009/38/EC.

7. Conclusions

As stated in the recitals of Directive 2009/38/EC, Para. 37, there is a need to link the Directives and the levels of informing and consulting employees established

44 Directive 2009/38/EC, Art. 6.

by Community and national law and/or practice to promote effectiveness, consistency and legal certainty. Priority must be given to negotiations on these procedures for linking information within each undertaking or group of undertakings. If there are no agreements on this subject and where decisions likely to produce substantial changes in work organisation or contractual relations are envisaged, the process must be conducted at both national and European level in such a way as to respect the competences and areas of action of the employee representation bodies. Opinions expressed by the European Works Council should be without prejudice to the competence of the central management to carry out the necessary consultations in accordance with the schedules provided for in national legislation and/or practice. National legislation and/or practice may have to be adapted to ensure that the European Works Council can, where applicable, receive information earlier or at the same time as the national employee representation bodies, but must not reduce the general level of protection of employees.

Romania has transposed the Community's provisions on the establishment of a European Works Council or a procedure in Community-scale undertakings and Community-scale groups of undertakings for the purposes of informing and consulting employees into national legislation.

A problem that might be brought into the discussion is the correlation between the meaning of "employees' representatives" as defined by the recast Directive on the one hand, and by Romanian legislation on the other. In the spirit of the Directive, employees' representatives are the employees foreseen by legislation and/or national practice. The republished Law no. 217/2005 refers to employees' representatives as being the representatives of the unions' organisations or, in case such a union doesn't exist, the persons chosen and assigned to represent the employees, in accordance with the law.

Taking into consideration the amendments of both the Romanian Labour Code[45] and the Romanian Social Dialogue Law[46] which regulate the institution of the employees' representatives, it seems necessary to harmonise the provisions of republished Law no. 217/2005 with the provisions of national labour law in respect of the term representatives of the workers/employees.

45 Law no. 53/2003 republished in May 2011 in the Romanian Official Journal no. 345 on 18.05.2011.

46 Law no. 62/2011, published in the Romanian Official Journal no. 322/10.05.2011, republished in the Romanian Official Journal no. 625/31.08.2012.

Bibliography

Ştefănescu, Ion Traian: Tratat teoretic şi practic de drept al muncii, Universul Juridic Publishing House, Bucharest, 2010.

Ovidiu, Ţinca: Observaţii referitoare la Legea no. 217/2005 privind instituirea comitetului european de întreprindere, Revista de Drept Comercial, Year XVIII, no. 2/2008.

Directive 94/45/EC, published in the EU's Official Journal L254/30.09.1994, modified by Directive 97/74/EC, published in the EU's Official Journal L10/16.01.1998, modified by Directive 2006/109/EC published in the EU's Official Journal L363/20.12.2006, abrogated by Directive 2009/38/EC, published in the EU's Official Journal L 122/28/16.05.2009.

Law no. 217/2005, published in the Romanian Official Journal, Part I, no. 628/19.07.2005, amended by the Government Ordinance no. 48/2006, published in the Romanian Official Journal, Part I, no. 1.028/ 27 December 2006, by Law no. 186/2011, published in the Romanian Official Journal, Part I, no. 763/28 October 2011, republished in the Romanian Official Journal, Part I, no. 889/15.12.2011.

Law no. 53/2003 republished in May 2011 in the Romanian Official Journal no. 345 on 18.05.2011.

Law no. 62/2011, published in the Romanian Official Journal no. 322/10.05.2011, republished in the Romanian Official Journal no. 625 / 31.08.2012.,

http://ec.europa.eu/social/, last accessed on 07.10.2012;

www.juridice.ro, last accessed on 07.10.2012.

Electronic Money, Means of Payment in Domestic and International Economic Exchanges. Statutory Changes at EU and EEA Level

Assistant professor Alexandru BULEARCĂ[1]

Abstract

Since the second half of the last century, worldwide, all sectors of the economy have experienced unprecedented growth, resulting in significant growth of economic exchanges globally. Considering that the exchange of goods and trade, regardless of the geographical space in which it takes place, is generally characterised by celerity, fast payment became a necessity, especially for trades conducted between partners from different countries or continents. In these conditions, the use of information technology processes in international payments came naturally, eventually culminating in the development of electronic money, the newest and fastest means of payment.

Keywords: payment, method of payment, payment services, electronic money, redemption.

1. General aspects concerning the legal status of payment

The obligational legal relationship gives the creditor the right to claim the right and timely execution of the benefit as committed from the debtor, under penalty of the coercive power of the state. In turn, the debtor, performing the obligation in favour of his creditor or a person expressly indicated therein, pays the debt, thus extinguishing the obligational legal relationship with the creditor.

As already known, obligations can be fulfilled in two ways, namely directly or in-kind and indirectly or by means of cash equivalents[2].

In principle, most obligations are performed directly, through payment. Therefore, payment designates the voluntary execution, in-kind, of the obligation undertaken. In plain language, payment designates the voluntary execution of a pecuniary obligation, meaning the remittance of a sum of money to the creditor. In legal terms, payment covers a much larger area of obligations of the borrower, such as the transmission or establishment of a right, the conclusion of

---

1 Alexandru Bulearcă, Athenaeum University of Bucharest, Romania, Email: office@officeatlaw.ro.

2 L. Pop, Treaty of civil law. Obligations. Vol. I General legal regime, CH Beck Publishing House, Bucharest 2006, p. 444.

a contract, the performance of a work, the provision of a service, the delivery of goods, documents, etc.[3].

Regardless of the concrete method of payment – cash, cheque or transfer – the institution of payment was subject to several doctrinal disputes to which we will refer briefly below, trying to elucidate this apparently simple but essentially complex operation.

Thus, according to classical theory, payment manifests the debtor's will to perform the obligation to which he is indebted, and takes the form of a legal and conventional transaction between payer and payee, in principle.

Opinions have emerged in literature claiming that payment is a unilateral act of the debtor[4], a theory that is criticised by one author[5] who bases his opinion on the distinction between payment as a means of executing obligations and payment as a means of extinguishing obligations.

As far as we are concerned, we rally to the doctrine which states that payment is always a legal act, as the debtor of a payment obligation always acts voluntarily and with the intention of settling an obligational legal relationship.

Therefore, based on the above considerations, we can say that payment represents a transfer of funds between the parties of an obligational legal relationship, respectively between the participants in a domestic or international economic operation, in order to extinguish the financial obligations undertaken.

For this purpose, the debtor of the legal obligational relationship will respect the conventions agreed with his creditor regarding the method, date, place and currency of payment.

Therefore we can state that the system of payments and remuneration is an important component of the monetary and financial system of the economy of a state, which provides financial cash flow and also enables the transfer of monetary assets between individuals and/or organisations involved in economic activity[6].

Under these circumstances, we can state[7] that the payment system, in general, is closely linked to the *currency of payment,* whose development as well as the development of technology transfer and storage of data associated with these

3 Idem, p. 446.

4 Fr. Terre, Ph. Simler, Yv. Lequette, Droit civil. Les obligations, Dalloz, Paris, 1999, p. 1223.

5 N. Cataluna, The legal nature of payment, Libraire generale de droit et de Jurisprudence, Paris, 1961.

6 Alexandru Bulearcă, Payment services in the EU and EEA market during the current economic crisis, in *Juridical Tribune*, Dec. 2011, vol. 1, no. 2, www.tribunajuridica.eu.

7 Ibidem.

operations has led to the emergence and improvement of the payment system, in order to complete the economic exchanges *with celerity*.

Thus, in commercial relationships with a third party element *payments have to be made in the currency agreed by the parties* in the contract. If the parties have not established a payment currency, the discharging currency will be the currency in circulation at the place of payment.

The problem of determining the payment currency is closely linked to monetary nominalism[8] as established by Article 1578 of the old Civil Code to which, as emphasised by the doctrine[9] and ruled in the practice of arbitration[10] of our country before 1990, is assigned the value of public order.

The idea of monetary nominalism expressed in the Romanian doctrine reflected the thesis of most French doctrine[11] as Article 1578 of the old Civil Code is a faithful translation of Article 1895 French Civil Code.

In legal literature has been written that the extent of monetary obligations cannot be determined other than by adopting monetary nominalism[12].

Moreover, arbitration practice has consistently ruled in the sense that the damage suffered by a creditor as a result of devaluation of the payment currency agreed by the parties in the contract cannot be located in the debtor's assets if he performed the payment obligation[13] in time.

However, if payment is late and the currency has depreciated in the meantime, the damage is localised at the creditor's level, and the debtor cannot take advantage of the situation, because it is based on the latter's fault that would invoke the principle of monetary nominalism[14].

Consequently, arbitration practice has constantly decided, even in the absence of a currency appreciation clause, that the debtor shall bear the risk of payment currency devaluation if the debtor has delayed payment, and shall owe

8 R. Vartolomei, Regimul juridic al plăților transfrontaliere în cadrul UE, Universul Juridic Publishing House, Bucharest, 2008, p.30.

9 O. Căpățână, B. Ştefănescu, Tratat de drept al comerțului internațional, vol II, RSR Academy Publishing House, Bucharest, 1987, p. 56.

10 CAB Decision no. 141 of 2 September 1977, commented by O. Căpățână in JRDCI (XL), in RRSI no. 6 (62) of 1982, pg. 449, which states that monetary nominalism is the buyer's obligation to pay the price of goods.

11 G. Ripert, J. Boulanger, Civil Law Treaty according to the Treaty of Planiol; Paris; LGDJ; vol: é; 1957; p. 572.

12 F. A. Mann, The legal aspects of money, 3rd edition, Oxford, Clarendon, 1971.

13 O. Căpățână, B. Ştefănescu, cited work, p. 56.

14 O. Căpățână, B. Ştefănescu, cited work, p. 59.

the creditor damages equivalent to the difference between the currency value on the due date and the payment date[15].

The French Supreme Court pronounced likewise and, after long discussions on monetary nominalism, stated that the provisions of Article 1895 of the French Civil Code does not have the character of public policy, being only a *suppletive* regulation[16]. Following this decision, the provisions of Article 1895 of the French Civil Code were interpreted as having been removed from application through a clause inserted in the contract by the parties[17].

Romanian legal literature[18], both pre-war and post 90s, inclined towards the legal standard qualification from Article 1578 of the old Civil Code, as being *suppletive*, basing its opinion on the provisions of Article 1579 of the old Civil Code, which was borrowed from the Italian Civil Code in 1865, repealed at the present time and which has no counterpart in the French Civil Code[19], according to which, if the intrinsic value of money is tainted with regard to a loan, the equivalent of the loan principal will be repaid.

We agree with the last point of view, because nothing prohibits the parties to a pecuniary legal obligational relation from agreeing to revalue claims in case of an obvious imbalance between the value of the payment currency on the date of conclusion of the contract and the payment date.

From the above it follows that the principle of monetary nominalism enshrined in Article 1578 of the old Civil Code is opposed to the principle of monetary value, provided by Article 1579 of the old Civil Code, both laws having suppletive character only.

As such, as far as pecuniary obligations are concerned, the parties to the contract may agree upon a clause stating that *in case the payment currency devalues by a certain percentage compared to the rate applying at contract conclusion*, the price indexing of that percentage shall be applicable de jure.

Relating to obligations stipulated by contract, the parties can also resort to another legal means by which to avoid the consequences of drastic depreciation

15 See Dec. CAB no. 36 of 30 September 1972 and Dec. CAB. no. 173 of 30 June 1979, in DPCI, no. 4/1983, p. 693.

16 See Cass. Civ. I, 27 June 1958, bull. Civ. no. 302.

17 L. Pop, cited work, p. 472.

18 D. Alexandresco, Theoretical and practical explanation of Romanian Civil Law compared to old laws and the relevant foreign law, volume V, National Printing House, Iasi, 1898, p. 494-495; C. Hamangiu, I. Rosetti-Bălănescu, Al. Băicoianu, Treaty of Romanian Civil Law, vol. II, All Pub. House, Bucharest, 1996, p. 373; I. Albu, Current issues concerning judicial reassessment of claims, conventional pecuniary obligations indexing and interest indexing, in Law no. 1/1994, p. 49.

19 L. Pop, cited work, p. 473.

of the currency of payment agreed, which gives the opportunity of revising the convention, but this is not the subject of our present work.

A controversial and long debated issue in literature is the presence or absence of the right recognised by legal authorities with whom a claim is filed concerning the obvious disproportion between the contractual obligations of the parties in a contract with sequential execution, *which occurred during its performance*, whereby the contract did not provide for price indexation clauses nor revision of the contractual obligations for such situations, to conduct a judicial indexing of monetary assets and liabilities, at the request of either party.

If until 1990 the response of Romanian law was negative, like that of French law, thereafter one can say that there is a real consensus on *judicial indexing* of claims[20] and pecuniary liabilities.

Considering that Articles 970, 981, 998, 1073, 1082 and 1084 of the old Civil Code *and also* Articles 1164, 1170, 1272, 1381, 1349, 1350, 1530, 1531 and 1489 of the new Civil Code provide legal grounds for judicial revaluation of pecuniary obligations, we can state that *indexing or revaluating* pecuniary claims *is entirely possible* under Romanian legislation, which is why we mention that it is *legal* when prescribed by the legislator in legal regulations, *conventional*, when it is the will of contracting parties or *judicial* (subsidiary) when the parties have failed to provide such clauses in their contract and one of them refuses to renegotiate their mutual obligations when performance becomes a burden for the other party.

However, in terms of the currency of payment, UNIDROIT Principles stipulate in Article 6.1.9. that the debtor of an obligation to pay a sum of money expressed in a currency other than that of the place of payment shall be held to settle the obligation exclusively in the currency agreed in the contract, unless the debtor is unable to make the payment in the currency in which the obligation is expressed, when it will be free to pay in the currency in circulation at the place of payment, in which case the exchange rate will be applied as of the due date of the claim or settlement, at the discretion of the creditor if the debtor has not paid at maturity.

Also, Article 6.1.10 of the UNIDROIT Principles establishes the rule whereby if the parties have not established the payment currency in their contract, the debtor could be released from obligation by making valid payment in

---

20 Supreme Court of Justice, Comm. Sec., dec. no. 445/4 April 1996, in R.D.C. no. 1/1998, p. 83; ibidem, dec. no. 562/February 1999, in RDC no. 4/2000, p.151; ibidem dec. no. 905/14 February 2001, in Law no. 3/2004, p. 192, which refers to the inflation indexing of compensation awarded in the event of termination of contract.

the currency of the place of payment. The same solutions are also found in Article 108 of the Principles of European Contract Law.

Regarding the currency in which a contractual payment is to be made, we hold that the debtor is bound to make pecuniary payment in the currency agreed between the parties in the contract and if the currency agreed is not legal at the place of payment, in the currency of the place of performance of the pecuniary obligation[21].

There are some exceptions to this rule, when the parties are allowed, by contractual agreement, to avoid payment in the currency of the performance place of the pecuniary obligation. Thus, Article 41 of the Commercial Code states that the parties can stipulate payment in a foreign currency by inserting the clause "effective" or other equivalent.

Article 1488 Para. 1 of Romania's New Civil Code provides that the debtor of an amount of money is discharged upon delivering the nominal amount due to the creditor. Basically, this law allows contracting parties to establish the payment currency in commercial contracts.

Promissory notes are another exception to compulsory payment in the currency of the place of performance of pecuniary obligations, where Article 45 Para. 4 of Law no. 58/1934 states that payment by the debtor in local currency cannot constitute discharge if the drawer has stipulated the payment must be made in a particular currency shown in the title[22]. Similar provisions are found in Law no. 59/1934 on cheques.

However, legislation governing promissory notes and cheques also provides rules of interpretation in relation to the payment currency specified in a title, when its value in the place of issuance differs from that of payment. Thus, in such a situation, it is assumed that the currency indicated in the title refers to the currency of the place of payment. One such typical situation is where the dollar is indicated as the payment currency without mention of the issuing country, dollars being the national currency of Canada, Australia and the USA. The same applies for the pound (English or Israeli).

---

21 O. Căpățână, B. Ștefănescu, cited work, p. 57.

22 E. Cristoforeanu, Treaty of law, vol. 2, Bucharest, 1936, p. 73-74; D. Gălățescu-Pyk, Bill exchange and promissory note, vol. 2, Bucharest, 1930, p. 337-339.

2. Electronic money institutions in view of Government Emergency Ordinance no. 99/2006 as further amended. Establishment, authorisation and operation

When Directive no. 2006/48/EC of the European Parliament and of the Council of 14 June 2006 relating to the taking up and pursuit of the business of credit institutions and Directive no. 2006/49/EC of the European Parliament and Council of 14 June 2006 on the capital adequacy of investment firms and credit institutions were adopted, there was no uniform regulation in the field of e-money issuers at EU and thus EEA level.

In Romania, the two Directives have been transposed into national legislation by Government Emergency Ordinance (GEO) no. 99/2006 relating to credit institutions and capital adequacy, (published in the Official Monitor no. 1027 of 27 December 2006, with effect from 1 January 2007). Pursuant to this regulation, electronic money institutions were only credit institutions, and the activity in question was governed by National Bank of Romania Regulation no. 6/2006 on the issuance and use of electronic payment instruments and relations between the participants in such transactions.

GEO no. 99/2006 has held that electronic money institutions are Romanian legal entities established and operating[23] as joint stock companies in accordance with Law no. 31/1990.

The activity of these entities had to be limited[24] to issuing electronic money and providing financial and non-financial services closely linked to the activity of issuing e-money, such as managing e-money by performing some operational and other functions related to the issuance of e-money, the issuance and administration of other means of payment and the provision of electronic information storage for certain public institutions or other entities.

Reading Article 323 and 324 Para. 3 of the GEO no. 99/2006 in conjunction, electronic money entities must immediately convert any reimbursed funds into e-money. In other words, electronic money entities are prohibited from any activity aimed[25] at accepting deposits or other repayable funds from the public, at raising and/or managing contributions from members of groups of people.

Moreover, electronic money institutions may not hold participations in other entities, except those whose main activity consists exclusively of the provision

23 Article 322 of GEO no. 99/2006, published in the Official Monitor (O.M.) no. 1027 of 27 December 2006.

24 Idem, Article 323.

25 Article 5 of GEO no. 99/2006, published in the O.M. no. 1027 of 27 December 2006.

of operational or other auxiliary services related to the issuance or distribution of e-money by the electronic money institution concerned[26].

According to Article 7 Para. 1, section 16 of GEO no. 99/2006, electronic money is a monetary value representing a claim on the issuer, stored on an electronic device, issued in exchange for the receipt of funds of an amount not less than the monetary value issued, and is also accepted as a means of payment by entities other than the issuer.

However, electronic money is issued for a specified period, and is recorded in a contract concluded between the issuer and the applicant, gnp2057which must document the terms of its redemption[27].

At the request of the holders, issuers are, moreover, under obligation of redemption at a value equal to its balance during the period for which the electronic money was issued. Electronic money is redeemed either by changing its value in cash or by transferring it to an account that is not subject to any fees or commissions other than those strictly necessary for the operation of redemption. In either of these two options, the legislator has stated a minimum redemption threshold of maximum ten euros or the equivalent in lei.

To obtain permission to operate from the National Bank of Romania, electronic money institutions must have an initial capital of one million euros or the equivalent in lei when filing for authorisation, and the own funds necessary for the business development must equal at least two percent of the highest amount or the average of the last six months of their financial obligations for issuing electronic money and must not fall below the level of the authorisation value[28].

On request, the National Bank of Romania may exempt an electronic money institution from some or all of the conditions imposed by GEO no. 99/2006, but only if the activity of issuing electronic money run by the issuing institution generates a total amount not exceeding the equivalent in lei of five million euros and never exceeds the equivalent in lei of six million euros, *or* when the electronic money issued by the institution is accepted as a means of payment only by its subsidiaries that provide operational or other auxiliary services related to the electronic money issued or distributed by the issuing institution, or the electronic money issued by the issuing institution is accepted as a means of payment by a limited number of entities in the same location or area or by institutions with close financial or business ties to the issuing institution[29].

26 Idem, Article 325.
27 Idem, Article 326.
28 Idem, Article 327.
29 Article 329 of Law no. 127/2011, published in the O.M. no. 437 of 22 June 2011.

In such situations, the documents supporting the issuance of electronic money must provide that the amount that can be stored on the electronic device available to holders in order to make payments is capped at the equivalent in lei of 150 EUR.

At the same time, the law allows electronic money institutions[30] to merge with banks, with other electronic money institutions or other companies providing auxiliary services only if their activity is restricted to the limited services mentioned in Article 323 of GEO no. 99/2006.

3. Changes to the original regulations relating to the establishment and operation of electronic money issuers

At EU level, the implementation of Directive no. 2006/48/EC of the European Parliament and of the Council of 14 June 2006 relating to the taking up and pursuit of the business of credit institutions and Directive no. 2006/49/EC of the European Parliament and of the Council of 14 June 2006 on the capital adequacy of investment firms and credit institutions has allowed regulatory authorities to gain practical work experience in the field at both Union and national levels, but also to identify issues related to electronic money issuing activities which were not covered in the initial regulations.

Consequently, the EU adopted Directive 2009/110/EC of the European Parliament and of the Council of 16 September 2009 on taking up, pursuit and prudential supervision of the business of electronic money institutions, published in the Official Journal of the European Union series L no. 267 of 10 October 2009. This legal document amended Directives 2005/60/EC and 2006/48/EC, and repealed Directive 2000/46/EC.

At national level, Law no. 127/2011 on the activity of electronic money issuance was adopted and published in the Official Gazette no. 437 of 22 June 2011, which transposes Article 1, Article 2, Paras. 1-3, Article 3, Paras. 1 and 3-5, Article 4, Article 5, Paras. 1, 2 and 5-7, Article 6, Article 7, Paras. 1, 3 and 4, and Articles 8-13, 18 and 22 of Directive 2009/110/EC of the European Parliament and of the Council of 16 September 2009 on the taking up, pursuit and prudential supervision of the business of electronic money institutions.

Below is a brief analysis of the changes contained in the new regulations in the field of electronic money issuers.

The *definition of electronic money institutions* has been expanded[31] and now, besides credit institutions regulated by Article 7 Para. (1) section 10 of the

30 Idem, Article 332.

31 Article 2 of Law no. 127/2011, published in the O.M. no. 437 of 22 June 2011.

Government Emergency Ordinance no. 99/2006 on credit institutions and capital adequacy, approved with amendments by Law no. 227/2007, and electronic money institutions as provided by Article 4 Para. (1) letter e) of the Law, also encompasses postal service providers that issue electronic money as defined by national legislation, and the European Central Bank and national central banks when not acting in their capacity as monetary authorities or in any other quality involving the exercise of public authority, and also Member States and their regional or local authorities, when acting in their capacity as public authorities.

However, the normative act stipulates that Law no. 127/2011 is not applicable for the monetary value stored on instruments referred to in Article 4 Para. (1) letter k)[32] of Government Emergency Ordinance no. 113/2009 on payment services, approved with amendments by Law no. 197/2010, as further amended and supplemented nor the monetary value designated for payment transactions referred to in Article 4 Para. (1) letter l)[33] of Government Emergency Ordinance no. 113/2009, approved with amendments by Law no. 197/2010, as further amended and supplemented.

Regarding the organisational form of electronic money institutions, Article 7 Para. 2 states that the National Bank of Romania may grant authorisation to operate to a Romanian entity established under Law no. 31/1990 on commercial companies, as further amended. Basically, this text provides that the entity requesting authorisation as an electronic money institution may be held in any corporate form regulated by law, and no longer requires the exclusive legal form of a joint stock company.

Also, the current regulation expressly mentions that issuers may conduct other commercial activities[34] besides issuing electronic money and providing payment services, but in this case, the regulator may require the establishment of a distinct entity for issuing electronic money and payment services if it considers that the other commercial activities may be prejudicial or detrimental to the strength of the financial situation of the electronic money institution or to the

---

32 Article 4 Para. (1) letter k) of GEO 113/2009 "services provided on instruments that can be used to purchase goods or services only in the premises used by the issuer or which, under commercial agreement with the issuer, can be used either within a limited network of service providers or for a limited range of goods or services".

33 Article 4 Para. (1) letter l) of GEO 113/2009 "payment transactions executed by means of any telecommunication, digital, IT devices, if the goods or services purchased are delivered to and are to be used by means of telecommunication, digital or IT devices, on condition that the operator of the telecommunication, digital or information services acts only as an intermediary between the payment service user and the supplier of goods and services".

34 Article 15 of Law no. 127/2011, published in the O.M. no. 437 of 22 June 2011.

NBR's ability to supervise whether the electronic money institution is complying with all obligations imposed by the relevant regulations.

In this respect, electronic money institutions may carry out activities such as payment services provided in Article 8 of Government Emergency Ordinance no. 113/2009, approved with amendments by Law no. 197/2010, as further amended, or providing operational and related services regarding the issuance of electronic money and payment services, such as ensuring the execution of payment transactions, foreign exchange services, safeguarding or storing data, and processing or administering payment systems, or any business other than the issuance of electronic money and payment services that is within the applicable legal framework[35].

However, under the new regulations, electronic money institutions may grant credits[36] related to payment services, as specified in Article 8 letter d)[37], e)[38] and g)[39] of Government Emergency Ordinance no. 113/2009, approved with amendments by Law no. 197/2010, as further amended.

Moreover, electronic money institutions may grant credits other than those referred to above in compliance with Law no. 93/2009 on non-banking financial institutions, as further amended and supplemented.

However, credits granted by the electronic money institutions may not be sourced from funds received in exchange for electronic money issued[40]. Basically, the enactment states unequivocally that the credits that can be given by electronic money institutions to their clients cannot come from amounts deposited by users or consumers for issuing electronic money.

Moreover, unlike the old regulation, the current ruling has reduced the minimum capital stock[41] required for authorising an electronic money institution to the amount of 350,000 euros or the equivalent in lei.

---

35 Idem, Article 21.

36 Idem, Article 22.

37 Article 8 letter d) of GEO 113/2009 "performing the following payment transactions if the funds are covered by a credit line for a payment service user: direct debits, including one-off direct debits, payment transactions through a payment card or a similar device, credit transfer operations, including programmed payment orders".

38 Article 8 letter e) of GEO 113/2009 "issuing and/or accepting payment instruments".

39 Article 8 letter g) of GEO 113/2009 "making payment operations in which the payer's consent to perform a payment transaction is given by any telecommunication, digital or IT means and the payment is made to the system or computer network operator or telecommunications provider that acts only as an intermediary between the payment service user and the supplier of goods and services".

40 Article 22 Para. 3 of Law no. 127/2011, published in the O.M. no. 437 of 22 June 2011.

41 Idem, Article 18.

However, the current regulation has maintained the obligation[42] of issuing electronic money immediately on receipt of the funds in return for which it is issued, and also the prohibition of deposits or other repayable funds from the public, in compliance with Government Emergency Ordinance no. 99/2006, approved with amendments and completions by Law no. 227/2007 as further amended.

Equally, electronic money institutions are prohibited from paying any interest or any other benefit whose value is directly related to the period during which the electronic money consumer or user holds that currency[43].

The current regulation also explicitly states that authorised institutions may issue electronic money before receiving the funds, if the electronic money issued is paid by means of a payment instrument[44], but are obligated to inform the electronic money applicants about the value and purchase price of the same.

In the absence of specific regulation, we believe that *de lege ferenda*, as far as the *purchase price of electronic money* is concerned, issuers shall be obliged to adopt *transparent procedures to include, without exception, only the actual costs of issuance without any other commissions or additional costs* that must be presented to applicants prior to agreement of any contract to issue electronic money.

Regarding the level of own funds of an electronic money issuer, the current regulation states that their value must not fall below the minimum threshold for authorisation, the equivalent in lei of 350,000 euros[45].

However, given the variety of business activities that electronic money issuers are permitted to pursue, the legislator has imposed an obligation to protect the funds received in exchange for the electronic money issued.

Thus it has stated that electronic money issuers are obliged to ensure the protection of the funds[46] received in exchange for the issuance of electronic money *either* by earmarking and separating them from the funds used in other activities of the issuing institution, and if the electronic money has not been redeemed or transferred to another electronic money issuer before the end of the business day after the day they were received, it shall be deposited in a separate account with a bank or invested in high quality assets as defined in regulations issued by the National Bank of Romania, *or* by purchasing insurance cover or some other comparable guarantee provided by an insurance company or bank that does not belong to the same group as the electronic money institution for an

42 Idem, Article 19 and 20.

43 Idem, Article 87.

44 Article 86 of Law no. 127/2011, published in the O.M. no. 437 of 22 June 2011.

45 Idem, Article 30 Para. 3.

46 Idem, Article 32.

amount equivalent to that which would have to be marked and kept separately in the absence of the insurance policy or other comparable guarantee, such insurance to pay out if the electronic money issuer is unable to meet its financial obligations.

Nevertheless, if only part of the monetary value issued is used as e-money and the rest is used for other purposes, the obligation to protect the funds is limited only to that amount used as electronic money.

Also, if it is not possible to estimate the share of monetary value to be used as electronic money or if it is variable, the obligation to protect the funds of the entity issuing electronic money will apply only to the representative part of the total funds estimated for use as electronic money, *based on historical activity*[47].

Furthermore, the current regulation states unequivocally that electronic money issuers are prohibited from outsourcing part or all of the activity of issuing electronic money. Nevertheless, electronic money issuers may use individuals or legal persons to distribute and redeem electronic money[48].

Yet, even if the normative act allows outsourcing of operational functions[49] related to the issuance of electronic money, the institutions concerned are under obligation to inform the regulatory authority, which is the National Bank, and to provide verification of the fact that the operation meets several cumulative conditions.

Thus, before outsourcing operational functions, electronic money issuers must ensure[50] *that* outsourcing does not constitute a delegation of management responsibility, *that* the obligations of the e-money issuer in relation to e-money holders are not affected; *that* compliance with the conditions to which the electronic money issuer is subject for authorisation is not harmed *and that* none of the conditions governing the authorisation of the electronic money institution is voided or altered.

The same obligatory character has been established for electronic money institutions who want to outsource certain operational functions related to payment services[51].

Regarding the redemption of funds, the normative act[52] stipulates that electronic money issuers are obliged to redeem, at the request of the electronic money holder, at any time, free and at nominal value, the electronic money which it holds.

---

47 Idem, Article 34.
48 Idem, Article 44.
49 Idem, Article 45.
50 Idem, Article 46.
51 Article 47 of Law no. 127/2011, published in the O.M. no. 437 of 22 June 2011.
52 Idem, Article 88.

Nevertheless, the legislator has given electronic money issuers the possibility of levying a tax on redemption only if this aspect is provided in the contract between the parties and *only* if the electronic money holder requests redemption before expiry of the contract, *or* if the parties have agreed a contract term of up to one year and that it cannot be terminated before a certain date *or* if redemption is requested more than one year after contract expiry[53].

In any of the redemption situations mentioned above, e-money issuers are required to establish the redemption fee[54] in proportion to the actual costs incurred in connection with the redemption, which is limited to covering costs and must not generate additional revenue or discourage the e-money holder from terminating the contract unilaterally.

Equally, if the electronic money holder requests redemption before expiry of the contract, he shall be entitled to choose between redemption of the full amount of e-money held or only of a part of it. This *option* no longer applies if the e-money holder requests redemption upon expiry of the contract or during a period of up to one year after expiry, in which case the entire amount of e-money must be redeemed[55].

However, if the e-money issuer is engaged in other commercial activities as regulated in Article 21 Para. 1, letter d) of the normative act[56] and does not know in advance the entire amount of money that was to be used as e-money, the electronic money institution shall redeem all funds requested by the electronic money holder[57].

In the absence of specific regulation we believe that, *de lege ferenda*, even if *the electronic money holder requests redemption more than one year after expiry of the contract*, the electronic money issuer must accept the redemption of the full amount of e-money held without fees or additional costs other than those established by Article 89 of Law no. 127/2011.

The electronic money holder may require unilateral termination of a contract governing the provision of electronic money that has been concluded for a period exceeding one year or indefinitely, without any charges, after 12 months from termination.

The normative act allows electronic money issuers to unilaterally terminate a contract[58] with the holder of electronic money only if it has been concluded for

53 Interpretation in conjunction of Articles 89 and 94 of Law no. 127/2011, published in the O.M. no. 437 of 22 June 2011.
54 Idem, Article 92 Para. 3 and Article 95 Para. 1.
55 Idem, Article 91 Para. 1.
56 Ibidem.
57 Idem, Article 91 Para. 2.
58 Idem, Article 96.

an indefinite period, and the user of electronic money has been notified at least two months before the effective termination date. In this case, the notification must be sent to the electronic money holder on paper or another durable medium, in understandable language, written in a clear, comprehensive and accurate manner, in Romanian or a language established by the parties in the contract.

At the same time, the current regulation also provides that – in the event of any litigation between the parties to a contract of e-money issuance and provision[59] – the party that believes its rights relating to the performance of contractual obligations have been injured, the consumer, consumers associations or other interested persons can contact the National Authority for Consumer Protection (ANPC), while legal entities can appeal to the Financial Guard (GF) concerning violations by electronic money issuers of the provisions of Article 86-92 and 94-97, or may initiate legal action. In their responses to the petitioners, ANPC or GF, where appropriate, have an obligation to inform the claimant of the existence of extrajudicial procedures for settling such litigation.

In this respect, the National Bank of Romania is empowered by the legislator to establish a specialised department to ensure the implementation of extrajudicial procedures for settling litigation arising between electronic money institutions and electronic money holders or users, and to adopt effective and adequate measures for resolving complaints brought before it.

The solution proposed by the specialised department of the National Bank of Romania is not binding on the parties concerned. Also, the specialised department of the National Bank of Romania may issue an advisory opinion on litigation that is not subject to mediation by the institution, if such points of views are requested by the courts[60].

In the event that the provisions of Law no. 127/2001 are violated or circumvented, the legislative act describes a series of acts[61] committed through negligence, which infringe the e-money issuance regime, in which can be resolved either by the ANPC in respect of complaints reported by individuals consumers, consumer associations or ex officio, or by the GF in cases brought by legal entities.

At the same time, deeds committed with intent in respect of the e-money issuance regime are qualified by the legislative act as infringements[62], namely *issuing electronic money unlawfully* and unlawfully *preventing the exercise of su-*

59 Article 100 of Law no. 127/2011, published in the O.M. no. 437 of 22 June 2011.

60 Idem, Article 101.

61 Idem, Article 102.

62 Idem, Article 105 and 106.

pervisory competencies by the National Bank of Romania, which are dealt with by the prosecution authorities.

Bibliography

Pop, L.: Tratat de drept civil. Obligațiile. Vol. I Regimul juridic general, CH Beck Publishing House, Bucharest, 2006.

Căpățână, O., Ștefănescu, B.: Tratat de drept al comerțului internațional, vol II, RSR Academy Publishing House, Bucharest, 1987.

Cunescu, C.: Clauze valutare, in ICE no. 43/1985.

Alexandresco, D.: Explicațiunea teoretică și practică a dreptului civil român în comparațiune cu legile vechi și cu principalele legislațiuni străine, volume V, National Printing House, Iasi, 1898.

Hamangiu, C, Rosetti-Bălănescu, I, Băicoianu, Al.: Tratat de drept civil român, vol. II, All Publishing House, Bucharest, 1996.

Cristoforeanu, E.: Tratat de drept cambial, vol. 2, Bucharest, 1936.

Gălășescu-Pyk, D: Cambia și Biletul la ordin, vol. 2, Bucharest, 1930.

Vartolomei, R: Regimul juridic al plăților transfrontaliere în cadrul UE, Universul Juridic Publishing House, Bucharest, 2008.

Bulearcă, Alexandru: Serviciile de plată pe piața UE și a SEE, în perioada actualei crize economice, in *Juridical Tribune* vol. 1, issue 2/2011, www.tribunajuridica.eu

Terre, Fr.; Simler, Ph.; Lequette, Yv.: Droit civil. Les obligations, Dalloz, Paris, 1999.

Cataluna: La nature juridique du paiement, Libraire generale de droit et de Jurisprudence, Paris, 1961.

Ripert, G., Boulanger J.: Traité de droit civil d'après le traité de Planiol; LGDJ, Paris, 1957.

Mann, F. A.: The legal aspects of money, 3rd Edition, Oxford, Clarendon, 1971.

Government Emergency Ordinance no. 113/2009 on payment services in the EU and European Economic Area, as amended by Government Emergency Ordinance no. 61/2010 and approved with amendments by Law no. 197/2010.

Law no. 127/2011, on the activity of issuing electronic money, published in Official Gazette no. 437 of 22 June 2011.

Directive 2007/64/EC of the European Parliament and of the Council of 13 November 2007 on payment services.

Directive 2009/110/EC on electronic money institutions.

Directive 2010/78/EU of the European Parliament and of the Council - Omnibus Directive.

Directive no. 2006/48/EC of the European Parliament and of the Council of 14 June 2006 relating to the taking up and pursuit of the business of credit institutions.

Directive 2009/110/EC of the European Parliament and of the Council of 16 September 2009 on the taking up, pursuit and prudential supervision of the business of electronic money institutions, published in the Official Journal of the European Union, series L no. 267 of 10 October 2009.

Combating Late Payments in Commercial Transactions: Transposition of EU Directives into the Laws of Croatia and Slovenia

Teaching and Research Assistant Ivan TOT[1]

Abstract

The aim of the paper is to evaluate the transposition of the EU Directives on combating late payments into the laws of Croatia and Slovenia. The research is restricted to the provisions of national laws which deal with the payment periods in commercial transactions, the notion of late payment and the private law consequences of the late payments. It is argued that, in some aspects, Croatia has failed to implement the Directives properly, while Slovenia's approach is perceived as being mostly in accordance with the conditions set forth in the Directives. Considering that the new laws brought into force in 2012, both in Croatia and Slovenia, contain provisions which are more favourable to the creditors than the provisions necessary to comply with the Directives, these original solutions are particularly examined in the paper. It is concluded that some of these solutions may serve as a model for future changes which could be made to Directive 2011/7/EU.

Keywords: payment period, late payment, interest, commercial transactions, Directive 2000/35/EC, Directive 2011/7/EU

1. Introduction

Late payments represent a major obstacle to the free movement of goods and services in the European single market. The first binding source of European Union law that tackles the problem of late payments was addressed to the Member States twelve years ago: Directive 2000/35/EC on combating late payment in commercial transactions[2]. Despite the efforts made through Directive 2000/35/EC, late payments in commercial transactions still remained a challenge to the proper functioning of the internal market. Therefore, the provisions of Directive 2000/35/EC were recast in 2011 with a new EU directive of the same name: Directive 2011/7/EU on combating late payment in commercial transac-

1 Ivan Tot, University of Zagreb, Faculty of Economics and Business, Republic of Croatia, itot@efzg.hr.

2 Directive 2000/35/EC of the European Parliament and of the Council of 29 June 2000 on combating late payment in commercial transactions, Official Journal, L 200, 8.8.2000, p. 35 – 38; hereinafter: Directive 2000/35/EC.

tions[3]. Directive 2011/7/EU made substantive changes to the legal mechanisms established in the earlier directive[4]. Although Directive 2011/7/EU was supposed to be transposed into national law by 16 March 2013 at the latest, the European Commission invited the Member States to step up their efforts at national level for early implementation of the new directive in 2012[5].

Slovenia joined the EU in 2004 and in 2007 became the first of the new Member States to enter the eurozone. Due to the already established statutory right to interest for late payment in the Obligations Code[6], the transposition of Directive 2000/35/EC into Slovenian law mainly consisted of amending the Act on Statutory Interest Rates for Late Payments in 2006[7]. In March 2011, the Act on Combating Late Payments was enacted[8], making Slovenia the first Member State to implement the new Directive 2011/7/EU. This act was replaced in July

---

3 Directive 2011/7/EU of the European Parliament and of the Council of 16 February 2011 on combating late payment in commercial transactions, Official Journal of the European Union, L 48, 23.2.2011, p. 1 – 10; hereinafter: Directive 2011/7/EU.

4 The new directive provided for a harmonisation of the period for payment by public authorities to businesses, while the contractual freedom in relations between undertakings was also limited to a lesser extent. The statutory interest rate for late payment was increased and a minimum fixed amount was introduced as statutory compensation for recovery costs.

5 With a view to assisting Member States in the challenging task of early transposition, the Commission established a Late Payment Expert Group – see the answer given by Mr. Antonio Tajani on behalf of the Commission to parliamentary question no. E-002295/2012 raised on 29.2.2012, in the document available online at: http://www.europarl.europa.eu/sides/getAllAnswers.do?reference=E-2012-002295&language=EN (last accessed on: 13.09.2012).

6 Obligations Code (Obligacijski zakonik), Official Gazette of the Republic of Slovenia (Uradni list Republike Slovenije), no. 83/2001, with amendments in no. 32/2004, 28/2006, 29/2007 and 40/2007, and an official consolidated version in no. 97/2007; hereinafter: Slovenian Obligations Code.

7 Act on Statutory Interest Rates for Late Payment (Zakon o predpisani obrestni meri zamudnih obresti), Official Gazette of the Republic of Slovenia (Uradni list Republike Slovenije), no. 135/2003, with amendments in no. 118/2005, 55/2006, 105/2006 and 11/2007; hereinafter: Slovenian Interest Act.

8 Act on Combating Late Payments (Zakon o preprečevanju zamud pri plačilih), Official Gazette of the Republic of Slovenia (Uradni list Republike Slovenije), no. 18/2011; hereinafter: Slovenian Late Payment 2011 Act.

2012 with a new Act on Combating Late Payments[9]. However, the text of these acts has still not been communicated to the European Commission[10].

Croatia is an acceding country which is expected to become a member of the EU on 1 July 2013. Former Directive 2000/35/EC was transposed into Croatian law through the provisions of the new Obligations Act in 2005[11]. In October 2011 a special act on combating late payments was enacted: the Act on Time Limits for Payment of Monetary Obligations[12]. The provisions of this act only partially transposed the new Directive 2011/7/EU into Croatian law which is why it was supplanted in September 2012 with the Act on Financial Operations and Pre-Insolvency Settlements[13] which announces the full harmonisation of Croatian law with the *acquis communautaire* in the field of combating late payments.

2. Time limits for payments in commercial transactions

Directive 2000/35/EC provided that

> "if the date or period for payment is not fixed in the contract, interest shall become payable automatically without the necessity of a reminder... 30 days following"

the date set forth in the directive[14].

The provision was interpreted by several authors arguing that Directive 2000/35/EC does not regulate the time limits for payments, but only the period as of which interest is due. Schulte-Braucks and Ongena had stated that

9 Act on Combating Late Payments (Zakon o preprečevanju zamud pri plačilih), Official Gazette of the Republic of Slovenia (Uradni list Republike Slovenije), no. 57/2012; hereinafter: Slovenian Late Payment 2012 Act.

10 According to the notice on national execution measures, in the document available online at: http://eur-lex.europa.eu/LexUriServ/LexUriServ.do?uri=CELEX:2011L0007 (last accessed on: 13.09.2012).

11 Obligations Act (Zakon o obveznim odnosima), Official Gazette (Narodne novine), no. 35/2005, with amendments in no. 41/2008 and 125/2011; hereinafter: Croatian Obligations Act.

12 Act on Time Limits for Payment of Monetary Obligations (Zakon o rokovima ispunjenja novčanih obveza), Official Gazette (Narodne novine), no. 125/2011; hereinafter: Croatian Late Payment 2011 Act.

13 Act on Financial Operations and Pre-Insolvency Settlements (Zakon o financijskom poslovanju i predstečajnoj nagodbi), enacted on 28.09.2012, not yet published in the Official Gazette (as of 28.09.2012), the document is available online at: http://www.sabor.hr/fgs.axd?id=21663 (last accessed on: 28.09.2012).

14 Art. 3.1 a) of Directive 2000/35/EC.

> "the Directive does not relate to the question when claims become due... but merely determines the point as of which interests are due"[15],

concluding that

> "as a result, national private law can continue to distinguish between the due date of the principal claim and that of the interests"[16].

Although not stating so directly, the same conclusion is reached by Zaccaria who writes about a 30-day period after which interest is due, rather than about a payment period after which the principal claim is due[17].

However, it should be borne in mind that interest is the legal consequence for late payment. The creditor is entitled to late payment interest only if he has not received the due principal amount after expiry of the payment period provided in the contract or in the statute. Therefore, by determining when interest is due, Directive 2000/35/EC has indirectly regulated the payment period after which the principal debt is due. This view is also expressed by Perales Viscasillas who stated that

> "if a reminder is no longer needed, it is because the debt is already due, so that only the moment when the debt becomes payable is deferred"[18].

Although not addressing the problem directly, it seems that both Milo[19] and McCormack[20] share the same view, as they refer to payment periods after which the debt is due, rather than to periods after which interest is due.

In this respect the provisions of the new Directive 2011/7/EU are more precise. For transactions between undertakings the directive provides that

---

15 Schulte-Braucks, Reinhard and Ongena, Steven, The Late Payment Directive – a step towards an emerging European Private Law?, "European Review of Private Law", vol. 11, no. 4, 2003, p. 530.

16 Ibid.

17 Zaccaria, Alessio, (EC) Directive 2000/35 on Combating Late Payments in Commercial Transactions, "The European Legal Forum (E)", vol. 5, no. 6, 2000-2001, pp. 388 – 389, the document is available online at: http://www.simons-law.com/library/pdf/e/92.pdf (last accessed on: 23.09.2012).

18 Perales Viscasillas, Pilar, Late Payment Directive 2000/35 and the CISG, "Pace International Law Review", vol. 19, no. 1, 2007, p. 134, the document is available online at: http://digitalcommons.pace.edu/pilr/vol19/iss1/8 (last accessed on: 23.09.2012).

19 Milo, John Michael, Combating Late Payment in Business Transactions: How a New European Directive Has Failed to Set a Substantial Minimum Standard Regarding National Provisions on Retention of Title, "European Review of Private Law", vol. 10, no. 3, 2003, p. 381.

20 McCormack, Gerard, Retention of Title and the EC Late Payment Directive, "Journal of Corporate Law Studies", vol. 1, no. 2, 2001, p. 502.

> "the creditor is entitled to interest for late payment upon the expiry of any of the following time limits"[21],

while regarding the transactions between undertakings and public authorities it obliges the Member States to ensure that

> "the period for payment does not exceed any of the following time limits"[22].

There is no doubt that, with these provisions, the new directive explicitly regulates the payment periods for the principal claim and not merely a date when interest becomes due.

When Directive 2000/35/EC was transposed into the laws of Croatia and Slovenia, the approach in both countries was to regulate the statutory payment periods in commercial transactions instead of determining only the date when interest is due. This position was maintained in the new laws set forth in the transposition of Directive 2011/7/EU into Croatian and Slovenian law.

2.1. Statutory payment periods in commercial transactions

Directive 2011/7/EU provides for a statutory payment period which is to be applied if the date or period for payment is not fixed in the contract. It does this in the same manner as the previous directive did when determining when interest is due, through setting forth that the creditor is entitled to interest for late payment upon the expiry of any of the following time limits:

- 30 calendar days following the date of receipt by the debtor of the invoice or an equivalent request for payment;
- where the date of the receipt of the invoice or the equivalent request for payment is uncertain, 30 calendar days after the date of receipt of the goods or services;
- where the debtor receives the invoice or the equivalent request for payment earlier than the goods or the services, 30 calendar days after the date of the receipt of the goods or services;
- where a procedure of acceptance or verification, by which the conformity of the goods or services with the contract is to be ascertained, is provided for by statute or in the contract and if the debtor receives the invoice or the equivalent request for payment earlier or on the date on which such acceptance or verification takes place, 30 calendar days after that date[23].

---

21 Art. 3.3 b) of Directive 2011/7/EU.

22 Art. 4.3 a) of Directive 2011/7/EU.

23 Art. 3.3 b) and 4.3 a) of Directive 2011/7/EU. The same time limits were set out in Art. 3.1 b) of Directive 2000/35/EC.

Regarding the statutory payment periods, Directive 2011/7/EU has imposed two additional duties on the Member States, which had not existed in the previous directive. The first one is a limit on the maximum duration of a procedure of acceptance or verification to 30 days from the date of receipt of the goods or services (unless otherwise expressly agreed in the contract and any tender documents and provided it is not grossly unfair to the creditor)[24]. The second new obligation of the Member States is to ensure in commercial transactions where the debtor is a public authority that the date of receipt of the invoice is not subject to a contractual agreement between debtor and creditor[25].

Member States are, however, allowed to extend the statutory payment period up to a maximum of 60 calendar days for public undertakings and for public entities providing healthcare[26].

2.1.1. Transposition into Croatian law

When implementing Directive 2000/35/EC, the Croatian Obligations Act introduced a provision which stated that

> "if a time limit for performance of a monetary obligation has not been stipulated in a commercial contract or contract between a trader and a public law person, the debtor shall, without having to be requested by the creditor, perform the obligation within the period of 30 days"[27].

This provision of the Croatian Obligations Act, which differs in style from the wording of Directive 2000/35/EC (and subsequent Directive 2011/7/EU) but is in line with the direction set in the directive, has been derogated by the Croatian Late Payment 2011 Act. However, an equivalent provision was inserted in the Late Payment 2011 Act[28], as well as in the new Late Payment 2012 Act[29].

---

24 Art. 3.4 and 4.5 of Directive 2011/7/EU.

25 Art. 4.3 b) of Directive 2011/7/EU.

26 Art. 4.4 of Directive 2011/7/EU.

27 Art. 174.1 of the Croatian Obligations Act. The 30-day payment period starts to run: as of the day on which the debtor receives the invoice or some other appropriate request for payment; as of the day on which the creditor performs his obligation, if it is not possible to determine the day of receipt of the invoice or some other appropriate request for payment with certainty, or if the debtor receives the invoice or some other appropriate request for payment before the creditor has performed his obligation; as of the day of expiry of the time limit for inspection of the subject of obligation, if a time limit for such an inspection has been stipulated by contract or law, and the debtor has received the invoice or some other appropriate request for payment prior to expiry of such time limit.

28 Art. 2.4 of the Croatian Late Payment 2011 Act.

29 Art. 11.4 of the Croatian Late Payment 2012 Act.

Although Directive 2011/7/EU provides for a statutory payment period in transactions between an undertaking and a public authority only for situations where the debtor is a public authority, the Croatian Late Payment 2011 Act prescribed the same statutory payment period of 30 days for transactions between an undertaking and a public authority where the debtor is the undertaking[30]. The intention was to emphasise that the same rules should apply to undertakings, irrespective of whether they owe debt to other undertakings or to public authorities. The same approach was held in the new Late Payment 2012 Act[31].

The maximum duration of a procedure of acceptance or verification, by which the conformity of the goods or services with the contract is to be ascertained, was regulated by the Late Payment 2011 Act in accordance with the provisions of Directive 2011/7/EU[32]. The maximum period was set at 30 days, providing that the parties to the contract can expressly agree on a longer period in their contract if such agreement is not grossly unfair to the creditor. When regulating the maximum duration of a procedure of acceptance or verification for commercial transactions between an undertaking and a public authority, the Late Payment 2011 Act overlooked that – according to Directive 2011/7/EU – the agreement on prolongation of the 30 days period has to be fixed in the contract and any tender documents. The mistake was corrected by the Late Payment 2012 Act, which included a new provision stating that such agreement has to be entered in any tender documents[33]. In other aspects, the Late Payment 2012 Act held almost the same provisions on this procedure as in the previous law[34]. A small novelty was the provision according to which the parties to the contract may prolong the duration of this procedure to more than 30 days only if such prolongation is justified by special circumstances of the case, such as a particular nature of the product or service[35].

In line with the duty imposed in Directive 2011/7/EU, the Late Payment 2011 Act prescribed that a contractual agreement between a public authority as a debtor and an undertaking as a creditor regarding the date of receipt of the invoice is *ex lege* null and void[36]. Although this was not an obligation under the directive, the new Late Payment 2012 Act established that a contractual agreement between undertakings regarding the date of receipt of the invoice is to be

30 Art. 3.3 of the Croatian Late Payment 2011 Act.

31 Art. 12.7 of the Croatian Late Payment 2011 Act.

32 Art. 2.5, 3.6 and 4.4 of the Croatian Late Payment 2011 Act.

33 Art. 12.6 of the Croatian Late Payment 2012 Act.

34 Art. 11.5 and 12.5 of the Croatian Late Payment 2012 Act.

35 Art. 11.6 of the Croatian Late Payment 2012 Act.

36 Art. 4.2 of the Croatian Late Payment 2011 Act.

null and void as well[37]. On the other hand, the new law mistakenly omitted to apply the same rule to transactions between undertakings and public authorities where a debtor is a public authority. The Croatian law in force therefore failed to implement Directive 2011/7/EU properly in this respect.

Another example of inadequate transposition of Directive 2011/7/EU into Croatian law is the exclusion of certain undertakings from the application of the provisions of the Late Payment 2012 Act. The new law exempted from its provisions financial institutions, credit unions, investment companies, investment fund management companies, credit institutions, insurance companies, reinsurance companies, leasing companies, payment services institutions and electronic money institutions[38]. The new law has basically exempted the whole Croatian financial sector, not only from the obligation to make payments in the statutory payment period, but also from all of the rules brought into force in transposing Directive 2011/7/EU, despite the nonexistence of any grounds for such approach in the text of the directive.

Moreover, regardless of a clear provision in Directive 2011/7/EU which states that liberal professions are covered by the directive[39], the Late Payment 2012 Act does not apply to liberal professions as they are not included in the notion of undertaking under this law.

2.1.2. Transposition into Slovenian law

The Slovenian Late Payment 2011 Act provided for a statutory payment period in which the debtor has to perform his monetary obligation if a payment period is not fixed in the contract: 30 days which start to run from the dates determined in the Act in a manner which is identical to the solution of Directive 2011/7/EU[40]. The only difference made in Slovenian law was the exclusion of the reference to "equivalent request for payment". The omission of the term is probably an intentional one, in order to emphasise the duty of sending invoices imposed by the tax laws. The new Slovenian Late Payment 2012 Act includes precisely the same provision[41].

Similarly to the approach in Croatian law, the Slovenian Late Payment 2012 Act as well as the previous 2011 Act provide for a statutory payment period of

---

37 Art. 14.2 of the Croatian Late Payment 2012 Act.

38 Art. 4.3 of the Croatian Late Payment 2012 Act.

39 Pt. 10 of the preamble of Directive 2011/7/EU states: "The fact that the liberal professions are covered by this Directive should not oblige Member States to treat them as undertakings or merchants for purposes outside the scope of this Directive".

40 Art. 7.1-2 of the Slovenian Late Payment 2011 Act.

41 Art. 12.1-2 of the Slovenian Late Payment 2012 Act.

30 days in commercial transactions between undertakings and public authorities, irrespective of whether a public authority is a debtor or a creditor.

The maximum duration of the procedure of acceptance or verification is set at 30 days in the Late Payment 2011 Act, unless otherwise expressly agreed in the contract and any tender documents and provided it is not grossly unfair to the creditor[42], which is all in accordance with

Directive 2011/7/EU. The same solutions are prescribed in the Late Payment 2012 Act as well[43].

In line with Directive 2011/7/EU, the Late Payment 2011 Act prescribed an irrebuttable presumption that a contractual agreement regarding the date of receipt is grossly unfair to the creditor and hence *ex lege* null and void[44]. Unlike Directive 2011/7/EU, the Slovenian law applied this provision both to contracts between undertakings and contracts between undertakings and public authorities. Surprisingly, this provision was left out of the new Late Payment 2012 Act. As a result of this omission, the Slovenian legislation which is now in force has failed to comply with the duty imposed by the directive in this respect.

Unlike the laws of Croatia, liberal professions are covered by the provisions of both Slovenian Late Payment Acts[45]. However, both laws have excluded the Slovenian Central Bank from the application of their provisions[46].

2.2. Payment period fixed in the contract between undertakings

Whereas Directive 2000/35/EC did not in any way limit the contractual freedom regarding the payment periods fixed in the contract between undertakings, Directive 2011/7/EU has obliged the Member States to ensure that the period for payment fixed in the contract does not exceed 60 calendar days, unless otherwise expressly agreed in the contract and provided it is not grossly unfair to the creditor[47]. In determining whether such or any other contractual term or practice is grossly unfair to the creditor, all circumstances of the case should be considered, while the directive imposes a duty on the Member States to provide that a

---

42 Art. 7.3-4 of the Slovenian Late Payment 2011 Act.

43 Art. 11.2-3 and 12.3-4 of the Slovenian Late Payment 2012 Act.

44 Art. 4.2 of the Slovenian Late Payment 2011 Act.

45 Explicitly through the provisions of Art. 2.1 of the Slovenian Late Payment 2011 Act and Art. 6.1 of the Slovenian Late Payment 2012 Act.

46 Art. 2.4 of the Slovenian Late Payment 2011 Act and Art. 5 of the Slovenian Late Payment 2012 Act.

47 Art. 3.5 of Directive 2011/7/EU.

grossly unfair term or practice is either unenforceable or gives rise to a claim for damages[48].

2.2.1. Transposition into Croatian law

In line with the directive, the Croatian Late Payment 2011 Act prescribed that undertakings as a general rule may agree on a payment period which does not exceed 60 days[49], allowing "exceptionally" a longer payment period[50]. The provision was highly criticised in Croatian legal literature by several authors stating that the law has omitted to explain in which exceptional cases the undertakings may agree on a payment period longer than 60 days[51]. Although the use of the phrase "exceptionally" might imply that the underlying idea was a restrictive approach according to which a payment period longer than 60 days would be allowed only rarely, the wording is merely the ill-chosen result of the intention to highlight that the legal norm on a 60-day payment period is not cogent in its nature. This was confirmed by a later statement by the Ministry of Finance explaining that a payment period of more than 60 days can be fixed in the contract if such a longer period is justified by the specific nature of a particular economic activity, for example production cycles in agriculture[52]. However, as intended in the directive, contractual payment periods of more than 60 days are subject to judicial review in order to determine if such longer payment period is grossly unfair to the creditor. A contractual term would be considered grossly unfair to the creditor if all of the circumstances of the case, particularly trade customs and the nature of the subject of obligation, indicate that such a stipulation is contrary

48 Art. 7.1 of Directive 2011/7/EU.

49 Art. 2.1 of the Croatian Late Payment 2011 Act.

50 Art. 2.2 of the Croatian Late Payment 2011 Act.

51 See: Gorenc, Vilim, Time limits for payment of monetary obligations after January 1st, 2012 (Rokovi ispunjenja novčanih obveza od 1. siječnja 2012.), "Accounting, auditing and finances" ("Računovodstvo, revizija i financije"), no. 12, 2011, p. 142; Pavičić, Damir, Application of the Act on Time Limits for Payment of Monetary Obligations (Primjena Zakona o rokovima ispunjenja novčanih obveza), "Accounting, auditing and finances" ("Računovodstvo, revizija i financije"), no. 1, 2012, p. 268; Pavičić, Damir, Current issues with the application of the Act on Time Limits for Payment of Monetary Obligations (Aktualna pitanja vezana za primjenu Zakona o rokovima ispunjenja novčanih obveza), "Accounting, auditing and finances" ("Računovodstvo, revizija i financije"), no. 5, 2012, pp. 126 – 127.

52 Response of the Ministry of Finance to a letter from the Croatian Association of Employers, no. 450-08/12-01/13, issued on 22.02.2012, the document is available online at: http://www.hup.hr/Upload/ZAKONODAVSTVO/2012/Z.o%20rokovima%20pla%C4 %87 anjami%C5% A1ljenje%201.pdf (last accessed on: 23.09.2012).

to the principle of good faith, resulting in an obvious inequality of the rights and obligations of the contracting parties to the detriment of the creditor[53]. If a contractual term would not stand the described test, which also includes examining whether the parties to the contract had justified reasons for deviating from the statutory payment period[54], the court would declare the contractual term null and void[55]. As a consequence of the invalidity, the creditor is entitled under the general rule of the Obligations Act to compensation for damages[56].

The new Croatian Late Payment 2012 Act is more rigid in limiting the contractual freedom of undertakings. While the general rule on 60-day payment periods remained[57], the new law specified that undertakings can agree on a longer period of payment only if the debtor issues a security instrument with the legal effect of an enforceable title to the creditor[58]. Moreover, even if this requirement is fulfilled, the law established the maximum payment period of 360 days[59]. The judicial test of fairness of a contractual term providing for a payment period of more than 60 days was kept on in the new law[60], adding that a payment period of more than 360 days would be null and void *ex lege* without the need for judicial review[61]. Although these provisions are stricter than those set forth in Directive 2011/7/EU, the new solutions 057under Croatian law are still in accordance with the directive, since the directive permits the Member States to bring into force provisions which are more favourable to the creditor than the provisions necessary to comply with the directive[62]. The condition of issuing a security instrument with the legal effect of an enforceable title even resembles a proposal for Directive 2000/35/EC that was abandoned: the amended proposal of this directive contained a provision under which the undertakings could agree on a payment period of more than 45 days only if the buyer provided the seller with a bill of exchange[63]. The Croatian law goes even further than the disregarded pro-

53 Art. 4.4 of the Croatian Late Payment 2011 Act. Equivalent provisions existed in derogated Art. 174.2 of the Croatian Obligations Act.

54 Art. 4.5 of the Croatian Late Payment 2011 Act. Equivalent provisions existed in derogated Art. 174.3 of the Croatian Obligations Act.

55 Art. 4.4 of the Croatian Late Payment 2011 Act.

56 Art. 323 of the Croatian Obligations Act.

57 Art. 12.1 of the Croatian Late Payment 2012 Act.

58 Art. 12.2 of the Croatian Late Payment 2012 Act.

59 Ibid.

60 Art. 14.5 of the Croatian Late Payment 2012 Act.

61 Art. 14.3 of the Croatian Late Payment 2012 Act.

62 According to Art. 12.3 of Directive 2011/7/EU.

63 See Art. 3.1 d) of the Amended proposal for a European Parliament and Council Directive on combating late payment in commercial transactions, COM/98/0615 final, Official Journal, C 374, 3.12.1998.

posal, considering that a bill of exchange does not have the legal effect of enforceable title under Croatian law.

2.2.2. Transposition into Slovenian Law

The Slovenian Late Payment 2011 Act also provided for more rigorous solutions when transposing Directive 2011/7/EU into Slovenian law. With a provision which is more favourable to the creditor than the one contained in the directive, it established that undertakings may exceptionally agree on a payment period of more than 60 days but not more than 120 days altogether, under the condition that the prolongation is set forth in a written form and that it does not represent a grossly unfair contractual agreement[64]. A grossly unfair contractual agreement is defined as an agreement which is grossly unfair to the creditor[65], while an agreement would be considered as such if it was determined by the court on the basis of all circumstances of the case[66]. The unfairness test particularly includes analysis of whether the agreement represents a deviation from good commercial practice, or from the good faith principle, the principle of prohibition of abuse of rights and the other principles of civil law, or from the nature of the product or the service, and whether the parties to the contract had justified reasons for deviating from the statutory payment period[67]. If it fails the fairness test, the contractual term is null and void[68]. Moreover, the law introduced an irrebuttable presumption that a contractual agreement providing for a payment period of more than 120 days is always grossly unfair[69].

However, the imposed limits of contractual freedom were short-lived as the new Slovenian Late Payment 2012 Act brought into force a softened approach. The new law provided that undertakings may exceptionally agree on a payment period of more than 60 days under the condition that the prolongation is set forth in a written form and that it does not represent a grossly unfair contractual agreement[70]. The maximum payment period, previously set at 120 days, is no longer prescribed. The irrebuttable presumption that a contractual agreement on payment period is null and void now applies only to agreements on payment periods of more than 60 days which are not laid down in written form[71]. All other

64 Art. 5.1 of the Slovenian Late Payment 2011 Act.
65 Art. 4.1 of the Slovenian Late Payment 2011 Act.
66 Art. 4.3 of the Slovenian Late Payment 2011 Act.
67 Ibid.
68 Art. 4.4 of the Slovenian Late Payment 2011 Act.
69 Art. 4.2 of the Slovenian Late Payment 2011 Act.
70 Art. 10.1-2 of the Slovenian Late Payment 2012 Act.
71 Art. 9.2 of the Slovenian Late Payment 2012 Act.

prolongations of the payment period in the contract between undertakings are subject to a judicial review of fairness which is regulated in the same manner as in the previous law[72]. Despite the provisions being weakened compared with the previous law, they still remain more severe and more favourable to the creditor than those contained in Directive 2011/7/EU.

2.3. Payment period fixed in the contract between an undertaking and a public authority

One major novelty of Directive 2011/7/EU compared with the earlier directive is a provision which obliges the Member States to ensure that the period for payment fixed in the contract between an undertaking and a public authority does not exceed 30 calendar days (following the date as explained *supra* regarding the statutory payment periods)[73]. The freedom of contract is not entirely disregarded, as an express agreement in the contract on a longer payment period is still allowed, yet on condition that such an agreement is objectively justified in light of the particular nature or features of the contract[74]. It is noted that the directive does not provide for a fairness test as it does with contracts between undertakings, but rather for a test of justifiability. Moreover, unlike the solution presented for contracts between undertakings, here Directive 2011/7/EU prescribes that a prolonged payment period must not exceed 60 calendar days[75]. Unlike Directive 2000/35/EC, which had not differentiated between contracts between undertakings and public authorities on the basis of whether a public authority is a debtor or a creditor, the provisions of Directive 2011/7/EU apply only to transactions between undertakings and public authorities where the debtor is a public authority[76].

2.3.1. Transposition into Croatian law

Pursuant to Directive 2011/7/EU, the Late Payment 2011 Act allowed the parties to a contract between undertaking and public authority to agree on a payment period of no more than 30 days where the debtor is a public authority[77]. Exceptionally, the payment period may be expressly extended, but to no more than 60

72 Art. 9.1, 3-4 of the Slovenian Late Payment 2012 Act.
73 Art. 4.6 of Directive 2011/7/EU.
74 Ibid.
75 Ibid.
76 Art. 4 of Directive 2011/7/EU. Compare to Art. 2.1 and 3.1 of Directive 2000/35/EC.
77 Art. 3.1 of the Croatian Late Payment 2011 Act.

days altogether[78]. If the parties agree on a payment period of more than 60 days, such contractual term is *ex lege* null and void[79]. A payment period fixed in the contract of more than 30 but less than 60 days has been made subject to judicial review of the fairness of such term, in the same manner as for contracts between undertakings. If this contractual term were deemed to be grossly unfair to the creditor, the term would be rendered null and void[80].

Aside from the aforementioned contracts, the Croatian Late Payment 2011 Act also regulates contracts between undertakings and public authorities where the debtor is the undertaking. However, the legal regime established for these contracts is the same as the contracts between undertakings[81].

The Late Payment 2011 Act allowed also for an exception which is not in line with Directive 2011/7/EU. Despite the fact that public entities providing healthcare should be subject to the same rules as other public authorities, the Croatian law applied the same legal regime to contracts where the debtor is a public entity providing healthcare as the one established for contracts between undertakings[82]. This approach was, however, abolished with the new Late Payment 2012 Act which does not exempt the healthcare system in any way from its provisions brought into force in transposition of Directive 2011/7/EU. In other aspects regarding contracts between undertakings and public authorities, the Late Payment 2012 Act kept on the same solutions provided in the earlier law[83].

2.3.2. Transposition into Slovenian law

The Slovenian approach shows strong determination to set the public authorities as an example of good payment practices. The Late Payment 2011 Act prescribed that the payment period cannot exceed 30 days in contracts where the debtor is a public authority[84]. An irrebuttable presumption that a contractual term specifying a longer payment period represents a grossly unfair contractual agreement has been established, with the consequence of such a term being null and void *ex lege*[85]. The same strict provisions were carried over to the new Late Payment 2012 Act[86].

78 Art. 3.2 of the Croatian Late Payment 2011 Act.
79 Art. 4.3 of the Croatian Late Payment 2011 Act.
80 Art. 4.4 of the Croatian Late Payment 2011 Act.
81 Art. 3.3 of the Croatian Late Payment 2011 Act.
82 Ibid.
83 Art. 12 and 14.4, 6-7 of the Croatian Late Payment 2012 Act.
84 Art. 6.1 of the Slovenian Late Payment 2011 Act.
85 Art. 4.2, 4 of the Slovenian Late Payment 2011 Act.
86 Art. 9.2, 4 and 11.1 of the Slovenian Late Payment 2012 Act.

3. The notion of late payment

Directive 2011/7/EU has defined "late payment" as

> "payment not made within the contractual or statutory period of payment and where the conditions laid down in Article 3(1) or Article 4(1) are satisfied"[87].

These conditions are that the creditor has fulfilled his contractual and legal obligations, and that he has not received the amount due in time, unless the debtor is not responsible for the delay. Substantially the same was prescribed in the previous Directive 2000/35/EC[88].

An argument arises on the basis of the first condition that a debtor of a monetary obligation is entitled not to perform his obligation until the creditor has performed his non-monetary obligation. It can be further argued that the rule *exceptio non adimpleti contractus*, which is well known in the national private laws of European countries[89], thus became a principle of EU contract law. On the opposite side, another argument could be that Directive 2011/7/EU has a limited scope of application, therefore it cannot be concluded just on the basis of this directive that the rule *exceptio non adimpleti contractus* became a principle of all EU contract law[90].

The phrase "contractual and legal obligations" of the creditor, as contained in the first condition, should be interpreted in a restrictive manner as meaning only the obligations which are in correlation with the debtor's obligations arising from the same contract, and not extensively as meaning any of the creditor's obligations to the debtor. The logic behind the provision of Directive 2011/7/EU is that it is not justifiable for a debtor to have to pay interest on late payment for

87 Art. 2.1.4 of Directive 2011/7/EU.

88 See Art. 2.1.2 and 3.1 c) of Directive 2000/35/EC.

89 See, e.g.: § 320 of the German Civil Code (Bürgerliches Gesetzbuch, Federal Law Gazette I (Bundesgesetzblatt I), no. 2/2002 with amendments in 53/2002, 21/2003 and 41/2011; hereinafter: BGB); Art. 101 of the Slovenian Obligations Code; Art. 358 of the Croatian Obligations Act. The synallagmatic principle is also recognised in the United Nations Convention on Contracts for the International Sale of Goods (11.04.1980, U.N. Doc. A/CONF.97/18, 1980; hereinafter: CISG) – Art. 58.1 of the CISG prescribes: "If the buyer is not bound to pay the price at any other specific time, he must pay it when the seller places either the goods or documents controlling their disposition at the buyer's disposal in accordance with the contract and this Convention. The seller may make such payment a condition for handing over the goods or documents".

90 Supporting the latter argument, in the context of provisions of 4 Directive 2000/35/EC, see e.g.: Zoll, Fryderyk, The Remedies for Non-Performance in the System of the Acquis Group, in: Schulze, Reiner (ed.), Common Frame of Reference and Existing EC Contract Law, Sellier, Munich, 2008, pp. 200 – 201.

a period of time during which the creditor was late with performance of his obligation.

The second condition governing a debtor's late payment is that the creditor had not received the amount due on time. The explanation of the term "received" is given in the preamble of Directive 2011/7/EU which states that a debtor's payment should be regarded as late

> "where the creditor does not have the sum owed at his disposal on the due date"[91].

This provision reflects, and is probably a direct consequence of, the interpretation given by the European Court of Justice in its landmark case *01051 Telecom*[92]. In this judgement, when interpreting the meaning of the term "received" in the context of the earlier Directive 2000/35/EC, the Court has held:

> "It is therefore explicit in the wording of that provision that a debtor's payment is regarded as late, for the purposes of entitlement to interest for late payment, where the creditor does not have the sum owed at his disposal on the due date. In the case of payment by bank transfer, only the crediting of the amount due to the creditor's account will enable him to have that sum at his disposal"[93].

According to Directive 2001/7/EU, the debtor of a monetary obligation will be exonerated from the legal consequences of his late payment, including from the duty to pay late payment interest, if he is not responsible for the delay. This is a subjective concept of late payment, as opposed to the objective concept according to which the debtor would be in delay irrespective of whether he is responsible or to blame for the delay.

The burden of proof should be carried by the debtor who should provide evidence that he is not responsible for the delay. This is the only interpretation that would be in line with the spirit of the directive, especially when bearing in mind

---

91 Pt. 17 of the preamble of Directive 2011/7/EU.

92 Judgement of the European Court of Justice of 3. April 2008, 01051 Telecom GmbH vs. Deutsche Telekom AG, case C-306/06, Official Journal, C 128, 24.5.2008, p. 7, document is available online at: http://curia.europa.eu (last accessed on: 10.09.2012). For more detailed information on this case see, e.g.: Cornelis, J. W. Baaij, Late Payments: Case: ECJ – 01051 Telecom, "European Review of Contract Law", no. 2, 2009, pp. 132 - 148; Micklitz, Hans-W., Cafaggi, Fabrizio (eds.), European Private Law after the Common Frame of Reference, Edward Elgar Publishing Ltd, Cheltenham, 2010, pp. 74 – 75; Tot, Ivan, Late Payment by Bank Transfer (Zakašnjenje s ispunjenjem novèane obveze plaæanjem putem banke), "Croatian Law Review" ("Hrvatska pravna revija"), no. 10, 2011, pp. 37 – 38.

93 §23 of the judgement in the case 01051 Telecom.

that the subjective concept of late payment is an exception from the general duty to pay on time[94].

The circle of reasons which exonerate a debtor from responsibility for late payment should be particularly narrow. A debtor could not use the argument that its own debtors did not pay or that public authorities failed to provide it with funding[95]. In fact, the only valid reason for the exoneration of the debtor should be an obstacle which is completely outside the sphere of the debtor's influence, such as *vis maior*.

3.1. The notion of late payment in Croatian law

The Croatian Obligations Act provides for an objective concept of late payment. A debtor is in delay if he has not performed his obligation in the given period of time[96], which period was set in the contract or provided by the law[97]. The question of whether the delay is his fault is not relevant, therefore a debtor's payment will be considered late even if the debtor is not responsible for the delay[98]. This objective concept of late payment is more favourable to the creditor than the subjective concept provided in Directive 2011/7/EU according to which the debtor may be exonerated from the legal effects of his late payment if he was not responsible for the delay. Although it is more favourable to the creditor than the directive's provisions, the approach of Croatian law is not contrary to Directive 2011/7/EU.

According to the Croatian Obligations Act, the debtor is in delay if he has not performed his obligation in the given period of time, even if the creditor has not performed his reciprocal obligations. However, one of the legal consequenc-

---

94 A similar conclusion was reached by Schulte-Braucks and Ongena in: Schulte-Braucks et al., cited work in ref. 15, p. 530. Also, Cornelis stated that the 01051 Telecom case showed that "it is the debtor who has to prove that he did everything necessary to ensure a timely payment in order to avoid the claim to interest for late payment by the creditor", in: Cornelis, cited work in ref. 92, p. 137.

95 Schulte-Braucks et al., cited work. in ref. 15, p. 530.

96 Art. 183.1 of the Croatian Obligations Act.

97 Art. 173.1-2 of the Croatian Obligations Act.

98 This interpretation is confirmed in the case-law of the Croatian Supreme Court, e.g. in the judgements VSRH Gzz 24/98 of 20.01.1999 and VSRH Gzz 69/98 of 04.02.1999; a full text is available in: Slakoper, Zvonimir (ed.), Case Law 1985-2005 and Bibliography on Obligations Act (Sudska praksa 1980 - 2005 i bibliografija radova uz Zakon o obveznim odnosima), RRiF Plus, Zagreb, 2005, pp. 118 – 119. This is also the prevailing interpretation in Croatian legal doctrine, see e.g.: Crnić, Ivica, Interest (Kamate), Informator, Zagreb, 1989, p. 4; Klarić, Petar, Vedriš Mladen, Civil Law (Građansko pravo), Narodne novine, Zagreb, 2009, p. 475; Tot, cited work in ref. 92, p. 36.

es of *mora creditoris* is that the late payment interest owed by the debtor is suspended as of the date from which the creditor is in delay[99]. Although different in concept from the solution of Directive 2011/7/EU, these provisions of Croatian law do achieve the same result as the provisions of the directive. Therefore, this approach of Croatian law is also not contrary to Directive 2011/7/EU.

3.2. The notion of late payment in Slovenian law

The Slovenian Obligations Code provides for the same legal solutions as in Croatian law. The established concept of late payment is an objective one[100], while late payment interest owed by the debtor is suspended as of the date of the creditor's delay[101].

Despite the narrow circle of reasons which could exonerate the debtor from the consequences of his late payment according to Directive 2011/7/EU, it would anyhow be more appropriate and more in line with the aims of the directive that the directive adopts the objective concept of the late payment. The provisions of both Croatian and Slovenian law could serve as a model in this respect for a potential recast of the directive in the future.

4. Legal consequences of late payment

The fundamental legal consequences of late payment which the Member States are obliged by Directive 2011/7/EU to ensure in national law are: a creditor's rights to late payment interest, compensation for recovery costs and reasonable compensation of other costs.

4.1. Late payment interest

Directive 2011/7/EU defines "interest for late payment" as

> "statutory interest for late payment or interest at a rate agreed between undertakings"[102].

"Statutory interest for late payment" means

99 Art. 185.2 of the Croatian Obligations Act.

100 See Art. 299.1 of the Slovenian Obligations Code which is identical to Art. 183. 1 of the Croatian Obligations Act.

101 See Art. 301.2 of the Slovenian Obligations Code which is identical to Art. 185.2 of the Croatian Obligations Act.

102 Art. 2.1.5 of Directive 2011/7/EU.

> "simple interest for late payment at a rate which is equal to the sum of the reference rate and at least eight percentage points"[103]

– in comparison with the earlier Directive 2000/35/EC, the margin was raised by one percentage point[104]. For Member States in the eurozone, a reference rate is either

> "the interest rate applied by the European Central Bank to its most recent main refinancing operations"

or

> "the marginal interest rate resulting from variable-rate tender procedures for the most recent main refinancing operations of the European Central Bank"[105].

The equivalent rate set by the national central bank is the "reference rate" for Member States outside the eurozone[106].

Directive 2011/7/EU allows for interest for late payment to be subject to a contractual agreement between debtor and creditor who can agree either a lower or higher interest rate for late payment. However, the directive obliges the Member States to ensure that such contractual agreement is not unfair to the creditor[107]. The agreement between debtor and creditor on a contractual rate of late payment interest might be regarded as unfair to the creditor only if the rate agreed is lower than the statutory rate, while a higher contractual rate is by nature more favourable to the creditor.

Permitting contractual agreement on the rate of interest for late payment was already criticised in the context of the earlier Directive 2000/35/EC[108]. It was argued that the contracting parties may, under certain circumstances, even reach agreement to the effect that no late payment interest will be owed[109]. For this reason a new provision was inserted in Directive 2011/7/EU according to which a contractual term or practice which excludes interest for late payment should always be considered grossly unfair[110].

---

103 Art. 2.1.6 of Directive 2011/7/EU.

104 Art. 3.1. d) of Directive 2000/35/EC.

105 Art. 2.1.7 (a) of Directive 2011/7/EU. Compared to the provision of Art. 3.1. d) of Directive 2000/35/EC, the definition of the "reference rate" was extended to include "the marginal interest rate resulting from variable-rate tender procedures".

106 Art. 2.1.7 (b).

107 Art. 2.1.5 and Art. 7 of Directive 2011/7/EU.

108 Art. 3.1. d) of Directive 2000/32/EC provided that the creditor is entitled to interest for late payment at a statutory rate, "unless otherwise specified in the contract".

109 Zaccaria, cited work in ref. 17, p. 392.

110 Art. 7.2 of Directive 2011/7/EU.

4.1.1. Late payment interest in Croatian law

The Croatian Obligations Act provides for a statutory rate of late payment interest in commercial transactions at a rate which is equal to the sum of the discount rate of the Croatian National Bank and eight percentage points[111]. This provision existed even prior to Directive 2011/7/EU, although the earlier directive insisted on an increase of the reference rate by seven percentage points.

In commercial transactions, debtor and creditor may agree on a rate of late payment interest which differs from the statutory rate. However, freedom of contract is limited as the highest rate fixed in the contract cannot exceed the sum of the statutory rate and one half of the statutory rate[112]. Further, such contractual agreement on a higher or lower rate of late payment interest is subject to a judicial review of fairness of such provision and would be rendered null and void if deemed unfair to the creditor – but also if deemed unfair to the debtor[113].

Following the provision of Directive 2011/7/EU according to which a contractual term or practice which excludes interest for late payment should always be considered grossly unfair, the Croatian Late Payment 2011 Act provides that such agreement is null and void[114]. The same provision exists in the new Croatian Late Payment 2012 Act, though it is applicable only to contracts between undertakings while contracts between undertakings and public authorities are excluded[115]. The Croatian law in force has therefore failed to implement Directive 2011/7/EU properly in this respect.

Like the solutions provided in the national laws of some Member States[116], the Croatian Obligations Act provides for a statutory rate of late payment interest not only for commercial transactions, but for all other transactions as well. The statutory rate is lower for the other relations (not of a commercial nature) and is equal to the sum of the discount rate of Croatian National Bank and five percentage points[117]. Although this approach is not contrary to Directive 2011/7/EU since the non-commercial transactions fall out of the directive's scope, here again the problem exists with regard to the liberal professions – contracts with people engaged in a liberal profession are not commercial contracts

---

111 Art. 29.2 of the Croatian Obligations Act.

112 Art. 29.3 and 26.2 of the Croatian Obligations Act.

113 Art. 29.4-6 of the Croatian Obligations Act. The test of fairness is the same as in the Late Payment 2011 Act – see supra in chapter 2.1.1. of this paper.

114 Art. 4.1 of the Croatian Late Payment 2011 Act.

115 Art. 14.1 of the Croatian Late Payment 2012 Act.

116 See e.g. § 288 of the BGB.

117 Art. 29.2 of the Croatian Obligations Act.

in the sense of the Obligations Act, therefore the lower interest rate is applied instead of the one for commercial transactions[118].

4.1.2. Late payment interest in Slovenian law

In Slovenian law the statutory rate of late payment interest in commercial transactions is prescribed as a rate which is equal to the sum of the reference rate and eight percentage points, the reference rate being the interest rate applied by the European Central Bank to its most recent main refinancing operations[119]. For contracts with consumers, the statutory rate of late payment interest is set at eight percent annually[120].

Debtor and creditor may agree on a rate of late payment interest which is lower or higher than the statutory rate, while limits to such agreement are not provided in the Obligations Code[121]. However, the Late Payment 2011 Act has limited the freedom of contract with regards to transactions between undertakings and public authorities where a public authority is the debtor: in these contracts, the contractual rate of late payment interest cannot be lower than the statutory rate[122]. This solution intends to show the public authorities as a model of good payment practices and may serve as a model for a new provision of some future EU legal act on combating late payments.

In line with Directive 2011/7/EU, the Late Payment 2011 Act has established an irrebuttable presumption that a contractual agreement which excludes interest for late payment represents a grossly unfair contractual agreement, with the consequence of such agreement being null and void *ex lege*[123].

---

118 Tot, Ivan, Late Payment Interest between Liberal Professions (Zatezne kamate između osoba slobodnih zanimanja), "Law in Economy" ("Pravo u gospodarstvu"), vol. 51, no. 3, 2012, pp. 850 – 852.

119 Art. 2 of the Slovenian Interest Act.

120 Art. 378.2 of the Slovenian Obligations Code and Art. 27.a.1 of the Slovenian Consumer Protection Act (Zakon o varstvu potrošnikovih, Official Gazette of the Republic of Slovenia (Uradni list Republike Slovenije), no. 20/1998, with amendments in 25/1998, 23/1999, 110/2002, 14/2003, 51/2004, 98/2004, 46/2006, 126/2007, 86/2009 and 78/2011.

121 Art. 379 of the Slovenian Obligations Code.

122 Art. 10 of the Slovenian Late Payment 2011 Act. The same is provided in Art. 13 of the Slovenian Late Payment 2012 Act.

123 Art. 4.2, 4 of the Slovenian Late Payment 2011 Act. The same is provided in Art. 9.2, 4 of the Slovenian Late Payment 2012 Act.

4.2. Compensation for recovery costs

A novelty in comparison with the earlier Directive 2000/35/EC is the provision of Directive 2011/7/EU which orders the Member States to ensure that the creditor is entitled to demand a minimum fixed sum of 40 EUR from the debtor, without the necessity of a reminder and as compensation for the creditor's own recovery costs incurred due to late payment[124]. Parties to a contract may exclude this creditor's right, but in the case of dispute the debtor would have to provide evidence that such contractual agreement is not grossly unfair to the creditor, since the directive establishes a rebuttable presumption that exclusion of compensation for recovery costs is grossly unfair[125].

4.2.1. Compensation for recovery costs in Croatian law

Whereas the Croatian Late Payment 2011 Act had not implemented the provisions of Directive 2011/7/EU on compensation for recovery costs, the new Late Payment 2012 Act established the creditor's right to compensation for recovery costs in the amount of 300 Croatian *Kuna*[126], which is roughly equal to the amount of 40 EUR. The new legal consequence of late payment in Croatian law has a more retributive than compensatory function, since it provides that a creditor is entitled to the compensation irrespective of whether any damage has been caused by the debtor's late payment[127], meaning the creditor is entitled to this additional amount even if no recovery costs are incurred.

Even though the creditor is entitled to compensation in the case of late payment of the obligations arising both from contracts between undertakings and contracts between undertakings and public authorities, a contractual agreement which excludes this creditor's right is *ex lege* null and void only in respect of contracts between undertakings[128]. Legislative intervention is therefore needed in order to transpose Directive 2011/7/EU properly, at least to establish a rebuttable presumption that exclusion of compensation in contracts between undertakings and public authorities is grossly unfair.

---

124 Art. 6.1-2 of Directive 2011/7/EU.

125 Art. 7.3 of Directive 2011/7/EU.

126 Art. 13.1 of the Croatian Late Payment 2012 Act.

127 Art. 13.2-3 of the Croatian Late Payment 2012 Act.

128 Art. 14.1 of the Croatian Late Payment 2012 Act.

4.2.2. Compensation for recovery costs in Slovenian law

The Slovenian Late Payment 2011 Act established the creditor's right to compensation for recovery costs in the amount of 40 EUR[129]. Instead of inserting a rebuttable presumption that a contractual agreement which excludes this right is grossly unfair, Slovenian law provided for a solution which is more favourable to the creditor: an irrebuttable presumption that such agreement is always grossly unfair to the creditor and as a result of unfairness is *ex lege* null and void[130]. The same provisions remained in the Late Payment 2012 Act[131].

4.3. Reasonable compensation of other costs

The 40 EUR compensation established in Directive 2011/7/EU is intended only for the recovery of administrative and internal costs incurred due to late payment, but not for any other recovery costs, such as those incurred by creditors in instructing a lawyer or engaging a debt collection agency[132]. However, in addition to this fixed sum, Member States are obliged to ensure a creditor's right to obtain reasonable compensation from the debtor for any recovery costs exceeding that fixed sum[133].

4.3.1. Compensation of other costs in Croatian law

In Croatia, the creditor is entitled to a fixed sum in compensation of recovery costs and to late payment interest, regardless of whether he has suffered any damage. The recovery costs exceeding the fixed sum of 40 EUR would be considered under Croatian law as damage incurred by the creditor due to the debtor's late payment. According to the Obligations Act, creditors are entitled to compensation for damages suffered as a result of a debtor's late performance of his obligation[134]. The creditor is not only entitled to full reimbursement of any incurred costs, but also to compensation for loss of profits and for non-pecuniary damages, if the late payment can be attributed to wilful intent or gross negligence on the part of the debtor[135]. In other cases where the debtor is to blame for late payment, the creditor is entitled to compensation of those damages that should have been foreseeable by the debtor at the time of entering into the con-

129 Art. 11 of the Slovenian Late Payment 2011 Act.
130 Art. 4.2, 4 of the Slovenian Late Payment 2011 Act.
131 Art. 14 and 9.2, 4 of the Slovenian Late Payment 2012 Act.
132 Pt. 19-20 of the preamble of Directive 2011/7/EU.
133 Art. 6.3 of Directive 2011/7/EU.
134 Art. 342.2 of the Croatian Obligations Act.
135 Art. 346.2 of the Croatian Obligations Act.

tract as the possible consequences of a breach of said contract, considering the facts the debtor knew or should have known at that time[136].

Unlike late payment interest and a fixed sum in compensation of recovery costs, where an objective concept of late payment is applied, Croatian law establishes the subjective concept of late payment in respect of the damage incurred by the creditor due to the debtor's late payment. The debtor may be exempted from liability for compensation if he provides evidence that the late payment occurred due to external, extraordinary and unforeseeable circumstances arising after entering into the contract, which circumstances he could not prevent, eliminate or avoid[137].

4.3.2. Compensation of other costs in Slovenian law

Regarding the creditor's right to compensation of costs as well as other damages suffered as a result of the debtor's late payment, the Slovenian Obligations Code provides identical solutions as the Croatian Obligations Act as explained above.

Directive 2011/7/EU explicitly states that the directive's provisions are without prejudice

> "to national provisions according to which a national court may award compensation to the creditor for any additional damage regarding the debtor's late payment"[138].

Therefore, the Croatian and Slovenian approach is in accordance with the directive. Moreover, in possible future amendments to Directive 2011/7/EU, it would be desirable to include a provision which would oblige the Member States to entitle the creditor to a right of full compensation of costs and other damages incurred due to late payment. Only in this manner would creditors be entirely protected from the negative effects of late payments.

5. Conclusion

When transposing the EU directives on combating late payments into their national laws, both Croatia and Slovenia showed a willingness to go beyond the minimum standards established in the directives in order to shift more rapidly from bad payment practices to a culture of prompt payment. Many of Croatia's and Slovenia's own legal solutions may serve as starting ideas when developing new measures of combating late payments at EU level.

---

136 Art. 346.1 of the Croatian Obligations Act.

137 Art. 343 of the Croatian Obligations Act.

138 Pt. 19 of the preamble of Directive 2011/7/EU.

Unfortunately, while concentrating on improving the provisions of the directives, Slovenia and Croatia failed to properly transpose the EU directives into their national laws in some aspects. Whereas Slovenia omitted to implement only one provision of Directive 2011/7/EU, Croatian laws on combating late payments contain a lot of errors and oversights, the major ones being the exclusion of the liberal professions and the whole of the financial sector from their provisions.

Legislative intervention is therefore needed in order to fully transpose Directive 2011/7/EU into the laws of Slovenia and Croatia. Until the directive is properly implemented, the national courts are expected to embrace a creative role in interpreting national laws in the light of the directive's provisions.

Bibliography

Cornelis, J. W. Baaij: Late Payments: Case: ECJ – 01051 Telecom, European Review of Contract Law, no. 2, 2009.

Crnić, Ivica: Interest (Kamate), Informator, Zagreb, 1989.

Gorenc, Vilim: Time limits for payment of monetary obligations after January 1st, 2012 (Rokovi ispunjenja novčanih obveza od 1. siječnja 2012.), "Accounting, auditing and finances" ("Računovodstvo, revizija i financije"), no. 12, 2011.

Klarić, Petar; Vedriš, Mladen: Civil Law (Građansko pravo), Narodne novine, Zagreb, 2009.

McCormack, Gerard: Retention of Title and the EC Late Payment Directive, Journal of Corporate Law Studies, vol. 1, no. 2, 2001.

Micklitz, Hans-W.; Cafaggi, Fabrizio (eds.): European Private Law after the Common Frame of Reference, Edward Elgar Publishing Ltd, Cheltenham, 2010.

Milo, John Michael: Combating Late Payment in Business Transactions: How a New European Directive Has Failed to Set a Substantial Minimum Standard Regarding National Provisions on Retention of Title, "European Review of Private Law", vol. 10, no. 3, 2003.

Pavičić, Damir: Application of the Act on Time Limits for Payment of Monetary Obligations (Primjena Zakona o rokovima ispunjenja novčanih obveza), "Accounting, auditing and finances" ("Računovodstvo, revizija i financije"), no. 1, 2012.

Pavičić, Damir, Current issues with the application of the Act on Time Limits for Payment of Monetary Obligations (Aktualna pitanja vezana za primjenu Zakona o rokovima ispunjenja novčanih obveza), "Accounting, auditing and finances" ("Računovodstvo, revizija i financije"), no. 5, 2012.

Perales Viscasillas, Pilar: Late Payment Directive 2000/35 and the CISG, "Pace International Law Review", vol. 19, no. 1, 2007, the document is available online at: http://digitalcommons.pace.edu/pilr/vol19/iss1/8 (last accessed on: 23.09.2012).

Schulte-Braucks, Reinhard, Ongena, Steven: The Late Payment Directive – a step towards an emerging European Private Law?, "European Review of Private Law", vol. 11, no. 4, 2003.

Slakoper, Zvonimir (ed.): Case Law 1985-2005 and Bibliography on Obligations Act (Sudska praksa 1980. - 2005. i bibliografija radova uz Zakon o obveznim odnosima), RRiF Plus, Zagreb, 2005.

Tot, Ivan: Late Payment Interest between Liberal Professions (Zatezne kamate između osoba slobodnih zanimanja), "Law in Economy" ("Pravo u gospodarstvu"), vol. 51, no. 3, 2012.

Tot, Ivan, Late Payment by Bank Transfer (Zakašnjenje s ispunjenjem novčane obveze plaćanjem putem banke), "Croatian Law Review" ("Hrvatska pravna revija"), no. 10, 2011.

Zaccaria, Alessio: (EC) Directive 2000/35 on Combating Late Payments in Commercial Transactions, "The European Legal Forum (E)", vol. 5, no. 6, 2000-2001, the document is available online at: http://www.simonslaw.com/library/pdf/ e/92.pdf (last accessed on: 23.09.2012).

Zoll, Fryderyk: The Remedies for Non-Performance in the System of the Acquis Group, in: Schulze, Reiner (ed.), Common Frame of Reference and Existing EC Contract Law, Sellier, Munich, 2008.

RECENT DEVELOPMENTS AND PERSPECTIVES IN THE REGULATION OF INTERNATIONNAL BUSINESS LAW

Considerations on the Need to Develop a Common Law on International Bankruptcy

Assistant professor Luiza Cristina GAVRILESCU[1]

Abstract

The need to harmonise the rules on insolvency has become prominent because bankruptcy procedure, as a legal institution, is mandatorily circumscribed to the procedural rules of the forum, which excludes the applicability of foreign rules; the application of foreign laws in resolving legal relations with a foreign element on insolvency was only allowed as an exception. Substantially different rules developed at national level for resolving insolvency procedure may impede the recovery of sustainable enterprises and thus may adversely affect the entire international competition framework. In doctrine, there were considered to be certain common principles of substantive law of insolvency, which would result from detailed analysis of the national laws. The contribution of international instruments seems significant in this regard. Taken together, the provisions of the abovementioned international instruments form a model for resolving the conflicts raised by international bankruptcy, through a combination of the main proceeding and secondary proceedings. Nevertheless, common law is not a set of predetermined rules with a firm content: it is the result of a work of interpretation, a result which, in turn, can become a useful tool for new interpretations. Jus commune is the expression of the goal to achieve harmonisation; a uniformisation that will respect differences and the values they represent.

Keywords: common law; harmonisation of rules; insolvency law; unified principles

Currently, companies tend to become multinational to benefit from the global phenomenon of the concentration of capital. To take advantage of business opportunities and attractive markets at a given moment, companies have significant assets and subsidiaries worldwide. Thus, commercial operators are forced to operate under the authority of multiple jurisdictions.

Each of the authorities involved requires the application of their rules, which are, of course, different. If a multinational company has financial difficulties, the restructuring or liquidation takes place within the jurisdiction of several authorities and leads to multiple insolvency proceedings. The courts before which the

1 Luiza Cristina Gavrilescu, "Alexandru Ioan Cuza" University of Iasi, Faculty of Law, Romania, Email: luiza.gavrilescu@uaic.ro.

dispute is brought must coordinate their collective proceedings and the states should harmonise their legal systems[2].

The current economic circumstances have necessitated a legislative framework for managing the problems caused by companies in financial difficulty. More specifically, the continued international expansion of trade and investments is conducted at a much faster pace than that at which various national laws adapt their regulations to meet the new current factual situations[3].

Insolvency regulations aim to ensure a balance in protecting the rights of all parties to the proceedings[4]. In particular, creditor equality must be respected, as well as the enforcement of appropriate treatment to the debtor[5].

How insolvency law protects the various parties involved can differ greatly from one state to another. Thus, one can identify significant differences in the structure and content of national insolvency regimes, due to fundamentally different domestic political considerations[6].

The need to harmonise the rules on insolvency has become prominent because bankruptcy procedure, as a legal institution, is mandatorily circumscribed to the procedural rules of the forum, which excludes the applicability of foreign rules; the application of foreign laws in resolving legal relations with a foreign element on insolvency was only allowed as an exception.

The lack of common rules on insolvency may cause differences in competitive treatment and difficulties in the operation of companies that engage in activities across borders or have foreign operations. Therefore, special attention should be paid to the regulation of the insolvency of groups of companies and the discouragement of *forum shopping*, consisting of strategic shifts in the centres of interest to obtain more favourable treatment[7].

---

2 See M. Natasha Labovitz, Jessica I. Basil, It's a Small World After All: A Survey of Recent Developments in US Bankruptcy Law and their Potential Multinational Impact, "Business Law International", vol. 7, no. 1/ 2006, p. 39.

3 See Mircea N. Costin, Angela Miff, Falimentul, Evoluţie şi actualitate [Bankruptcy, Evolution and Current Situation], Lumina Lex Publishing House, Bucharest, 2000, p.41.

4 See Gheorghe Piperea, Insolvenţa: legea, regulile, realitatea [Insolvency: Law, Rules, Reality], Wolters Kluwer Publishing House, 2008, p. 279.

5 See Ana Birchall, Procedura insolvenţei. Reorganizarea judiciară şi procedura falimentului. Note de curs incluzând procedura concordatului preventiv şi a mandatului ad-hoc [Insolvency Proceedings. Judicial Reorganisation and Bankruptcy Proceedings. Lecture Notes Including Arrangement Procedure and Ad-hoc Mandate], Universul Juridic Publishing House, Bucharest, 2010, p. 10.

6 See Dragoş Alexandru Sitaru, Dreptul comerţului internaţional [International Trade Law], Lumina Lex Publishing House, Bucharest, 2004, p.446.

7 See R. Goode, Principles of Corporate Insolvency Law, Sweet /Maxwell, London, 2005, p. 35.

The activity of uniformisation in the field of insolvency is reflected in the conclusion of international agreements, the adoption of regulations, and the development of model laws that are transposed into national laws. The results of the process of assimilating a set of common principles were outlined in the Report prepared by *INSOL EUROPE*[8] in April 2010, at the request of the Committee on Legal Affairs of the European Parliament, titled *Harmonisation of Insolvency Law at EU Level*. The specialists who prepared the document based their analysis on country reports from Poland, France, UK, Germany, Spain, Italy and Sweden. Material from the Netherlands and Belgium was also considered[9].

The purpose of the report was to assess whether the harmonisation of insolvency law at EU level is possible as well as necessary. Among the immediate benefits of eliminating the differences in the legal regime of insolvency are: preservation of insolvency value; increase in predictability regarding the real possibilities of debt recovery; attracting potential investors to ensure business growth; reducing costs involved in managing the proceeding.

The uniformisation of the rules does not aim to achieve total homogeneity, the existence of differences in insolvency law is a postulate which cannot or should not be applied. Analyses carried out in the field of cooperation on international bankruptcy confirmed that the unification of legislative solutions of the states would be justified only in a few sectors of insolvency[10]. Among these, the following were identified, in particular:

- establishing common criteria for identifying insolvency as a prerequisite for opening bankruptcy proceedings[11];
- development of similar rules on the conditions for formulating and processing requests for opening insolvency proceedings[12];

8 INSOL EUROPE – The Professional Association for European Restructuring and Insolvency Specialists.

9 See Giorgio Cherubini, Neil Cooper, Daniel Fritz, Emmanuelle Inacio, Katarzyna Ingielewicz, Guy Lofalk, Miriam Mailly, David Marks Q.C., Anna Maria Pukszto, Barbara F.H. Rumora Scheltema, Robert Van Galen, Miguel Virgos, Bob Wessels, Nora Wouters, Harmonisation of Insolvency Law at EU Level, report of the Policy Department C – Citizens' Rights and Constitutional Affairs. European Parliament. B-1047 Brussels, available at: http://www.europarl.europa.eu/studies, accessed on 10.08.2012.

10 See Ian F. Fletcher, Insolvency in Private International Law, Oxford University Press, New York, 1999, p. 3.

11 Vasile Pătulea, Sfera de aplicabilitate a prevederilor Legii nr. 64/1995 privind procedura reorganizării judiciare şi a falimentului [The Scope of Law no. 64/1995 on Judicial Reorganisation and Bankruptcy Procedure], in "Dreptul", no. 2/2005, p. 47.

12 Aspru, L.O., Insolvenţa transfrontalieră în statele Uniunii Europene [Cross-Border Insolvency in EU States], in "Pandectele Române", supplement, 2006, p. 16.

- establishing distinctions in the subject of the proceeding: reorganisation or liquidation, to be made in order to achieve common goals;
- determining the effects of the proceeding according to the same criteria regarding property or non-property elements.

The relative inability of traditional mechanisms of normative technology, represented by the substantive approach[13], led to the identification of other ways of unifying substantive international bankruptcy law, including the creation of a common law, *jus commune*[14].

The homogenisation of substantive international bankruptcy law can be achieved starting from a deeper form of coordination which would highlight the complementarity between the legal systems and the originality of current rules. Such an approach is based on the intellectual link between the international regulations, which are based on common principles and methods.

In fact, private international law presupposes that each of the legal systems involved in international relations has a certain potential legitimacy to solve a given legal situation. This constant characteristic was termed by a large portion of the European doctrine *jus commune*[15]. Its origin is recognised as being in *Justinian's Compilations*, but there is some dispute about its evolution and the distinct realities to which this notion was related over time. Thus, the unity of the notion was called into question and is even sometimes regarded as a "historical fantasy".

The EU has become a formidable factor of uniformisation and in recent years its actions have appeared to exceed its traditional competence. Since the Resolution of 26 May 1989[16] by which the European Parliament called on Member States to standardise their entire private law, scientific initiatives have multiplied and the reality of the project has become more tangible. Some materials have already been the subject of extensive research, several of which are of undeniable interest for international bankruptcy[17].

---

13 See Ioan Macovei, Drept internaţional privat în reglementarea Noului Cod civil şi de procedură civilă [Private International Law in Regulating the New Civil Code and Civil Procedure], C.H. Beck Publishing House, 2011, p. 24.

14 A se vedea L.C.Gavrilescu, Tehnici normative de omogenizare a reglementărilor falimentului internaţional [Normative Techniques for the Homogenisation of International Bankruptcy Regulations], in "Analele Ştiinţifice ale Universităţii Al. I. Cuza" Iaşi, Tomul LVI, no. II Ştiinţe Juridice, 2010, p. 68.

15 See Francessco Calasso, Introduzione al diritto comune, Giufre, Milan, 1970, p. 391.

16 The resolution was published in the Official Journal of the European Union, 26 June 1989, no C158/400.

17 See Jurgen Basedow, European private law: Company and labour law, Kluwe, La Haye, 1999, p. 704.

As noted, Europe

> "appears to be a melting pot of social aspirations that sometimes raises problems difficult to solve, even at national level"[18].

Law is more of an identity factor, rather than normative, just as

> "different languages are instruments for the patterns of thought and feeling characteristic to nations"[19].

Thus, the interest in a study of *jus commune* is due to the fact that internationalists feel the need to overcome the difficulties posed by the differences between national systems, especially in the regional integration of the European Union. At the same time, the internationalisation of relations underlies a diminishing of the coding ideal, just as it generates the fear of a loss of identity. From this point of view, the example of *The European Contract Code*, with the polarisation of representations it created within the doctrine, is entirely relevant[20].

The communication and then the action plan presented by the European Commission gave the controversy between Thibaut and Savigny[21] a topical character: in fact, the question is now linked to the merits of codification and the forms in which it has to be adopted. Within Europe, the relevance of this question seems to be confirmed by the ambiguities of expression of European bankruptcy law. Thus, an autonomous system of rules can be identified that radiate outward from the centre, the institutions of the European Union, towards the laws of the Member States. In fact, the same expression designates a pluralistic system but uniform vocation and standardised system.

Jus commune is therefore the expression of the desire to allow harmonisation and uniformisation that will respect the differences and the values they represent. Certainly, some common points can be highlighted between *jus commune* and European law: the latter is a common law for all, but it also admits peculiarities, as the national law of the Member States continues to exist.

As noted by some authors,

> "European common law changed its nature, so it is no longer an actual law, but only the idea of a common legal legacy, a simple heritage. But this legacy has also

18 See Giulio C. Giorgini, Methodes conflictuelles et regles materielles dans l`application de nouveaux instruments de reglement de la faillite internationale, Dalloz, 2006, p. 39.

19 Ibidem, p. 41.

20 See C. Macovei, Dreptul european al contractelor. Modernizarea normelor de drept conflictual [European Contract Law. Modernisation of the Rules of Conflict Law], "Alexandru Iona Cuza" Publishing House, Iaşi, 2005, p. 102.

21 Positivist, Thibaut was a proponent of codification, while Savigny, the founder of the historical school, was a supporter of customary law.

> changed its contents: once based mainly on the idea of classical natural law, it is based later on the ideas expressed by modern liberal and capitalist society"[22].

It is therefore recommended to make use of the lessons offered by *jus commune* and its study, given the vitality of such an ancient notion.

The appropriateness of such an approach is based on the consideration of a future phenomenon, at least in appearance, shaped by a distant past glory. Moreover, this historical approach is already familiar in practice. Thus, it is said that

> "he who seeks success in *Court* should forget national codifications of the last three centuries and relate to the old common law of Europe, as it was developed in Latin, and is thus intelligible to all"[23].

This observation demonstrates that *jus commune* is not only a dream of humanist academics. Conversely, it should be emphasised that such a study does not focus only on certain, more general subjects, such as the law of obligations, but can be extended to more technical fields, namely that of intellectual property or, for my part, international bankruptcy, although often, in fact, the technicality of a subject seems to be an insurmountable obstacle for any attempt to generalise or pass to a higher level of abstraction.

Roman law has preserved a surprisingly vital force in commercial matters, especially in terms of arbitral jurisdiction. In fact, sometimes the parties ask the arbitrators to apply Roman law to resolve their dispute. Moreover, as arbitration is based on *lex mercantoria*, I must stress that it borrows much from Roman law and in general from *jus commune*. One may think that this reference to Roman law does not refer to the law of collective proceedings: the practice, however, offers some examples to the contrary. Thus, the arbitral tribunal established under the *Permanent Court of International Justice at The Hague* in the Venezuela case has applied the provisions of Roman law on bankruptcy[24]. It is true that, in that case, the parties themselves chose the application of Roman law, a choice which seems more difficult today, but it is also true that – in the absence of direct references to *jus commune* – it would have been taken into account within *lex mercantoria.*

The conclusions reached during the debates on the *European Code of Obligations* currently tend to act as a catalyst and extend their influence far beyond

22 See Olivier Beaud, Ouverture: L`Europe entre droit commun et droit communautaire, in "Droits", nr. 14/1991, p. 9.

23 See G.C. Giorgini, cited work, p. 51.

24 See Hersch Lauterpacht, Private Law Sources and Analogies of International Law (with special Reference to International Arbitration), Longmans, Green and Co, London, 1927, p.250.

the original scope[25]. However, if the studies on the European Code are extremely numerous, the idea of a European code of bankruptcy or even a European law of bankruptcies is less frequently mentioned[26].

The complexity and formalism of the subjects with procedural elements are probably some of the reasons for this relative lack of interest. Even so, at a general level, some authors have demonstrated the need to accompany the harmonisation of substantive law with a harmonisation of procedural law[27]. The opposition between the continental *civil law*, Roman-inspired, and the *common law*, Anglo-Saxon, legal systems is presented as an insurmountable barrier blocking the path of successful uniformisation. Many observers think that, if uniformity must be achieved, it will be done by sacrificing the heritage of one of the two legal cultures.

This approach, which reduces to extinction the specific elements of the various systems, thus constitutes a significant barrier to *jus commune*. However, the proponents of this sacrifice ignore the fact that, although the Anglo-Saxons did not welcome the tenets of *jus commune* like others, English law undoubtedly underwent a phenomenon of *Romanisation*, and then of *civilisation*. Today, the process of unification tends to intensify, so that we are witnessing a phenomenon described by some authors as the *hybridisation* of the law systems.

In this context, international bankruptcy presents a remarkable opportunity. Its complexity, the weight of its imperatives, its special place in the legal policy of each state, have provided a tremendous urge to remove the traditional views which are impeding progress[28].

International instruments regulating international bankruptcy can contribute to building a *jus commune* and thus open the way for the homogenisation of substantive bankruptcy law[29]. The construction of such a common law involves highlighting the principles of unity and common interpretation methods[30].

---

25 See Klaus Peter Berger, The Principles of European Contract Law and the Concept of the Creeping Codification of Law, in "European Review of Private Law", 2001, p. 21.

26 See Titia M. Bos, The European Insolvency Regulation and the Harmonization of Private International Law in Europe, in "Netherlands Law Review", no. 1/2003, p. 49.

27 See Andreas Schwartze, Enforcement of Private Law: The Missing Link in the Process of European Harmonization, in "European Review of Private Law", 2000, p. 135.

28 See John A. E. Pottow, Greed and Pride in International Bankruptcy: The Problems of and Proposed Solutions to Local Interests, in "Michigan Law Review", no. 8/2006, p. 1899.

29 See Carl Felsenfeld, International Insolvency, Juris Publishing, New York, 2005, p. 25.

30 See W.W. McBryde, A. Flessner, S.J. Kortmann, Principles of European Insolvency Law, Series Law of Business and Finance, vol. 4, Kluwer Legal Publishers, Deventer, 2003, p. 28.

It should be noted in this regard that *Regulation (EC) No. 1346/2000* on insolvency proceedings and *OHADA Uniform Act* relating to proceedings to cover the liabilities of the insolvent debtor[31] are both regional instruments and, therefore, present some analogies. The *Regulation* achieves a compromise between the universality and the territoriality principles of bankruptcy[32].

The situation is more complex for the *UNCITRAL Model Law* on Cross-border Insolvency[33] and the *Concordat of the International Bar Association*[34], both international in origin. The first-mentioned instrument is intended to become incorporated in a legal system, thus entailing a kind of *naturalisation*. This will give the provisions of this instrument the quality of internal rules. Thus, despite its international origin, the same *Model Law* to be built by two different states will lead to two rules, emphasising the two distinct legal systems. As for the *Concordat*, its provisions usually require an agreement, a protocol to produce a legal effect. The word "usually" is used because, if certain provisions are considered transnational public rules, this recognition will attract the obligation to observe them, even in the absence of such an act.

In doctrine there are considered to be certain common principles of substantive insolvency law, which would result from detailed analysis of national laws[35]. The contribution of international instruments seems significant in this regard. In fact, the list of principles covered includes: limited universality of bankruptcy, the role of the legislation on opening the proceeding, the right to appoint a liquidator who is responsible for overall treatment of the debtor's insolvency, reducing the scope of public order, the principle of creditor equality, and others[36].

Taken together, the provisions of the abovementioned international instruments form a model for resolving the conflicts raised by international bankruptcy, through a combination of the main proceeding and secondary proceedings.

---

31 The Uniform Act adopted by the Organization for Harmonization of Business Law in Africa in April 1998.

32 See Hirsch, A., Vers l`universalité de la faillite au sein du Marché commun, in "Cahiers de droit européen", no. 1/ 1970, p. 56.

33 Legislative Guide on Insolvency Law, UNCITRAL, United Nations Commission on International Trade Law, United Nation' s Publication, New York, 2005, p. 1.

34 Cross-border Insolvency Concordat, developed within the Insolvency and Creditors Rights Committee of the International Bar Association in 1995.

35 P.R. Wood, Principles of International Insolvency, Thomson, Sweet /Maxwell, London, 2007, p. 121.

36 Goode, R.M., Principles of Corporate Insolvency Law, Sweet /Maxwell, London, 2005.

The four instruments are noted to focus on the idea of extraterritorial effect given to the main proceeding opened under the same or similar criteria[37].

Nevertheless, common law is not a set of predetermined rules with firm content: it is the result of a work of interpretation, a result which, in turn, can become a useful tool for new interpretations.

The circulation of the models provided by international instruments should be accompanied by a circulation of the decisions, which are also to be integrated into a *jus commune*[38]. The difficulty is that a community of opinions should be created. The role of the doctrine is, from this point of view, fundamental. In international law, interpretation is not supported by a legal system. Notable in this respect is the interest of the *International Monetary Fund* through its project regarding an international bankruptcy tribunal.

The rebirth of the concept of *jus commune*, noted by many commentators, is rooted in a community of legal rules which emphasised the existence of common methods of analysis. This *jus commune* of international bankruptcy is thus established, not as a set of rules of substantive law, but as a common approach to the legal issue.

Bibliography

Aspru, L.O.: Insolvenţa transfrontalieră în statele Uniunii Europene, in "Pandectele Române", supplement, 2006.

Basedow, J.: European private law: Company and labour law, Kluwe, La Haye, 1999.

Beaud, O., Ouverture: L'Europe entre droit commun et droit communautaire, in "Droits", n. 14/1991.

Berger, K.P.: The Principles of European Contract Law and the concept of the Creeping Codification of Law, in "European Review of Private Law", 2001.

Birchall, A.: Procedura insolvenţei. Reorganizarea judiciară şi procedura falimentului. Note de curs incluzând procedura concordatului preventiv şi a mandatului ad-hoc, Universul Juridic Publishing House, Bucharest, 2010.

Bos, M.,T.: The European Insolvency Regulation and the Harmonization of Private International Law in Europe, in "Netherlands Law Review", n.1/2003.

McBryde, W.W.; Flessner, A.; Kortmann, S.J.: Principles of European Insolvency Law, Series Law of Business and Finance, vol. 4, Kluwer Legal Publishers, Deventer, 2003.

Calasso, F.: Introduzione al diritto comune, Giufre, Milan, 1970.

---

37 C.G. Paulus, A Theoretical Approach to Cooperation in Transnational insolvencies: A European Perspective, in "European Business Law Review", November/December, 2000, p. 435.

38 Dicker, R., Segal, N., Cross-Border Insolvencies and Rescues: The English Perspective, in "International Insolvency Review", no. 8/1999.

Cherubini, G.; Cooper, N.; Fritz, D.; Inacio, E.; Ingielewicz, K.; Lofalk, G.; Mailly, M.; Marks D.; Pukszto, A.; Rumora Scheltema, A.; Van Galen, R.; Virgos, M.; Wessels, B.; Wouters, N.: Armonizarea legislaţiei privind insolvenţa la nivelul Uniunii Europene, - Report of the Political Directorate C - Citizens' Rights and Constitutional Affairs European Parliament Brussels B-1047, available at: http://www.europarl.europa.eu/ studies, last accessed on 07.08.2012.

Costin, M.N.; Miff, A.: Falimentul, Evoluţie şi actualitate, Lumina Lex Publishing House, Bucharest, 2000.

Dicker, R.; Segal, N.: Cross-Border Insolvencies and Rescues: The English Perspective, in "International Insolvency Review", n. 8/1999.

Felsenfeld, C.: International Insolvency, Juris Publishing, New York, 2005.

Fletcher, I.F.: Insolvency in Private International Law, Oxford University Press, New York, 1999.

Gavrilescu, L.C.: Tehnici normative de omogenizare a reglementărilor falimentului internaţional, in "Analele Ştiinţifice ale Universităţii" Al. I. Cuza" Iaşi, Tome LVI, n.II Juridical Sciences, 2010.

Giorgini, G.C.: Methodes conflictuelles et regles materirlles dans l`application de nouveaux instruments de reglement de la faillite internationale, Dalloz, 2006.

Goode, R.: Principles of Corporate Insolvency Law, Sweet /Maxwell, London, 2005.

Hirsch, A.: Vers l'universalité de la faillite au sein du Marché commun, in "Cahiers de droit européen", n.1/ 1970.

Labovitz, M.N.; Basil, J. I.: It's a Small World After All: a Survey of Recent Developments in US Bankruptcy Law and their Potential Multinational Impact, in "Business Law International", vol. 7, n. 1/ 2006.

Lauterpacht, H.: Private Law Sources and Analogies of International Law (with special Reference to International Arbitration), Longmans, Green and Co., London, 1927.

Macovei, I.: Drept internaţional privat în reglementarea Noului Cod civil şi de procedură civilă, C.H. Beck Publishing House, Bucharest, 2011.

Macovei, C.: Dreptul european al contractelor. Modernizarea normelor de drept conflictual, Publisher University "Alexandru Iona Cuza", Iasi, 2005.

Paulus, C.G.: A Theoretical Approach to Cooperation in Transnational insolvencies: A European Perspective, in "European Business Law Review", November/December, 2000.

Pătulea,V.: Sfera de aplicabilitate a prevederilor Legii nr. 64/1995 privind procedura reorganizării judiciare şi a falimentului, in "Dreptul", n. 2/2005.

Piperea, Gh.: Insolvenţa: legea, regulile, realitatea, Wolters Kluwer Publishing House, Bucharest, 2008.

Pottow, J.A.E.: Greed and Pride in International Bankruptcy: The Problems of and Proposed Solutions to Local Interests, in "Michigan Law Review", n. 8/2006.

Sitaru, D. A.: Dreptul comerţului internaţional, Lumina Lex Publishing House, Bucharest, 2004.

Schwartze, A.: Enforcement of Private Law. The Missing Link in the Process of European Harmonization, in "European Review of Private Law", 2000.

Wood, P.R.: Principles of International Insolvency, Thomson, Sweet/Maxwell, London, 2007.

Legislative Guide on Insolvency Law, UNCITRAL, United Nations Commission on International Trade Law, United Nation's Publication, New York, 2005.

Dignity at Work - Contemporary Challenges

Assistant professor Cristina SÂMBOAN[1]

Abstract

The present article aims to clarify the legal significance of the notion of "dignity at work", to present the way in which this significance has evolved over time – from the moment of its introduction into international legislation up to the present - and finally, to explain the causes that have determined the major changes in the perception of this notion over the last two decades.

Key words: dignity at work, social and economic rights, harassment, post-Fordism, flexible organisation.

Once the Universal Declaration of Human Rights was adopted in 1948, the notion of "dignity" officially entered the domain of law and became one of the central values that lie at the core of the structure made up of the other rights[2].

As for the notion of dignity at work, it expectedly represents an application of *dignity* to the domain of labour relations. We do not find the concept as such mentioned and rigorously defined in international legislation, but we do find dignity as an explicitly stated fundamental value in all international legal systems for the protection of economic and social rights, starting with the very Universal Declaration of Human Rights. Article 23 of the above-mentioned Declaration is regarded by most authors as the core of the right to dignity at work in international legislation: the text identifies the right to work, to free choice of work, to satisfactory and fair payment and the freedom of assembly as manifestations of human dignity[3].

---

1 Cristina Sâmboan, ARTIFEX University of Bucharest, Romania, Email: cristina@samboan.ro

2 On the impact and significance of this "encounter", I have tried to reach some conclusions in the article entitled "How dignity entered the field of law and what it brought to it" published in "Juridical Tribune" no. 2/2012 (www.tribunajuridica.eu).

3 Mariann Arany Toth, The Right to Dignity at Work: Reflections on Art. 26 of the Revised European Social Charter, accessible online at the following website address : http://www.law.illinois.edu/publications/cllpj/archive/vol_29/issue_3.pdf; last accessed : Sept 22nd 2012.

The protection of dignity is also stated as a fundamental value in the *Declaration of Philadelphia*[4], in a context that emphasises the double dimension of work: material and non-material (moral). The ILO conventions, recommendations and practice codes take over this view, which links worker's *dignity* (also) to the development of personal skills in the working environment or to the support of personal value (self-respect) – without being reduced to that, however. The prohibition of forced labour and discrimination, the minimum obligatory standards regarding wage and salary levels, the number of paid holidays, working hours, health and safety at the workplace, the compulsoriness of advance notices, etc. – they all make up the material dimensions of work. Together with the (previously mentioned) non-material ones, they complete the foundation of human dignity in the context of workplace relations.

The notion of *dignity* plays an essential role in evaluating the manner of implementing the rights stipulated by the text of the *European Social Charter*[5] on a national level, as well as in interpreting these rights[6]. In fact, the Committee[7] has repeatedly emphasised the "fundamental principle" and "keystone" value that *human dignity* has in interpreting and enforcing the provisions of the Charter[8]. These provisions refer to a wide range of social rights, which also include (apart from the right to work, to fair payment, safe and healthy working environment, labour union rights, etc.) a number of rights such as the protection of the worker's and his family's private life, the right to professional training and career guidance (in other words, rights related to the worker's personal development),

---

4 Adopted on 10 May 1944, it developed the basic goals and principles of the International Labour Organisation (ILO).

5 Adopted with the support of the Council of Europe, the European Social Charter is considered the outcome of the European Convention for Human Rights in the field of social and economic rights protection. Signed in Turin (Italy) on 18 October 1961, the Charter came into force in 1965 and was subsequently amended and completed, so on 3 May 1996, the Revised European Social Charter was adopted, to replace the 1961 version.

6 Mariann Arany Toth – the above-quoted article (see footnote 3), p. 280-281.

7 This is the European Committee for Social Rights, which ensures the control apparatus for enforcing the Charter by the signatory states, together with the Governmental Committee and the Ministers' Committee of the European Council. This apparatus is based on both the analysis of the general reports drawn up by the signatory states, as well as on solving collective complaints. The Committee's analyses and case law represent an important source of information regarding the way in which the significance of the dignity notion is understood at this level in the enforcement and interpretation of the Charter stipulations.

8 "The essence of the Social Charter consists in guaranteeing and respecting the dignity of all human beings (...)" (1 Conclusions XIV-2, at 63 – General Introduction) – cited by Mariann Arany Toth, the above-quoted article, p. 280-281.

as well as the right to be protected from workplace and "workplace-related" moral and sexual harassment. In the analyses and conclusions of the Committee, phrases like "the right to personal dignity" and "respect for human dignity" repeatedly occur in relation to social protection and welfare, the right to housing or the right to be protected against poverty and social exclusion[9].

One can draw the following conclusions from the facts explained above:

- *dignity at work* represents a crucial value for economic and social rights, assumed and stated as such by the main international right protection systems (UN, ILO, the Council of Europe);
- the right to *dignity at work* is a complex right, which "subsumes a wide range of the worker's rights"[10].
- the actual significance of the protected value (i.e. *dignity*) is not obvious from the normative content of international rules and regulations. As highlighted in literature[11], if we wish to find out exactly what the text writers understood by *dignity*, the documents underlying the final versions of such texts are much more useful, interesting and information-packed sources (i.e. drafts, memoranda, statements of purpose, reasoning and argument texts, etc.) – in other words, the documents that record the preparatory meetings taking place before the conventions. The aim and scope of the present paper prevent us from getting into such detailed analysis. We will only flag here the importance and usefulness of such analysis in any attempt to elaborate the legal concept of *dignity at work*.

In other words, in international legislation, the notion of *dignity at work* appears as a core value of the entire set of economic and social rights which, each one in its turn, represents a manifestation of dignity. As for these rights, their (substantial) number expresses very well the multi-faceted structure of *dignity at work*, hence the necessity of multiple protection.

To this end, we present a tentative classification of some means of protecting *dignity at work*, starting from the general etymological significance of the word – more precisely, from its Kantian interpretation (since his expression in-

9 Apart from these references, the Charter stipulates, in Art. 26, a so-called "right to dignity at work". Its content refers to protection against "workplace and workplace-related" sexual and moral harassment. In the given context (as shown above), to reduce the essence of dignity at work to the text of Art. 26 would be a serious mistake!

10 Raluca Dimitriu, "Respecting the worker's private life and dignity at work", Romanian Revue of Employment Law, no. 7/2011, p. 45.

11 Mariann Arany Toth – the quoted article, p. 284-289. The author's analysis on dignity at work is one of the most articulate and complex juridical (legal) analyses we have ever come across and we will refer back again to this extremely useful text.

troduced the notion of *dignity* in the field of law[12]) which relies on the notion of self-respect in literature[13] (and here we particularly consider sociological literature, which has always attached special importance to this issue):

To sum up[14], *dignity at work* presupposes the guarantee of *self-respect* by means of:

- *a harmonious relationship with one's self*: the possibility of performing an appropriate activity (type of work), which fits the individual skills, a meaningful activity, able to provide self-fulfilment, personal satisfaction, social usefulness; the possibility of performing an activity in such conditions that ensure the necessary autonomy for an optimal outcome (a kind of protection ensured legally by the right to career guidance and the right to professional training);
- *a harmonious relationship with the environment*: working under appropriate (physical and material) conditions, which are meant to protect health and ensure a degree of comfort that enables the best working conditions (this kind of protection is legally guaranteed by means of: the right to health and safety at work, the legal regulations regarding working hours and paid holidays, the protection of children, teenagers and mothers in the context of workplace relations etc.);
- *a harmonious relationship with society, the social status*: the possibility to put to use and capitalise one's personal and professional abilities (work itself gives *social dignity*), the possibility to enjoy the results of one's work by means of fair payment, meant to ensure an appropriate social insertion, depending upon the quantity, quality and usefulness of the performed activity (this kind of protection is legally ensured by means of: the right to work, the right to fair payment, the right to workplace safety and social services, the right to housing, the right to be protected against poverty and social exclusion, the prohibition of discrimination, etc.);

---

12 Kant interpreted dignity in a universalistic "key", i.e. as an intrinsic value derived from the very quality of being human, regardless of status or achievements, as any human being is entitled to the others' respect. "To always treat the person as goal, not as means" was one of the great philosopher's favourite catchphrases, meant to illustrate his perspective.

13 Sharon C. Bolton, Dignity in and at work: why it matters, in Dimensions of dignity at work, Elsevier Ltd., Oxford, 2007, p. 8.

14 The proposed classification is not entirely identical with those encountered in literature (which are also relatively varied), but we have considered it useful in order to perform a comparative analysis of the dignity at work notion on its two inseparable levels: juridical (legal) and social.

- *a harmonious relationship with the working partners – both co-workers and employers*: the possibility of avoiding the abuse of power by means of discrimination, harassment, psychological pressure, in the context of the typical asymmetry of industrial relations (this kind of protection is legally ensured by means of: the prohibition of discrimination, harassment, the right to private life, trade union rights).

In the context of the above-mentioned facts, several remarks are in order:

1. firstly, one can easily notice that the lines separating the rights corresponding to the four dimensions of *dignity at work* (as shown above) are partially flexible. Thus, for instance, the rights concerning the limitation of working hours and paid holiday do not ensure just the physical protection of the worker (the b) area), but also the psychological one, protecting the worker from pressures regarding overtime, the assignment of excessive workload, etc. Similarly, the rules and regulations prohibiting discrimination aim to ensure protection not only in the d) area (corresponding to the *employment time*), but also in the c) area (the social status), since the prohibition of discrimination also refers to the time *before* the employment and aims to eliminate the unfair obstacles barring the way to employment opportunities;
2. secondly, it is interesting to note that, in the light of international acts and bills that introduced the concept of *dignity* in relation to economic and social rights (namely, the Universal Declaration of Human Rights, The European Social Charter, the conventions and directions of ILO), the least regulated area is the one under paragraph d), i.e. the one that refers mostly to the worker's *individual* relations at the workplace, or, to be more precise, that element of *dignity* that is most affected by the *psychological* dynamics of social relationships. It is true that both the prohibition of discrimination and trade union rights are related to the early stages of international normative activities in the domain of social relations, as they are to be found in the convention texts from the very beginning. However, this is not true of regulations concerning the prohibition of harassment or regarding the worker's private life. Thus, Article 26 regarding *dignity at work* (the very one that forbids sexual and moral harassment at the workplace) was introduced only later (in 1966), with the adoption of the *Revised Social Charter*. There is no similar text in the original form of the Charter.

In other words, in their initial stages, international conventions seem to have almost completely disregarded this vulnerable aspect of *dignity*, namely the one concerning the worker's *personal*, *individual* relations in the workplace. The legal protection established by these normative acts is obviously conceived to protect not so much the worker's *individual person*, but rather the *social catego-*

ry of workers. The norms that regulate workplace *harassment* occur relatively late in both national[15] and also (as we have seen) international legal systems.

Actually, concerns on the issue of (sexual and moral) "harassment" at work first occurred on the researchers' agenda only as late as the '80s and '90s – at first, only at the level of sociological debates and psychological research[16]. These were followed by the adoption, at national level, of legal regulations meant to prevent and impose sanctions on this type of manifestation at the workplace. Both social studies and legal texts have started to use the term "dignity at work"[17] increasingly in such contexts, to mean a protected value with respect to such types of behaviour. As sociological research has advanced, it has identified multiple facets of harassment at work (expressed by terms like "mobbing", "bullying" or "stalking")[18]. The interest in the phenomenon started to grow in the middle of the last decade, so at present, the debates on the issue are in full swing!

To sum up, it would seem that, starting with the '90s, "dignity at work" is increasingly associated (both at the level of academic debates and in the legal field[19]) with psychologically aggressive types of behaviour that occur as part of the individual workplace relations and progressively less with material elements (related to health, safety, remuneration or social status), as emphasised by international conventions.

This change of perspective is certainly not casual. At first sight, *it is highly probable that it may coincide with the occurrence of a specific social phenomenon*, consisting of an increasing rate of psychologically aggressive behaviour at the workplace. What is the phenomenon that was able to cause such a large scale development? Because it is obvious that psychological abuse cannot have been a novelty in the field of industrial relations, which are essentially asymmetrical and (leaving any doctrinary gibberish aside), they are basically power relations! But since, until this moment, psychological harassment does not seem to have held an important place either on the sociologists' or legislators' agenda, it means that such forms of behaviour (if they existed – and it is highly unlikely

15 1984, Canada; 1987, Great Britain – to quote just a few examples...

16 Thus, for instance, the psychologist and professor Heinz Leymann uses the term "mobbing" for the first time during the '80s to denote a certain type of harassment at the workplace (http://en.wikipedia.org/wiki/Mobbing#cite_note-Westhues-1 – last access: 22.09.2012).

17 or, to be more precise, "dignity at the workplace" (in French, "dignité au travail").

18 All these terms are actually quite recent; they started being used on a larger scale at the beginning of the last decade ...

19 For example, the Dignity at Work Bill (2001) in Great Britain ...

that they did not) took place within "reasonable" limits, without creating any noticeable imbalances at the higher social level.

The answer is not so mysterious: in the mid '90s, we are in the middle of the "post-Fordist" era. Economists know the phenomenon very well, but even us lay people had the opportunity to identify it, if not at a conceptual and direct level or "live" (given its typical features, the Romanian economic and social space takes over and assimilates the echoes of such mass phenomena in a specific manner), at least at a cultural level. Thus, TV productions such as *The Firm* or movie protagonists like Ally McBeal (career women with a difficult private life, debilitated by excessive involvement in her professional life, etc.) are just a few examples in an impressive line of Hollywood productions and characters conceived according to the same pattern, who have captured our interest since the '90s and who were actually only cultural reflections of a social reality that was undergoing substantial changes.

Let us now very briefly resume the characteristics of the "post-Fordist" period – naturally contrasted with the typical features of the "Fordist" period (which preceded it and to which it indirectly owes its name):

"*Fordism*" (named of course after the famous Henry Ford, the first mass producer of automobiles) is a term used by economists to denote the impact that the assembly line (first used by Ford to mass produce his cars) had in the field of economic and social relations between 1945 and the '70s. The assembly line made possible the rapid mass production of standardised goods at low production costs.

In the field of industrial relations, Fordism meant a high level of employment in the sector of industrial production (in other words, the prevalence of the so-called "blue collars", i.e. skilled or unskilled manual workers), standardised, technical, highly specialised work, dependent upon industrial machinery, taking place within bureaucratic organisational structures, strictly hierarchical, with a limited managerial elite (senior management), strong labour unions and a prevailing seller's market[20].

Faced with the challenges of globalisation, Fordism gradually fell into decline in the '70s, when the level of profitability and innovation in American mass production dropped considerably. The social perception of the economic crisis became very intense during the '80s and '90s with the market penetration of more flexible and innovative competitors, such as Japan (a representative model of the so-called "Asian tigers"). Initially, the Japanese success was at-

---

20 Sorin-George Toma, Fordism, post-fordism şi globalizare, available online at: http://www.amfiteatrueconomic.ase.ro/ arhiva/pdf/no17/articol_fulltext_pag135.pdf, last access: 22 September 2012.

tributed to a particular type of organisational culture, which meant a collective involvement in reaching the goals of the organisation (expressed by the so-called TQM – total quality management). Subsequent analyses have led to the conclusion that the Japanese success was also due to a business system based on a pyramid-like structure of sub-contractors (outsourcers).

In response to the challenges of global competition, political leaders from the US and UK implemented a series of neo-liberal policies, which were meant to "free" the markets from the "rigid rules" imposed by "much too strong" labour unions. Market flexibility was stimulated by privatisation, adopting anti-unionist legislation and insistent efforts to impose the discipline and rules of the free market on the sector of public services in order to render them more efficient and more adaptable to consumers' demands. As a result, a large part of the activity performed by this sector was sub-contracted to private services companies. In an economy thus increasingly dominated by the service sector, the new market rhetoric may be epitomised in the catchphrase "The client is always right". In modern jargon, the "white collars" have become the "pink collars", hint at the excessively accommodating attitude towards the client-consumer. The economy has thus become increasingly dominated by the various and unpredictable fads of demand and an increasingly aggressive philosophy of consumerism[21] has developed as a consequence. We are already in the middle of the *post-Fordist* era.

Getting back to the issue of *dignity at work* and in order to better understand the dynamics of post-Fordism labour relations, it is necessary to make a succinct analysis of the *typical organisation* that is representative of this system. It is the famous model of the "*flexible organisation*", that is meant to be the opposite of the rigid hierarchical structures specific to the previous period.

Theory shows us that this kind of organisation is characterised by the following features: the prevalence of the service (tertiary) sector, network-like corporate relations, flexible hierarchies, declining power of the labour unions, team work, flexible specialisation, emphasis on knowledge, information, training and learning, large scale use of communication systems, getting employees involved in the decision-making process and autonomy at work ("*empowerment*"), a high level of competitiveness, performance rewarding systems, the logic of eliminating any elements that fail to "add value" to the organisation (such as staff, struc-

---

21 Karen Legge, Putting the missing "H" into HRM: the case of the flexible organisation, in vol. Searching for the Human in Human Resource Management, Palgrave Macmillan, 2007, p. 121-122.

tures, ngnp2057technologies, materials. etc.), the absence of standard labour contracts[22].

The structure of the *flexible organisation* generally involves the existence of two categories of employees: on the one hand, there is the "hard core", which is "functionally flexible", i.e. employees with standard (ongoing) employment contracts, who are considered capable of responding to various tasks, are adaptable to changes in working methods and technology, able to be substituted from one position to another; on the other hand, there is the "side-line", which are "flexible in number": employees with non-standard (fixed term) employment contracts, who are liable to be laid off depending on fluctuations in demand[23].

Apart from the discourse level, the studies underline a series of effects, reactions and behavioural patterns that this type of organisational structure has brought about in the domain of social relations. Thus:

- firstly, the flexible organisation brought about a major and significant change at social level, with respect to the previous Fordist period, i.e. it generated the large-scale phenomenon of *job insecurity*. The feeling of insecurity determined a certain work-related *behavioural pattern*. Apparently, not even the employees that make up the so-called organisational "hard core" (i.e. the ones that enjoy a certain degree of security) are exempt from this pattern. On the contrary, this category seems to be the most exposed to this type of reaction. It is a "*culture of long hours and presenteeism*"[24], a type of work pressure caused by the so-called "*survivor's syndrome*"[25], a strong need to prove "commitment", either to ensure job security or to get promoted. Naturally, such a reaction to the challenges of competitiveness on the labour market – competitiveness which is overtly promoted by post-Fordist organisations – leads to a serious work life – private life imbalance, with a major impact on family life, the psycho-social development of children, personal identity and stability, etc. Moreover – and this is of particular interest for our subject matter – it builds up a significant amount of tension in the workplace relations, as the individual naturally regards his co-workers as virtual competitors.
- secondly, studies emphasise the fairly illusive character of the so-called "empowerment", i.e. the supposed work autonomy and involvement in the decision-making process. It is true that, within the *flexible organisation* (unlike with the Fordist structures), employees enjoy a higher degree of operational autonomy, but the results of their activity continue to be assessed against

22 Sorin George Toma, quoted article (see footnote 20) and Karen Legge, cited work, p. 121.

23 Karen Legge, cited work, p. 120.

24 Ibidem, p. 125.

25 Ibidem, p. 125.

standards that are firmly set at an executive level. Organisational studies have shown that, in the (above analysed) highly competitive environment and due to the intense promotion of teamwork (a specific feature of the *flexible organisation*, as we have seen), this type of "autonomy" is actually extremely harmful at an interpersonal level. The result is team members supervising and imposing sanctions on each other according to very strict criteria and in a manner that is eventually much harsher than the older forms of technical and bureaucratic control[26]. Analysts warn about the power relations that are subversively developing under the cover of this pseudo-autonomy: behind the appearance of cooperation and mutual respect and in the context of varied short-term projects, which do not allow the development of relations based on loyalty and mutual trust, responsibilities are shunned, success is claimed, individuals undermine each other, subject to the pressures of an intensely competitive environment[27].

- finally, the consumerist culture – also a specific feature of the post-Fordist "era" – with its emphasis and importance attached to "customer enchantment"[28], exerts additional pressure on the employee. Apart from having communicative skills, the employee must also be up to the supposed aesthetic and emotional demands of the customer, i.e. he has to "look good", dress and behave "adequately". Basically, consumerism has turned the customer-employee relationship into a relation of unequal force, in which the advantage is held by the former, at the emotional "expense" of the latter.

In the light of the above mentioned facts, *the causes that have led to the major change in the perception* of the notion of *dignity at work* (as mentioned in the beginning of this article) finally begin to take shape. This change of perception started in the '90s and consisted of the increasing importance attached to interpersonal psychological pressures in the workplace: we are actually dealing with *the major social changes brought about by the post-Fordist era.*

Essentially, the main alteration brought about by post-Fordism (which is relevant for our discussion) was that of *destructuring workplace relations* in a way that eliminated all those intermediary elements that, during the Fordist period, mediated the relations between employer and employee on the one hand and those among employees, on the other hand. These mediating elements consisted of:

---

26 Ibidem, p. 127.

27 Sennett, R., The Corrosion of Character, New York, Perennial, quoted by Karen Legge, cited work, p. 127.

28 Korczinsky, M., Human Resources Management in the Service Sector, Palgrave Macmillan, 2002 – quoted by Karen Legge, cited work, p. 128.

a) hierarchical barriers;
b) "technical" barriers: basically, the machinery – since the main activity consisted of physical labour ("working the machinery"), the direct contacts with co-workers were relatively sporadic and irrelevant on a personal level;
c) functional barriers: we are dealing here with a clear assignment of the working tasks, which was able to stabilise workplace relations, without generating any competitive risks; but such barriers are almost gone in the post-Fordist period (which, as we have seen, is very much focused on flexibility);
d) social and cultural barriers: globalisation generates an intensely competitive environment at a societal level.

In actual fact, post-Fordism has created *non-mediated (direct) contacts in the workplace, but in an intensely competitive context*, which is still *not regulated authority-wise*. Since the power lines are not clearly marked in such an environment, they are created spontaneously, as relations unfold. This is the best possible ground for "thriving" psychological pressures of all kinds! The workplace has become a battlefield.

This picture has dominated the social space since the '90s and it continues to dominate it these days. But has anything changed since then? Are we still there? Is post-Fordism unwaveringly continuing its "triumphant march"? Have any challenges, obstacles or (why not?) opportunities come up in the meantime?

I join those authors[29] (and, I tend to believe, a general trend that is not necessarily part of the academic mainstream) who say that yes, indeed, *two major events* have come up in the meantime and they are likely to generate *major, unprecedented changes* in the field of social hence also workplace relations. These changes have not yet taken place in a way that might significantly alter the picture we have described above. However, they are silently germinating, in the hustle and bustle of the globalised world.

What these events are, as well as the impact that they might have on *dignity at work* in the future – in another article…

Bibliography

Bolton, C. Sharon: Dignity in and at work: why it matters (in Dimensions of dignity at work), Elsevier Ltd., Oxford, 2007.

Donkin, Richard: The future of work, Palgrave Macmillan, 2010.

Dimitriu, Raluca: Respectul vieţii private a lucrătorului şi a demnităţii la locul de muncă, in Revista Română de Dreptul Muncii (The Romanian Revue of Employment Law) no. 7/2011.

---

29 Richard Donkin, The Future of Work, Palgrave Macmillan, 2010.

Legge, Karen: Putting the missing "H" into HRM: the case of the flexible organisation, in the vol. Searching for the Human in Human Resource Management, Palgrave Macmillan, 2007.

Toma, Sorin-George: Fordism, post-fordism şi globalizare, available online at: http://www.amfiteatrueconomic.ase.ro/ arhiva/pdf/no17/articol_fulltext_pag135.pdf.

Toth, Mariann Arany: The right to dignity at work: Reflections on Art. 26 of the Revised European Social Charter, accessible online at: http://www.law.illinois.edu/publications/cllpj/archive/vol_29/issue_3/totharticle29-3.pdf.

The Romanian Adherent, Party to the Transnational Adhesion Contract

Associate professor Carmen Tamara UNGUREANU[1]

Abstract

The Romanian adherent[2], party to a transnational adhesion contract, deals with clauses specific to this, more precisely with jurisdiction clauses and with choice of law clauses, which can prove to be abusive or invalidly concluded. In the case of the first category of clauses, when it comes to designating a state court, the Romanian adherent is submitted to the provisions of the Brussels I Regulation or to Romanian legislation governing jurisdiction, as the case may be; if an arbitration court is indicated, the provisions of Romanian legislation apply, combined with those from the international conventions to which Romania is a party. Regarding the second category of clauses, through which the applicable law is indicated, the Romanian adherent is submitted to the Rome I Regulation. If the Romanian adherent considers the clauses through which the competent court or the applicable law is imposed on him/her to be abusive, he/she may bring proceedings in Romanian courts, which will decide on their validity and, if this is the case, will impose the sanction of nullity on them (or with another sanction provided by law), applying instead the jurisdiction rules and competent law in the absence of choice according to the Romanian Private International Law.

Key words: adhesion contract, adherent, abusive clause, weak party, Brussels I Regulation, Rome I Regulation

1. The conclusion of contracts is based on the principle of party autonomy. According to Article 1169 Romanian Civil Code[3]

> "The parties are free to conclude any contracts and to determine their contents, within the limits imposed by the law, public order and good morals".

The contracting parties negotiate the contract and its clauses within the limits of the contractual freedom permitted by the objective law.

---

1 Carmen Tamara Ungureanu, "Alexandru Ioan Cuza" University of Iaşi, Faculty of Law, Romania, Email: carmen.ungureanu@uaic.ro.

2 The term "Romanian adherent" used in the present material refers to an adherent living in Romania or having his/her habitual residence or seat in Romania, and not an adherent with Romanian citizenship or Romanian nationality; this, because – according to Romanian Private International Law and the laws of the European Union (U.E.) – nationality/citizenship cannot be used to determine the competent court or the applicable law.

3 Law no. 287/2009 regarding the Civil Code, published in the Official Gazette of Romania, Part I, no. 511 dated 24 July 2009, with subsequent changes and modifications.

Adhesion contracts emerged in economic-legal life with the goal of ensuring the celerity of execution of the contractual relations and in order to satisfy economic necessities, and their importance is growing. The parties, i.e. stipulant and adherent, conclude a pre-written contract[4]; it is imposed by one of the parties, by the stipulant, and the other party, the adherent, can only accept it as it is (not being able to negotiate it) or refuse to conclude it[5].

Adhesion contracts are: contracts concluded by *consumers*[6] *with professionals* (frequently, adhesion contracts are identified with the contracts concluded by consumers)[7]; *individual employment contracts*; contracts concluded *between professionals*, where one is economically inferior to, or intellectually or techni-

4 What in Common Law is known by the suggestive and widespread name of "take-it or leave-it". See also Mo Zhang, Contractual Choice of Law in Contracts of Adhesion and Party Autonomy, in "Akron Law Review", 2008, p. 123 and the following, the document is available online at: http://waynedev.uakron.edu/law/lawreview/v41/docs/MoZhang_final08.pdf (consulted on 3/08/2012).

5 See also Tudor Vlad Rădulescu, Sources of Obligations, in The New Civil Code. Comments, Doctrine and Jurisprudence, vol. II, Hamangiu Publishing House, Bucharest, 2012, p. 410.

6 In Romanian legislation, into which the European Directives in the field were transposed, consumer means any natural person or group of natural persons constituted in associations, who buys, acquires, uses or consumes products or services outside its professional activity (point 13 of the Appendix to Law 296/2004 regarding the Consumer Code, published in the Official Gazette of Romania, Part I, no. 593 dated 1 July 2004); in the European Regulations, the notion of consumer is a more restrictive one, meaning that associations of consumers are not included in this category, but only the natural person contracting for a purpose which can be considered as not being connected with his/her professional activity (Art. 15 line (1) of the Brussels I Regulation; Art. 6 line (1) of the Rome I Regulation). In the decision of the Court of Justice of the European Union (CJEU) in the case Verein für Konsumenteninformation vs. Henkel (C-167/2000) of 1 October 2002, it was decided that the term consumer did not include a consumers' protection association; for details, see Peter Stone, EU Private International Law, Elgar European Law, Second Edition, U.K., 2010, pp. 131-134. The text of the Brussels I Regulation is available online at: http://eur-lex.europa.eu/LexUriServ/LexUriServ.do?uri=OJ:L:2001:012:0001:0023:en:PDF (consulted on 2/08/2012). The text of the Rome I Regulation is available online at: http://eur-lex.europa.eu/LexUriServ/LexUriServ.do?uri=OJ:L:2008:177:0006:0006:en:PDF (consulted on 1/08/2012). CJEU decisions can be found online at: http://curia.europa.eu/.

7 This category also includes contracts between consumers and service providers (electricity, gas, water, fixed and mobile phones, cable television, transportation contracts, bank contracts, entertainment contracts, hotel contracts, lottery contracts); contracts between consumers and commercial entities, such as sale contracts, rental contracts, etc.; insurance contracts.

cally dependent on, the other[8]. Another (extreme) type of adhesion contract is a so-called "*shrink wrap*" contract[9], which is very often used in logistics business[10], whereby the adherent accepts all the clauses of a sale contract, unknowingly consenting merely by opening the software packet.

Most adhesion contracts are contracts concluded with consumers; and there is a legislative need to regulate these contracts in detail for the purpose of protecting the weak party, the consumer.

2. In the Civil Code, the Romanian legislator dedicated certain texts to the adhesion contract[11], adopting some of the regulation in this field of the Civil Code of Québec. *The adhesion contract* is defined in Article 1175 Civil Code as being a contract in which the *essential* stipulations (clauses) are imposed or drawn up by one of the parties, on his behalf or upon his instructions, and are not negotiable, the other party accepting them as they are[12]. Considering that the definition is similar to that given to the adhesion contract in Article 1379 line 1 of the Civil Code of Québec, its comments from legal literature and relevant legal practice will be taken into consideration.

Thus, qualifying a contract as an adhesion contract presupposes that two elements be cumulatively present/two conditions be met: a) *the essential* clauses of the contract have to be *imposed* by one of the parties; b) the other party has to be *incapable of negotiating (bargaining)* the contract. The nature of the contract or the quality of one of the parties was deemed not to be relevant, only an analysis of these two elements could characterise a contract as being one of adhe-

8 See, Sylbette Guillemard, Dieudonné Édouard Onguene Onana, Le contrat d'adhésion : actualités et droit international privé, în "Les Cahiers de droit", vol. 48, no. 4, 2007, p. 641, the document is available online at: http://id.erudit.org/iderudit/043948ar (consulted on 29/07/2012).

9 For details, see Jiao Xue, A Comparative Study of Shrink-Wrap License, in "Journal of Politics and Law", vol. 2, no. 2, 2009, pp. 86-93, the document is available online at the address: ccsenet.org/journal/index.php/.../2167 (consulted on 30/07/2012).

10 See Sylbette Guillemard, Dieudonné Édouard Onguene Onana, work cited, p. 643.

11 The following articles of the Civil Code refer to adhesion contracts: Article 1175, Article 1269 line (2), Article 1671 and Article 2515.

12 In legal literature, it was considered that, from the definition of the adhesion contract it follows that a contract can be qualified as being an adhesion one, either when the essential clauses were imposed by one of the parties or when they were drawn up by one of the parties; from the final part of the text it can be deduced that there is no adhesion contract unless the essential clauses are imposed on the adherent; see, for this, Alin-Adrian Moise, Sources of Obligations, in The New Civil Code. Comments on articles, C. H. Beck Publishing House, Bucharest, 2012, p. 1229.

sion[13]. The inequality between the parties regarding their economic, legal or informational power does not justify *in abstracto* considering a contract to be one of adhesion; it has to be established if one of the parties was unable to negotiate the clauses of the contract[14]. It is not sufficient for a contract to be drawn up by one of the parties or by a third party (for example, a lawyer) on their behalf; it has to be *imposed* on the other party, on the adherent.

As a consequence, the adherent is *always* in a position of inferiority vis-à-vis the stipulant.

Regarding the *essential character* of the contractual clauses, this has to be examined in each case (in particular) by the court; what is not essential for one contractual party might prove to be for the other. In the Québec jurisprudence, the courts ruled what is meant by essential clauses in different situations[15].

3. Adhesion contracts include *the risk* of adherents accepting *abusive clauses*, either because they unknowingly consent to the contractual clauses (adherents frequently sign contracts without reading all the clauses or without having the possibility to discover them, as in the case of "*shrink wrap contracts*"), or because, despite being aware of them, they accept them because they have to conclude the contract[16].

Romanian law only defines the concept of *abusive clause* in respect of relations between consumers and professionals[17], as being clauses not negotiated directly with the consumer and which, individually or together with other provi-

---

13 See Brigitte Lefebvre, Le contrat d'adhésion, in "La Revue du Notariat", Montréal vol. 105, September 2003, p. 444, the document is available online at: https://papyrus.bib.umontreal.ca/jspui/bitstream/1866/1386/1/Contrat%20d'adhesion.pdf (consulted on 25/06/2012).

14 See Brigitte Lefebvre, op. cit., p. 446.

15 Thus, in an intellectual property contract (Rousse c. Dion, J.E. 2001-1213 (C.Q.)) the court considered four clauses to be essential: the exclusiveness clause, the penal clause, the amount of money which the artist should receive and the duration of the contract. See in this context Brigitte Lefebvre, op. cit., p. 447, footnote 24. See also, Renaud Baudouin, Code civil du Québec annoté, tome II, 14th Edition, Wilson & Lafleur Itée Publishing House, 2011, p. 1649 et seq.

16 See Sylbette Guillemard, Dieudonné Édouard Onguene Onana, work cited, p. 646.

17 The abusive clause is defined in Article 4 line (1) of Law 193/2000 regarding the abusive clauses of contracts concluded between commercial entities and consumers (republished in the Official Gazette of Romania, Part I, no. 305 dated 18 April 2008; Law 193/2000 transposes the provisions of Directive 93/13/EEC of 5 April 1993 on unfair terms in consumer contracts, published in the Official Journal of the European Union L 095, 21/04/1993 and available online at: http://eur-lex.europa.eu/LexUriServ/LexUri Serv.do ?uri=CELEX:31993L0013:en:HTML); the same definition is also found in Law 296/2004 regarding the Consumer Code, in point 6 of the Appendix to the Law.

sions of the contract, create a significant unbalance between the rights and the obligations of the parties, to the detriment of the consumer and in contradiction of the principles of good faith. The court decides which sanction to impose for an abusive clause in a contract on a case by case basis. The phrasing used by the legislator in the legal text[18], according to which the abusive clauses *do not produce effects* on the consumer and the contract continues if possible after *elimination* of the clauses, was interpreted in legal literature as meaning that the applicable sanction[19] is *partial absolute nullity*[20].

In the case of adhesion contracts not concluded by consumers[21], *the abusive clauses*, not being expressly regulated by a specific provision[22], are penalised by applying *the general rules* that contracts have to fulfil: respecting public order and good morals (Article 1169 Civil Code), good faith (Article 1170 Civil Code) and the other validity conditions imposed by law; recourse to the vices of consent (error, fraud, violence, lesion[23]) is therefore possible, to the cause of the

18 Article 6 of Law 193/2000 regarding the abusive clauses of contracts concluded between commercial entities and consumers.

19 In order to impose sanctions on the inefficiency of an invalid clause in a contract, legislation uses terms such as: the clause is considered not written, the clause is without any effect, the clause is inoperative and, rarely, the clause is null. All these phrases used in Romanian legislation were taken from EU legislation (where, considering the diversity of the sanctions in the Member States, neutral terms were used, such as the lack of effects of the abusive clauses of Directive 93/13/EEC of 5 April 1993 on unfair terms in consumer contracts; see in this context Sophie Gaudemet, La clause réputée non écrite, Economica Publishing House, Paris, 2006, pp. 75-76) and of the states' legislation, source of inspiration for the new Romanian Civil Code or the new Romanian Civil Procedure Code. The definition of these sanctions and the distinctions between them do not make the subject of the present material.

20 See to this end, Liviu Pop, Treaty of Civil Law. The Obligations. Vol. II. The Contract, Universul Juridic Publishing House, Bucharest, 2009, pp. 333-335.

21 The adherents, when they are not consumers, are not especially protected against abusive clauses. Generally, there is a reluctance in protecting professionals, who do not seem to be vulnerable in the relations between them; but, they are not, in economic, legal, technical terms, equal between them; in their contractual relationships they can be affected by abusive clauses, imposed by one party in the adhesion contract, the other party not having the power of bargaining them. See also Gheorghe Piperea, Introduction to the Law of Professional Contracts, C. H. Beck Publishing House, Bucharest, 2011, p. 79.

22 The special one referring to consumers not being able to be applied in a general manner, because, according to Article 10 Civil Code, the laws which derogate from a general provision are applied only in express and limitatively indicated cases.

23 The Civil Code regulates the lesion as a general vice of consent, for the situations in which there is a contractual unbalance between the obligations fulfilled by the parties, no matter of their quality, even if they are professionals, (Articles 1221-1224). The funda-

contract, which has to be lawful and moral. At the same time, the Civil Code provisions dedicated to contracts can be cited to eliminate the abusive clauses[24], that is Article 1671 Civil Code, which, in the *contract of sale*, provides that any *doubtful clauses* must be interpreted in favour of the buyer, with consumers and adherents being included in this category[25].

The sanction applied to abusive clauses is their *nullity*, which is evaluated case by case by the court[26]. The rule is *partial nullity*[27], whereby the contract

---

mental feature of the lesion is the economic violence, vice of consent. The economic violence is defined as being „the abusive exploitation by a dominant party of his/her state of intellectual superiority within the negotiations, characterized by material or psychological pressures attempting at the liberty of consent of the other party, in a manner strong enough to justify the annulment of the unbalanced contract resulted from these negotiations, which generate unjust advantages for the dominant party". See in this respect, Jean Rovinski, Le vice contractuel de violence dans le droit moderne des contrats, thèse, 1987, as it was quoted by Fabrice Piollet, La réception de la violence économique en droit compare, Mémoire, Université Paris II Panthéon-Assas, 2008, pp. 19-20, document available online at the address: http://www.freewebs.com/mjaparis2/MEMOIRES%202008/Violence%20.pdf (consulted on 18/06/2012) and by Sache Neculaescu, Liviu Vasilescu, A New Approach Regarding the Legal Contract Lesion, in „European Integration Realities and Perspectives", Volume 5, 2010, p. 97, document available at the address: http://www.proceedings.univ-danubius.ro/index.php/eirp/article/view/610 (consulted on 20/06/2012).

24 In the Civil Code of Québec protection against abusive clauses is ensured to all, no matter of their standing at the conclusion of the contract (consumer, employee, insured professional, etc.) (Articles 1435-1438 Civil Code of Québec). See, Sylbette Guillemard, Dieudonné Édouard Onguene Onana, work cited, p. 651. The Romanian Civil Code did not adopt these provisions.

25 The text of Article 1671 Civil Code specifies that doubtful clauses must beinterpreted in favour of the buyer, "subject to the rules applicable to contracts concluded with consumers and adhesion contracts"; this last part of the text seems useless and confusing, as in such contracts it is generally the buyer – or consumer – who is the adherent and needs protection.

26 See Liviu Pop, work cited, p. 336.

27 From the provisions of the Civil Code it follows that the legislator opts for the favor contractus principle according to which all measures stipulated by the objective law must pursue the purpose of ensuring the validity and execution of the contract, and the survival of the contractual relationship. These measures consist of limiting or diminishing the causes of nullity or dissolution of contracts in order to produce the effects intended by the parties. See in this respect Louise Rolland, Les Principes d'UNIDROIT et le Code civil du Québec : variations et mutations, in "„Revue Juridique Thémis", Québec, 2002, p. 595, the document is available online at: https://papyrus.bib.umontreal.ca/jspui/bitstream/1866/1362/3/Les%20principes%20DUNIDROIT.pdf (consulted on 25/07/2012).

survives to produce its intended effect once the abusive clauses have been "cleaned up".

4. In these days of technological development, concluding an adhesion contract does not take borders into consideration. Thus, for example, electronic contracts – concluded through a web page or website – can only be adhesion contracts[28], where the contracting parties are frequently resident or domiciled in different states, the currency is foreign, the goods or services under contract are situated in a different state than that of the adherent's residence, etc. So when the adherent consents to the conclusion of such a contract, they are, in fact, signing *a transnational adhesion contract;* thus triggering the mechanism of Private International Law. A transnational adhesion contract is one with foreign element(s)[29], and which is subject to two or more legal orders.

5. Transnational adherents deal with two clauses that are specific to Private International Law:

- clauses regarding *the choice of the competent authority* to settle any disputes between the adherent and the stipulant, and
- clauses through which *the applicable law* is chosen for the adhesion contract.

The two types of clauses specific to transnational adhesion contracts will be analysed briefly, considering that their stipulation could be to the detriment of the adherent and therefore abusive.

6. As each state has its own Private International Law, and there is no universally applicable, supranational Private International Law, transnational adherents *with domicile/residence or seat in Romania* are subject to Romanian Private International Law, which prioritises the application of European Union (EU) legislation[30].

The general rule requires examination of whether any dispute with a foreign element relates to EU Member States or to states outside the EU If the foreign element concerns EU territory, EU Regulations govern the competent court and applicable law to which the adhesion contracts are subject. If it refers to systems of law outside the EU area, the competent court is governed by Articles 148-157 of Law 105/1992 regarding the regulation of Private International Law relations[31]; they will be replaced by Chart VII-a (International Civil Trial), Article

28 Adherents cannot negotiate; they can only click the answers, without the possibility of continuing if they ignore a question asked by the stipulant.

29 See Ioan Macovei, Private International Law in the Regulation of the New Civil Code and New Civil Procedure Code, C. H. Beck Publishing House, Bucharest, 2011, p. 4.

30 As Article 5 Civil Code stipulates.

31 Published in the Official Gazette of Romania, Part I, no. 245 dated 1 October 1992.

1064 et seqq, once the new Civil Procedure Code[32] enters into force. The Romanian Civil Code (Articles 2637-2640) determines which law is applicable to contracts.

7. *Clauses regarding the competent authority* for settling disputes between parties to transnational adhesion contracts.

Stipulants can include a clause indicating the competent court in case of possible disputes between the parties in adhesion contracts. The designated court can be a *state* or *arbitration* tribunal.

A) When the designated court is a state court

a. In the *EU* area, the competent court in the case of the adhesion contracts is established by applying Regulation 44/2001 on jurisdiction and the recognition and enforcement of judgements in civil and commercial matters, known as Brussels I[33]. For a jurisdiction clause[34] to be governed by the *Brussels I Regulation*[35], three conditions have to be fulfilled: the contract has to have an *international character* (for example, the execution of the contractual obligation has to take place on the territory of a Member State other than that of the parties' domicile); at least one of the parties has to be *domiciled* on the territory of a Member

32 Law 134/2010 regarding the Civil Procedure Code, republished in the Official Gazette of Romania, Part I, no. 545 dated 3 August 2012. Competence rules relating to Romanian Private International Law are stipulated in the new Civil Procedure Code; when it enters into force, the corresponding provisions of Law 105/1992 will be abrogated (as it results from Article 83 letter e) by Law 76/2012 for enforcing Law 134/2010 regarding the Civil Procedure Code, published in the Official Gazette of Romania, Part I, no. 365 dated 30 May 2012). The entry into force of the new Civil Procedure Code was postponed until 1 February 2013 by the Urgent Act of Government no. 44/2012, published in the Official Gazette of Romania, Part I, no. 606 dated 23 August 2012.

33 In 2009, the EU signed the Hague Convention of 30 June 2005 on Choice of Court Agreements, which has still not entered into force. The EU signed the Convention by means of the decision of the Council of 26 February 2009 (2009/397/CE), published in the Official Journal of the European Union L 133/1 of 29/05/2009. A further decision of the Council on the ratification of the Convention has to follow before the Convention enters into force (see Peter Stone, work cited, p. 164).

34 Other terms with the same meaning are used to specify the jurisdiction clause: clause on competent authority, prorogation of jurisdiction agreement, clause referring to the choice of the competent authority.

35 In 2010, the European Commission proposed amendments to Brussels I Regulation COM (2010) 748 final 2010/0383 (COD), available online at: http://eurlex.europa.eu/Lex UriServ/LexUriServ.do?uri=COM:2010:0748:FIN:EN:PDF (consulted on 28/07/2012), which also contains changes to Article 23 (prorogation of jurisdiction) and to articles aimed at protecting the weak parties; one of the proposed changes abolishes the condition for the defendant or one of the parties to be domiciled on the territory of an EU Member State.

State[36]; *the court designated* by the jurisdiction clause has to be a court in a *Member State*, or generally, courts in a Member State (if a court from a third state is designated, the Regulation is not applicable).

The general rules regarding the prorogation of jurisdiction to the Brussels I Regulation are based on the parties' agreement, manifested expressly by concluding a jurisdiction clause (Article 23).

Adherents domiciled in Romania are subject to these general rules, if they conclude a contract including a foreign element, and the court designae1031ted by the stipulant is situated in an EU Member State[37].

Adherents classified as *insured*, *consumers* or *employees* are assured of protection by the Regulation. trchEuropean legislation contains detailed regulations of contracts concluded with a party who is considered weak, with the purpose of ensuring protection of that party.

As a principle, jurisdiction clauses cannot be inserted in such adhesion contracts. There are exceptions, expressly stipulated, which are considered incapable of harming the weak party (the insured, the consumer or the employee)[38]. First of all, *jurisdiction clauses agreed after a dispute has arisen* are allowed, as the weak party is considered to be acting consciously, acknowledging the negative effects they risk by designating jurisdiction to a certain court (Article 13 point 1; Article 17 point 1; Article 21 point 1, Brussels I Regulation). Certain jurisdiction clauses are permitted for each type of contract (insurance, concluded with the consumers or employment contracts).

The following clauses are permitted in *insurance contracts*:

- clauses which allow the policyholder, the insured or a beneficiary to bring proceedings in courts other than those indicated in section 3 of the Regulation

---

36 If neither of the parties is domiciled in a Member State but they agree to designate as competent the court or the courts of a Member State, this agreement produces its effects, if the chosen court declares itself competent by applying its own law, lex fori; according to Article 23 line (3), if the chosen court declares itself competent and does not decline its competence, no other court from another Member State can settle the dispute. See Peter Stone, work cited, p. 179.

37 See decision no. 3308/2010, Commercial Section, High Court of Cassation and Justice (H.C.C.J.), in which the provisions of the Brussels I Regulation regarding the choice of court are mentioned in a reinsurance contract, which was qualified as being one of adhesion, the document is available online at: http://www.scj.ro/cautare_decizii.asp (consulted on 30/07/2012); in the same vein, decision no. 3307/2010, Commercial Section, H.C.C.J.; decision no. 1425/2011, Commercial Section, H.C.C.J.

38 See Hélène Gaudemet-Tallon, Les Conventions de Bruxelles et de Lugano, Compétence internationale, reconnaissance et exécution des jugements en Europe, Librairie Générale de Droit et de Jurisprudence, Paris, 1996, p. 184.

(Article 13 point 2); these clauses can also be concluded before the dispute has arisen since weak parties are believed to benefit from supplementary options regarding jurisdiction, which can be more favourable for them;

- clauses which confer jurisdiction to the court in the Member State, where both the policyholder and the insurer are resident/domiciled at the time of conclusion of the contract, even if the dispute arises abroad, provided that such an agreement is allowed by the law of the chosen court (Article 13 point 3)[39];
- clauses concluded with a policyholder, *who is not domiciled in a Member State*, with two exceptions: the insurance is compulsory and the insurance relates to immovable property in a Member State (Article 13 point 4);
- clauses concluded in case of *major insurance* contracts, when these cover one or more risks enumerated in Article 14 (Article 13 point 5); by admitting that the contracting parties are of comparable economic standing, and the policyholder, the insured or the beneficiary does not need particular protection, such clauses are allowed without restrictions; the risks enumerated in *Article 14* relate to maritime and aircraft insurance, with some exceptions when protection of the weak party (the passenger) is intended.

In the case of *contracts concluded with consumers,* jurisdiction clauses can be designated which:

- allow consumers to bring proceedings in courts other than those stipulated in section 4, which are more favourable to them (Article 17, point 2);
- if the professional and consumer are domiciled or have their habitual residence in the same Member State at the time of concluding the contract, they can agree to confer jurisdiction on this court (Article 17, point 3); professionals are thus not obliged to defend themselves against claims asserted by consumers in another Member State, such as the new residence of the consumer; for such an agreement to be valid, it must be permissible pursuant to the law of the designated court[40].

---

39 In the decision Pelux vs. Axa Belgique of 12 May 2005 (C-112/2003), CJEU ruled that a jurisdiction clause concluded on the basis of Article 12 point 3 of the Brussels Convention (Article 13 point 3 of Brussels I Regulation) is not opposable to the beneficiary of the insurance, who did not consent expressly to this clause and who is domiciled in a different Member State than that of the insured or of the policyholder. See Peter Stone, op. cit., p. 129.

40 See in this respect the decision Benincasa vs. Dentalkit, CJEU, of 3 July 1997 (C-269/95); Jean-Paul Beraudo, Convention de Bruxelles du 27 septembre 1968. Competence. Règles ordinaires de compétence, in Juris-Classeur, Europe, Éditions du Juris-Classeur 5, 1999, no. 50 - 51; Hélène Gaudemet-Tallon, op. cit, p. 192. The designated

In the case of *individual employment contracts*, jurisdiction clauses are allowed, providing that they permit the employee to bring proceedings in courts other than those indicated in section 5 and which are more favourable to them (Article 21).

b. *If a transnational adhesion contract is connected with states which do not belong to the EU* and the jurisdiction clause designates a court outside the EU, the provisions of Law 105/1992 regarding the regulation of Private International Law relations apply; these provisions will be abrogated and replaced with new ones in the new Civil Procedure Code (once it enters into force). Article 154 of Law 105/1992 specifies only that, if a jurisdiction clause was concluded, the designated court has competence, unless another court, Romanian or foreign, has exclusive jurisdiction to settle that dispute. The new Civil Procedure Code contains detailed provisions on this matter. According to the Article 1067 line (1) of the new Civil Procedure Code, the parties can conclude a jurisdiction clause on a patrimonial matter in favour of a court which shall have jurisdiction on an actual or future, potential dispute with foreign elements. *The form* of jurisdiction clause can be in writing, telegram, telex, fax or any other communication means which allows it to be proven by hard copy. In the absence of a contrary stipulation, the competence of the chosen forum is exclusive.

Article 1067 line (2) of the new Civil Procedure Code stipulates that the choice of court is *without effect* if it leads to an *abusive* deprivation of one of the parties of the protection ensured by a court according to Romanian legislation. Adherents are deprived of the protection ensured by Romanian law when stipulants designate a foreign court for settling disputes between the parties. At the same time, the choice is *without effect* if the chosen court is foreign and the Romanian courts have exclusive jurisdiction on the dispute and *vice versa*[41]. Romanian courts have exclusive jurisdiction based on Article 1079 of the new Civil

court can invalidate the agreement, declaring the clause conferring jurisdiction as abusive, as it follows from the case CJEU Océano Grupo Editorial vs. Quintero of 27 June 2000 (C-240/98).

41 In line (3) of Article 1067 of the new Civil Procedure Code, the legislator stipulates that: "The chosen court cannot declare of its own motion that it has no jurisdiction if: a) one of the parties is domiciled/has the habitual residence, respectively a secondary seat in the area of this court; b) Romanian law is the applicable law with regard to the dispute according to Romanian Private International Law". I consider that this text refers to the situation in which the Romanian court is chosen and it complements the preceding article (Article 1066, regulating the voluntary prorogation of jurisdiction in favour of the Romanian court).

Procedure Code[42]. As far as *adhesion contracts* are concerned, they have exclusive jurisdiction in the case of immovable property, when the property is situated on Romania's territory (Article 151 point 7 of Law 105/1992 and Article 1079 point 1 of the new Civil Procedure Code); also, Romanian courts have exclusive jurisdiction on *consumer contracts*, when consumers

> "are domiciled or have their habitual residence in Romania, for obligations of current consumption for personal or family use of the consumer and without connection with their professional or trade activity, if: a) the supplier received the consumer's order in Romania; b) the conclusion of the contract was preceded in Romania by a specific invitation addressed to them or by advertising, and the consumer had taken all the steps necessary on their part for conclusion of the contract". (Article 1079 point 3 of the new Civil Procedure Code).

If these conditions are fulfilled, a jurisdiction clause designating a foreign court in an adhesion contract in which the adherent is a consumer is *inoperative*, null, the Romanian court being the competent one.

B) When the designated court is an arbitration tribunal[43]

The subject of arbitration is not covered by the Brussels I Regulation[44], nor is it dealt with in any other EU regulation or legislative act[45]. As a consequence, domestic legislation applies to arbitration, more precisely, the provisions of the Civil Procedure Code (Article 369 et seqq of the Civil Procedure Code in force

42 See, for example, decision no. 1500/2010, Commercial Section, H.C.C.J., when the court decided that: "In case of the conclusion, by correspondence, of an international commercial contract of reinsurance containing a jurisdiction clause in favour of a foreign court and a choice of law agreement, those clauses not being renegotiated by the contractual partners, the Romanian courts have no jurisdiction to settle the dispute, unless the exception hypotheses stipulated in Article 154 of the Law 105/1992 are incident": the article refers to the exclusive jurisdiction of the Romanian courts; the document is available online at: http://www.scj.ro/cautare_decizii.asp (consulted on 30/07/2012).

43 Arbitration is not analysed in any detail in this paper.

44 For example, in the case Allianz vs. West Tankers of 10 February 2009 (C-185/2007), CJEU ruled that it is incompatible with the Brussels I Regulation for a court of a Member State to issue an order restraining a person from commencing or continuing proceedings before the courts of another Member State on grounds that such proceedings would be contrary to an arbitration agreement.

45 In the proposal to modify the Brussels I Regulation, improving the rapport between regulation and arbitration is mentioned, as well (see footnote no. 35). For details, see Olga Troshchenovych, Jakob B. Huebert, Samy Julien Hamama, Brussels I Regulation and Arbitration – Trading Torpedoes for Trust?, in "Themis" 2011, Judicial cooperation in civil matters, the document is available online at: http://www.ejtn.net/Documents/ Themis%202012/Written%20paper%20Lisbon/Written_paper_Germany_2_International_Co operation_in_Civil_Matters%20%20%20.pdf (consulted on 2/08/2012).

and Article 1110 et seqq of the new Civil Procedure Code[46]), the New York Convention of 1958 on the Recognition and Enforcement of Foreign Arbitral Awards[47] and the European Convention on International Commercial Arbitration of 1961, agreed in Geneva[48]. Both conventions stipulate that the arbitral clauses[49] inserted in contracts[50] have to be fulfilled.

8. Jurisdiction or arbitral clauses in transnational adhesion contracts are deemed effective if they respect the legal provisions governing their conclusion. In case of claims that these clauses were not validly concluded, regarding their *formal* or *material validity conditions*[51], the question arises as to which *court has jurisdiction* to rule on their validity and based on *which law*.

Regarding the *jurisdiction clauses,* the *Brussels I Regulation* establishes more formal validity conditions, [stipulating that a jurisdiction clause can be concluded in one of the following *forms* (according to Article 23): in writing;

---

46 According to Article 1111 of the new Civil Procedure Code, "(1) Any dispute of a patrimonial matter can become the object of arbitration if it concerns rights on which the parties may dispose and the law of state where the arbitral tribunal has its seat does not reserve exclusive jurisdiction to the state courts". Article 1112 of the new Civil Procedure Code enumerates the formal and material validity conditions that the arbitration agreement has to fulfil. As regards formal validity conditions, like the jurisdiction clause, arbitration agreement are deemed valid if concluded in writing, telegram, telex, fax, email or any other communication means which allows it to be proven by hard copy. Regarding the material validity conditions, unlike the jurisdiction clause, (referring to which the legislator does not specify which law the seised court has to apply in order to establish its validity), the arbitration agreement is valid if it fulfils the provisions imposed by one of the following laws, all of which are equally competent: a) the law chosen by the parties; b) the law governing the object of the dispute; c) the law applicable to the contract which contains the arbitral clause; d) Romanian law.

47 Convention on the Recognition and the Enforcement of Foreign Arbitral Awards, New York, 10 June 1958, to which Romania adhered with the Decree no. 186/1961.

48 European Convention of International Commercial Arbitration, agreed in Geneva on 21 April 1961, ratified by Romania through Decree no. 281/1963.

49 The arbitral clause or the arbitration agreement represents the agreement of the parties in a contract to submit a potential dispute, which might occur between them, to arbitration; for details, see Ioan Macovei, work cited, p. 281 et seqq.

50 See also decision no. 3111/2009, Commercial Section, H.C.C.J., in which the Romanian court declared of its own motion that it has no jurisdiction, as the parties agreed an arbitral clause in their contract, the document is available online at: http://www.scj.ro/cautare_decizii.asp (consulted on 30/07/2012).

51 For details, see Jan-Jaap Kuipers, Party Autonomy in the Brussels I Regulation and Rome I Regulation and the European Court of Justice, in "German Law Journal", no. 11/2009, vol. 10, p. 1512, the document is available online at: http://www.germanlawjournal.com/pdfs/Vol10-No11/PDF_Vol_10_No_11_15051525_Developments_JK.pdf (consulted on 27/07/2012).

evidenced in writing; in a form which accords with practices established between the parties; according to the practices, usages, of the international trade; in any communication by electronic means which provides a durable record of the agreement] and a single material validity condition, which refers to the object of the clause: any disputes which have arisen or which may arise in connection with a particular legal relationship[52]. Regarding the other material validity conditions, for example, the parties' consent, it is the seised court which will settle the matter.

The Court of Justice of the European Union (CJEU) ruled in the decision *Benincasa vs. Dentalkit* of 3 July 1997 (C-269/95) that the validity of a jurisdiction clause is examined independently of the situation of the contract in which it is inserted[53], i.e. without considering whether the contract was validly concluded or not.

The seised court (whether designated or not by the parties in the jurisdiction clause) decides on *the validity* of the jurisdiction clause. *The applicable law* for determining its validity is either *lex fori*[54], or *lex causae*[55], the practice of EU Member State courts not being harmonised in this field.

---

52 The condition for the dispute to concern a particular legal relationship leads to the conclusion that the parties cannot conclude jurisdiction clauses governing all the disputes which might arise between them; this avoids the party with the greater economic power being able to impose a particular court for any dispute on the other party.

53 See Michael Bogdan, Concise Introduction to EU Private International Law, Europa Law Publishing House, 2nd Edition, Groningen, 2012, p. 64. Also see Peter Stone, work cited, p. 175.

54 The validity of the jurisdiction clause is decided by applying the law indicated by the private international law of the seised court; see in this respect Peter Stone, work cited, p. 175; Michael Bogdan, work cited, p. 64.

55 Lex causae, the applicable law to the clause, as derived from the CJEU decision in the case Elefanten Schuh vs. Jacqmain, of 24 June 1981 (no. 150/80), is the one indicated by the designated court in the jurisdiction clause; thus, from the moment the clause is concluded, it is known if it was validly signed or not. See Jean-Paul Beraudo, op. cit., no. 38, 41; Hélène Gaudemet-Tallon, op. cit., p. 93. If other laws were applied, such as the law of the excluded court or the law of the seised court, the jurisdiction convention will be uncertain, doubtful, the parties not knowing if the convention is validly signed; Hélène Gaudemet-Tallon, op. cit., p. 93. The practice of the courts of the EU Member States is not unitary in the field; some states apply lex fori, considering that the jurisdiction convention is a procedural matter and others apply lex causae with the consequence that the same jurisdiction clause can be considered valid in a Member State and not valid in another. See in this respect Thomas Pfeiffer, Choice of Forum Agreements, in Burkhard Hess, Thomas Pfeiffer, Peter Schlosser, Report on the Application of the Regulation Brussels I in the Member States, 2007, pp. 158-159, document available online at the address: http://ec.europa.eu/civiljustice/news/docs/study_application_brussels_1_en.pdf.

If the court seised by the adherent, whether designated or not in the jurisdiction clause inserted in the adhesion contract, is a *Romanian court,* Romanian private international law is initially applicable for verifying its competence. Before the enngfe1031try into force of the New Civil Procedure Code, the practice of the High Court of Cassation and Justice (H.C.C.J.) has shown that, after verifying its competence, it applies *lex causae* in order to establish the validity of the jurisdiction clause[56]. The new text of the Civil Procedure Code, which stipulates that the choice of court is *without effect* if it leads to an *abusive* deprivation of one party of the protection that a court assures them according to Romanian legislation [Article 1067 line (2)], will oblige the seised Romanian court, on the request of the adherent, to verify if the foreign court imposed on the adherent, deprives them of the protection of Romanian law, i.e. the court will apply *lex fori* in order to establish the validity of the jurisdiction clause. The adherent may also request determination of the Romanian court's jurisdiction on the basis of Article 1069 of the new Civil Procedure Code, which regulates *the forum of necessity*:

> "The Romanian court from the place with which the dispute has a sufficient connection becomes competent to settle it, even though the Romanian court has no jurisdiction to hear the dispute, if it is proved that the proceedings cannot possibly be instituted abroad or the institution of such proceedings abroad cannot reasonably be required"[57].

The jurisdiction clauses in Romanian law are qualified by the legislator in Civil Code (Article 1203) as being *non-usual clauses*, with a special regime. Thus, according to Article 1203 Civil Code, the standard clauses, included in a contract, which stipulate in favour of the party proposing them

> "(...) arbitration clauses or clauses of prorogation of jurisdiction *are ineffective* unless they are expressly accepted in writing by the other party".

Standard contractual clauses mean

---

56 See, for example, decision no. 1916/2011, Commercial Section, H.C.C.J. The court appreciates that, "jurisdiction is not determined in relation with Article 149 point 4 of Law 105/1992, but in relation with Article 154 of this law, in accordance with which, if the parties agree to submit disputes arising from their legal relationship to a particular court, this court will have general jurisdiction; since the insurance policy MAR 91 was submitted to the exclusive jurisdiction of the English courts, these courts are responsible for ruling on the contract validity, as well", the document is available online at: http://www.scj.ro/cautare_decizii.asp (consulted on 30/07/2012); in the same vein, decision no. 1500/2010, Commercial Section, H.C.C.J.

57 The provision regarding the forum of necessity was taken over from the Civil Code of Québec (Article 3136).

> "the stipulations established previously by one of the parties in order to be used generally and repeatedly and which are included in the contract without having been negotiated with the other party". [Article 1202 line (2) Civil Code].

In order to be considered validly concluded, jurisdiction clauses have to be expressly accepted by the adherent, the signing of the contract not being sufficient. So if the adherent consents to the conclusion of a contract, for example on the internet, but does not expressly and undoubtedly accept such clauses, they are deemed not to have consented to them and they are therefore *without effect for the adherent.* The sanction which is deduced from this text is *the nullity of clauses*[58]*,* and the seised court will decide on the sanction, according to the characteristics of each case in particular.

As far as *arbitration clauses* in transnational adhesion contracts are concerned, both the New York Convention of 1958 and the Geneva Convention of 1961 establish that – in order to determine clause validity – the court will apply the law chosen by the contractual parties; failing any indication by the parties as to the applicable law[59] it will apply the proper law under the rules of conflict that it deems applicable. According to Article 1112 line (2) of the new Civil Procedure Code, *the seised Romanian court,* whether designated by the arbitration clause or not, applies, at its own choice, one of the following laws, all of which are equally competent, when determining validity: the law chosen by the parties, the applicable law to the object of the dispute, the applicable law to the contract which contains the arbitration clause, or Romanian law. If the court chooses to apply Romanian law (that it knows best), then it will also apply Article 1203 Civil Code, according to which the adherent has to expressly accept the arbitration clause, this being a *non-usual clause*.

In situations where adherents are *consumers*, any choice of forum other than a Romanian court is inoperative (Article 1081 of the new Civil Procedure Code),

---

58 As far as sanctions in comparative law, more precisely in French law, are concerned, the sanction is to consider/deem the clauses as not written; for example, recently, in France, the Pau Appeal Court, in a decision of 23 March 2012, ruled that a jurisdiction clause designating the courts of California in Facebook's general terms of use was deemed non written, and declared of its own motion that it has jurisdiction, based on Article 48 of the French Civil Procedure Code, (which stipulates that any clause which, directly or indirectly, derogates from the territorial jurisdiction rules is deemed not written, unless the clause is concluded between commercial entities and specified in an obvious manner in the contract. See also Cédric Manara, Facebook n'est pas ami avec le Code de procédure civile français, in "Dalloz actualité", 16 April 2012; the decision is available online at: http://md.netiris.fr/telecharger/mirror/CA-Pau_20120323_facebook.pdf (consulted on 31/07/2012).

59 See Ioan Macovei, work cited, pp. 284-285.

as Romanian courts have exclusive jurisdiction, if the conditions included in Article 1079 point 3 of the new Civil Procedure Code are fulfilled. At the same time, according to Romanian law, an arbitration clause[60], inserted in a contract concluded with a consumer is deemed abusive[61].

9. The clause designating the applicable law to which the adhesion contract is subject.

a. In the *EU* area, *Regulation 593/2008* on the law applicable to contractual obligations (also called *Rome I*) applies, whereby *party autonomy* is a fundamental principle

> "a contract shall be governed by the law chosen by the parties" [Article 3 line (1) first sentence of the Regulation].

In situations involving a conflict of laws, the Regulation applies to contractual obligations in civil and commercial matters [Article 1 line (1)], and therefore also to transnational adhesion contracts[62]. According to Article 2, the law specified by the Regulation is applied regardless of whether it is the law of a Member State[63], which gives the Regulation a universal character. *The universal character* means that its provisions become uniform law, replacing the Private International Law of all the Member States with regard to contractual obligations in

---

60 The appendix to Law 193/2000, letter l) stipulates that clauses which "exclude the right of the consumer to take legal action or to exercise any another legal remedy, particularly by requiring the consumer to take disputes exclusively to arbitration, are considered abusive".

61 See also Jean-Philippe Moiny, Cloud computing: validité du recours á l'arbitrage ? (partie I) Droits de l'Homme et clauses abusives, in "Revue Lamy Droit de l'Immatériel" no. 77, December 2011, p. 95 et seqq, the document is available online at: http://alexandrie.droit.fundp.ac.be/GEIDEFile/6876.pdf?Archive=193935791111&File=6876_pdf (consulted on 23/07/2012); Carmen Tamara Ungureanu, Private International Law. Consumers Protection and Products Liability, All Beck Publishing House, Bucharest, 1999, pp. 42-45.

62 The Regulation is also applicable to contracts featuring all the characteristics of a domestic contract but given international character by the parties choosing a foreign law as the applicable law. See in this respect Paul Lagarde, Convention de Rome (obligations contractuelles), Rép. Dalloz, Droit communautaire, April, 1992, no. 12. There are also authors who consider that, although the Regulation does not exclude such a possibility, as a principle the parties cannot submit an internal contract to a foreign law. See Antoine Kassis, Le nouveau droit européen des contrats internationaux, Librairie Générale de Droit et de Jurisprudence, Paris, 1993, pp. 268 - 276.

63 See also Codrin Macovei, The European Law of Contracts. Modernizing the Provisions of Conflictual Law, Publishing House of "Alexandru Ioan Cuza" University Iaşi, 2005, pp. 48-50.

civil and commercial matters[64]. Romanian Private International Law [Article 2640 line (1) Civil Code] refers to the Regulation to designate the applicable law in the matter of contractual obligations. In order for the provisions of Rome I Regulation to apply, the contracting parties – domiciled in the EU or outside the EU - can agree a jurisdiction clause designating a court from a Member State.

The parties may choose any law which better suits their common interests, without justifying the reasons for their choice[65]. As a consequence, the stipulant can impose any law on the adherent. The choice of applicable law has to be *expressly* or clearly demonstrated in the terms of the contract or the circumstances of the case.

If adherents act in specific capacities in *transnational adhesion contracts* (passenger, consumer, insured or employee)[66], party autonomy is limited when choosing the law applicable to the contract, with the purpose of protecting the adherent, who, in such cases, is considered to be the weak party.

In *contracts governing the carriage of passengers,* Article 5 line (2) Para. 2 of the Rome I Regulation states that, according to Article 3, the parties can only choose one of the following laws as applicable to the contract: the law of the country where the passenger has their habitual residence; the law of the country where the carrier has its habitual residence; the law of the country where the carrier has its central administration; the law of the country of departure; the law of the country of destination.

As regards *contracts concluded with consumers*, party autonomy is limited to a choice which cannot result in deprivation of the consumer of the protection afforded them by the mandatory provisions of the law of the country where the consumer has their habitual residence[67]. In this conflict rule, governed by Article

64 See Hélène Gaudemet-Tallon, Convention de Rome du 19 juin 1980. Champ d'application. Clauses générales, in Juris-Classeur, Editions du Juris-Classeur, 1996, no. 32; Report Giuliano-Lagarde, in Richard Plender, The European Contracts Convention. The Rome Convention on the Choice of Law for Contracts, Edition Sweet & Maxwell, London, 1991, p. 255.

65 See Hélène Gaudemet-Tallon, Convention de Rome ..., cited work, no 6; Paul Lagarde, work cited, no 31.

66 In comparison with the Brussels I Regulation, the Rome I Regulation also protects the passenger.

67 This text was interpreted in many ways in legal literature; see in this respect Carmen Tamara Ungureanu, European Private Business Law, Junimea Publishing House, Iași, 2002, pp.166-169; Jean-Christophe Pommier, Principe d'autonomie et loi du contrat en droit international privé conventionnel, Editions Economica, Paris, 1992, pp. 157 – 165; Antoine Kasssis, work cited, pp. 334 - 342; Jean-Yves Carlier, Autonomie de la volonté et statut personnel. Etude prospective de droit international privé, Etablissements Emile

6 of the Rome I Regulation, party autonomy can be used only when it does not deprive the consumer of the protection afforded them by the mandatory provisions of the law that is objectively applicable; the law of the consumer's habitual residence ensures minimum protection, but the parties may choose another law, which will protect the consumer better[68].

The special conflict rule governing consumer protection does not function in all contracts concluded between consumers and professionals, but only if the conditions stipulated in Article 6 line (1) are fulfilled: the professional is either engaged in its commercial or professional activities in the country where the consumer has their habitual residence, or, by any means, *directs* its activities in that country or in several countries including that country, and the contract falls within the sphere of such activities[69].

With the purpose of protecting the weak party from *insurance contracts* covering *risks situated inside the territory of the Member States*, the parties can choose from among several laws laid down in Article 7 line (3) Rome I Regulation: the law of any Member State where the risk is situated at the time of conclusion of the contract; the law of the country where the policyholder has their habitual residence; in the case of life assurance, the law of the Member State of which the policyholder is a national; for insurance contracts covering risks limited to events occurring in one Member State other than the Member State where the risk is situated, the law of that Member State; where the policyholder of a contract falling under this paragraph [Article 7 line (3)] pursues a commercial or industrial activity or a liberal profession and the insurance contract covers two or more risks which relate to those activities and are situated in different Member States, the law of any of the Member States concerned or the law of the country of habitual residence of the policyholder. In case the laws of the Mem-

---

Bruylant, Brussels, 1992, p. 97; Hélène Gaudemet-Tallon, Convention de Rome...cited work, no. 50.

68 See Hélène Gaudemet-Tallon, Convention de Rome ...cited work, no. 50. The seised court is responsible for examining which law is more favourable for the consumer, identifying the laws to be compared and effectively comparing them in respect of the full range of advantages and disadvantages in the general interest of all consumers (and not just of the consumer involved in the dispute). This conflict of law method gives the court widespread 077614 liberty to determine the more favourable law for the consumer, which makes the system of applicable law flexible, but also unpredictable; see also Carmen Tamara Ungureanu, Private International Law..., cited work, pp. 124 – 128.).

69 Even if the conditions imposed by Article 6 line (1) of the Rome I Regulation are fulfilled, the special conflict rule aimed at consumer protection does not apply to all the contracts concluded by consumers; for excluded contracts, see Article 6 line (4), letter (a)-(e), Rome I Regulation. See also Carmen Tamara Ungureanu, The European Private ...cited work, pp. 167-168.

ber States mentioned in the first, second and last situation grant more liberty regarding the choice of law applicable to insurance contracts, the parties can use this possibility.

Article 8 line (1) of the Rome I Regulation stipulates that *the individual employment contract* is governed by the law chosen by the parties in accordance with Article 3 of the Regulation. However, such a choice cannot deprive employees of the protection afforded them by provisions that cannot be neglected by agreement under the law that, in the absence of choice, would have been applicable. The principle is one of party autonomy, but limited, meaning that the choice of another law than that objectively applicable in the absence of choice cannot have the effect of depriving employees of the protection ensured by the mandatory provisions of the objectively applicable law as provided for in Article 8 lines (2) – (4). Article 8 line (1) has to be interpreted in the same manner as for contracts concluded by consumers: the law objectively applicable must ensure minimum protection; the parties can choose another law that is more favourable to the employee. The law objectively applicable in the case of the employee is determined through certain presumptions that indicate the country with which the employment contract is most closely connected[70].

b. *Outside EU territory,* the Romanian Private International Law provisions of the Civil Code (Article 2637)[71], which establishes party autonomy in choosing the applicable law, are applicable. No protective conflict rules are expressly stipulated for adherents, regardless of their status. In the situation analysed in this paper (transnational adhesion contracts), which is governed by the Rome I Regulation, the provisions of Article 2637 Civil Code are not applicable in Romania; since – as demonstrated above – the Regulation has universal character, it supersedes the private international law of all the Member States.

10. If the seised court in the transnational adhesion contract is an arbitration court, the stipulant can also impose the *law applicable to* the contract. If an applicable law is not chosen, the arbitrators will apply the law indicated by the conflict rule they consider appropriate[72].

11. The validity of the clause designating the law applicable to the contract (*electio juris*) is subject to the same law as the main contract [Article 3 line (5) of the Rome I Regulation].

According to Article 10 of the Rome I Regulation, *the existence and the validity of a contract*, or of any term of a contract, so including a clause designat-

70 See Paul Lagarde, cited work, no. 85.

71 Article 2637 Civil Code contains, partially, similar provisions to those of Article 3 of the Rome I Regulation.

72 See in this respect Ion P. Filipescu, Private International Law, Actami Publishing House, Bucharest, 1997, vol. II, p. 257.

ing the law applicable to the transnational adhesion contract, are determined by the law which would govern it under the Regulation if the contract or term were valid. Nevertheless, in order to establish lack of consent, a party may rely on the law of the country of their habitual residence if the circumstances indicate that it would not be reasonable to determine the effect of their conduct in accordance with the law of the contract. *Romanian adherents* can use this provision *in transnational contracts* to apply Romanian law, according to which the choice of law clause has to comply with the conditions of Article 1203 Civil Code: the clause has to be expressly accepted by the adherent.

The law applicable *to the formal validity* of the choice of law clause is established by opting between *lex causae* and *locus regit actum*, both of which are competent. When *adherents* are *consumers*, Article 11 line (4) of the Rome I Regulation aims to ensure their protection by stipulating that consumer contracts, including the choice of law clause, have to have the form stipulated by the law of the country in which the consumer is habitually resident; it is the same law which governs the contract in substance, in the absence of choice of the applicable law or, when the chosen law deprives the consumer of the protection afforded by the mandatory provisions of the law of their habitual residence and which is justified by the very close connection which exists between the substance and the form in consumer contracts. The Regulation does not contain special provisions governing other contracts concluded with a party who is considered to be weak but not a consumer.

When the choice of law clause in the transnational adhesion contract is not valid according to the Rome I Regulation, the seised court will remove it, by applying the sanction specific to the law which established the invalidity of the clause. If a Romanian court applies Romanian law to settle the validity of the clause, it will either sanction it with nullity, or it will be deemed not written, inoperative, without effect.

12. *In conclusion*, when entering into transnational adhesion contracts that are imposed on them without their having the power to negotiate, Romanian adherents must deal with clauses specific to such contracts, more precisely with jurisdiction and choice of law clauses. If the first clause concerns designation of a *state court*, the Romanian adherent is subject to the provisions of the Brussels I Regulation or to domestic Romanian jurisdiction rules, accordingly; if an arbitration court is indicated, the provisions of Romanian legislation apply in conjunction with the New York Convention of 1958 and the Geneva Convention of 1961. As far as choice of law clauses are concerned, the Romanian adherent is subject to the Rome I Regulation.

The principle of party autonomy functions/applies in both categories of clauses, with *limited* scope in cases where the Romanian adherent is *a weak party*. Professionals do not benefit from any special protection.

When Romanian adherents consider the jurisdiction or choice of law clauses imposed on them to be abusive, they may seise the Romanian courts, which will settle their validity and, if this is the case, will sanction them with *nullity* (or with another sanction stipulated by law), applying instead the jurisdiction rules and competent law in the absence of choice as stipulated by Romanian Private International Law.

Compared to the rules applicable to adhesion contracts in the European Regulations, which only protect the party considered weak (consumer, employee, insured, passenger), Romanian law ensures *minimum protection* of adherents regardless of status (which, by definition, is inferior to that of the stipulant) in the new rules introduced in the Civil Code and in the new Civil Procedure Code (except for the protective rules applicable to consumers). Thus, regarding competence, Article 1067 line (2) of the new Civil Procedure Code allows the Romanian court to have jurisdiction over the dispute, if the choice of a foreign court leads to a*busive* deprivation of the adherent of the protection afforded by the Romanian court; at the same time, the Romanian adherent can appeal to the forum of necessity (Article 1069 of the new Civil Procedure Code). Pursuant to Article 1203 Civil Code, jurisdiction agreements and choice of law or arbitration clauses in contracts are *unusual clauses*, which do not produce effects upon adherents unless expressly accepted by them. The Civil Code regulates the *lesion* as a *general vice of consent* for situations of contractual imbalance between the obligations fulfilled by the parties, regardless of their status, even if they are professionals (Articles 1221-1224). If seised by a Romanian adherent in a transnational adhesion contract dispute, the Romanian courts will be able to appeal to these provisions in order to take fair decisions.

Bibliography

Baudouin, Renaud: Code civil du Québec annoté, volume II, 14th edition, Wilson & Lafleur Publishing House Itée, 2011.

Beraudo, Jean-Paul: Convention de Brussels du 27 septembre 1968. Competence. Règles ordinaires de compétence, in Juris-Classeur, Europe, Éditions du Juris-Classeur 5, 1999.

Bogdan, Michael: Concise Introduction to EU Private International Law, Europa Law Publishing, 2nd Edition, Groningen, 2012.

Carlier, Jean-Yves: Autonomie de la volonté et statut personnel. Etude prospective de droit international privé, Etablissements Emile Bruylant, Brussels, 1992.

Filipescu, Ion P.: Private International Law, vol. II, Actami Publishing House, Bucharest, 1997.

Gaudemet, Sophie : La clause réputée non écrite, Economica Publishing House, Paris, 2006.

Gaudemet-Tallon, Hélène : Les Conventions de Bruxelles et de Lugano, Compétence internationale, reconnaissance et exécution des jugements en Europe, Librairie Générale de Droit et de Jurisprudence, Paris, 1996.

Gaudemet-Tallon, Hélène: Convention de Rome du 19 juin 1980. Champ d'application. Clauses générales, in Juris-Classeur, Editions du Juris-Classeur, 1996.

Guillemard, Sylbette, Onguene Onana, Dieudonné Édouard : Le contrat d'adhésion: actualités et droit international privé, in "Les Cahiers de droit", vol. 48, no. 4, 2007, the document is available online at: http://id.erudit.org/iderudit/ 043948ar (consulted on 29/07/2012)

Kassis, Antoine: Le nouveau droit européen des contrats internationaux, Librairie Générale de Droit et de Jurisprudence, Paris, 1993.

Kuipers, Jan-Jaap: Party Autonomy in the Brussels I Regulation and Rome I Regulation and the European Court of Justice, in "German Law Journal", no. 11/2009, vol. 10, the document is available online at: http://www.germanlawjournal.com/ pdfs/ Vol10No11 /PDF_ Vol_10_No_11_1505-1525_Developments_JK.pdf (consulted on 27/07/2012).

Lagarde, Paul: Convention de Rome (obligations contractuelles), Rép. Dalloz, Droit communautaire, April, 1992.

Lefebvre, Brigitte: Le contrat d'adhésion, in "La Revue du Notariat", Montréal vol. 105, septembre 2003, the document is available online at: https://papyrus.bib.umon treal.ca/jspui/bitstream/1866/1386/1/Contrat%20d'adhesion.pdf (consulted on 25/06/ 2012).

Macovei, Codrin: European Law of Contracts. Modernising the Provisions of Conflictual Law, "Alexandru Ioan Cuza" University Publishing House, Iaşi, 2005.

Macovei, Ioan: Private International Law, in the Regulation of the new Civil Code and the new Civil Procedure Code, C. H. Beck Publishing House, Bucharest, 2011.

Manara, Cédric: Facebook n'est pas ami avec le Code de procédure civile français, in "Dalloz actualité", 16th April 2012.

Moiny, Jean-Philippe: Cloud computing: validité du recours á l'arbitrage ? (partie I) Droits de l'Homme et clauses abusives, in "Revue Lamy Droit de l'Immatériel" no. 77, December 2011, the document is available online at: http://alexandrie.droit.fundp.ac.be/ GEIDEFile /6876.pdf?Archive=193 935791111&File=6876_pdf (consulted on 23/07/2012).

Moise, Alin-Adrian: Sources of Obligations, in The New Civil Code. Commentary on articles, C. H. Beck Publishing House, Bucharest, 2012.

Neculaescu, Sache, Vasilescu, Liviu: A New Approach Regarding the Legal Contract Lesion, in „European Integration Realities and Perspectives", Vol. 5, 2010, the document is available online at: http://www.proceedings.univdanubius.ro/index.php/eirp/article/view/ 610 (consulted on 20/06/2012).

Pfeiffer, Thomas: Choice of Forum Agreements, in Burkhard Hess, Thomas Pfeiffer, Peter Schlosser, Report on the Application of the Regulation Brussels I in the Member States, 2007, the document is available online at: http://ec.europa.eu/civiljustice/news/docs/ study_application_brussels_1_en.pdf (consulted on 30/07/2012).

Piollet, Fabrice: La réception de la violence économique en droit compare, Mémoire, Université Paris II Panthéon-Assas, 2008, the document is available online at: http:// www.freewebs.com/mja-paris2/MEMOIRES%2020 08/Violence%20.pdf (consulted on 18/06/2012).

Piperea, Gheorghe: Introduction in the Law of Professional Contracts, C. H. Beck Publishing House, Bucharest, 2011.

Pommier, Jean-Christophe: Principe d'autonomie et loi du contrat en droit international privé conventionnel, Editions Economica, Paris, 1992.

Pop, Liviu: Civil Law Treaty. Obligation. Vol. II. The Contract, Universul Juridic Publishing House, Bucharest, 2009.

Rădulescu, Tudor Vlad: Sources of Obligations, in the New Civil Code. Comments, Doctrine and Jurisprudence, vol. II, Hamangiu Publishing House, Bucharest, 2012.

Rolland, Louise : Les Principes d'UN I D R O I T et le Code civil du Québec : variations et mutations, in "Revue Juridique Thémis", Quebec, 2002, the document is available online at: https://papyrus.bib.umontreal.ca/jspui/bistream/1866/1362/3/Les%20principes%20 DUNIDROIT.pdf (consulted on 25/07/2012).

Stone, Peter: EU Private International Law, Elgar European Law, Second edition, U.K., 2010.

Troshchenovych, Olga, Huebert, Jakob B., Hamama, Samy Julien: Brussels I Regulation and Arbitration – Trading Torpedoes for Trust?, in "Themis" 2011, Judicial cooperation in civil matters, the document is available online at: http://www.ejtn.net/Documents/ Themis%202012/Written%20paper%20Lisbon/Written_paper_Germany_2_International _Cooperation_in_Civil_Matters%20%20%20.pdf (consulted on 2/08/2012).

Ungureanu, Carmen Tamara: European Private Business Law, Junimea Publishing House, Iași, 2002.

Ungureanu, Carmen Tamara: Private International Law. Consumers Protection and Products Liability, All Beck Publishing House, Bucharest, 1999.

Xue, Jiao: A Comparative Study of Shrink-Wrap License, in "Journal of Politics and Law", vol. 2, no. 2, 2009, the document is available online at: ccsnet.org/journal/index.php/.../ 2167 (consulted on 30/07/2012).

Zhang, Mo: Contractual choice of law in contracts of adhesion and party autonomy, in "Akron Law Review", 2008, the document is available online at: http://waynedev. uakron.edu/law/lawreview/v41/docs/MoZhang _final08.pdf (consulted on 3/08/2012).

Rising Importance and Significance of International Commercial Arbitration

PhD Harsh PATHAK[1]

Abstract

With trade and commerce increasing rapidly between nations, there has been a significant rise in disputes, leading to an urgent need for an effective and unified dispute resolution system which can sufficiently settle disagreements/issues among parties in dispute and which has to be arrived at keeping in mind the differences in laws of every nation, hence, immensely increasing the scope of private international law, or conflict of laws as called by different nations. Such urgency has led to many conventions, one of the most important being The New York Convention of 1958 (Convention on the Recognition and Enforcement of Foreign Arbitral Awards) and the UNCITRAL Model Law promulgated in 1985 and amended as recently as 2006, which has been the source for international arbitration, the most widely used dispute resolution method for international commercial trade and transactions, and many countries like India have also based their legislation on the rules of the UNCITRAL Model Law. Most European countries as well as India have ratified the New York Convention of 1958 (Convention on the Recognition and Enforcement of Foreign Arbitral Awards) for the purposes of international trade and commercial transactions therefore opening the gateway for easier execution of international commercial transactions among such countries.

Keywords: International Commercial Arbitration, UNICITRAL, Indian Arbitration law, Alternate Dispute Resolution, Foreign Direct Investment, New York Convention 1958.

There has been a significant rise international commercial transactions, leading to an urgent need for an effective and unified dispute resolution system which can sufficiently settle disagreements/issues among parties in dispute and which has to be arrived at keeping in mind the differences in laws of every nation, hence, immensely increasing the scope of private international law, or conflict of laws as called by different nations. Such urgency has led to many conventions, one of the most important being The New York Convention of 1958 (Convention on the Recognition and Enforcement of Foreign Arbitral Awards) and the UNCITRAL Model Law promulgated in 1985 and amended as recently as 2006 which has been the source for international arbitration, the most widely used dispute resolution method for international commercial trade and transactions, and many countries like India have also based their legislation on the rules of the UNCITRAL Model Law.

---

1 Harsh Pathak, Advocate, Supreme Court of India, Delhi, India, Email: info@harshpathak.com.

India with approximately 1.22 billion people[2] is the second most populous country in the world. The economy of India is the eleventh largest in the world by nominal GDP and the third largest by purchasing power parity (PPP)[3]. The country is one of the G-20 major economies and a member of BRICS. On a per capita income basis, India ranked 140th by nominal GDP and 129th by GDP (PPP) in 2011, according to the IMF[4]. India is one of the world's fastest growing economies and of major interest to foreign investors as a popular investment hub. As per IMF figures, the FDI in India for the year 2011 was 34.2 billion USD and 4.2 billion USD for the first quarter of 2012[5].

In 1991, the Indian economy was opened to FDI under the New Industrial Policy 1991, and since then the Government has liberalised the exchange control regulations, and moved from a strict regime allowing investments only in particular sectors, to a much freer approach with the objective of inviting and facilitating foreign investments. Investments are approved through two routes - 'automatic route' (requires no prior approval) and 'government approval route' (applications must be made to the Foreign Investment Promotion Board). One hundred percent foreign ownership is permitted in most activities under the automatic route. Such ownership is subject to compliance with certain conditions, except inter-alia in certain sectors such as airports, asset reconstruction companies, atomic minerals, broadcasting, postal services, courier services, print media, single brand retail, and telecoms. In these sectors there are specified sectorial caps/thresholds on foreign ownership. FDI is prohibited in agriculture, atomic energy, retail trading (except single brands up to 51%), lottery, betting and gambling.

India therefore has a system for foreign investors that is straightforward, and rarely requires government approval beyond an investment notification. There are still a number of restrictions that the US and Europe are trying to encourage the government to change, in sectors such as legal, insurance and banking, and those efforts remain ongoing. India's attraction to foreign investors is tempered only by its sometimes unclear legislation. The problem with legislation arises when government policy is changed, since new laws can often be badly drafted.

Investors face another problem with the Indian judicial system because the pleadings system is archaic, and therefore most court proceedings require large volumes of paperwork since everything needs to be pleaded. As a result, there is large volume of pending cases and therefore it can take as much as a decade for

2 Office of the Registrar General of India, Ministry of Home Affairs.
3 International Monetary Fund website – www.imf.org (as retrieved on 26.09.2012).
4 International Monetary Fund website – www.imf.org (as retrieved on 26.09.2012).
5 International Monetary Fund website – www.imf.org (as retrieved on 26.09.2012).

a trial to complete. Therefore, from a business perspective, the Indian courts are used more as a means of achieving interim results rather than definitive decisions. Most companies will go to court to get injunctions but will otherwise avoid them where possible.

In India, access to courts is relatively easy as litigation costs are relatively low, given that access to courts is a fundamental right enshrined in the Constitution of India. The Indian courts usually do not award realistic costs and as a result arbitration is the preferred option for dispute resolution. Litigators advise investors to include arbitration clauses in their contracts so as to provide for a dispute resolution mechanism in case differences/disputes arise.

India has been one of the fastest growing economic powers in recent times and has seen many changes in its economic policies leading to many foreign companies and corporations investing in the country's various profitable sectors. It has thus become a global economic power whose international commercial arbitration system required overhaul to reflect the changing times. Arbitration is governed by the Arbitration and Conciliation Act 1996 in India which is based for most parts on the Model law on International Commercial Arbitration adopted by the United Nations Commission on International Trade Law (UNCITRAL) in 1985. This Act has resulted in facilitation of Foreign Direct Investment (FDI) in India in a big way by providing for interim measures, implementation of foreign awards in India and appeal against awards in certain cases in matters of arbitration.

India's Arbitration Act is based on the UNCITRAL model, thereby forbidding the local courts from taking any view on the merits of a case where there is an arbitration clause. The Indian Arbitration Act is divided into two parts, domestic and international, based on the venue of arbitration. The Indian courts' ability extends to governing international arbitrations as well. Therefore, if arbitration takes place outside India, the parties in dispute can very well approach the Indian Courts for interim relief. An important case law in this regard *is Bhatia International vs. Bulk Trading S.A., (2002) 4 SCC 105. On page 120, it has been held*[6]*:*

> "*23.* That the legislature did not intend to exclude the applicability of Part I to arbitrations, which take place outside India, is further clear from certain other provisions of the said Act. Sub-section (7) of Section 2 reads as follows: "2.(7) An arbitral award made under this Part shall be considered as a domestic award".
>
> As is set out hereinabove the said Act applies to (*a*) arbitrations held in India between Indians, and (*b*) international commercial arbitrations. As set out hereinabove international commercial arbitrations may take place in India or outside India. Outside India, an international commercial arbitration may be held in a conven-

6 Bhatia International vs. Bulk Trading S.A., (2002) 4 Supreme Court Cases 105, India.

tion country or in a non-convention country. The said Act however only classifies awards as "domestic awards" or "foreign awards". Mr Sen admits that provisions of Part II make it clear that "foreign awards" are only those where the arbitration takes place in a convention country. Awards in arbitration proceedings which take place in a non-convention country are not considered to be "foreign awards" under the said Act. They would thus not be covered by Part II. An award passed in an arbitration which takes place in India would be a "domestic award". There would thus be no need to define an award as a "domestic award" unless the intention was to cover awards which would otherwise not be covered by this definition. Strictly speaking, an award passed in an arbitration which takes place in a non-convention country would not be a "domestic award". Thus the necessity is to define a "domestic award" as including all awards made under Part I. The definition indicates that an award made in an international commercial arbitration held in a non-convention country is also considered to be a "domestic award".

In Rashtriya Ispat Nigam Ltd. vs. Verma Transport Co., (2006) 7 SCC 275, on page 284, it has been held[7]:

"22. The scope and purport of such a clause was considered in *Heyman* vs. *Darwins Ltd. (1942) 1 All ER 337* and it was stated: (All ER pp. 339 H-340 A):

"The answer to the question whether a dispute falls within an arbitration clause in a contract must depend on (*a*) what is the dispute, and (*b*) what disputes the arbitration clause covers. To take (*b*) first, the language of the arbitration clause in this agreement is as broad as can well be imagined. It embraces any dispute between the parties 'in respect of' the agreement or in respect of any provision in the agreement or in respect of anything arising out of it. If the parties are one on the point that they did enter into a binding agreement in terms which are not in dispute, and the difference that has arisen between them is as to their respective rights under the admitted agreement in the events that have happened—e.g. as to whether the agreement has been broken by either of them; or as to the damage resulting from such breach; or as to whether the breach by one of them goes to the root of the contract and entitles the other party to claim to be discharged from further performance; or as to whether events supervening since the agreement was made have brought the contract to an end so that neither party is required to perform further—in all such cases it seems to me that the difference is within such an arbitration clause as this. In view, however, of phrases to be found in the report of some earlier decisions, the availability of the arbitration clause when 'frustration' is alleged to have occurred will require closer consideration".

In Gas Authority of India Ltd. vs. Keti Construction (I) Ltd., (2007) 5 SCC 38, on page 52, it has been held[8]:

---

7 Rashtriya Ispat Nigam Ltd. vs. Verma Transport Co., (2006) 7 Supreme Court Cases 275, India.

8 Gas Authority of India Ltd. vs. Keti Construction (I) Ltd., (2007) 5 Supreme Court Cases 38, India.

> "*21.* The Preamble to the Act makes it amply clear that Parliament has enacted the Arbitration and Conciliation Act, 1996 almost on the same lines as the Model Law, which was drafted by the United Nations Commission on International Trade Law. In *Sundaram Finance Ltd.* vs. *NEPC India Ltd (1999) 2 SCC 479.* it has been observed that the provisions of the Arbitration and Conciliation Act, 1996 should be interpreted keeping in mind the Model Law as the concept under the present Act has undergone a complete change. It will, therefore, be useful to take note of the corresponding provisions of the UNCITRAL Model Law".

In Fuerst Day Lawson Limited vs. Jindal Exports Limited, (2011) 8 SCC 333, on page 353, it has been held[9]:

> "*54.* The Arbitration and Conciliation Act, 1996 that has repealed the Arbitration Act, 1940 and also the Acts of 1937 and 1961, consolidates and amends the law relating to domestic arbitration, international commercial arbitration, enforcement of foreign arbitral awards and defines the law relating to conciliation and provides for matters connected therewith and incidental thereto taking into account the UNCITRAL Model Law and Rules".

International commercial arbitration is taking place rapidly all across the globe and is being preferred over, and hence replacing, traditional methods of dispute resolution, such as litigation, for international commercial transactions by corporations making foreign investments or making investments in collaboration with foreign parties. The enormity and complexity of business trade transactions and globalisation in today's age is a clear indicative of an increase in unexpected and unforeseen problems and disputes and therefore any state or corporation intending to make foreign investment or investment in collaboration with a foreign party as well as governments of nations across the globe are in dire need of an effective dispute resolution system to ensure the smooth functioning of their agreements, policies and economies.

There are various methods and forums of dispute resolution but arbitration is definitely preceding in usage of such forums for settlement of disputes and is a relatively modern technique as practiced today even though the concept has been around for many years as the methods and techniques of conducting arbitration as well as the laws governing such arbitration have been updated and modernised by nations from time to time to meet modern-day requirements and to bring them in line with internationally accepted principles and laws.

Arbitration is a form of alternative dispute resolution (ADR) and is a legal technique for resolving disputes between parties outside the courts in private wherein the parties to a dispute refer it to one or more than one person, as may

9 Fuerst Day Lawson Limited vs. Jindal Exports Limited, (2011) 8 Supreme Court Cases 333, India.

be stipulated by the arbitration clause incorporated by the parties in the contract itself, for dispute redressal, called 'Arbitrators' or the 'arbitral tribunal' by whose decision they agree to be bound, such decision being the award and being legally enforceable. Arbitration has established itself as the best method of determining complex commercial disputes all over the world. Countries such as India and Singapore have come a long way in this aspect and arbitral centres are being set up and established, and there has been a rise in the study of the law and practice of international commercial arbitration as an important subject among students at universities and law colleges.

International commercial arbitration is an effective way of putting an end to disputes between parties, without recourse to the courts of law, as arbitration usually takes much less time as compared to trial in a court of law, is less costly and usually results in fair and realistic awards. Furthermore, the laws governing arbitration proceedings in a particular matter, the arbitral tribunal and the seat of arbitration can be agreed upon and predetermined by the parties as convenient to them, making dispute resolution easier, effective and practical. Parties can agree to conduct arbitration proceedings in a totally independent country if the laws governing arbitration in such country are suitable to the parties and any award passed by such arbitral tribunal is legally binding upon such parties. Arbitration is conducted in different countries and against different legal and cultural backgrounds, on neutral grounds, and is not a formal proceeding like trials in courts. Therefore, arbitration has the advantages of fairness, bias-free decisions, practicality, speed, efficiency, control, cost effectiveness, can be made confidential as proceedings are generally non-public, and the advantage of awards being internationally enforceable, unlike orders of traditional courts, due to various agreements and conventions entered into between countries to encourage international arbitration, such as the New York Convention 1958 (Convention on the Recognition and Enforcement of Foreign Arbitral Awards).

Another major advantage of arbitration over traditional methods of dispute resolution is that – since the parties are free to choose the arbitrator(s), in today's world where technology, research, commodities, finance, among various other fields, are complex to understand and need fact finding and the expertise of someone who has the required capabilities of make a well-reasoned decision – arbitration allows the parties to choose an arbitrator with such requisite technical knowledge and experience, thus enhancing the quality of decision-making in many cases. Each party in arbitration is free to choose procedural matters to be employed and also the rules pertaining to taking testimony, language, interim measures, substantive law, evidentiary matters, presiding arbitrators and the degree of procedural formality.

In today's age, arbitration procedure has advanced so much that arbitration has become more sophisticated to the extent that it is even being conducted online with a system known as Online Dispute Resolution or ODR where the parties file disputes online, proceedings take place over the internet, and judgements are given on the basis of documents submitted online.

Various conventions and protocols have been entered into by various countries to harmonise the rules governing international commercial arbitration. In the past there have been various conventions, such as:

The Geneva Protocol of 1923

The Geneva Convention of 1927

The European Convention of 1961

The Washington Convention of 1965

In recent times, the UNCITRAL Model Law, promulgated in 1985 and amended as recently as 2006, has been the source for international arbitration and many countries like India have also based their legislation on the rules of the UNCITRAL Model Law. The New York Convention of 1958 (Convention on the Recognition and Enforcement of Foreign Arbitral Awards) is the most important convention to date in the field of arbitration. As of September 2012, 145 of the 193 United Nations Member States had adopted the New York Convention of 1958 (Convention on the Recognition and Enforcement of Foreign Arbitral Awards)[10]. India as well as most European countries have ratified the convention, therefore making it easier for prospective parties to engage in trade and commerce with each other.

The growth of international commercial arbitration has also given rise to various private and state run associations that conduct arbitration, most of them having their own rules and procedures allowing parties to select them as their choice of institutions to conduct and take care of the procedural aspects of arbitration, which is also known as institutional arbitration. A few of the prominent associations conducting arbitrations in the international arbitration sphere are:

1. The London Court of International Arbitration (LCIA)
2. The International Chamber of Commerce. (ICC)
3. American Arbitration Association (AAA)
4. International Centre for Settlement of Investment Disputes (ICSID)

Therefore, there has been widespread growth in the field of international commercial arbitration for which various countries have associated themselves with this new phenomenon in the legal field to enhance their economy and de-

10 UNCITRAL website - http://www.uncitral.org/uncitral/en/uncitral_texts/arbitration/NY Convention.html (as retrieved on 26.09.2012).

velop their country's judicial system through providing alternative forums for businesses and states.

But arbitration as a dispute resolution method is not free from disadvantages, including the fact that arbitration may become highly complex and may take up as much time to resolve the dispute as a trial in court. Further, if there is a predetermined and incorporated arbitration clause in an agreement, the parties are bound by it and it is therefore mandatory and binding in nature, and the parties waive their rights to access the courts and to have a judge or jury decide the case. Sometimes, arbitration costs much more than a trial in court would, added to which, both parties usually have to bear the cost of arbitration equally, which reduces the award of the winning party accordingly.

Another major disadvantage of arbitration is that there are very limited avenues for appeal, which means that an erroneous decision cannot be easily overturned especially in cases of international commercial arbitration, and in some legal systems, arbitral awards have fewer enforcement options than judgements. Although usually thought to be speedier, when there are multiple arbitrators on the panel, arbitration proceedings may take very long to be concluded as the proceedings – being informal in nature – are conducted at the convenience of all parties and arbitrators.

Nonetheless, international commercial arbitration is without doubt one of the most effective methods of dispute resolution in a world of complex and ever growing global business transactions between nations governed by different commercial laws. International commercial arbitration provides a platform where parties of different nations engaging in commercial trade can agree upon the method of dispute resolution by giving them flexibility in terms of applicable laws, the venue of dispute resolution, and more practical proceedings presided over by competent persons, where the final award is legally enforceable.

Bibliography

James, H., Gould, N.: International Commercial Arbitration: A Handbook 9, 2nd Edition, LLP, 1999.

Rubino-Sammartano, Mauro: International Arbitration Law and Practice, Kluwer Law International, 2nd Edition (Revised), 2001.

Redfern, A., Hunter, M.: International Commercial Arbitration, Sweet & Maxwell, 4th Edition, 2004.

Reddy, V, Nagaraj, V.: Arbitrability: The Indian Perspective. 19 J. Int'l 117, 118 (No. 2, 2002).

Bansal, A. K.: International Arbitration in India, 6Am. Rev. Int'l Arb. 191 (1995).

Krishan, Ranbir: An Overview of the Arbitration and Conciliation Act 1996. 21 J. Int'l Arb. 263, 265 (No. 3, 2004).

Work, Tracy: Student Author, India Satisfies Its Jones for Arbitration: New Arbitration Law in India, 10 Transnat'l Law, 217, 220 (1997).

Sood, S.: Finding Harmony with UNCITRAL Model Law: Contemporary issues in International Commercial Arbitration in India after the Arbitration and Conciliation Act of 1996.

Raghavan, V.: New Horizons for Alternative Dispute Resolution in India: The New Arbitration Law of 1996. 13 J. Int'l Arb. 5, 9-24 (No. 4, 1996).

On Dissenting Opinions in International Arbitration

Lecturer Cristina FLORESCU[1]

Abstract

When an arbitral tribunal is a collegiate body comprised of an uneven number of arbitrators, usually three members, the arbitrators can decide the case and render an award by majority vote. However, one arbitrator may express his disagreement with the majority view, issuing a concurring or a dissenting opinion. A dissenting opinion generally expresses disagreement with the result, while a concurrent opinion disagrees with the reasoning behind that result, which is not contested, both separate opinions being known and analysed as dissenting opinions. Few arbitration laws and rules deal with dissenting opinions expressly, but it is generally accepted that even if they should not form part of the award, they are communicated for scrutiny to the institution, in case of institutional arbitration, and to the parties afterwards. Dissenting opinions may improve the quality of majority awards and, instead of weakening the arbitral tribunal's authority, can promote arbitration. This means that a good faith, balanced and harmonious dissenting opinion, may prove to the losing party that all arguments were carefully and exhaustively examined by the arbitral tribunal during the stage of deliberation and later, when rendering the award.

Keywords: arbitration, dissenting opinion, concurring opinion, award.

1. Introduction

Dispute resolution processes can be consensual processes, such as mediation, conciliation, or negotiation, in which the parties attempt to reach agreement or adjudicative processes, such as litigation or arbitration, in which a judge, jury or arbitrator determines the outcome.

Arbitration is a process mainly for business disputes, by which two parties can settle a dispute in front of an arbitral tribunal specially constituted for that dispute, outside the traditional courtroom, while litigation is conducted inside a court of law.

Litigation is a lawsuit or other legal resort to the state courts to determine a lawful question or matter[2].

---

1 Cristina Florescu, Spiru Haret University of Bucharest, Faculty of Law and Public Administration, Romania, Email: crisflorescu@gmail.com.

2 For more details on the issue related to the benefits of arbitration see Alan Freeman, Litigation: Arbitration vs. litigation, 7 factors to consider before you draft a mandatory arbitration clause, 19 April 2012, available online at http://www.insidecounsel.com/2012/04/19/litigation-arbitration-v-litigation.

Arbitration involves settling a dispute by neutral and impartial persons outside the state courts and without proceeding to a court trial, as an alternative to litigation. It is sometimes preferred as a means of settling a matter in order to avoid the expense, delay, and acrimony of litigation[3].

International arbitration is no longer a form of alternative dispute resolution, but has nowadays become a more preferred and appropriate alternative to litigation in domestic and international courts. These days, it is the primary procedure for the resolution of international commercial and investment disputes.

Arbitration is a process by which the parties agree to the binding resolution of their disputes by arbitrators, who are usually selected and appointed by the parties or by the appointing authority, which is a mechanism chosen directly or indirectly by the parties for this task.

Unlike court litigation, where the judges cannot be selected or elected by the parties and are always appointed by the state mechanism, arbitration can be referred to by means of an arbitration agreement concluded between the parties. Moreover, the arbitration dispute is settled by binding resolution which finally disposes of the substantive disputed issues, having the legal effect of *res judecata* as regards those issues.

In this paper, international arbitration refers to both commercial and investment arbitration, although the first one is a private and the other a public matter and there is a substantial difference between those two kinds of arbitration, but here is not the place to discuss this subject that has been studied separately[4].

2. About deliberation and arbitrators in close conjunction with dissent

The arbitrators' duties in rendering an enforceable award are to decide the dispute in accordance with the applicable rules of law[5] and procedure, in view of the evidence before them and also in line with their beliefs. Prior to making the

---

3 http://wiki.answers.com/Q/What_is_the_difference_between_Arbitration_and_Litigation #ixzz270I3BAQe.

4 Cristina Florescu, Aspecte privind investirea instanței de arbitraj în arbitrajul privind investițiile străine (Aspects related to the constitution of arbitral tribunals in investment arbitration), "Revista Română de Drept al Afacerilor" no. 9/2011 ("Romanian Journal of Business Law" no. 9, 2011), p.13.

5 If the parties request the case to be decided *ex aequo et bono* then the case is to be decided by principles of what is fair and just. An arbitrator who is authorised to decide *ex aequo et bono* is not bound by legal rules but may take account of what is just and fair.

award and after closing the proceedings, the arbitrators deliberate, considering carefully and thoroughly the pros and cons of the grounds for the decision.

Deliberation is the process through which the members of the arbitral tribunal make their decision and the parties, the lawyers and other specialists in arbitration are particularly interested in the decision-making process and the inherent difficulties that may arise during deliberation, which may lead to dissenting or concurring opinions.

Deliberation is the phase of the arbitral process during which the members of the arbitral tribunal discuss and draft a decision in a very professional manner, which implies specific skills, prudence and firmness while at the same time avoiding the breach of confidentiality, in a manner that permits each arbitrator to freely express their opinion.

The deliberation process is a not a facile one, as arbitrators are not only judges, with a jurisdictional function; as arbitrators they are confronted with less formalism and limitations than those imposed by court litigation[6]. The arbitral tribunal is not a permanent body and its competence is limited to a certain case. Usually in international arbitration, the arbitrators come with different technical and cultural backgrounds and have different nationalities, speak different languages and have various specialisations in several legal fields. As every arbitrator has their own methods of judging and thinking about a case, deliberation can sometimes become a difficult process, taking into consideration all the above mentioned factors which can contribute to the decision-making process.

The collegiate principle governs the activity of the arbitral tribunal in each of its stages and is the basis on which all arbitrators participate in the deliberation process after closing the proceedings. This means that the arbitrators not only have the opportunity to express their opinion but a prerogative that results from the arbitrator's status.

As deliberation is an obligation incumbent on the arbitrators, the arbitral tribunal should take a decision after the discussion between. The normal and ideal situation is to reach a unanimous decision, but in practice there are cases when this cannot be reached, due to the size, complexity, the number of claims and the particular circumstances of the case in discussion, not to mention possible problems that may inherently arise in the proceedings. In this case, as the award must be legally rendered by a collegiate tribunal formed of more than one arbitrator (usually three arbitrators), it is necessary for the decisions to be made by the majority of the members of the arbitral tribunal or, if no majority is reached, by the president of the arbitral tribunal (presiding arbitrator), according to applicable norms.

6 Lord Bingham, The business of Judging, Oxford University Press, 2000, p. 4.

Thus, in deliberation, problems may arise when the arbitral tribunal comprises three arbitrators and the two co-arbitrators do not agree on the same opinion, even if the president of the arbitral tribunal is generally striving to achieve unanimity or when, according to the applicable rules to the proceedings, the presiding arbitrator does not have sole power of decision in the absence of a majority. The presiding arbitrator's possibility to deliver exclusively the award was considered the best option

> "because if the law only provided for the decision by the majority, a deadlock could occur when delivering the award, since each one of the arbitrators could have a different opinion"[7].

Although the author cited above considers that this possibility protects the effectiveness of the arbitration proceedings, on the contrary, I consider that each arbitrator of the tribunal is forced by professional deontology and personal moral duty to review the whole case and, in order to obtain the best result, the arbitral tribunal must try to reach a common opinion or at least a majority of two arbitrators of the tribunal. In any case, most arbitration rules stipulate a majority in order to render the award. But it is a good opportunity to reassess the dispute, because disagreement among a tribunal's members shows that the case is really difficult, and raises complex issues that need to be re-analysed with careful consideration. Arbitrators do not need to rush in finding a common solution, which they otherwise might make in haste and in fear of expressing the own ideas. That is why, sometimes, the separate opinion can make a difference, which should form the basis for the rest of the tribunal's possible reconsideration and ensures the parties that the case was properly evaluated.

Throughout the process, and especially during deliberation, the presiding arbitrator plays a special role in respect of reaching a unanimous decision. He must diligently perform the most important task of leading, first the procedure and then the discussions between the arbitrators in a civilised manner and with collegial respect, considering the factual and legal issues presented by the parties. The tribunal's analysis should reflect the arbitrators' ability to reach a consensus on the outcome of the case. The presiding arbitrator mainly has the duty of mediating between the co-arbitrators to find a balanced solution that is not obviously biased in favour of one party and not of creating an opportunity for divergence.

Even if presiding arbitrator is not able to obtain unanimity, the pressure is on the co-arbitrator who disagrees with the presiding arbitrator, given that decisions

---

7 Jose Maria Alonso, Deliberation and drafting awards in international arbitration, in Liber Amicorum Bernardo Cremades, Ed. La Ley, grupo Wolters Kluwer, 2010, p. 139

by the tribunal require a majority of the votes of all its members[8]. This is because sometimes one of the co-arbitrators, usually the arbitrator appointed by the party that loses the case, does not agree with the decision or the reasoning of the majority or with the presiding arbitrator. In that situation, the disagreeing co-arbitrator has the option to formulate and issue a separate opinion explaining the reasons for his divergence, notwithstanding that even party-appointed arbitrators are expected to be impartial and to act without bias, partisanship or appearances thereof. Dissention must be a matter of conviction and not convenience or politics. Dissents should not be a criticism of the majority, but rather a factual detached statement. The opinions should be concentrated, clear, detecting the issues of disagreement, and should reasonably encompass the arguments in support of the divergent opinion. It is intended to be an intellectual exercise and not an admonitory or moralising discourse. The co-arbitrators have a duty to ensure that the arguments on each side are fully and fairly considered, but the arbitrators should not argue points which counsel could have or should have argued, if they had been there. The decision-making process is not a matter of right or wrong with respect to the issues under consideration, but rather of different views on the same subject[9].

3. General considerations on the history of dissenting opinions

The history and tradition of common law taught specialists, and especially lawyers, to consider generally the issuance of dissenting opinions to be normal practice or even an obligation. Conversely, specialists in civil law tradition have been implicitly considering dissenting opinions to be improper, if not unlawful[10]. Nevertheless, as with many other issues in international arbitration, the distinct differences between common law and civil law traditions have faded over time.

Yet some practitioners and notorious scholars[11] have expressed their conviction that dissenting opinions should still be hindered in spite of the widespread

8 Article 47 of the ICSID Arbitration Rules.

9 Dissenting in Arbitration, available online at http://www.maritimeadvocate.com/arbitration/dissenting_in_arbitration.htm.

10 Peter J. Rees Q.C., Patrick Rohn, Dissenting Opinions: Can They Fulfil a Beneficial Role?, "Arbitration International", vol. 25, 2009, p. 329, pp. 329-346.

11 For example, see Jean-Francois Poudret, Sebastien Besson, Comparative Law of International Arbitration, 2nd ed., 2007, at para. 754, where it is stated that dissenting opinions should be avoided wherever possible. Philippe Fouchard, Emanuel Gaillard, Berthold Goldman, On International Commercial Arbitration, Emmanual Gaillard and John Savage (eds.), 1999, para. 1401, give the opinion that it would be unfortunate for dissenting

practice and open-minded view of the arbitral institutions, as the ICC (International Chamber of Commerce located in Paris, with special reference to the Court of Arbitration) does mostly.[12] Nowadays, however, dissenting opinions are more widely accepted and admitted. But I consider that the admissibility and the necessity of delivering a personal dissenting opinion should depend on the examination of interest[13].

Dissenting opinions are and will remain a reality, and they operate as a regulator that reduces the pressure in cases when the arbitrators have different views and cannot issue a common opinion. Therefore, the need for dissenting opinions cannot be denied and their prohibition is neither desirable nor productive. The ability to give a dissenting opinion helps focus disagreement into more constructive and valuable forms[14].

Decisions by arbitral tribunals and judicial bodies, in general, are often the result of complicated and dense debate arising out of differing assessments of law and evidence. Rendering the decision, especially in a complex and major dispute, is the most delicate task of the tribunal. This undoubtedly requires not just legal skills but also, and perhaps especially, a great deal of balance and common sense[15], irrespective of different legal and cultural backgrounds.

---

opinions to become common practice. Alan Redfern, Martin Hunter, Nigel Blackaby, Constantine Partasides, Law and Practice of International Commercial Arbitration, 4th ed., 2004, para. 8-79, assert that the arbitral process militates against the giving of dissenting opinions other than in exceptional circumstances. W. Laurence Craig, William W. Park, Jan Paulsson, International Chamber of Commerce Arbitration, 3rd ed., 2000, p. 374, affirm that while dissenting opinions may exceptionally be justified, they are generally to be discouraged.

12 The Statistical Report of the ICC Court published each year shows the number of awards that were made by majority and/or that were accompanied by, or included, dissenting opinions. In 2006, 293 awards were approved by the court, of which 179 were final awards, 82 partial awards and 32 awards by consent. In 23 awards, unanimity was not reached by the tribunal but the award was made by majority. Ten years earlier, in 1996, 19 awards (as compared with 12 in 1995) were accompanied by dissenting opinions. By comparison, however, dissenting opinions were produced in only two of the 76 LCIA awards issued in 2008. Data collected from Peter J. Rees Q.C., Patrick Rohn, cited work, p. 330.

13 See also Jose Maria Alonso, Deliberation and drafting awards in international arbitration, cited work, p. 140.

14 Richard Mosk, Tom Ginsberg, Dissenting Opinions in International Arbitration, "Mealey's International Arbitration Report" vol. 15, no. 4, 2000, p. 31.

15 Domenico de Pietro, The Controversial Role of Dissenting Opinions In International Arbitral Awards, October 24, 2011, available online at http://blogs.law.nyu.edu/trans national/2011/10/the-controversial-role-of-dissenting-opinions-in-international-arbitral.

It is very hard in a collegiate tribunal to reach a solution agreed by consensus because of the very nature of such a body, since every arbitrator as an individual has personal and separate approaches, views and configurations of the facts of a dispute, especially as each party presents the case in its favour. But the arbitrators have to also be prepared to make concessions and to waive some of their beliefs for the sake of a common result. But not at any price; if an arbitrator feel it is impossible to overcome some different points that may appear during the debates in the tribunal's deliberation, he is free to explain why he disagrees in a separate opinion.

When the arbitrator disagrees with the reasons but not with the result, the separate opinion is a concurring one. But as long as it is a disagreement, most specialists and scholars also call them dissenting opinions.

Dissenting opinions are therefore those in which one of the tribunal's arbitrators proposes and issues a different solution or different legal grounds from those raised by the majority of the tribunal. A concordant solution with different reasoning is called a concurring opinion, while a solution that differs from the one adopted by the majority is called a dissenting opinion. Both are individual opinions in which the dissenter expresses a different view from the other colleagues, so both are dissenting opinions generally.

More commonly seen in common law jurisdictions, and less so in the civil law tradition, the dissenting opinion in international commercial arbitration remains a controversial subject[16].

In arbitration matters decided by a tribunal of multiple arbitrators, the preferred result in all situations is, of course, an award unanimously reached by all of the arbitrators[17].

I consider that there should be no incentive to constrain the issuance of dissenting opinions to a particular type of decision, *i.e.* only to awards, regardless of whether they are interim, partial or final. The arbitral tribunal issues several procedural orders and decisions to which dissent can be applied if the arbitrator is unsatisfied with that decision. These can include issues such as determination

16 Peter J. Rees Q.C., Patrick Rohn, cited work, p. 329.

17 Richard M. Mosk, The Debate over Dissenting and Concurring Opinions in Arbitration, "University of West Los Angeles Law Review", vol. 26, 1995, pp. 51-55; Hans Smit, Dissenting Opinions in Arbitration, "ICC International Court of Arbitration Bulletin", 2004, pp. 37-39; Richard M. Mosk, Tom Ginsburg, Dissenting Opinions in International Arbitration, "Mealey's International Arbitration Report", Vol. 15, no. 4, April 2000, pp. 30-35; Laurence Shore, Kenneth Juan Figueroa, Dissents, Concurrences and a Necessary Divide Between Investment and Commercial Arbitration, "Global Arbitration Review" vol. 3, 2008, pp. 18, 20; Jacques Werner, Dissenting Opinions Beyond Fears, "Journal of International Arbitration", vol. 9, 1992, pp. 23-29.

of the place of arbitration, possible stay of the proceedings, other issues related to the procedural schedule, the production of documents or other kinds of procedural approaches that arbitrators might consider justify a separate, dissenting opinion.

Given the conflicting approaches, in 1985, the International Chamber of Commerce (ICC) Commission on International Arbitration established a Working Party on Dissenting Opinions on Interim and Partial Awards (Working Party) to examine the very subject. The Working Party invited commentary, deliberated on the desirability of dissenting opinions in international arbitration, issued preliminary reports, and then a final report in 1988, published in 1991[18].

This report's conclusions[19] of the ICC Commission on International Arbitration do not amend or supersede the ICC Rules of Arbitration or bind the ICC Court or its Secretariat. Instead they are just a 'practical guide' and held that:

- the presiding arbitrator's duty should be to establish a procedure for the internal working of the tribunal, designed to ensure that he is able to send any dissenting opinion to the Secretariat at the same time as sending the draft majority award;
- a dissenting opinion should only be communicated to the Court of Arbitration if it is received by the Secretariat before the date on which the award comes to the Court for scrutiny in the normal course of events and a dissenting opinion received after the award has been scrutinised by the Court should simply be notified to the parties and placed on file;
- dissenting opinions should normally be sent to the parties by the Court of Arbitration at the same time as notification of the award under the ICC Rules; exceptionally, a dissenting opinion should not be notified where the Court of Arbitration concludes that such communication is prohibited by law, or where the validity of the award may be imperilled, in the country in which the arbitration took place or in any country in which (so far as the Court can reasonably foresee) recognition or enforcement of the award is likely to be sought;

18 Fourth Report on Dissenting and Separate Opinions, Working Party on Partial and Interim Awards and Dissenting Opinions, ICC Commission on International Arbitration, Doc. No. 420/293 Rev. 2 (23 February1988). The Working Party's conclusions from its earlier reports are included in the final report. Final Report issued by the Work Group on Dissent Opinions, [hereinafter ICC Final Report], "ICC International Court of Arbitration Bulletin", vol. 2, no. 1, 1991, p. 32.

19 ICC Final Report para. 24-31.

- the Court of Arbitration may draw the attention of dissenting arbitrators to any circumstances which may prohibit the communication of a dissenting opinion to the parties, or may imperil the validity of the majority award.

4. National and international rules applicable to dissenting opinions

Regarding the legal regime governing dissenting opinions, the position in national arbitration laws and under major arbitration rules is not expressly defined. Most laws and rules are silent on the issue of dissenting opinions[20] and, in practice, arbitration agreements rarely, if ever, contain any guidance or rule on the issuance of dissenting opinions[21]. A very complete examination and comparative perspective of law and rules containing provisions regarding dissenting opinions can be found in Manuel Arroyo's paper, where he examined 107 national arbitration laws and most of the arbitral rules for his survey and concluded that modern arbitration laws and rules – though differing on how dissents may be treated in the award – normally allow dissenting opinions[22].

In Romanian legislation and practice, Article 360^2 of the Romanian Civil Procedure Code and Article 68 of the Romanian Arbitration Court Rules stipulate that, when the arbitral tribunal is composed of an odd (uneven) number of members, the arbitrator who has expressed a view that differs from the majority

20 Even the UNCITRAL Model Law does not mention dissenting opinions explicitly, Art. 31(1) of the Model Law provides that the reasons for which an arbitrator omits to sign the award have to be stated if the award is only signed by the majority. This provision has been interpreted as mandating the minority arbitrator to set out the reasons for his dissent. See also Jacques Werner, Dissenting Opinions: Beyond Fears, cited work, p. 24.

21 For example, some legal texts that mention aspects related to dissenting opinions: Article 37(3) of the Spanish Arbitration Act, Article 24(2) of the Brazilian Arbitration Act, Article 53 of the Chinese Arbitration Law, Article 39(1) of the Bulgarian Arbitration Law, Article 47(3) of the ICSID Arbitration Rules, Article 48(4) of the Netherlands Arbitration Institute Rules, Article 47(5) of the CIETAC Rules. Other important arbitral organisations or laws are silent, as ICC, LCIA, SCC, ICDR, UNCITRAL, Swiss Rules.

22 Manuel Arroyo, Dealing with Dissenting Opinions in the Award: Some Options for the Tribunal, "ASA (Swiss Arbitration Association) Bulletin", Kluwer Law International, vol. 26, no. 3, 2008, pp. 439-445 (pp. 437-466). At the same time, the authors Mosk and Ginsburg (cited work, p. 35) stated, in 2000, that dissenting opinions had apparently become "prevalent in international arbitration. They are here to stay. It therefore makes sense for arbitral institutions to address them directly through the inclusion of provisions for dissenting opinions in procedural rules and codes of ethics". In view of the sets of rules issued or amended thereafter, it would seem that several institutions took action accordingly.

of the arbitral tribunal will draft and sign a separate opinion, explaining the reasoning behind such an opinion. Moreover, if a separate opinion is expressed, the dispositive part of the award will mention that fact. The arbitral award will be signed by all arbitrators, excepting the case when a separate opinion has been expressed; in that case, the majority will sign the draft and the dissenting arbitrator will sign only the dissenting opinion[23].

For the sake of good order, Article 594 of the new Code of Civil Procedure, which will come into force on 1 February 12013, upholds the rules stated above and mentions that the same rules apply accordingly for concurring opinions.

Under the auspices of any law or rule, the dissenter is nevertheless free to sign the majority award if he wishes, as some parts of it may be in agreement with its opinion. Consequently, the dissenter may sign the award at his discretion, even when delivering a dissenting opinion[24]. In procedural terms, dissenting opinions are not even considered as being part of the award but, normally, they are made available to the parties[25].

Where an arbitrator is given the opportunity to participate in the drafting of the final award but refuses to do so, choosing instead to issue a dissenting opinion, the award issued is a proper award and not an award by a truncated tribunal[26].

Regarding other arbitral norms and rules, dissenting opinions are expressly permitted under the ICSID (International Centre for Settlement of Investment Disputes) Convention (Article 48(4) of the Convention). The Iran-US Claims Tribunal incorporated an amendment to the UNCITRAL (United Nation Commission on International Trade Law) Rules to allow for dissenting opinions (Article 32 of the Rules). These express references in the ICSID Rules and the modification by the Iran-US Claims Tribunal are based on the observation that dissenting opinions prove to be more appropriate in cases where a State is a party[27].

---

23 Ioan Schiau, Disagreeing on Parties' Disagreement: The Arbitral Award and the Dissenting Opinion, available online at http://aspeckt.unitbv.ro/jspui/bitstream/123456789/194/1/schiau%20i.pdf.

24 See also footnote no. 17, with reference to Art. 31(1) of the Model Law.

25 J.D.M. Lew, L. A. Mistelis, S. Kroll, Comparative International Commercial Arbitration, Wolters Kluwer, 2003, p. 641.

26 Philipp Peters, Presiding Arbitrator, Deciding Arbitrator: Decision-Making in Arbitral Tribunals, in Christian Klausegger, Peter Klein et al. (eds), Austrian Yearbook on International Arbitration 2011, (Manz'sche Verlags- und Universitätsbuchhandlung 2011) p. 158.

27 Philippe Fouchard, Emanuel Gaillard, Berthold Goldman, cited work, p. 766; Manuel Arroyo, cited work, pp. 443.

Scholars and some of the world's most experienced and well-known arbitrators also present different opinions regarding the permissibility of dissenting opinions in international commercial arbitration. Some of them share Redfern's view[28] against the prevalence of dissents in arbitration, although he accepts the reality that dissents cannot be prohibited and are here to stay, while others support their permissibility, like Born[29], who argues that the right to provide a dissenting or separate opinion is a natural corollary of the adjudicative function and the obligation to provide a reasoned award. That is certainly the better view[30], even the reasons and arguments for and against are linked to each other as regards the duties to be fulfilled by the arbitrators.

Another paper analysing dissenting opinions[31] distinguishes between arbitrations involving bilateral investment treaties and those involving general commercial arbitration. In the latter, they say, "a dissenting opinion is rarely advisable". In arbitrations involving investment treaties, however,

> "an arbitrator should state his or her view both to develop the law and to demonstrate his or her thinking to the broader investment treaty community".

The opinions of other authors on the issue of dissenting opinions are also mentioned in this paper when analysing several aspects, advantages and disadvantages of such separate opinions[32].

ICC practice in this respect has become clearer since the Final Report issued in 1991, as stated above[33]. The ICC Court does not especially promote or sup-

---

28 Alan Redfern, The 2003 Freshfields Lecture, Dissenting Opinions in International Commercial Arbitration: the Good, the Bad and the Ugly, "Arbitration International" vol. 20, no. 3, 2004, p. 223-242, also available online at http://ciarb-european branch.com/ training/Paris2012/A15.%20Redfern%20on%20Dissents.pdf; Alan Redfern, Dangerous Dissents, 16 March 2005, available online at http://www.brownwelsh.com/Archive/2005_Master_Redfern.pdf; W. Laurance Craig, William W. Park and Jan Paulsson, International Chamber Of Commerce Arbitration, 3rd ed., 2000, para. 19.06, p. 374.

29 Gary Born, International Commercial Arbitration, Kluwer Law International, 2009, p. 2466.

30 Jeff Waincymer, Procedure and Evidence in International Arbitration, Kluwer Law International, 2012, p. 1303, pp. v-1348.

31 Laurence Shore, Kenneth Juan Figueroa, Dissents, cited work, p. 18.

32 Several of these authors' views have also been studied by Ilhyung Lee, Introducing International Commercial Arbitration And Its Lawlessness, By Way Of The Dissenting Opinion, "Contemporary Asia Arbitration Journal", vol. 19, no. 1, 2011, p. 19- 35, available online at: http://ssrn.com/abstract=1867886; See also Philipp Peters, cited work, pp. 129 – 160, especially section E, pp. 157, 158 where dissenting opinions are briefly presented.

33 Final Report issued by the Work Group on Dissent Opinions, "ICC International Court of Arbitration Bulletin", vol. 2, no. 1, 1991, p. 32.

port the issuance of dissenting opinions but allows dissenters to make their opinion known to the Court for its use in the scrutiny of the draft award. However, the Court takes it into consideration only when scrutinising the draft award, on condition that the dissenting opinion is submitted to the court at the same time as the draft award by the majority members of the tribunal. There is also the possibility that such dissenting opinion may change the faith of the majority award when the dissenting opinion appears strongly persuasive and alerts the Court to the possibility of the award being insufficiently reasoned, inconsistent or contrary to provisions of applicable law[34]. In this circumstance, the Court can draw the arbitrators' attention to those specific points of substance and invite them to reconsider their draft in view of the dissenter's opinion, as provided in Article 33 of the new ICC Rules, former Article 27[35]. Such a comment by the Court in light of the dissenting opinion may require new or further deliberation by the arbitrators, who will need to consider whether they want to adopt some parts of the dissenting opinion and make some changes to their award[36].

Although the dissenting opinion does not form a part of the award and is therefore neither formally reviewed nor approved, the form and structure of the dissenting opinion must be clear and strong, as the duty of the arbitrator is to fully explain his reasons, as in any award. The dissenting opinion should not be too long nor contain again the initial parts and abbreviations already set out in the majority award, but needs to adequately explain what the arbitrator did in the interpretative process, with particular care and with a special duty of caution for the proposals and solution he finds as the basis of the interpretative outcome. At the same time, the finding has to be the result of a proper fact-finding procedure; and the elements and steps in this procedure must be spelled out in the opinion as they must in the award[37].

In deciding whether to send the dissenting opinion to the parties or not, the ICC Court is guided by its own Final Report and, therefore, usually communicates the dissenting opinion to the parties along with the award, unless dissenting opinions are prohibited by the arbitration law, or where the validity of the award might be endangered, either in the place of arbitration or (to the extent that this could be foreseen) in the country of enforcement[38]. However, the Working Party did not identify in its Final Report any country in which, under its na-

34 Peter J. Rees Q.C., Patrick Rohn, cited work, pp. 333, 334.

35 Francis Patrick Donovan, Dissenting Opinions, ICC International Court of Arbitration Bulletin vol. 7 no. 2, 1996, p. 76.

36 Peter J. Rees Q.C., Patrick Rohn, cited work, p. 334.

37 Pierre Lalive, On the Reasoning of International Arbitral Awards, "Journal of International Dispute Settlement", vol. 1, no. 1, 2010, p. 60, pp. 55-65.

38 ICC Final Report para. 29.

tional laws, the validity of the award would be endangered by the communication of the dissenting opinion[39], therefore, in practice, dissenting opinions are sent out by the ICC with the majority award, attached after the signature page of the award. Generally, the tribunal is simply informed that the dissenting opinion will be sent to the parties when publishing the signed award[40]. However, if the majority arbitrators can argue convincingly why they consider the communication of a dissenting opinion to be improper or inadmissible under the arbitration law or that it would endanger the validity of the award, the Court will refrain from communicating the dissenting opinion to the parties. In such cases, the dissenting arbitrator may still be permitted to communicate his dissenting opinion to the parties, informally[41].

5. Advantages and disadvantages of the dissenting opinion

Historically, dissenting opinions have been an important aspect or – better – tool of international courts for many years, especially those rendered in the jurisprudence of the International Court of Justice have played a significant role in the development of international law[42]. Such dissenting opinions have added to the prestige and reliability of the Court and – if well-reasoned and serious – such dissents ensure the parties that the case was thoroughly assessed[43].

Dissenting opinions have substantially contributed to the development of international law by their new approaches and, particularly, to the authority of international justice. Furthermore, according to Sir Hersch Lauterpacht, dissenting opinions maintain the independence and impartiality of the judges and provide a better understanding of the Court's judgements[44]. Equally, dissenting opinions

39 Ibidem, para. 22.

40 Alan Redfern, The 2003 Freshfields Lecture, Dissenting Opinions in International Commercial Arbitration: the Good, the Bad and the Ugly, cited work, p. 241, referring to the conclusions of a Working Session in September 2000 where the ICC reviewed its procedure in relation to dissenting opinions.

41 ICC Final Report para. 22. See also Peter J. Rees Q.C., Patrick Rohn, cited work, p. 334.

42 R.P. Anand, The Role Of Individual And Dissenting Opinions In International Adjudication, "International and Comparative Law Quarterly", vol. 14, 1965, pp. 788-808. See also Domenico de Pietro, cited work.

43 Domenico de Pietro, cited work.

44 Sir H. Lauterpacht, The Development of International Law by the International Court, being a revised edition of "The Development of International Law by the Permanent Court of International Justice, 1934", London, Steven and Sons Limited 1958, reprinted edition published by Grotius Publications Limited, Cambridge, 1982, p. 68. Also availa-

have served the important purpose of developing domestic law over time[45], where they are seen as tools through which the law managed to move to a higher and more civilised stage. This kind of dissenting opinion offers different solutions, analyses more in tune with new developments, therefore contributing to the continuing adjustment of the law to new conditions. The dissenter often is perceived as more ready to take the next step and to propose novel solutions, perhaps in part because, as dissenters, they are not responsible for the final result[46]. Unfortunately, bearing in mind that dissenting opinions in arbitration are generally not published, except for investment arbitration, this benefit of contributing to law development is of reduced importance in arbitration.

Some specialist and authors[47] argue that arbitral decisions should be published in their entirety. To some of them, this regime is applied by a number of arbitral institutions, as for example several arbitral awards issued under the auspices of the ICC International Court of Arbitration are published. In order to maintain the secrecy and the long debated confidentiality of arbitration, in addition to demonstrating the necessary transparency, a selection, rather than all of them, are published, primarily in the Collection of ICC Arbitral Awards, co-published by ICC Publishing and Kluwer Law International, the ICC Interna-

---

ble online at http://books.google.ro/books?id=hrBp85NknioC&pg=PR3&hl=ro&source=gbs_selected_pages&cad=3#v=onepage&q&f=false.

45 In his above quoted paper The Controversial Role of Dissenting Opinions in International Arbitral Awards, Domenico de Pietro reminded of a very interesting case in 1896 when Justice Harlan rendered a dissenting opinion in a Supreme Court racial segregation case that was at the heart of the decision, almost fifty years later, in the case of Brown vs. Board of Education, which ended racial segregation in American schools. Another dissenting opinion, in the United Kingdom, contributed to a radical change in the law on arbitration. In the 1995 Ken Ren case, the Supreme Court, which back then was the House of Lords, addressed the issue as to whether or not to make an order for security for costs in an arbitration. The Lord Justices agreed that the English courts had the discretionary power to issue any such orders. In Lord Mustill's dissenting opinion, which Lord Browne-Wilkinson also supported, it was argued that an order for security for costs did not conform to the type of procedure that the parties had selected for the protection of their rights and that any court application to that effect should have been denied. Interestingly, the 1996 English Arbitration Act, which was enacted one year after the Ken Ren decision, took the power to order security for costs in arbitration away from the English courts and vested it in the arbitrators. See also Alan Redfern, The 2003 Freshfields Lecture – Dissenting Opinions in International Commercial Arbitration: The Good, the Bad and the Ugly, cited work, p. 223-242.

46 Hans Smith, Dissenting Opinions in Arbitration, "ICC International Court of Arbitration Bulletin" vol. 15 no. 1, 2004, p. 37.

47 Ibid. p. 38

tional Court of Arbitration Bulletin, the ICCA's[48] Yearbook Commercial Arbitration and the French Journal du droit international, commonly known as Clunet.

I appreciate also that – by publishing and making them available – arbitral awards can increase the promotion and acceptance of arbitration in general, and can help the development of arbitration practice and law, thus ensuring transparency and fostering the necessary social and cultural acceptability of arbitration. For the same reason, dissenting and concurring opinions should be published, emphasises another author[49]. Moreover, the minority opinion of a dissenter, in particular, can provide a more comprehensive overview of the case; even if the dissenting opinions are not part of the award, I believe they complete it and should be perceived as providing clarification of the dissenting arbitrator's view on the majority award, which can ensure comprehensive understanding of the case.

In recent years most laws and rules in international arbitration have been adapted and developed especially to cope with the reality of international circumstances. And dissenting and concurring opinions can contribute to this development, providing the resources for finding better new solutions and principles to the real issues and aspects that appear every day in the business and cor-

48 ICCA is the acronym for International Council for Commercial Arbitration.

49 Peter J. Rees Q.C., Patrick Rohn, cited work, pp. 339-346. A special section addresses the circumstances under which a dissenting opinion can and should be published. The authors made some consideration of the points for ensuring better and more efficient issuance of a dissenting opinion, as follows: Guideline No. 1 (Principle): No issuance of dissenting opinion if arguments of the minority are set out in the award (fall-back solution); Guideline No. 2 (Subject Matter): Criticism must concern relevant issues of fact, law and/or procedure. And here it is so well said: "The purpose of dissenting opinions in arbitration is, first, to inform the parties that an alternative evaluation and interpretation of relevant facts and laws was considered, even if ultimately rejected by the majority, and, secondly, to inform the parties and the appellate and enforcement courts about procedural irregularities and blatant errors of law that may constitute a violation of public policy and lead to the vacation and non-enforcement of the award"; Guideline No. 3 (Procedure and Timing): Circulation to majority prior to adoption of the award; Guideline No. 4 (Form and Style): short, polite, restrained and not imperilling the award's authority by its polemical style; Where to regulate: should the issuance of dissenting opinions be regulated in a professional code of ethics? To the last question I consider that the rules have to take this issue into consideration, and some of them already have. The authors very well concluded that "although every case has its particularities which need to be taken into consideration, the general principles and mechanisms set out above, if applied with robust common sense, should help to ensure that if a dissenting opinion has to be issued it can serve a meaningful purpose and play a beneficial role".

porate arena[50]. They potentially play the same role that the great dissenters played in the development of law in common law and especially in American courts[51] as mentioned above.

Another advantage of the dissenting opinion may be considered the judicial and arbitral responsibility of the arbitral tribunal to clearly and completely analyse all the facets of the factual and legal aspects of the case when taking the final decision. Bearing in mind that an arbitral award is only subject to review on exceptional, limited grounds, and cannot be revised on the merits, this should motivate the arbitrators to provide a coherent, convincing and sound award. Therefore, the force of a dissenting opinion should not be neglected, as the arbitrators that form the majority can reconsider their position, which might ultimately produce a unanimous decision in an efficient settlement.

A dissenting opinion criticising ordinary issues of fact and law should not actually imperil the authority of the award and its ability to be recognised and enforced under the New York Convention[52], bearing in mind that most national arbitration laws generally do not provide for a review of the award on its merits. And especially when the dissenting opinion reveals deficiencies, such as faults, omissions, oversights and other irregularities, it is to the parties' benefit to be protected against such possible awards and to try to set aside or refuse recognition of such awards. The position expressed by the scholars Redfern and Hunter[53] is that the very objective of arbitration is to arrive at a determinative decision, regardless of whether all the arbitral tribunal is of the same decision and even if the decision is improper[54]. I cannot subscribe less to this view, as long as a decision is the result of a properly conducted procedure.

After seeing the disappointing result, the losing party is more interested in how the tribunal reached that conclusion and why the dispute was settled in opposition to its own views and arguments. This is where the dissenting opinion can enlighten the losing party and increase its willingness to voluntarily comply with the award. After careful examination of the whole award and the separate opinion, the losing party may decide that the case was properly taken into consideration, even though the result is unsatisfactory, or whether it wants to take further action (like an action to set aside the award or objections to be raised at the stage of recognition and enforcement).

50 See also Alan Redfern, The 2003 Freshfields Lecture – Dissenting Opinions in International Commercial Arbitration: The Good, the Bad and the Ugly, cited work, p. 224.

51 Hans Smith, Dissenting Opinions in Arbitration, cited work, p. 39.

52 Peter J. Rees Q.C., Patrick Rohn, cited work, p. 340, the footnote no. 43.

53 Alan Redfern, Martin Hunter, Nigel Blackaby and Constantine Partasides, cited work, para 8-82, pp. 391-392.

54 Peter J. Rees Q.C., Patrick Rohn, cited work, p. 340, the footnote no. 43.

Even in such a case, the dissenting opinion does not have a decisive impact, and the court reviewing the majority award may take the dissenting opinion only as evidence without any assurance that its interpretation of the facts and/or law will be exactly followed.

In case the award is subject to scrutiny – as in ICC practice where this process is realised in more depth and the Court Secretariat is called upon to assess the appropriateness of attaching the dissenting opinion to the award – the Court may indicate some points where the majority should pay additional attention in the interests of a complete and efficient award.

Another aspect is that a dissenting opinion may sometimes create a more extensive record of the entire proceedings. Nowadays, in most international arbitrations involving significant values and higher interest disputes, this record of the proceedings is already achieved by the complete transcript of the hearings, including examination of the witnesses. The dissent is, however, likely to stress the points that have not supported the majority opinion, highlighting them based on the facts and arguments that may have been neglected by the arbitrators in order to reach a majority decision more easily. An assertion in a dissenting opinion where there is no contemporaneous evidence may support some challenges that could not otherwise be successfully made[55].

One might consider that a dissenting opinion is not exactly a benefit, as it may create the basis for offsetting aside the award, especially since the dissenting arbitrator is usually the one appointed by the losing party. But here particularly the arbitrator's duty of neutrality, independence and impartiality should prevail and – governed by intellectual honesty – an arbitrator is unlikely to risk his reputation by presenting a passionate view in spite of the majority just to disrupt the process and satisfy the party that appoint him. A dissenter should be driven by the need to ensure complete analysis of the case while being convinced that his personal integrity prevents him from fully subscribing to the majority award. A watchful eye cast by the institution when scrutinising draft awards would appropriately redress possible abuses in this regard[56].

As regards the scrutiny process, a dissenting opinion may alert the institution to the fact that the case is complicated and needs special attention in order to detect any possible issues that may be redressed and, if considered appropriate, the Court can invite the majority to reconsider some aspects in this respect. If well-reasoned and drafted in good faith, such dissenting opinions can increase the level of the award and may stimulate a more thorough reasoning in the ma-

55 Jeff Waincymer, cited work, p. 1305.

56 Hans Smith, Dissenting Opinions in Arbitration, cited work, p. 40.

jority's award[57]. Moreover, it has also been assessed[58] that the free and open-minded manifestation of differing views improves and consolidates the authority and legality of the arbitral proceedings by demonstrating, especially to the losing party[59], that alternative arguments have been thoroughly assessed, even if ultimately discarded by the majority. This approach should strengthen confidence in the proceedings and thus encourage the losing party to voluntarily comply with the award without enforcement proceedings being necessary.

It has been asserted that a dissenting opinion, a pure and unaltered statement of opinion, can be issued to demonstrate to the appointing party that its position has been staunchly defended[60]. While this may indeed be the case, it is not necessarily a bad thing. An analysis of the fundamental arbitral principle of the parties' possibility to appoint their arbitrators shows that one duty of a party-appointed arbitrator is to be sure that the legal and factual position of the party that nominates him is fully taken into consideration, properly analysed when determining and settling the case, and featured in the reasoning behind the award. Dissenters should not exaggerate this duty by feeling absolutely compelled to issue a separate opinion, their main duty still being to strive for unanimity.

The issue of breaching the secrecy of the arbitration decision-making process and the deliberation confidentiality has long been debated. But confidentiality in arbitration generally relates to the publication of the arbitration process and does not limit the differing evaluation of the facts and/or application of the law by an arbitrator through a dissenting opinion. I am of the opinion that the secrecy rule encompasses the arbitrators' discussions and arguments exchanged in the deliberation process to find a decision, *i.e.* the deliberative process is confidential, but not the voting process through which an arbitrator may express a

57 Richard M. Mosk, Tom Ginsburg, cited work, p. 30.

58 Ibid.

59 Alan Redfern, The 2003 Freshfields Lecture, Dissenting Opinions in International Commercial Arbitration: the Good, the Bad and the Ugly, op.cit., p. 234, shows that in 2001 there were 24 dissenting opinions issued in ICC arbitrations. In 22 of these the dissenting arbitrator was identified as the one appointed by the losing party. This statistical evidence cannot be simply attributed to the fact that parties are careful to select arbitrators with views similar to theirs and that the statistics therefore only reflect the dissenter's shared outlook with the appointing party. See, Werner, Dissenting Opinions: Beyond Fears, cited work, pp. 25, 26, and Mosk and Ginsberg, cited work, p. 32, who argue in that direction. A rare exception to the rule is Tokio Tokeles vs. Ukraine, ICSID Case No. ARB/02/18, IIC 258 (2004), where the chairman Prosper Weil issued a dissenting opinion to the majority decision on jurisdiction.

60 Peter J. Rees Q.C., Patrick Rohn, cited work, p. 336.

view that differs from the rest of the tribunal, *i.e.* the reasons for decisions need to be transparent.

The risk of the parties being informed about the very substance of the deliberations is not facilitated by the issuance of a dissenting opinion, which is restricted to a differing evaluation of the facts and/or application of the law[61] by the dissenter and does not impede over the confidentiality in arbitration[62].

6. Conclusions

In international arbitration one should bear in mind the different nationalities, cultures and legal systems of the arbitrators that influence attempts to arrive at a common result. This is why, in practice, it is not easy to reconcile all the tribunal's interpretations and views regarding a unanimity award on a case that is differently perceived and presented by the parties themselves. It is therefore the climate inside the tribunal and the relations among its members that matter most of all, as the individual background, personality, professionalism, reputation and ethics of each arbitrator should smooth rather than impede progress towards a permissive decision during deliberation, despite the inherent tensions existing within the tribunal.

In striving to achieve unanimity of the arbitral tribunal, a dissenting opinion can be used by a co-arbitrator during the deliberation process to arrive at a compromise, an award that comes closer to the outcome that the co-arbitrator be-

61 Ibid., p. 338.

62 A contrary opinion is expressed by an eminent scholar: "It would be difficult, if not impossible, for arbitrators to have a frank and open exchange of views, to advance ideas and proposals, to change their mind and then perhaps to change it back again, if what they had said and what they had not said, what they had thought and what they had not thought, was to become known to the parties – particularly in a situation in which two of the three members of the tribunal are chosen by the parties themselves ... Arbitrators should be able to discuss freely and openly the case that they have to decide. Yet it is difficult for arbitrators to do this if there is a risk, real or imaginary, that one of their number will break the confidence of their discussions, whether by communication with his or her appointing party, or by means of a dissenting opinion". Alan Redfern, The 2003 Freshfields Lecture, Dissenting Opinions in International Commercial Arbitration: the Good, the Bad and the Ugly, cited work, p. 239. But my interpretation is that, indeed, the arbitrators should communicate with each other freely and without prejudice in the process of exchanging views during deliberation, but this is not altered by any dissenting opinion. This does not breach the confidentiality of the deliberation and decision-making process, but just expresses the different view of the dissenter from the majority. On the contrary, in fact, it is the dissenter who should not fear disclosure of his views and criticism of the majority decision in issuing an individual opinion according to his beliefs, as it is his duty to render a correct and complete decision.

lieves in and also to the view held by the majority[63]. In practice, the dynamics of a collegiate tribunal in search of unanimity may result in a more nuanced award than a sole arbitrator might decide in the same situation[64].

Whatever the criticism may be, issuing dissenting opinions is nowadays considered widely permissible and achieves several goals in practice[65]. By expressing disagreement, an arbitrator might compel the majority members to reconsider their opinion by debating and taking his ideas into consideration, which may lead to a unanimous award, or might result in the dissenter signing the award despite disagreeing with it. Eventually, dissenting opinions may even help to flag serious irregularities of the majority, enabling these flaws to be remedied before issuing the award.

As far as the procedural requirements for dissenting opinions are concerned, there is no required form; they are attached to the award or provided separately to the parties, although the dissenting opinion is not part of the award itself and is also not attributed any direct legal effect. However, depending on the circumstances of each case, a dissenting opinion might play a role in proceedings to set aside or enforce an award.

Finally, recent years have revealed an increasing demand for publication of arbitral awards in order to create a uniform, reliable and coherent jurisprudence on specific persistent issues of international trade law. Without doubt, the more 'public' arbitral decisions are, the stronger would be the case for dissenting opinions, as the situation of dissenting opinions in international and domestic courts would become increasingly applicable and relevant to international commercial arbitration[66].

Overall, I consider that a dissenting arbitrator is advised to issue a dissent when he has tried his best to reconcile with his colleagues on the panel, as an effective and conscientious arbitrator has the professional obligation to do as thorough and competent a job as possible, including delivering a dissenting opinion if necessary. Dissenting opinions may also support settlement negotiations and avoidance of claims in future transactions[67], because if some uncertainty surrounds the terms and conditions of the parties' dealings, then it might

63 For example, a tribunal may issue unanimity by splitting a portion of the claims and rendering a balanced decision in favour of both parties, or deny the recovery of costs for one party in favour of the other.

64 Michael McIlwrath, John Savage, International Arbitration and Mediation, A Practical Guide, Wolters Kluwer, 2010, p. 323, pp. 1-515.

65 Philipp Peters, cited work, p. 158.

66 Domenico de Pietro, cited work.

67 Jeff Waincymer, cited work, p. 1306.

be advisable to ensure greater transparency and clarification to prevent future disputes.

Consequently, for the benefit of arbitration, if dissenting opinions are issued under current legislation and practice in good faith, and are well-reasoned and responsible, they are allowed and should also be published to further scholarly analysis. Furthermore, with due respect for the integrity of the process, dissenting opinions should not be used to destabilise the purposes and principles of arbitration, especially its neutrality and confidentiality, or to constitute improper grounds for any judicial attack on the award.

Bibliography

Alonso, Jose Maria: Deliberation and drafting awards in international arbitration, in Liber Amicorum Bernardo Cremades, Ed. La Ley, grupo Wolters Kluwer, 2010.

Arroyo, Manuel: Dealing with Dissenting Opinions in the Award: Some Options for the Tribunal, "ASA Bulletin", Kluwer Law International, vol. 26 no. 3, 2008.

Berg van den, Albert Jan: Chapter 42, Dissenting Opinions by Party-Appointed Arbitrators in Investment Arbitration, in Looking to the Future: Essays on International Law in Honor of W. Michael Reisman, Mahnoush Arsanjani et al. (eds.), 2010.

Born, Gary: International Commercial Arbitration, Kluwer Law International, 2009.

Fouchard, Philippe, Gaillard, Emanuel, Goldman, Berthold: On International Commercial Arbitration, Emmanual Gaillard and John Savage (eds.), 1999.

Lalive, Pierre: On the Reasoning of International Arbitral Awards, "Journal of International Dispute Settlement", vol. 1, no. 1, 2010.

Lee, Ilhyung: Introducing International Commercial Arbitration And Its Lawlessness, By Way Of The Dissenting Opinion, "Contemporary Asia Arbitration Journal", vol. 19, no. 1, 2011.

Lew, J.D.M., Mistelis, L. A., Kroll, S.: Comparative International Commercial Arbitration, Wolters Kluwer, 2003.

Mosk, Richard M.: The Debate over Dissenting and Concurring Opinions in Arbitration, "University of West Los Angeles Law Review" vol. 26, 1995.

Mosk, Richard, Ginsberg, Tom: Dissenting Opinions in International Arbitration, "Mealey's International Arbitration Report" vol. 15, no. 4, 2000.

Peters, Philipp: Presiding Arbitrator, Deciding Arbitrator: Decision-Making in Arbitral Tribunals, in Christian Klausegger, Peter Klein et al. (eds), Austrian Yearbook on International Arbitration 2011, (Manz'sche Verlags- und Universitätsbuchhandlung 2011).

Redfern, Alan, Hunter, Martin, Blackaby, Nigel, Partasides, Constantine: Law and Practice of International Commercial Arbitration, 4th edn, 2004.

Redfern, Alan: Dangerous Dissents, 16 March 2005, available online at http://www.brownwelsh.com/Archive/2005_ Master_Redfern.pdf.

Redfern, Alan: The 2003 Freshfields Lecture, Dissenting Opinions in International Commercial Arbitration: the Good, the Bad and the Ugly, "Arbitration International" vol. 20, no.

3, 2004, p. 223-242, also available online at http://ciarbeuropeanbranch.com/ training/Paris2012/A15.%20Redfern%20on%20Dissents.pdf.

Rees Q.C., Peter J., Rohn Patrick, Dissenting Opinions: Can They Fulfil a Beneficial Role?, "Arbitration International", vol. 25, 2009.

Shore, Laurence, Figueroa, Kenneth Juan: Dissents, Concurrences and a Necessary Divide Between Investment and Commercial Arbitration, "Global Arbitration Review" vol. 3, 2008.

Smit, Hans: Dissenting Opinions in Arbitration, "ICC International Court of Arbitration Bulletin", 2004.

Waincymer, Jeff: Procedure and Evidence in International Arbitration, Kluwer Law International, 2012.

Werner, Jacques: Dissenting Opinions Beyond Fears, "Journal of International Arbitration", vol. 9, 1992.

Final Report issued by the Work Group on Dissent Opinions, "ICC International Court of Arbitration Bulletin", vol. 2, no. 1, 1991.